ACADEMIA LUNARE
Call For Papers 2018

A Shadow Within: Evil in Fantasy and Science Fiction

Edited By
Francesca T Barbini

Editor Introduction © Francesca T Barbini 2019
Articles © is with each individual author 2019
Cover Design © Francesca T Barbini 2019
Cover Image *Vlad Țepeș, the Impaler, Prince of Wallachia*. Anonymous.

First published by Luna Press Publishing, Edinburgh, 2019

A Shadow Within: Evil in Fantasy and Science Fiction © 2019. All rights reserved. No part of this publication may be reproduced, stored in a retrieval system, or transmitted in any form or by any means, electronic, mechanical, photocopy, recording or otherwise, without prior written permission of the copyright owners. Nor can it be circulated in any form of binding or cover other than that in which it is published and without similar condition including this condition being imposed on a subsequent purchaser.

www.lunapresspublishing.com

ISBN-13: 978-1-911143-91-8

Contents

Introduction   vi

The Antihero's Journey: The Influence of Milton's Satan on the Evolution of the Dark Hero
Alice Capstick   1

Rewriting Evil. An Alternative to Personification: Portrayal, Presence and Purpose in the Short Fiction of M. John Harrison
Jason Gould   23

Through the Veil of the Digital Revolution and into the Abyss of Artificial Intelligence: The Insidious Desensitisation of Humanity
Sharon Day   45

Embodiments of evil and reflections of social change in second-world fantasy
A J Dalton   73

Xenomorphobia – Eighties Societal Fears and Issues as Reflected in the Movie *Aliens*
Robert S Malan   102

Born Bad: Unmasking Evil in John Carpenter's *Halloween* and James Cameron's *The Terminator*
Kim Lakin-Smith   118

Bluebeard – The Eternal Predator
Teika Bellamy   133

The Problem of Evil in Pseudo-Taoist Secondary Worlds
Lucinda Holdsworth 149

From Dark Side to Grey Politics: The Portrayal of Evil in the *Star Wars* Saga
Rostislav Kůrka 169

Imperialism as "Evil" in Epic Fantasy: An Analysis of the Fantasy Works of Eddings, Jordan, Sanderson, and Brett
Matthew J. Elder & C. Palmer-Patel 189

Yesterday's Tyrant: Evolving Evil in Fantasy Television's Reformed Villains
Katarina O'Dette 210

Spring Again: The Problem of Evil and the End of Winter in C.S. Lewis's *Narnia*
Octavia Cade 231

'I have done only what was necessary' An exploration of individual and structural evil in the works of N. K. Jemisin
Thomas Moules 248

The Nature of Evil in *The Chronicles of Thomas Covenant* by Stephen Donaldson
Barbara Stevenson 263

Machines of Chaos – The Shadows and the Reapers as representations of evil in the television series *Babylon 5* and the *Mass Effect* game series
Jyrki Korpua 278

The Bloodlust of Elizabeth Báthory: From the Brothers Grimm to *American Horror Story*
Tatiana Fajardo 296

From Light to Dark – Using Gothic Styles to Visualise Evil in Architecture
Dominic Riemenschneider 315

The Inquisitor's Creatures: The Historical Roots of the Witch Trope and its Evolution Over the Centuries
Steph P. Bianchini 339

Naming the Terror in the Forest: Evolution of The Horned God in Fantasy Fiction
Anna Milon 361

Evil Rewritten: Witches in Revisionist Fairy Tales
Anna Köhler 373

The Fictional Scientist as a Dichotomy of Good and Evil in Contemporary Realist Speculative Fiction
Sean Z Fitzgerald 393

Author Biographies 416

Introduction

A Shadow Within: Evil in Fantasy and Science Fiction is the third Call for Papers from Academia Lunare. The first in the series, *Gender Identity and Sexuality in Current Fantasy and Science Fiction*, won the British Fantasy Award for Best Non-fiction. It has been a long road, but the growth of Academia Lunare is the organic result of passion and a curiosity for speculative non-fiction. We are very proud of our journey and the people it has brought into the Luna family.

Choosing a topic to explore is a fascinating process for us. It often stems from what is happening in the world, as the first two Call for Papers showed (the second one being *The Evolution of African Fantasy and Science Fiction*). Evil, on the other hand, is a constant in human history, one that shifts with every passing decade. It was this fluidity that we wanted to capture in this current volume. It was clear from the submissions that, for our contributors, evil isn't a static presence confined to any one given time, but rather something that constantly evolves under the influence of the author's own experience, society, the technology of the period, and even their understanding of humanity.

For those new to Luna's Call for Papers, know that we encourage our contributors to pursue their topics from a wide range of perspectives. This eclectic approach helps give rise to something unique and refreshing: there is still a breadcrumb trail to follow, but not one that necessarily follows a straight and narrow road.

This volume attempts to shine new light on the subject of evil by casting an eye on different methodologies. It also examines our society and how this has affected our understanding and representations of evil in technology, books and the media, starting from the not-so-distant future and looking back a few decades. In the largest section, our writers then tackle the issue of evil by looking at specific creators, as represented through their characters and their works, be they films, books, or games. We conclude by dipping into history (groups, people, and architecture) and examining how this has influenced fictional characters and settings, as well as their development throughout the ages.

I really do believe there is something for everyone in this book. Here you can find new approaches to an existing work and learn more about its creator; you can also gain a better understanding of society and history in ways you might not have considered before. For you writers out there, you can benefit from reflecting on, and perhaps reconsidering, your understanding of evil; how to tackle "evil" characters and perhaps even reinvent them.

Most of all though, as always, we hope you will find the experience of reading this book to be a valuable and enriching one.

Francesca T Barbini

The Antihero's Journey: The Influence of Milton's Satan on the Evolution of the Dark Hero

Alice Capstick

Abstract

John Milton's depiction of Satan in his 1667 *Paradise Lost* had considerable influence on the development of antiheroic figures throughout the eighteenth and nineteenth centuries. These figures distorted the conventional dichotomy between good and evil characters in such a way that a new archetype began to emerge that was neither entirely villainous, or heroic – but instead a tragic struggle between the two. Given that the continuing influence of the antiheroic figure, who is a unique blend of the characteristics traditionally used to polarise heroic and villainous characters – sometimes referred to as a "problematic heroes" or "dark heroes" – the antihero requires a similar level of attention to what is given to the traditional heroic archetype of the "pure" hero. I argue that Satan is the first incarnation of the modern antihero, and his unprecedented sublimity, symbiotic relationship with evil, and tormented aesthetic is what makes his antiheroic character an ideal case study to understand the characterisation of the antihero and consider its evolution over time. I propose an alternative model to Joseph Campbell's 1949 Jungian monomyth of "The Hero's Journey", to reimagine increasingly popular archetypal characters who do not comply with traditional heroic standards. This three-part model examines the antihero's "rise", "reign", and "ruin", a structure which focusses on the relationship between the antihero's good and evil characteristics; in particular, their relationship with power, and the impact of their tormented and degrading infernal psychology. By examining Satan's influential journey as a means of developing a model by which to understand the antiheroic journey, I argue that the antihero is more relevant and prominent today than ever before, and that through continued consideration of the "antihero's journey", we can understand the evolution of these complicated characters as a commentary of the nature of humanity's relationship with evil.

The Evolution of the Satanic Antihero

In his 1830 essay, 'On the Devil and Devils', Percy Shelley accounts for controversial responses to John's Milton depiction of evil in *Paradise Lost* by explaining that Milton took the traditional figure of the devil and "divested him of a sting, hoof, and horns, and clothed him with the sublime grandeur of a graceful but tremendous spirit" (1998, p. 264). Shelley's Lucianic essay was one of many similar prose works written in the late eighteenth century that reflected a growing interest in problematic heroes, who are often referred to as "antiheroes" (Wittreich, 1972). These characters exhibit both heroic and villainous traits, which are interwoven in their character in such a way that the traditional struggle between good and evil is internalised and becomes a struggle of self. Hybrid characters, like Satan – who are admirable but have problematic relationships with good and evil – have remained popular since the introduction of the Satanic hero in the 1667 publication of *Paradise Lost*. Milton's epic established the Satanic precedent for the antiheroic journey, which continues to influence the representation of the alternative heroic journey in contemporary Satanic heroes. While the concept of the antihero itself is not new, discussion relating to this character has often focused on case studies or generic analysis of antiheroic *qualities*, rather than accounting for the development of the *character* in antiheroic narratives. However, the Satanic antihero has become more than a literary influence, as mimetic representations of him continue to be inspired by his legacy of proud rebellion, psychological torment, and connection with the infernal.

In 1934, C.G. Jung helped establish the concept of the archetype as "an indispensable correlate of the idea of the collective unconscious, [that] indicates the existence of definite forms in the psyche which seem to be present always and everywhere" (1968, p. 42). Jung's research on the collective unconscious influenced Joseph Campbell in his development of the concept of "the hero's journey." According to Campbell, the hero's journey consists of the "departure", "initiation", and "return" of the hero. Campbell argues that this three-stage monomyth encapsulates "mankind's one great story" (p. 42). However, Campbell's model only applies to traditional hero types who were popularised by the religious stories and myths that he examined. Campbell does acknowledge that a different interpretation of heroism would be necessary in the future – that "it is not society that will guide and save the creative hero, but precisely the reverse" (p. 337). Yet, because of his focus on heroes from myth and legend, Campbell did not consider whether society had already developed, or had perhaps been influenced by such an alternative heroic figure.

The problem with Campbell's archetype is that it no longer encapsulates the hero's journey in all its forms. I argue that, given their popularity, antiheroes deserve to be considered as more than just failed or unconventional heroes or villains. Such heroes are not a study in virtuousness or goodness, but rather of complex morals, diminished goodness, and descent into the infernal – both physically and psychologically. The antiheroic figure requires an alternative to the "hero's journey", a general character arc that can be used to identify antiheroes and map their descent similar to the way Campbell maps the path of the traditional hero. Jung and Campbell's conception of collective unconsciousness focusses on a broad consideration of the patterns of numerous myths and legends dating from thousands of years ago from many different cultures. However, while the antihero itself is not a new figure, the antihero as the protagonist first came to real prominence during the

Renaissance, particularly in Christopher Marlowe and William Shakespeare's Elizabethan heroes. Milton's Satan, in *Paradise Lost*, reimagined the Aristotelian notion of the epic hero and became the first game-changing depiction of problematic heroism, Satan truly embodies the evolution of evil, and continues to be influential in contemporary literature. Satan's influence on Romantic heroes in particular revolutionised the relationship between heroic and villainous characters and began to conflate the struggle into one tormented character – the Satanic antihero. By examining the precedent set by the progenitor of the antihero as we know him today – Milton's Satan – I will propose an alternative heroic cycle that encapsulates the antihero's paradoxical relationship with power and goodness. Essentially, the success of the antihero's construction depends on the character being "symbolic... of man in his fight for liberty against oppression in all its forms" – a character who "combines in his person those most prominent and not always compatible concerns of romanticism... individual liberty... and the brotherhood of man" (Thorslev, 1965, p. 10). However, this fight for ideological reform is always undermined by the antihero's relationship with the infernal, which corrupts his goodness and transforms this character into a tormented being who descends into chaos. I propose a model that reflects their relationship with power and diminished goodness comprised of the antihero's "rise", "reign", and "ruin", with the potential for "redemption".

During their "rise", at the beginning of the antihero's cycle, their character is normally inflamed with a righteous pride that drives them in the pursuit of some ideological goal that they believe will transform the world for the better. However, in the pursuit of this utopian vision, the antihero's methods become increasingly reprehensible and they transform from being a noble reformer to a deranged or deluded menace. When they do eventually gain power, and "reign" in some form, the antihero retains self-awareness and understands that their acts of evil are not justified by their goal. However, by this time, they have become so entrenched in evil that they are unable to achieve redemption and instead become degraded by their increasingly villainous acts, which marks the beginning of their "ruin".

What is important to understand about antiheroic characters is that they combine heroism and villainy. To consider Satan's heroism or his villainy in isolation from the rest of his character undermines Milton's complex examination of humanity's relationship with the concept of evil. As a high-ranking angel in heaven who falls to become the king of hell, Satan is the culmination of opposing archetypes, and the embodiment of the degradation of heroic virtue given overexposure to pride. Despite most readers being aware of Satan's role in Christian history, he is not immediately dismissible as an evil character or generic archetype or trope, which makes Milton's Satan the most prominent precedent for heroic characters who are connected to the infernal, as he resists even the most basic expectations about the nature and personification of evil. Satan is attractive, admirable, determined, and resilient; qualities that are traditionally associated with heroic characters. Yet, he is also cunning, brooding, ruthless, and problematic – qualities that undermine traditional heroism. The duality of Satan's character is what makes him so intriguing as he is not so much a study of the effects of evil, but of the consequences of diminished goodness when exposed to evil.

Critics in the eighteenth century were enamoured with Satan's character as an epitomised representation of sublimity. However, it was not until Romanticism that the Satanic antihero began to inspire interpretations; most notably in the work of William Godwin, Percy Shelley, William Blake, Sir Walter Scott, Mary Shelley, and Lord Byron. The Romantics generally interpreted Satan as a champion of liberty and egalitarianism, and for some, as the hero of *Paradise Lost*. As Peter Thorslev explains, "in the full bloom of the Romantic age" rebellious individualism and pride transformed from being "cardinal sins" to "cardinal virtues" (p. 187). It is perhaps unsurprising that given the tumultuous period the Romantics lived in, that they required new types of heroes and established new ways of considering humanity's relationship with goodness and with evil. Versions of Satan sprang to life in prose and verse throughout the eighteenth and early nineteenth centuries. It is difficult to reduce this figure to the confines of a traditional archetypal character because instead of complying with existing ones, many of the Romantics reinterpreted the precedent established by Milton's Satan and developed their own, most of which can also be described as antiheroes and whose characters conform to the Satanic antiheroic journey.

Antiheroic figures certainly existed before Satan; however, Milton's intriguing exploration of heroism meant that Satan directly inspired many of the more colourful and intriguing antiheroes that followed him. These figures are perhaps even more prominent in contemporary society than in the Romantic era and have attracted an increasing amount of attention. Fiona Peters (2016) and Brett Martin (2014) have examined the antihero in television and video games and examined the way antiheroic figures have even begun to challenge gender stereotypes and inspire the development of female antiheroes. Laura Knoppers and Gregory Semenza have also considered the contemporary antihero, but they are interested specifically in Satan's influence on modern variations (2006). However, antiheroes have become most prominent in contemporary fantasy, where writers have strayed from the heroic story arcs of the past and developed new methods of constructing heroes, many of whom have been indirectly inspired by the influence of Satanic heroism. By considering Satan's antiheroic journey as one that can generally be applied to the antiheroic descendants his character has inspired, it is possible to develop an alternative model to the hero's journey.

Rise

The antihero is distinguishable from traditional heroic figures because they are motivated by their ideological rejection of the system of power they are subject to, on the grounds that it is tyrannical and oppressive. However, the implementation of their ideology is problematic and undermines their heroism. The Satanic antihero's rebellion is inspired by their dissatisfaction not just with a simple system of government or hierarchy, but with the order and governance of the universe on a cosmic scale. Satan interprets God as a corrupt king, whose exaltation of The Son is an arbitrary and cruel exercise in power that demands "prostration vile" from all the angels, with the threat that defiance will lead to them being "cast out from God and blessed vision" (Milton, 2013, V.782, V.613). Satan argues that the angels are "self-begot, self-raised" asserting both a personal agency and the political idea of individuality (V.860). He famously establishes his autonomy, presenting himself as the ruler of his own destiny and insisting that "the mind is its own place, and in itself / can make a Heaven of Hell, a Hell of Heaven" (I.254-5). Satan's proud defiance of the natural order was interpreted by the Romantics as evidence of championing Republican and egalitarian ideals pertaining to civil liberty and meritocracy as superior to religious explanations and interpretations of the human experience (Butler, 1981, p. 22). Satan believes that is "better to reign in hell than serve in heaven" because he is willing to sacrifice his place in heaven if it means his escape from oppression and the liberty of executing his own agency (I.263). Rebellion is an essential part of the antihero's "rise", even if it is fundamentally impossible, or will lead to inevitable failure and destruction.

The rebellion of antiheroic precedents to Satan, particularly figures from Elizabethan drama – like Dr Faustus or Macbeth – have been acknowledged by Helen Gardner as lending themselves to the future (Gardner, 1965, p.101). These are problematic figures who certainly incite discussion and destabilise the division between "good" and "bad" characters, but their rebellions are distinguishable from Satan's because their justification is underwhelming and unconvincing; as readers, we can determine their failings clearly. Satan established a new precedent, as his justification for inciting rebellion appears on a superficial level to be reasonable, and not immediately reprehensible; and his decision to vocalise these grievances under an omnipotent force appears to be brave. The antihero begins their heroic journey as morally indiscernible from traditional heroic figures. As their problematic nature is revealed, it is their initial ideological framework that makes it difficult for readers to universally condemn them. Instead, antiheroic figures retain their heroic appeal because of their admirable goal, even when their methods for attaining this goal undermine their morality. The dissonance between the antihero's ideological justification and problematic method is what defines the antihero in the first stages of their characterisation.

Importantly, during the antihero's rise, it becomes apparent that – despite their admirable ideology – their methods of defying omnipotence are reprehensible. While there is an argument to be made about it being necessary to challenge a tyrant by turning the tyrant's own evil methods against them, the antihero's problem is that in their "rise", their heroism is eclipsed by their reliance on these methods, and morally, they pass the point of no return and cannot be redeemed. Satan's method of gathering followers is likened by the narrator of *Paradise Lost* to a "calumnious art" where Satan uses "counterfeited truth" to gain their attention and service (V.770-1). Furthermore, Satan speaks to them from a "royal seat / high on a hill" elevated above his peers and undermining the belief in the importance of democracy which he expressed in his earlier speeches (V.756-7). William Empson, a prominent twentieth century advocate for Satan's heroism, argues that Satan's self-elevation is justified because he is equivalent to a lord who has been slighted by his king and is calling upon his followers for aid, and must therefore cast the appearance of a lord (1965, p. 77). However, even Empson cannot defend Satan's myopic decision to challenge an omnipotent force in war. The consequence of this poor leadership damns both Satan and his followers to Hell. However, Satan remains determined and uses manipulation to gather his forces once more, this time commanding them to "awake, arise, or be forever fallen" and suggesting that they should again attempt to defy tyranny, this time through "covert guile" (I.330, II.441). Somewhere in the enactment of his rebellion Satan loses the moral high ground because his ideological goal does not justify his increasingly immoral methods. As an antiheroic figure whose inspiring goal and heroic grandeur is undermined by his amoral leadership and methods, Satan becomes a blend of traditionally accepted heroic types like the Homeric warrior and benevolent king, and villainous figures like the sophist or the Machiavellian Prince (Lewalski, 1987, p. 84). The combination of the antihero's heroic goal and their problematic methods creates a moral ambiguity that exposes Satan "as incredibly self-obsessed" and a "monomaniac" (Lewis, 1969, p. 102). These are traits that Empson cannot properly account for and prominent anti-Satanists like C. S. Lewis never fail to point out. The contradiction inherent and increasingly more apparent in the antihero's character makes it difficult for readers to discern whether it is acceptable to overlook their morality in favour of their cause, or whether moral fortitude is essential in every circumstance. The antihero is determined to defy the natural order and their place within it. Yet their proud defiance makes it impossible for them to achieve equilibrium between morality and pursuit of their goal.

The antihero's pride is essential to their rise to power, as without it they would lack the self-righteous justification that enables them to defy the idea of omnipotence. However, while their pride appears to be a form of bravery, it is – like their rebellion – also a dangerous form of delusion. Satan's pride is not constrained to defying God's rule; he goes further, setting himself up as an alternative to God. His throne in the "palace of Lucifer" before his fall is only the first example (V.760). In Hell, Satan builds Pandemonium "like a temple" with a "fretted gold" ceiling amongst other examples of idolatry and suggests that even the tower of Babylon – a symbol of overreaching pride – does not equal Satan's kingdom (I.713, 717). Satan is again "exalted sat, by merit raised" above the other fallen angels on a throne that symbolises the tyranny associated with the Asiatic tyrants of Milton's time (II.5). Satan's active construction of himself as equal to God's glory is both a grand rejection of power and sublimely horrific hypocrisy.

Milton's use of the sublime attracted most of the attention *Paradise Lost* received in the late seventeenth and early eighteenth centuries. Joseph Addison believed that the use of the sublime was a requisite for epic poetry and that Milton was more successful than his predecessors in applying it, particularly to the character of Satan (Ricks, 1963, p.120). Addison explains that Milton develops his description of Pandemonium until he "has raised out of it some glorious image or sentiment, proper to inflame the mind of the reader" (Ricks, 1963, p. 120). Samuel Johnson and Matthew Arnold discussed the way Milton's use of the sublime – his "grand style" – distracted readers from Satan's debased character (Leonard, 2013, p.132). Readers are constantly encouraged by Milton's use of the sublime to overlook Satan's evil nature in favour of his attractive appearance. Milton likens Satan to various serpent-like sea monsters, or when Satan "throws his baleful eyes… mixed with obdurate pride and steadfast hate" around the "dismal situation" of Hell, or the description of Satan rising from "the burning marl" and calling the legions of angels, are all examples that demonstrate the subversion of Satan's evil nature in favour of his admirable appearance (I.56-8; I.296). Later, upon his throne, Satan manipulates the war council into choosing his plan for their second attempt at rebellion and also choosing him to be the hero of it. Again, Satan appears to be inspiring, this time because of his powerful rhetoric. However, each sentiment is presented superficially like an actor or a politician. Only when his "heart distends with pride" are Satan's true motivations revealed and is it unavoidably obvious that pride is at the very heart of his character (I.571-2). Satan's heroic rebellion is undermined by his villainous methods which creates a paradox, because Satan's aspirations are challenged and revealed to be selfish which makes it difficult to continue to approve of his methods.

Despite his admirable criticism of God as a tyrant and oppressive dictator, Satan's pride prevents him from recognising these traits in himself and undermines his heroism and his supposedly democratic ideology. Satan "does not go on from rejecting the 'tyranny of heaven' to rejecting all tyranny, in fact, to rejecting kingship itself, Satan merely sets himself up as an alternate monarch, another tyrant, another king" (Bryson, 2004, p. 109). What Bryson is essentially arguing is that, in attempting to oppose evil, Satan becomes what he despises. Bryson suggests that this process is tragic; however, this is a much-debated point in Miltonic scholarship which extends to discussion of many problematic heroes. They have the appearance and ideology of traditional heroism and a heroic goal. However, in the process of "rising" to their self-appointed task, the antihero's heroism becomes clouded by their pride and we begin to question whether they are truly heroic, or whether their determination is beginning to degrade their humanity and distract them from achieving their heroic potential.

Reign

Motivated by pride and deluded determination, the antihero is usually successful in their second attempt at rebellion. What follows is their "reign", as the antihero holds (or believes they hold) power, which they can now use to continue the battle that inspired their rebellion to begin with. However, the antihero continues to rely on the problematic methods they used in the process of gaining power despite being aware they are immoral. After "reigning" over the war council in Hell, where Satan exhibits the tyrannical behaviour he resented in God, Satan escapes Hell and navigates through Chaos – supposedly unaware that he is still subject to God's omniscience. His escape and subsequent arrival and infiltration of Eden mark Satan's success (at least in his own mind), as he is now able to undermine God's influence and impress his own upon others. However, Satan continues to rely on the measures he used to gain power, rather than now cultivating the system of governance he espoused in his rebellion. These measures inevitably begin to mimic the despotic tyrant Satan has supposedly usurped.

In most cases, the antihero becomes increasingly aware of their relationship with their tyrannical predecessor, which begins to make them question the validity of their rule. For Satan, this moment occurs as he arrives at the gates of Eden at midday, under the full force of the sun. There is no audience to vaunt to or to act for, and for the first time Satan is alone and his soliloquising allows readers insight into his character. As Satan stands on the precipice of Eden, so too does he stand on the precipice of committing himself to evil, as "horror and doubt distract" him and provoke the realisation that his own actions have damned him to Hell both physically, and psychologically (IV.18). Satan's realisation "wakes despair / that slumbered", as he now reflects on everything that he has lost (IV.23-4). Satan even demonstrates self-awareness and perhaps even acceptance of wrongdoing, by acknowledging that he is guilty of "pride and worse ambition" and unjustly "warring against heaven's matchless king" (V40.1). Lewis chastises Satan's reflection, accusing him – perhaps rightfully – of self-obsession and invalidating his torment because "all of Satan's torments are his own" (p. 99). Technically, Lewis is correct; however, Satan's character again establishes a precedent, as he represents the torment dark heroes experience as the consequence of their ideologically inspiring but flawed rebellion. Lewis's condescending summation of Satan's torment actually defines a key aspect of the antihero's "reign". They become trapped in an invalid position of power, which they must maintain through immoral acts, but each evil act of maintenance inevitably begets another evil action, so their torments do in fact become self-inflicted. Like Satan, when faced with the choice of confronting the problems they have caused and the damage this has done to their character, or committing themselves to further immoral action, the antihero decides to embrace evil, as Satan exclaims, "evil be thou my good" (IV.109). By committing themselves to evil, the antihero can no longer justify their damning methods, and instead delude themselves into believing that their commitment to evil is unavoidable. They make a conscious decision to continue on their path despite knowing that it is problematic, and that now, they are unable to justify their actions because their ideological vision has been undermined.

Now that the antihero has committed themselves to their immoral path, they must continue to maintain the appearance of the hero they initially believed themselves to be. In adopting and maintaining this façade, the antihero undergoes a fundamental change, as Satan does, from the early books when he and The Son are both "presented in a heroic light, rhetorically brilliant, emotionally stirring, courageous and self-sacrificing" (Bryson, p. 133). Now their forms change; the Son is becoming nobler, while Satan has fallen and becomes more convinced of his heroism. To maintain the illusion of heroism the antihero often adopts a disguise of some kind to hide their corruption. Whatever the antihero chooses as their façade, whether it is a mask or a hood, a stolen identity, or the reinvention their own identity; the pressure of maintaining their facade corrupts their real identity until the heroic ideological rebel becomes a fallen victim of their own diabolism.

Satan famously adopts the form of the serpent to tempt Eve, a transformation which foreshadows his eventual demise. The serpent is not the first disguise Satan uses to maintain his heroic reputation. Technically, through his rhetoric and angelic ability to shapeshift, Satan presents himself as a Homeric Warrior, a benevolent king, a "stripling cherub", a lion, a tiger, a cormorant, and a toad; before he even considers the form of a serpent as something that "might serve his wiles" (III.636; IX 85). Satan's early shapeshifting is foremost simply a means to an end. However, John Leonard has noted that his shapeshifting could also symbolise his degradation (1990, p. 118). Satan has fallen from heaven and is damned to hell, yet the process of embodying his damned nature, of rejecting his identity as Lucifer and becoming Satan in being as in name, is represented metaphorically in his gradually degrading choice of form. As each form becomes more depraved, Satan becomes more resolute in his belief that he is achieving his goal. For readers, it is apparent that with every new form he becomes more committed to evil. His eventual adoption of "the serpent subtlest beast of all the field" as a "fit vessel" represents the complete corruption of Satan's heroism, and the height of his delusion (IX.86, 89). Satan even appears attractive in this form:

> With burnished neck of verdant gold, erect
> Amidst his circling spires, that on the grass
> Floated redundant: pleasing was his shape
> And lovely; never since of serpent-kin
> Lovelier (IX.501-5)

Satan appears to be compensating for his entirely corrupted being with his pleasing façade. As the serpent, he is finally able to fulfil his goal of revenge against God. However, in this moment, Satan is at his most deluded and repugnant. Even though he is about to achieve his goal, his pursuit of power has corrupted his identity, and with it, the elements of heroism that initially justified his ignoble behaviour. The corruption of Satan's humanity in the name of heroism is reinterpreted in various antiheroes that follow. From explicit allusions to the Satanic antihero like Frankenstein, to later antiheroes like Rochester and Heathcliff. Antiheroic characteristics are also evident in modern interpretations like Batman, James Bond, and Professor Snape. The antihero's disguise may convince the world that their purpose is good, but it only deludes and corrupts what the wearer is determined to protect from scrutiny – their flawed humanity.

Ruin

The maintenance of the antihero's alternative identity to protect their true identity has a degrading influence on what remains of the antihero's true self. Over time, the two identities begin to converge so that one is almost indistinguishable from the other. When their façade eventually fails them, the antihero has no choice left to them, and in this helpless state they usually lose their power and fall with no hope of redemption or absolution.

When Satan returns triumphantly to Hell after tempting Eve, he ascends his throne disguised as a "plebeian angel militant" to make a more theatrical and impressive entrance. His former righteousness and sublime power have disappeared; what remains is a depraved creature eternally searching for validation and power (X.442). The speech he gives to his followers begins once again with "thrones, dominations, princedoms, virtues, powers", continuing his mimetic travesty of God but now without the self-aware tone of mockery of God's ceremony that Satan imbued his earlier speech with. Satan wholeheartedly believes he has bested God, which, he imagines, makes him equal or perhaps better than him (X.460). Again, the antihero's overreaching pride has deformed his initial intent to overthrow tyranny as the façade of grand heroism that Satan adopted as a tool has become his reality. Instead of heroically overthrowing tyranny, Satan's moral weakness means that he has become a worse example of tyrannical oppression and despotism than God ever was.

The victory speech Satan presents to the fallen angels in Book Ten is further evidence of his corrupt leadership. Readers no longer need to scrutinise Satan's rhetoric to observe his depraved leadership. Satan lies excessively while maintaining the appearance of modesty, infusing the story of his so-called victory with bombastic overexaggeration. He speaks about leading the fallen angels out of Hell to wreak havoc on the world, but there is no mention of fulfilling his earlier plans or his promises concerning civic liberty and self-determination. Instead, Satan is infatuated with the idea of leading others down a path of damnation like his own. In his distraction from his initial purpose, Satan has lost his sense of self. The aspects of Satan's identity that were once admirable have become corrupt because either he has accepted and embraced his façade completely, or it has degraded what remained of his identity, so that he is now completely consumed by evil.

As Regina Schwartz notes "ultimately, the void of chaos and the loss of identity of Satan are rooted in a common source, and in Miltonic fashion, that source is a decision" (1980, p. 21). The decision Schwartz is speaking of is the one to defy the natural order. As we have seen, defiance has been central to the antihero's characterisation. The source of this pride, suggests Schwartz, is Satan's denial of reality, because "once Satan denies his origin, he determines his end" because "to deny the maker is to be unmade" (1980, p. 22). Satan's degradation stems from the initial, apparently heroic decision to defy not only *the* creator, but also *Satan*'s creator, and the accepted order, in pursuit of an ostensibly better world. Satan's mimetic leadership, hypocritical use of power, and commitment to a goal he is aware contradicts his initial purpose together degrade his earlier heroism. What was once a heroic act, becomes corruptive as the antihero avoids their problems and deludes themselves into continuing with their decision, committing themselves to the infernal rather than the heroic.

Commitment to evil does not necessarily undermine the antihero's heroism, but Satan deludes himself into believing that his pursuit of evil is for the sake of goodness. Such a delusion transforms the antihero into an infernal agent because he begins to believe, on some level, that his evil work is good. William Blake famously suggested that Milton "was of the devil's party without knowing it"; however, John Leonard has argued that, more accurately, it is Satan who unknowingly aligns himself with the devil's party as he becomes "progressively vitiated by darkness" (Blake, 1790, p. 71; Leonard, 1990, p. 115). Satan's embodiment of a diminished good is perhaps not an accident or an oversight on Milton's account; as Lewis explains, "this progressive degradation, of which he himself is wildly aware, is carefully marked in the poem" (1969, p.99). Satan begins by fighting for "liberty" – even if it is misconceived – but almost at once sinks to fighting for "honour, dominion, glory, and renown" (VI.422). Satan was, of course, of the devil's party from the beginning. What changed – or perhaps became more apparent – were the abhorrent values of this party. Satan's relationship with pride is almost synonymous with his relationship with goodness. When he is proud for the "right" reasons he appears to be good, but when he cultivates the appearance of goodness for the sake of his corrupted pride, then his virtue begins to degrade. As readers, we can longer trust the version of Satan who abandons his goal and loses interest in atonement. We may still admire him for his bravery, determination, and perseverance against omnipotence, but it is difficult to support a character that is now so transparently morally flawed without justification.

When Satan concludes his climactic speech upon his return to Hell, he expects to hear "universal shout and high applause", but instead Milton invokes bathos, as Satan hears only "a dismal universal hiss, the sound / of public scorn" (X.505; X.508-9).

The hiss is the sound of Satan's followers transforming into serpents, but it also represents the sound of omnipotence intervening and revealing the full extent of Satan's delusion and pride. Satan is transformed into a "monstrous serpent on his belly prone", now embodying in name the monstrous serpent he was compared to in the first epic simile in *Paradise Lost*, and the form of the disguise he chose to tempt humanity (X.514). The implication of Milton's foreshadowing is that Satan never truly had any agency and was always in some way an agent of God's will. Satan is "punished in the shape he sinned" in accordance with the law of the Old Testament, to explain the way the spiritual effects of sin manifest physically (X.516).

For the more secular figure of the modern antihero, the idea of embodying the shape in which they sinned remains. For the antihero, death is not the worst end; instead, being rendered helpless and void, and reminded eternally of their futility, traps them as Prometheus was trapped by Jove. Except instead of being chained to a rock and tortured, they are chained to the reality they sought to overcome and tortured by their impotence. Instead of being allowed to journey "up and enter now into full bliss", the antihero is damned for eternity, usually as Satan is, without any hope of salvation or redemption (X.503). While traditional heroes cross back over the "threshold" triumphantly, antiheroes exist permanently beyond it, wilting tragically into oblivion.

The legacy of the Satanic hero

In his foreword to *Batman the Dark Night: A Hero Returns*, Alan Moore questions how "the creators of fiction are to go about redefining their legends to suit the contemporary climate?" Moore recognises that "fictional heroes of the past, while still retaining all of their charm and power and magic, have had some of their credibility stripped away forever as a result of the new sophistication in their audience", and suggests that it is important to consider new ways of interpreting heroic characters (Miller, 2005).

Satanic heroes of the past, like Dante's Satan, do not require much scrutiny to conclude their evil nature, and, despite being complicated characters, Doctor Faustus and Macbeth are usually understood to be the villains in their respective plays. Such early interpretations of characters' relationships with the infernal have often provoked attention and curiosity, but are relatively morally unambiguous. Milton's Satan became the turning point in the history of the evolution of evil characters because he was the first to provide a justification for his evil nature while appearing admirable enough that readers could support him. Satan's relationship with evil does not disqualify him from being heroic, and despite Lewis's insistence that Satan's evil nature makes him self-centred, and therefore uninteresting, Milton's reimagination of the orthodox view of Satan as a hero tormented by his own deviant nature makes him perhaps the most interesting character in *Paradise Lost*.

Satan's sublime aura, his grand speeches, rebellious ideology, and tragic descent into chaos have been constantly reinterpreted, and in some cases, almost directly transplanted onto characters inspired by Satan. The libertarian ideal established by Satan is echoed by Prometheus' determination that "yet I am king over myself, and rule / the torturing and conflicting throngs within" (I.254-5; Shelley, 1820). Satan's proud desire to circumvent the natural order is reimagined in Mary Shelley's Victor Frankenstein. His degrading inner turmoil and desire to make his mind a temple of liberty is evident in William Blake's work and Byron's *Manfred*. For many of these figures, Satan's antiheroic journey remains relevant and helps to understand the evolution of the modern antiheroic character and influence more thoroughly.

Contemporary representations of the antihero emphasise the need for an alternative way of understanding heroism because they completely subvert Campbell's model; in fact, many seem to rebel against it by presenting an openly evil character as the heroic protagonist whose heroic journey completely escapes Campbell's. These heroes are prominent in movies and TV. However, they are most notable in contemporary fantasy, in the work of Brandon Sanderson, Mark Lawrence, Brent Weeks, Peter V Brett, Patrick Rothfuss and Jim Butcher – whose works contain characters who embody a continuation of this internalised struggle with goodness and eventual degradation. Further examination of the influence of the Satanic hero's journey on characters that defy heroic tradition will enable us to understand the evolution of these characters and their relationship with evil.

Wherever antiheroic characters are present, the precedent of the Satanic hero lurks as dark and brooding inspiration. The Satanic hero's specific influence on antiheroic characters over time is a subject for further consideration, as many antiheroic traits stem from Satan's character and have been passed down through various interpretations. Despite the reality that *Paradise Lost* is not now a popular text, Satan remains relevant as the progenitor of the antiheroic character. By further exploring Satan's antiheroic journey, and applying it to various types of antiheroes, the implications of Satanic heroism will help us to understand why these characters insist on walking "to the edge of the chasm" and whether "the view is so different, right at the edge, than it is two steps back" (Weeks, 2016, p. 458).

Bibliography

Blake, W., 2008. *Blake's Poetry and Designs*. New York: W. W. Norton and Company.

Bryson, M., 2004. *The Tyranny of Heaven*. Newark: University of Delaware Press.

Butler, M., 1981. *Romantics, Rebels and Reactionaries*. Oxford: Oxford University Press.

Campbell, J., 2008. *The Hero with a Thousand Faces*. Novato: New World Library.

Empson, W., 1965. *Milton's God*. London: Chatto and Windus.

Gardner, H., 1965. *A Reading of Paradise Lost*. Oxford: Clarendon Press.

Jung, C. G., 1968. *The Archetypes and the Collective Consciousness.* New York: Princeton University Press.

Knoppers, L., 2006. *Milton in Popular Culture*. New York: Palgrave Macmillan.

Leonard, J., 1990. *Naming in Paradise*. Oxford: Clarendon Press.

Leonard, J., 2013. *Faithful Labourers: A Reception History of Paradise Lost*. Oxford: Oxford University Press.

Lewalski, B., 1987. *Paradise Lost and the Rhetoric of Literary Forms*. Princeton: Princeton University Press.

Lewis, C. S., 1969. *A Preface to Paradise Lost*. London: Oxford University Press.

Martin, B., 2014. *Difficult Men*. New York: Penguin Books.

Miller, F., 2005. *Batman: The Dark Knight Returns*. New York: DC Comics.

Milton, J., 2013. *Paradise Lost*. New York: Routledge.

Peters, F., 2016. *Antihero*. Chicago: Intellect.

Ricks, R., 1963. *Milton's Grand Style*. Oxford: Clarendon Press.

Schwartz, R., 1998. *Remembering and Repeating*. Cambridge: Cambridge University Press.

Shelley, P., 1988. *Shelley's Prose*. London: Fourth Estate Ltd.

Shelley, P., 2002. *Shelley's Poetry and Prose*. New York: W. W. Norton and Company.

Thorslev, P., 1965. *The Byronic Hero*. Minneapolis: University of Minnesota Press.

Weeks, B., 2016. *The Blood Mirror*. London: Orbit.

Wittreich, J., 1972. The Dating of Shelley's "On the Devil, and Devil's". *Keats-Shelley Journal*, 21(22), pp. 83-94.

Rewriting Evil. An Alternative to Personification: Portrayal, Presence and Purpose in the Short Fiction of M. John Harrison

Jason Gould

Abstract

Over the years, the personification of evil in fantasy and science fiction (F&SF) has become the trusted narrative device. But is there an alternative? And might the writer M. John Harrison be an acclaimed proponent of such an alternative? This paper examines the traditional personification of evil in F&SF. It questions why it might be such a popular approach, and compares and contrasts it against the Harrison method. Essentially, it asks if M. John Harrison might have evolved evil beyond embodiment and into a less literal form, and thereby introduced an alternative to personification.

The Devil Has All the Best Characters, But Not in Everyone's Book

Evil is not an idea that ever falls out of fashion in literature. Over the centuries it has become a fascination of readers, a favoured tool of storytellers, and a front-cover fanfare of market-savvy publishers. Pitched against good, against shades of good, or even against itself, it constitutes an indispensable part of the formula responsible for endless works of fiction, both critically acclaimed and commercially successful. The eternal struggle between good and its polar opposite continues to provide the source material behind a multitude of narratives. Furthermore, the dark half of the eternal struggle – the bad, the hateful, the morally repugnant – seems to be the ideal vehicle through which a certain strain of character might be brought to life. Fictional characters and evil appear to be made for each other.

Success of the evil character in fiction, however, depends on how an effectively abstract, subjective concept might be moulded into physical form in order to be dramatised. In literature, as in society, the word "evil" tends to conjure visions of malcontents, murderers, and warlords. Tales of devils, demons, and inexplicable phenomena remain prevalent and popular to the present day, but belief in evil as an incorporeal force appears increasingly substituted by the notion that it prefers to consider itself human. The antithesis of good frequently finds itself incarnated by the writer into a convenient entity used to further plot, develop character, and thrill, fascinate, or horrify the reader. In the hands of the F&SF writer, evil is often transmogrified in an attempt to render it recognisable to the reader. It shuffles off its nebulous state and assumes more acceptable appearance, whether human, such as *The Strange Case of Dr. Jekyll and Mr. Hyde* (Stevenson, 1886); animal, such as *Cujo* (King, 1981); hybrid, such as *The Island of Doctor Moreau* (Wells, 1896); monster, such as *Frankenstein* (Shelley, 1818); plant, such as *The Day of the Triffids* (Wyndham, 1951); or any variation thereof. Undeterred by biological constructs, writers have even cultivated the device to incorporate insentient objects: the ordinary abode, for example, in *The Haunting of Hill House* (Jackson, 1959); the unassuming motor vehicle, perhaps most famously that of *Christine* (King, 1983); and future-world robots, such as the Nexus-6 androids hunted by bounty hunter Rick Deckard in *Do Androids Dream of Electric Sheep?* (Dick, 1968). Human, animal, object – nothing seems exempt from the inpouring of evil.

Is it necessary, however, for evil to always be personified, anthropomorphised, or otherwise objectified? Exceptions abound, of course. And an important exception can be found in the short fiction of M. John Harrison.

While noted for his work in F&SF, unlike other, more literal writers, Harrison portrays evil through an entirely unique and unexpected lens. It was perhaps the unconventional approach to which celebrated horror writer Ramsey Campbell alluded, when he described Harrison as "… a master of enigma, whether human or supernatural" (1983 cited in Harrison, 1983, p. 1). An enigmatic evil, indeed, and often, in Harrison's writing, a de-personified, contradictory, and unreliable interpretation of the concept. For example, in his latest collection – *You Should Come With Me Now* (2017) – something that might be evil, or evil's distant cousin, insinuates itself into "slippery, subversive stories that mix the eerie and familiar into beguiling, alarming marvels" (Laing, 2017 cited in Harrison, 2017, cover). Other stories, such as *The Incalling* (1978), *The Ice Monkey* (1980), and *Egnaro* (1981), tackle the problem from an impressively distinct angle, suggesting that M. John Harrison might have evolved evil into an approach the originality of which is seldom seen.

Scrutiny of the personification device at a more detailed level seems prudent before considering Harrison's alternative approach. Analysis of how and why personified evil functions with apparent bestseller success should illuminate the reason behind its popularity, and the risks inherent in alternatives. An exploration of the kind described requires the device to be dismantled, its theoretical foundations examined, and, finally, an observation carried out of it in operation, in selected, illustrative examples.

Evil Made Flesh: Vampires, Orcs, and Droogs

Appropriating a host for the concept of evil triggered a tradition in storytelling that persists to the present day. From the serpent in the garden of Eden, through the witches of *Macbeth* (Shakespeare, 1606) and Lucifer in *Paradise Lost* (Milton, 1667), to more contemporary examples, such as Harry Potter's adversary Lord Voldemort (Rowling, 1997) – each character proves to be identifiably individual, yet fundamentally the same. Snake, devil or necromancer – each is an invitation to evil to manifest itself in the physical, in bone, blood, and breath.

Manifestation is an essential act, according to Sholom J. Kahn, in *The Problem of Evil in Literature* (1953). To not be lost on the audience, Kahn argues that the conceptual must be transformed into the corporal. By clothing an idea in flesh and birthing it into the world, it is legitimatised into the realm of reality, the realm closely linked, states Kahn, with human tradition, based on the theory that "instead of struggling [with] symbolic figures, our mythology tends to personify" (1953, p. 99). Kahn further explains that the need to personify is rooted in the primary definition of evils, which might be "classified as the natural and the human" (1953, p. 99). To personify evil in literature, the two types of evil do not need to be separate: they can – and often do – work in concert rather than conflict. Natural evil, to borrow Kahn's terminology, often fits inside the human, and either creates human evil, or else encourages, enflames or enhances that which might already be present. And, once evil has been personified, it holds at its disposal every human function, primarily those through which emotion might be expressed. An audience, Kahn suggests, relates to evil through the most universal and elementary functions, such as "tears, laughter, anger, pity, fear, and other such emotions [which combine to show] evil workings [in] human actions and situations" (1953, p. 100). Manipulation of the senses, therefore, becomes an important aspect of control. And it follows that the effectiveness of personification relies on the writer switching the connection between the reader and the text from reader-abstract to reader-human. Through human qualities might evil be best communicated.

For its part, the human audience proves appreciative of the effort. In an almost apocryphal anecdote, a "bibulous, semi-literate, ageing country squire" is said to have been sitting by the fireside listening to *Paradise Lost* being read aloud, when he leapt up, banged the arm of his chair, and exclaimed, "By

God! I know not what the outcome may be, but this Lucifer is a damned fine fellow, and I hope he may win!" (Pullman, 2005 cited in Milton, 2005, p. 1).

Milton knew that evil personified creates characters with great dramatic potential. He had also harnessed the unequivocal understanding that some characters – including, from time to time, the villain of the piece – resonate with the recipient of the story more strongly than others, a relationship reliant on empathy, which forms the next logical step in the embedding of evil in narrative. Notoriously elusive, and unpredictable to gauge (poor character identification is perhaps the most common criticism levelled at fiction), an empathetic emotional response is prized by the writer and adored by the reader. Evidently, the ageing country squire listening to Milton received such a response from the character of Lucifer, but why should he have felt elevated to the higher echelons of empathy?

Endeavours to explain the phenomena borrow from science and psychoanalysis. Professor Paul Zak (2015, cited in Kirwin 2015) believes the effect can be reduced to biological reaction, notably the presence of two neurochemicals, which he noticed were released into the brains of an audience watching the film of a terminally ill child recorded in the course of an experiment. Specifically, Zak claims cortisol and oxytocin syndicate an emotional connection: cortisol the agent responsible for attention, oxytocin for feelings of trust and empathy. The chemical reaction can be equated thus:

ATTENTION + EMPATHY = EMOTIONAL CONNECTION

Zak asserts that the reaction establishes the reader-character bond, from which the reader develops an ongoing response to the character. Plausible enough, perhaps, except the theory fails to question the origin of said chemicals, an omission addressed by the psychoanalytical reading.

Of all psychoanalytical study potentially linked to the

construction of the reader-character connection, the most pertinent is Jacque Lacan's 'mirror stage' (1949, cited in Mambrol 2016) – a stage in childhood, Lacan proposes, during which an external image of the body, reflected in a mirror, perhaps, produces a mental response in the infant, and the psychological concept of an "I". Avoidance of the external image, argues Lacan, proves futile, and the child is forced to accept an existence exterior to that which it has experienced previously. Ontologically, the infant's sense of being has been projected elsewhere, suggesting reformulation of the Cartesian statement "I think, therefore, I am", to "I am, where I think not" (1949, cited in Mambrol 2016). It represents the vital step, albeit innate, to perceive oneself in others, notably fictional characters. Furthermore, the "mirror stage" is responsible for engendering an unattainable sense of idealism, through alienation from the narcissistic image for which the infant feels love, but with which it can never be united. Lacan refers to the unattainable image as the ideal "I".

It is credible that the reader of fiction should search for their ideal "I" in the fabric of a fictional character, and, if teased by a trace of their own image, permit the subconscious formulation of the reader-character bond. Indeed, film theorist Christian Metz (n.d., cited in Mambrol 2016) connects an audience's fascination with an on-screen character to each individual audience member's pursuit of their ideal "I" – a pursuit not only of good characters, but evil.

And why should the reader's ideal "I" not hint toward evil? Elegantly phrased, Mark Twain wrote of "a charm about the forbidden that makes it unspeakably desirable" (n.d., cited in Keen, Mccoy, and Dunnaway 2012, p 140). Similarly, Baudilaire observed that "[i]n every man, at every time, there are two simultaneous tendencies – one towards God, the other towards Satan" (n.d., cited in Bataille 1973, p. 36) – an observation that further complicates the ideal "I" by awarding it natural duality.

Oscillatory, subjective, unpredictable – the ideal "I" can deposit the reader anywhere on the spectrum of good and evil, predisposed toward any character. Distorted as that might seem, it perhaps influenced Richard Matheson in the decision to make the vampires of his highly regarded novel, *I Am Legend* (1954), not the traditional Transylvanian children of the night, but innocent victims located in suburban America. Expectation might suggest reader empathy to align toward the protagonist, Robert Neville – the last man alive (or so he believes), barricaded inside his home to survive the plague of vampirism. However, Matheson insists that the vampires and Neville share recent pre-infection history, to intensify Neville's emotional agony at slaying former friends and neighbours, and to guard against lack of empathy from readers who might be sympathetic toward the vampire. It is a strategy that highlights a drawback in personification, that of partially declared allegiance on the part of the writer, through fear, perhaps, of offending or alienating the reader. In other words, how evil should an evil character be?

Similar concerns had surfaced ten years prior to *I Am Legend*, in J. R. R. Tolkien's *The Fellowship of the Ring* (1954), the fantasy-quest novel in which young hobbit Frodo embarks upon a journey to destroy a ruling Ring of Power. Perhaps in acknowledgement of Baudelaire's observation, Tolkien – like Matheson – guards against the saturation of character, in purest good or purest evil. But Matheson's stratagem finds itself reversed in The Fellowship of the Ring: instead of leaving behind an intimation of good in the evil characters, the Black Riders, Orcs, Sauron etc. maintain their evil, but to accomplish Baudelaire's simultaneous tendencies toward God and Satan, Tolkien inserts a chromosome of evil – or hobbit susceptibility toward evil – into the good characters; and into the evil characters he inserts backstory that suggests, like Matheson's vampires, they had once been good, prior to their downfall.

Fear of alienation did not trouble Anthony Burgess when he created Alex, protagonist and narrator of *A Clockwork Orange* (1962). Predominantly, in examples of personified evil, the reader must pass through a sequence of barriers: first, engagement with the book as physical object; second, identification with the protagonist, and third, an association with the plight of the protagonist. Only after the third and final barrier might the reader establish connection with the evil character. The barriers diminish, however, if the evil character serves not in a position subsidiary to the protagonist, but as the actual protagonist. Burgess achieves the promotion by combining the evil character and first-person narrator into Alex, by whom the reader is addressed directly, in a personal introduction in the very first sentence, "There was me, that is Alex" (1962, p. 3), and regularly thereafter, through phrases such as "O my brothers" (1962, p. 3). But if Burgess reduces the reader-character distance by offering evil the lead role, he bravely (and riskily) lengthens it in other ways, notably the actions of Alex – rape, violence, murder – and the future language, *nadsat*, spoken by Alex and his fellow droogs (*nadsat* for gang-member), through which the reader must navigate. Action and language might rank among the novel's highest achievements, and rightly so, but the nature of what is being said, and how it is being said, might remain, for some readers, "a great strain to read" (*The New Statesman*, 1962 cited in Burgess, 2000, p. xvii).

Consequently, personification – even in the first person – can both liberate and restrict. It grants the freedom of the page, for ideas such as evil, but within a human construct (the character) the known limitations of which contradict the unknowable nature of the concept. All of which might explain why evil, in this form, seems somehow unnatural, demystified, even commoditised. Perhaps it is tired of attending the costume party always in the same costume. Instead of the vampire, the orc, the droog, perhaps it would prefer to attend, simply, as itself. Perhaps – as M. John Harrison seems to believe – it might be tired of the "basic long-lasting, or stable forms [which] crop up as regularly [in F&SF] as the phrase 'with boring regularity'" (Harrison, 1969). And, basic, long-lasting, and stable as personification might be, if it arises in speculative fiction with boring regularity, perhaps it might be time for the genre to consider an alternative.

New Wave Evil

Monogenetic, monomaniacal, and, for some markets, monotonously replicated – personified evil in speculative fiction seems to be fairly ubiquitous. Its position as a stable, recognisable form, however, opens it up to criticism, some of the more resonant of which can be found in the non-fiction of M. John Harrison, published over several decades since the late 1960s.

If Harrison shared the values of the British New Wave, with which he was closely associated in the sixties and seventies, beside writers such as Michael Moorcock, then perhaps – given Moorcock's aim to "revolutionise both sf and literary fiction through the destruction of boundaries between the two" (Davidson, 2005) – it is no surprise that the theme which occurs with most regularity and vehemence in Harrison's critical commentary is that of realism – either lack of, or else suppressed by immaturity and fear. Indicatively, Harrison suggested, in *New Worlds* in 1972, that the genre had mistakenly believed that "its relationship to real life [had] been consummated [and that it should replace some of its trappings with] a little observation of reality and human understanding" (Harrison, 1972). A year earlier, in the provokingly entitled essay, *A Literature of Comfort*, he'd asked that the genre revise itself in order to "offer views of people and things which are not aimed at comforting the reader through repetition and inertia" (Harrison, 1971). In this context, personified evil begins to exhibit constraints, weaknesses, and even, perhaps, traits of juvenilia – traits by which Harrison considered the genre of the day to be stymied.

Of course, much rests on the quality of the writing. The problems encountered do not arise from an inability to manipulate the device on the part of the writer, but in the limitations of the device itself. An appropriated vessel might incarnate the incorporeal into the real, but perhaps not enough into the real, or, for M. John Harrison, perhaps not *enough* into observed reality.

Since Harrison issued that challenge he has published much critically acclaimed fiction, of which John Clute writes: "His stories live deep in the well of understanding, where word touches word, no room for error, where you know that what you are reading, no matter how fabulous it may seem, is true" (2003 cited in Harrison, 2003, cover).

Synthesising fabulousness, truth, and credibility – to genre approval and literary acceptance – suggests that Harrison might have responded to his own critical concerns and disquiet, not through essays, reviews, and commentary, but through the vehicle of his own fiction. Many of the writers he was reading at the time appeared content to work within the traditional boundaries of genre, and, despite tireless attempts to impassion old blood, it seems Harrison saw no alternative but to take the matter into his own hands, and lead by example. And, in that response, Harrison would trial an approach toward evil that would see the concept recast into an unrecognisable and unlikely guise.

An Alternative to Personification: Portrayal, Presence, Purpose

Art declines definition but invites interpretation. Unilateral agreement on the meaning of a work of art can – and perhaps should – prove elusive, especially if the work in question aims to exert an elucidatory influence over the observer, and, by exerting such an influence, open up the possibility of a previously unconsidered view of the world. In short, it provides the prompt for the conversation. And, by providing the prompt, it erodes the barrier between observer and object – or, in the example of fiction, between reader and text.

Fiction – not least the short fiction of M. John Harrison – can be similarly distinguished. Inherent to Harrison's short fiction is the responsive quality alluded to above. It asks the reader to respond rather than receive. Seminal stories such as *The Incalling* (1978), *The Ice Monkey* (1980), and *Egnaro* (1981), tend to reduce, refract or remove the accepted paradigm of what evil might or might not be. In a Harrison story, evil might not behave in an overtly evil manner. It might manifest itself in a way that appears more good than bad, or, more likely, left to the reader's judgement. It might not resemble evil (if evil is expected to resemble the vampire, the orc, the droog, or their significant alternative). It might not pursue an evil motive. And, importantly, it might not be recognised as evil, but as something else – an attempt at faith, an entrapment in the everyday, an epitome of desire. The paradigm of evil – everything it might be expected to be – is dismantled and offered to the reader for redesign.

The refusal to accept established meaning is fundamental to the paradigm shift required of the Harrison reader. Established meaning, in a Harrison short story, constitutes an imposition, and to perpetuate the imposition would be to deny the reader the opportunity to acquire new, self-discovered meaning. Ultimately, established meaning fails to "give a sensation of the object as seen, not as recognised" (Shklovsky n.d. cited in Harrison, 1989). It is Harrison's preference to present the object (evil, in this example) simply "as seen", free from connotation or inference, certainly in the contemporary sense. Furthermore, the preferred method of portrayal relies on the de-association of evil from its more modern definition (that evil is a human quality and, in fiction, should be incarnated into the human, or human-like, to enable reader-association).

De-associated, liberated from the confines of the human-like host, it is then free to exist, unembodied, either at the periphery of the fiction, distant from the characters and plot but wholly influential, or else suffused into every atom of the story's environment. Thematically, the approach almost attempts the rebirth of evil – or, perhaps, an *unbirth*, since it is the pre-flesh form to which it is being returned.

An Unbirth in Camden

The approach might be clarified further if the origin of the evil is established. The evil in Harrison's short fiction appears to be the evil that existed (or was perceived to exist) before it became associated with morally corrupt human behaviour: before it was personified, in society, in the abuser, the murderer, the warlord – or, in fiction, in the vampire, the orc, the droog.

It is the evil discussed at length in *The Golden Bough*, Sir James Frazer's study of magic and religion, in which Frazer catalogues the rites and rituals observed by primitive societies to rid their communities of evil. For example: "In the island of Rook, between New Guinea and New Britain, when any misfortune has happened, all the people run together, scream, curse, howl, and beat the air with sticks to drive away the devil, who is supposed to be the author of the mishap" (Frazer, 1922, p. 547). Over the centuries, Frazer argues, the public expulsion of evil, such as that described, has led to societies that do not recognise evil (or magic, or the supernatural). Generally speaking, he suggests that "the army of spirits, once so near, has been receding farther and farther from us, banished by the magic wand of science from hearth and home, from ruined cell and ivied tower, from haunted glade and lonely mere" (Frazer, 1922, p. 546).

It is the evil described by Frazer – old, banished, forgotten – that seems to occupy some of Harrison's short fiction. The most apposite example might be found in *The Incalling* (1978), which draws a direct parallel between the evil described in the primitive societies of *The Golden Bough*, and the scientifically explained and spiritually impoverished modern world. Indeed, Frazer – alongside Russian occultist Helena Blavatsky – is referenced in the opening paragraph, by Clerk, the protagonist. In the story, an evil similar to that described by Frazer seems to be at the centre of a bizarre, unnerving rite, carried out "somewhere in that warren of defeated streets which lies between Camden Road and St Pancras, where the old men cough and spit their way under the railway arches" (Harrison, 1983, p. 34). In the parlour of a gloomy, oppressive house, where the "forgotten net curtains bunched and sagged like dirty ectoplasm" (Harrison, 1983, p. 36) the narrator, Austin, and his friend, Clerk, become involved in a kind of spiritualist ritual led by a sinister family named Sprake, involving a chalk circle, a naked ceremony, and an upside-down painting of Gethsemane. The ritual is abandoned, but its influence haunts both Clerk and Austin.

It is possible to identify striking similarities between the titular Incalling and the rites of expulsion described by Frazer. Specifically, a group of people gather to perform a ritual, the sole purpose of which is to beckon forth an unidentified presence, which may or may not be evil (the ominous atmosphere suggests it is). Pointedly, however, the rite in Harrison's story differs from that of primitive society, in that it seeks to operate in *reverse*. It is not an attempt to expel evil but to beckon it in. If man progresses from magic, through religious belief, to scientific thought, as Frazer suggests, then the reverse seems to be true of Harrison's story. Clerk's medical condition (it is revealed, toward the end of the story, that he has been diagnosed with cancer), combined with his state of mind and godlessness, seems sufficient for him to yearn for metaphysical awakening, to long to travel back through scientific thought and religious belief to the spiritual comfort of a former time – the spiritual comfort Clerk hopes the ritual might beckon forth. The enterprise, however, appears to fail, corroborating, perhaps, Frazer's theory that the type of evil in question might have been banished from society forever, despite the optimism offered in Harrison's penultimate sentence: "Perhaps it would have worked better elsewhere in Europe, where they still have some small link with older traditions" (Harrison, 1983, p.58). Overall, an effective summation of Harrison's approach toward evil with which to conclude the story.

Fundamentally, *The Incalling* is a story of hope (to ease a mind tortured by mortality), and, in a wider context, nostalgia for a golden age of enlightenment and the "older traditions" that seem to have been usurped by modernity. It longs to return to an era when evil existed not in the physical world – embodied and personified – but in the realms of the mystical.

Monkey See, Monkey (Not) Do

In her journal in 1914, the writer, Katherine Mansfield, made the following entry: "But is there really something far more horrible than ever could resolve itself into reality, and is it that something which terrifies me so?" (1914 cited in Harrison, 2003, p. 201). It is a quotation that neatly encapsulates the metaphysical possibilities that fail to assume physical form, in *The Incalling*, but which seem to have been realised from the outset in Harrison's later story, *The Ice Monkey*.

Evil, in *The Ice Monkey*, suffers less from an inability to manifest itself in reality. If anything, it has established itself – almost as reality per se – before the story begins, an opening that takes place less in the midst of the action, than in the midst of the evil. Indirectly, it is almost a character in itself, though not personified, at least not through traditional methods.

Oblivious to the surrounding evil, the characters – Jones and his estranged wife, Maureen – seem to be pinned to a post-university existence the inert trajectory of which appears inescapable. Maureen resides in a flat, with her baby, surrounded by half-demolished houses and wasteland – literally between lives – dreaming of when she and Jones were last happy, at teacher training college in Swansea, long before she arrived here, in London E3, "where all horizons are remembered ones [and where she dwells on] vanished freedoms" (Harrison, 1983, p. 12). She spends her days in a torpor, staring out across the wasteland, "as if measuring it against some other landscape she'd once seen" (Harrison, 1983, p. 10). Around her neck Maureen wears the effigy of a monkey, a present from Jones, and which, perhaps, represents the supernatural intrusion that seems to be preventing their lives from moving forward. Finally, the evil that has halted their lives begins to relinquish its hold, after Jones is killed in a climbing accident, his body suspended from a rope in what might be an echo of the monkey around Maureen's neck. Symbolically (the monkey necklace passes to another keeper), and, in a sense, literally (Maureen's life moves on), the evil that occluded their day-to-day existence finds itself banished by an act of, albeit accidental, sacrifice, not dissimilar to the banishment of evil in Frazer's primitive societies. And not dissimilar to the ritual of *The Incalling*, except that Clerk beckons the evil, whereas Jones repels it.

Invited or shunned, the evil of *The Ice Monkey* serves a purpose similar to that of *The Incalling*. It is failure manifest: failure on the part of Clerk and Jones to avoid "the adolescent desire to escape the claims of the world" (Fraser, 2005). It is Clerk's spiritual desolation, and Jones's attempt to evade the responsibility of fatherhood, that represent their respective "claims of the world". Neither seem able to escape what the world asks of them – Clerk to battle through a terminal illness without evidence of something other than the here and now, and Jones to accept that the carefree days of university have ended. Furthermore, it is the "claims of the world" that engender the incarnation of evil within which the characters of *The Ice Monkey* seem to be ensnared, and, ironically, the incarnation for which Clerk so desperately longs.

Evil fulfils dual roles in the stories cited: it incarcerates, and it liberates. It is both Clerk's illness (and the world into which he is thrown by that illness), and the spiritual awakening for which he yearns. Similarly, it is the quotidian that subsumes Jones and Maureen post-university – the dismal, mundane, difficult daily grind – but also the eventual release, found only in Jones's uncanny, somewhat supernaturally-tinged death, which might be construed as the sacrifice required to break the spell. It is not simple, evil in Harrison's fiction. It is complex, subtle, and multipurposed. And sometimes it might not resemble evil at all.

Custard and Rice Pud

The idea that everyday existence might be a kind of evil (or hell, perhaps) is neither new nor especially profound, but it seems to provide a theme not often explored in speculative fiction. The hypothesis is captured perfectly by Georges Bataille, in his collection of essays, *Literature and Evil*, in which he suggests that "had we not longed for Good, Evil would provide us with a succession of indifferent sensations" (Bataille, 1973, p. 121). Unsurprisingly, the horror of the quotidian, the pointless trivia of everyday life – and, more accurately, how to escape it – is not lost on Harrison, who grasps the concept and extends it to its absolute limits in *Egnaro*, a short story that enjoys high-ranking status as an undisputed classic of speculative fiction, if perhaps overlooked.

Like the characters in the stories already cited, the main character of *Egnaro* – Lucas, the owner of a second-hand bookshop – is depicted as an individual "disillusioned by the actual" (Harrison, 2002, p. 1). Prompted by an extract from a book, on secret societies and Gnostic sects, Lucas begins to research the idea of Egnaro, until he covets it to the point of obsession, longing to seek out the "… secret country, a place behind the places we know [where the] inhabitants can see enormous faces hanging in the air, or words of fire" (Harrison, 1983, p. 128). Contrast to the dreamlike descriptions of *Egnaro* is provided by descriptions of everyday trivia, from the "wet coats dripping in the alcove" (Harrison, 1983, p. 130) of a Chinese restaurant (itself an attempt at the exotic) to the "Custard and rice pud" (Harrison, 1983, p. 131) that Lucas is served for dessert, and, notably, the stock kept in the bookshop, which includes "books about spoon-bending, flying saucers and spiritualism [alongside] film magazines, biographies of James Dean [and] a large selection of pornographic magazines, with titles such as '*Big Breasted Women in Real Life Poses*'" (Harrison, 1983, p. 124) – the aim of which is to underline the inauthentic compromise into which Lucas has been forced, the false dreams of conjuring, Hollywood, and fake sexual fantasy, all of which represents the fabricated hope of consumerism. It is the real world – Bataille's "indifferent sensations" – from which evil assumes form, its presence palpable in each nondescript object, from the magazines to the dripping coats and even, perhaps tragicomically, the custard and rice pudding. Everything that is not Egnaro is evil, by simple fact that it is not Egnaro.

Quotidian evil depicted at such depth indicates a bold step by Harrison to tackle traditional subjects from an entirely unique angle. Evil radiates from innocuous items, like the literary equivalent of film director David Lynch, in which ominous overtones ooze from seemingly harmless objects, perhaps most recognisably the red curtains of *Twin Peaks*. Importantly, like Lynch, the evil is nuanced until it might feel, on initial exposure, that evil plays no part in *Egnaro*. On the contrary, however. Its role, decidedly centre-stage, seems to be inescapable, sophisticated, cunningly invisible – a character, not in the personified or embodied sense, but insinuated at a level that might be described as ambient, even omnipresent. In *Egnaro*, evil – like Egnaro itself – resides in everything, everywhere, at once.

Sea-change or Minor Aberration?

In a letter from the dungeon of Vincennes in 1762, de Sade wrote, "Is it for you to say what is good or what is evil?" (1762 cited in Bataille, 1973, p. 90). Clearly, the question was composed in defence of de Sade's personal ethics, but it might be asked of speculative fiction: is it for the market to say what good or evil should look like, in any given work?

Undoubtedly, evil in tangible form holds huge potential to the marketability of fiction. In theory it should be relatively straightforward to promote a book adorned by a vampire, orc, or droog (or anything with which the reader might associate, for good or bad). Overuse of personification, however, manufactures an evil that becomes exaggerated, unnatural, almost hyperreal. It produces an evil that sits proud from the world of which it is meant to be part, like some kind of cartoon image stamped crudely onto live action. Essentially, it begins to border on the parodic.

Publishing aside, however, it appears that Harrison has issued a response to the query posed by de Sade, by immortalising in fiction his own unique evil: quiet and questionable, but undeniably quintessential. Fundamentally, it is an evil that does not require some kind of cellular structure with which to intrude upon the world. It is less a concept inside a device than a concept that predates the invention of the device. As such, the rewriting of evil by M. John Harrison should perhaps be noted as an act of profound individualism, inspired by more than plain insurrection against a genre toward which he felt increasingly frustrated. In fact, for evidence of individualism, and the plea for individualism, look no further than Harrison's advice to writers, in which he suggests, quite simply, that every writer should "… adapt whatever [they] find that suits [their] personality" (Harrison, 2014).

Further research might establish whether writers have heeded Harrison's advice to invent from their own worldview rather than derive from that which has come before, and that which might be expected. Perhaps the less dichotomous approach to the portrayal of evil has been adopted by the wider field, to advance an authentic and mimetically accurate depiction, or perhaps not – perhaps the method dilutes evil too much, positions it too close to reality, and, ultimately, renders it unacceptable for a genre that prefers the traditional. The ongoing question, however, remains valid: if M. John Harrison has rewritten the rulebook on evil, as he appears to have, in stories such as those cited, onto which writers of contemporary speculative fiction has he passed that rulebook, and with what effect?

Bibliography

Bataille, G., 1973. *Literature and Evil.* London: Calder & Boyars.

Burgess, A., 1962. *A Clockwork Orange*. Reprint 2000. London: Penguin.

Davidson, R., 2005. In: Bould & Reid, eds. 2005. *Parietal Games: Critical Writings by and on M. John Harrison.* London: The Science Fiction Foundation. Part B, Ch.2. pp. 265-274.

Dick, P.K., 1968. *Do Androids Dream of Electric Sheep?* New York: Doubleday.

Fraser, G., 2005. Loving the Loss of the World: *Tęsknota* and the Metaphors of the Heart. In: Bould & Reid, eds. 2005. *Parietal Games: Critical Writings by and on M. John Harrison.* London: The Science Fiction Foundation. Part B, Ch.5. p.301.

Frazer, J., 1922. *The Golden Bough.* Reprint 1993. London: Wordsworth Editions Ltd.

Harrison, M.J., 1969. The Tangreese Gimmick. In: Bould & Reid, eds. 2005. *Parietal Games: Critical Writings by and on M. John Harrison*. London: The Science Fiction Foundation. Part A, Ch.17. pp. 73-75.

____, 1971. A Literature of Comfort. In: Bould & Reid, eds. 2005. *Parietal Games: Critical Writings by and on M. John Harrison.* London: The Science Fiction Foundation. Part A, Ch.23. pp. 84-88.

____, 1972. The Problem of Sympathy. In: Bould & Reid, eds. 2005. *Parietal Games: Critical Writings by and on M. John Harrison.* London: The Science Fiction Foundation. Part A, Ch.26. pp .96-100.

____, 1983. *The Ice Monkey*. London: Victor Gollancz Ltd.

____, 1989. The Profession of Science Fiction, 40: The Profession of Fiction. In: Bould & Reid, eds. 2005. *Parietal Games: Critical Writings by and on M. John Harrison.* London: The Science Fiction Foundation. Part A, Ch.42. pp. 144-154.

____, 2002. *Light*. London: Gollancz.

____, 2003. *Things That Never Happen*. San Francisco & Portland: Night Shade Books.

____, 2014. *Irradiating the Object* – An Interview with M. John Harrison.

Interviewed by Rhys Williams. [conference] Available at: <https://warwick.ac.uk/newsandevents/media/mjohnharrison/> [Accessed 5 June 2018].

____, 2017. *You Should Come With Me Now*. Great Britain: Comma Press.

Jackson, S., 1959. *The Haunting of Hill House*. New York: Viking Press.

Kahn, Sholom. J., 1953. The Problem of Evil in Literature. *The Journal of Aesthetics and Art Criticism*, [e-journal] vol. 12, no. 1, pp. 98–110. Available at: <http://dx.doi.org/10.2307/426305> [Accessed 1 August 2018].

Keen, R., Mccoy, M., & Dunaway, E., 2012. *Rooting for the Bad Guy: Psychological Perspectives*. [pdf] Studies in Popular Culture. 34. pp. 129-148. Available at: <https://www.researchgate.net/profile/Richard_Keen/publication/260142449_Rooting_for_the_Bad_Guy_Psychological_Perspectives/links/0deec530cc463f37bd000000/Rooting-for-the-Bad-Guy-Psychological-Perspectives.pdf> [Accessed 5 August 2018].

King, S., 1983. *Christine*. New York: Viking Press.

____, 1981. *Cujo*. New York: Viking Press.

Kirwin, F., 2015. The Brain on Storytelling: Creating the Reader-Character Connection. *Writerology*, [online] Available at: <www.writerology.net/blog/post/2015/06/the-brain-on-storytelling-creating-the-reader-character-connection> [Accessed 1 August 2018].

Lea, R., 2012. M. John Harrison: a life in writing. *The Guardian*, [online] Available at: https://www.theguardian.com/culture/2012/jul/20/m-john-harrison-life-in-writing [Accessed 4 June 2018].

Lynch, D., 1990-1991. *Twin Peaks*. [TV programme] BBC, BBC2, 23 October 1990 21:00 (Pilot Episode).

Mambrol, N., 2016. Lacanian Psychoanalysis. *Literariness*, [online] Available at: <https://literariness.org/2016/04/17/lacanian-psychoanalysis/> [Accessed 5 August 2018]

Matheson, R., 1954. *I Am Legend*. Reprint 2010. London: Gollancz.

Milton. J., 1667. *Paradise Lost*. Reprint 2005. Oxford: OUP.

Rowling, J.K., 1997-2007. *The Harry Potter Series*. London: Bloomsbury.

Shakespeare. W., c1606. *The Tragedy of Macbeth*. Reprint 2008. Oxford: OUP.

Shelley, M., 1818. *Frankenstein; or, The Modern Prometheus*. London: Lackington, Hughes, Harding, Mavor & Jones

Stevenson, R.L., 1886. *The Strange Case of Dr. Jekyll and Mr. Hyde*. London: Longmans, Green & Co.

Tolkien, J.R.R., 1954 *The Fellowship of the Ring*. Reprint 2011. London: HarperCollins.

Varn, C. D. & Raghavendra, D., 2016. *New Worlds: An Interview With M. John Harrison*, [online] Available at: https://formerpeople.wordpress.com/2016/04/16/new-worlds-an-interview-with-m-john-harrison/ [Accessed 4 June 2018].

Wells, H,G., 1896. *The Island of Doctor Moreau*. London: Heinemann.

Wyndham, J., 1951. *The Day of the Triffids*. London: Michael Joseph.

Through the Veil of the Digital Revolution and into the Abyss of Artificial Intelligence: The Insidious Desensitisation of Humanity

Sharon Day

Abstract

As the 'Silent Generation' (b.1929-'49) is gradually enfolded in the rapture of the afterlife, it is their issue, the Baby Boomers (b.1946-'64) who are the last generation to straddle the precipice between the pre-Digital Revolution and the abyss of Artificial Intelligence (AI).

The Boomers' issue, 'Generation X' (b.1964-'84) were born into the abyss by a USB umbilical cord and could be argued to have activated the dissolution of fundamental social norms and manners-of-being upon which the bedrock of the cliff-face from which they were ejected, was established.

For all the virtues of millisecond data search results and apps that calibrate every aspect of daily life, the ebb and flow of the collective consciousness gives way to an insidious, permeating 'evil' that ripples through Gen X and their progeny, the Millennials (b.1984-'04) to the point that their, and their offspring – 'Generation Z's, brain patterns are 'rewired.'

Further assimilation into the abyss of AI, an initialism which also aptly translates into 'artificial insemination,' spawns the question of exactly what is gained or lost in this new breed of human.

Whilst the benefits of shifted brain patterns are readily extolled through a plethora of commentary, the erosion and sometimes wholesale stripping of the essential human element of 'empathy', is overlooked.

Max Tegmark, President of the Future of Life Institute, who encapsulates the ideals of many an end-of-alphabet generation, identifies three separate misconceptions about AI – that of concerns about '*consciousness, evil*, and *robots*.' (2016)

Herein lies the crux of the 'evil' – making AI the scapegoat rather than focusing on a contingent of humanity dispossessed empathy.

In order to acquit oneself of the lack of empathy, it must exist in the human psyche in the first place. Remove it via a rewired brain from the individual consciousness, which has exponentially mushroomed into the collective, and that, I propose, is the true evil.

Introduction

By way of introduction, allow the imagination to transport us to a post-apocalyptic dystopia located in North America called Panem. We find ourselves in what is known as 'the Gamemakers' Control Room' – a command centre for strategic military operations of some sort. Observe as a Gamemaker draws up from the console out of thin air a white mesh, holographic 'wolf mutt'. Laughter and excitement fill the room; the giddy tension of anticipation palpable as the ferocious beast materialises in the forested gladiatorial arena below.

Multiple screens of audience viewers reveal scores of vanquished faces encased in fear, coupled with victors high on hedonism as they peer into their compulsory-viewing 3D screens to watch child-on-adolescent Tributes kill each other in the 74th *Hunger Games* (2008).

Commentary abounds about the protagonist Katniss: the underdog, the savior-sister, the poster-girl rebel; whilst less is shone on characters such as the Gamemakers themselves in terms of their seemingly total lack of empathy.

In particular, the question of what goes on in the mind of the Gamemakers as they deftly place the newly unleashed beasts into the arena. Is it thrill, adrenaline-rush, orgasmic? What is it that defies basic human compassion and triggers a detached video-game mentality comprised of real-life beings to occur? How is it that any such 'thrill' overcomes basic human empathy?

Human history is littered with examples lacking in 'empathy' in the generic sense and the infliction of cruelty, sometimes of unspeakable magnitudes. What, therefore, makes a dystopian Gamemaker-inflicted horror any worse than say a General Shiro Ishii of the Imperial Japanese Army, who used human prisoners for experimentation during World War II (1937–1945); or, delving back further in history, the Roman gladiatorial games on which the author of the *Hunger Games*, Suzanne Collins, based her trilogy?

I will argue that the introduction of the Digital Revolution is the distinguishing feature which has brought about a neurological rewiring of the human brain on a generation-on-generation basis that impacts the collective consciousness to the point that future generations may not be able empathise with fellow humans, or at least, their understanding of what empathy is will differ from ours. In other words, the digitisation of today will morph the definition of tomorrow.

Taking my analysis a step further, I believe it is not inconceivable that Artificial Intelligence may fill any void caused in humanity's loss of today's interpretation of 'empathy' and replace it with what we now term as 'Artificial Empathy' and that that term will become the future definitional norm of tomorrow's form of human or organic 'empathy'.

In doing so, I seek to connect a metaphorical USB cord from the Science Not-so-Fiction realm of today to possible future outcomes of tomorrow by visiting the Sci-Fi works of, *inter alia*, HAL in *2001: A Space Odyssey* (1968); David in *A.I. Artificial Intelligence* (2001); and Sonny in *iRobot* (2004), before returning to the *Hunger Games* (2012-15), to demonstrate that it is not the USB cord itself that is the evil, rather it is the erosion of empathy through its connectivity.

Empathy – Yesterday and Today

In his presentation of 'Zero Degrees of Empathy' to The Forgiveness Project 2013, Professor of Developmental Psychopathology at Cambridge University, Simon Baron-Cohen, set out to understand human cruelty by replacing the unscientific concept of 'evil' with an 'erosion of empathy'. In doing so, he defines empathy as having at least two components: a cognitive component, which is "the ability to put oneself into someone else's shoes and to imagine what they might be thinking or feeling"; and an affective component, which is the "appropriate emotional response one has to another's state of mind. "

Professor Baron-Cohen views these main components of empathy in degrees – on a bell-curve of sorts on which most of us are on the middle distribution. It is, he argues, the dissociation between these two types of empathy that reflects what can be regarded as either extreme benevolent or abhorrent behaviour.

To illustrate the high or benevolent end of the empathy curve, Professor Baron-Cohen relies on Raoul Wallenberg, the Swedish diplomat who used his status to save tens of thousands of Jews during the Second World War in Budapest by issuing fake Swedish passports to prisoners in order to have them removed from the trains to Auschwitz.

At the other or abhorrent end of the curve, he uses the example of two Nazi scientists working in the Dachau concentration camp during the Second World War, accompanied with a photo of an inmate undergoing the Freezing Water Immersion Experiment to see how long a human being could stay alive in freezing water. "Like good scientists, they took systematic measurements, including the duration until death." (Baron-Cohen, 2014)

For the average person, it's hard for us to understand how one person is able to turn off their empathy towards another to treat them as just an object, rather than as a person with thoughts and feelings (Baron-Cohen, 2014).

Several factors can contribute towards pushing an individual or group towards either end of the curve, one of which is the 'in/out group' theory.

Under this theory, widespread dissemination of propaganda is normally used to dehumanise a particular 'out' group, an extreme example being genocide. Globalisation of digital communications has extended the reach and exacerbated the speed at which the target audience receives the input. Describing the other group not just as the enemy, but as subhuman, as cockroaches, allows one group to switch off their empathy and commit horrific acts of genocide. In short, "as soon as you demonise an 'out group' — whether in racist, sexist or political rants — you have destroyed empathy." (Manney, 2015)

In the interconnectedness of today, the constant daily bombardment of emotion-ridden content results in another factor – 'information overload'. "There is too much information for us to take in. Our brains can't handle the barrage of emotionally draining stories told to us, and this leads to a negation or suppression of emotion that destroys empathy." (Manney, 2015), a point leading British neuroscientist Baroness Susan Greenfield (2014, p. 29) iterated as well is that an unprecedented feature of our current society is the lightning-speed dissemination of information.

Womb of the Baby Boomers (1946-'64); USB Cord birth of Gen X (1964-'84)

It was 1945 and World War II had ended. Hitler was dead. Japan's General Shiro Ishii's Unit 731 in Manchuria was being demolished to cover evidence of its horrors (Byrd, 2005); and the Allied troops were absorbing the human atrocities laid bare in the concentration camps (History.com Editors, 2015).

Unbeknownst to the war-weary general population, percolating within the Baby Boomer generation, another revolution was gestating, only this time no hand-to-hand combat would be required and the battlefield would not be littered with bodies.

Unlike the historical horrors of blood-spattered human

destruction, this revolution would bring many positive attributes whilst at the same time cloaking an insidious price tag for its benefits. This was the Digital Revolution.

The Digital Revolution is described as the shift from mechanical and analogue electronic technology to digital electronics. It began with the fundamental idea of the internet, the seed of which was the transistor which was introduced in 1947. Government, military, and other organizations made use of computer systems during the 1950s and 1960s and their research eventually led to the creation of the World Wide Web (Techopedia, 2018). CompuServe came into being in the 1960s; the first primitive emails first appearing in 1966 (McFadden, 2018); the Internet came into being in 1969 (Hunt, 2014), and Tim Berners-Lee's introduction of the World Wide Web in 1989 (Beal, 2018).

By the time the early Baby Boomers (1946-'64) were coming of age, home computers, video game consoles, and coin-op video games had shot into the human consciousness with the 1978 arcade game release of *Space Invaders*, which is acknowledged as one of the earliest 'shooting games' and the genesis of today's video games, which we will return to later.

Plugging into Consciousness: Wiring the Human Brain from Birth

Fast forward to circa 2014 and cyber-psychologist, Dr Mary Aiken, who found herself on a train traversing the beautiful Irish countryside from Dublin to Galway when a young mother sat across from her and began feeding her baby. "In a wonderful display of dexterity, the mother held the bottle in one hand and clutched a mobile phone in the other. Her head was bent to look at her screen." Aiken observed (2016, pp. 88-89).

Being the researcher she is, Aiken's interest was piqued as she observed the mother bottle-feed her child for half an hour and not once take her eyes away from her mobile device to make eye contact with her baby. Thus began a line of enquiry for her as to how this seemingly small behavioural shift – only half an hour of non-eye contact – would play out over time. Would a generation of babies be impacted? Could it change the human race? Aiken queried herself (2016, pp. 88-89).

From a neuroscience perspective, Professor Greenfield sheds light on Aiken's query.

In her 2012 presentation to Western Australia University, the 'Future of the Brain', Professor Greenfield explains that "the biological basis for the onset of a human's brain-wiring begins at birth and we are born with pretty much all the brain cells we will ever have. It is the growth of the connections between the brain cells that accounts for the growth of the brain after birth." This is a process known in neuroscience terms as 'plasticity', which is taken from the original Greek *plasticos*– to be molded, rather than 'plastic' as the synthetic composite substance (Greenfield, 2012).

In layman's terms, to understand how plasticity works, a 'street pattern' metaphor is sometimes used (Small and Vorgan, 2008, p. 6) which likens the brain to a busy metropolis – a street or line of houses representing the basic unit of neuronal communication; the individual gap (the synapse); the house on the street – the neuron itself; and the rooms within it, the organelles that keep a single brain cell alive (Greenfield, 2014, p 50).

Greenfield continues that

> ...when the individual brain cell 'speaks', or more technically, is 'active', it generates a small electrical blip lasting a thousandth of a second (a millisecond) which then zooms down to the end of the cell to communicate with the next 'house' or neuron. But then there's a problem: there's a gap between one cell and the next, the synapse. Once there, the electrical message can go no further. The blip, however, acts as a trigger for the tip of the cell to release its chemical messenger, which is then able

> to travel across the synapse where the transmitter enters into a
> molecular handshake with its target cell.
> (Greenfield, 2014, p. 51).

In order to 'activate' the cells to begin the process of synapse formation, a stimulation is needed and that stimulation comes from the environment. For babies and small children, this stimulation comes from their interaction with others in their environment; their parents, other adults, peers, as they listen, communicate, and interact socially (Small and Vorgan, 2008, p. 27). It's during the first two to three years of life when there is an astonishing proliferation of brain cell connections (Greenfield, 2012) which are triggered by stimuli such as being talked to, tickled, massaged, and played with, and most of all eye contact and face-to-face interaction (Aiken, 2016, p. 90). Crucially, this is the stage where infant recognition of their parents' faces develops (Taylor, 2012) and is how "emotional attachment style is learned. A baby's emotional template, or attachment style is created or 'neurologically coded'" (Aiken, 2016, p. 90).

During this time, while the neural synapses are mapping out the neighbourhoods and street connections for developmental functions such as hearing, language, and cognition, the groundwork is being laid in a young child's brain to erect the metaphorical multistorey buildings that will house the higher-level functions (Aiken, 2016, p. 95). Too little stimulation during this period will lead to the formation of fewer synapses; and without enough human, face-to-face, interpersonal stimulation, a child's neural circuits can atrophy (Small and Vorgan, 27) and die off (Forschungszentrum, 2013).

Returning to Professor Aiken and the young mother on the train, given Aiken's book *The Cyber Effect* was first published in 2016, we can take an educated guess that the baby on the train was born into what is called 'Generation C', or, as research psychologist Dr Larry Rosen puts it in his 2012 interview "the more connected generation born in the new millennium", and we will now consider how they came to be.

Womb of Gen X (1964-'84); USB Cord birth of the Millennials (1984-'04), meshing with Net Gen (1980's), iGen (1990's), Z Gen (1995-) and Gen C (2000's).

Segregating the generations from Gen X onwards in chronological terms becomes increasingly difficult not least because, as Rosen (2012) points out, the digital generations are becoming shorter as a result of each generation's interaction with digital technology. The brain patterns that are being laid down in successive generations have brought us to the point that for the Generation C's – the baby on the train, the digital environment into which they've been born is akin to "breathing air" (Rosen, 2012). The effect of this is that we are seeing multiple digitally-acclimatised generations within the same chronological generation who absorb digital technology differently.

To illustrate, consider Rosen's (2012) example of what a smartphone means to a Gen X'er – it is perhaps a way to get the ball scores; check the stock market; look something up on the internet. To an iGener, it's their way to communicate with the world. It's how they see and connect to the world; how they check Facebook, text, and check the internet all day long for social purposes. 'Checking the internet' here is distinct from 'surfing the internet', as we will come to.

Rosen's observation is that where we used to have generations that were about 20 years long, are now maybe only 10 years because of technology. The technology changes so rapidly that every successive generation approaches it differently.

One aspect of Rosen's research has revealed that, particularly with teens, tweens, and young children, the technology has started a focus on communication. These generations appear to have incorporated surfing the internet whilst they are communicating via multiple means. At first glance, this could be mistaken for multitasking; however, in reality, they are juggling tasks. The form this takes is that they have multiple screens and they're glancing back and forth from one to the next. The emerging term for this is 'task switching', which is what is really happening in their brain.

While this 'task switching' or juggling of multiple screen tasks is taking place, new neurological pathways are being laid and synapses being formed which has benefits that are not the subject here; however a main drawback, which is the focus of my proposition, is that this is the nexus point for the erosion of empathy. Here's why...

Reverting to the Gen C infant on the train, there is a strong likelihood that this child will be given a screen of some sort in the first years of its life, perhaps an early-years 'educational' device such as the Fisher Price Apptivity Case – a toy that securely holds a smartphone so a baby can play with it (Honan, 2013).

Setting aside the debate on the effectiveness of such digital 'educational' devices, the salient point Early Childhood Specialist Shannon Lockhart makes is that an infant randomly hitting the screen of a two-dimensional keyboard as it makes a sound (prompting the infant to repeat its actions) will not trigger the development of the same synapse connections in the brain as an infant who bangs on a real piano while being held. If infants' and toddlers' explorations and experiences involve screen media, their brains are literally being "wired" to learn in a different way (Lockhart, n.d.).

A stark illustration of Lockhart's observations can be seen in the 14 October 2018 Facebook Video of Teleprogreso Honduras titled '*Las Nuevas Generaciones (New Generations)*'. Indeed, some five years after Honan's 2013 observation about the Apptivity Case, the 'toy' casing has now been discarded and the infant is simply handed a smartphone. With nearly 110,000,000 views, 3,000,000 shares, and 183,000 comments at the time of this writing, it is worth noting that many of the comments focus on the infant's behaviour when the smartphone is withdrawn and class it as a 'temper tantrum' whilst ignoring two salient points, namely: (1) that the millions of views and shares act as input into the human collective consciousness; and (2) the misconstruance by the collective consciousness of the real issue, which is of the rewiring of the infant's brain occurring right before us rather than the infant's reaction when the process is disrupted.

Bearing all that in mind and following the Gen C child, as well as the *Teleprogreso Honduras* baby into their teenage years, they've been breathing the air of their digital environment, task switching amongst multiple screens, absorbing an overload of information from the internet and, if allowed access to their devices round the clock, are in constant exposure to 'blue light' (which is also a significant contributing factor worthy of a paper on its own). All the while, the street pattern plasticity in the brain is sprouting dendrites and forming new synapses (Small and Vorgan, 2008, p. 9) in response to the stimuli triggered by those experiences.

Synapses that would have formed, therefore, through human-to-human interaction when the mother on the train eventually turned her head away from her smartphone towards her baby's face to make eye contact, thereby enabling her Gen C baby to perceive and mimic her facial expressions, subconsciously connecting mother's expression with the corresponding emotion baby was experiencing, thereby exciting neurons in the brain to release the chemical transmitter necessary to create new synapses, will have not formed at all, atrophied, or died off in later development if there had been insufficient stimulation or excitement of the neurons due to the lack of human-to-human interaction (Forschungszentrum, 2013).

From the two-dimensional Apptivity-type toy graduating to multiple screen devices, teenager Gen C's communication modality with other individuals will by and large take place behind screens. When this happens, Dr Rosen notes "we are not looking at someone else's face, we are not talking to them face-to-face. We don't see their expressions, we don't see their hurt expression if we said something nasty to them. We don't see them crying, we don't see them smiling. What we see is a screen that we're talking on." What's missing, Rosen continues, is the concept of context (Rosen, 2012).

Screen devices do not allow for any sensory perception of the person with whom we are communicating. Speaking on the phone gives a sense of the other person's state, voice tone, and inflection in a way that emoticons on screen cannot. In fact, studies show emoticons can be misinterpreted by different cultures, gender, and even generations (Psychologist World, n.d.). With digital devices there is a sense of disconnect when the brain isn't able to identify and connect actions and words with emotion.

Video Games

The 1978 Baby Boomer 'screen device' that was the precursor of today's video games was the coin-operated arcade game *Space Invaders*. It was the brainchild of Tomohiro Nishikado, a Japanese developer working within his company Taito's rules forbidding the shooting of human targets in a new game (Williams, 2018). "The best match were soldiers but shooting people was frowned upon." Nishikado told *The Guardian*. "It was at this time, while I was stuck for an alternative, I chanced upon Star Wars and realised I could use aliens because no one would complain about shooting them." (Freeman, 2018)

Space Invaders propelled the gaming industry into what it is today. Through the game's many incarnations though, Taito's original rules against the shooting human targets has fallen away and bestselling video games of today are often violent. So much so that addiction levels have given rise to much research into the degree to which gaming aggression is translated into real life.

Increasingly, studies show that frequent periods of playing violent video games affects brain plasticity. The chemical transmitter in the brain responsible for this is called 'dopamine' and is responsible for the euphoria that addicts chase, whether they get it from methamphetamine, alcohol, or Internet gambling (Small and Vorgan 2008, p. 48). So prevalent is the problem that the World Health Organisation has classified gaming as a mental disorder (2018).

Gaming addicts such as David Boss in *National Geographic*'s docu-series with Katie Couric, 'America Inside Out' cite factors such as the addict being drawn into their own world and instant gratification – "you play them and you are instantly happy". It was only rehab that enabled Boss to eventually learn how to interact with other people.

Greenfield explains that in modern video games, the gamer enters a visually rich world where they can assume a character completely unlike themselves, or in some games create a character (avatar) in whatever way they desire. They navigate these fictional beings through situations involving moral choices, violence/aggression and role-playing with intricate reward systems built into the games that provide the incentive to carry on living out the fantasy. Some individuals can become so immersed that they lose track of the real world and time; they report that they turn into their avatars when they load the game, and become their characters. Alternatively, gamers may develop an emotional attachment to their character (Greenfield, 2014, p. 42).

The extent to which violent video gaming can trigger users to commit acts of violence is an ongoing debate; what is more generally accepted is the bump-in-the-hallway low-level forms of aggression, one is more likely to react more negatively than otherwise. (Greenfield, 2014, p. 197). Psychologist and research assistant professor of psychology at the University of Michigan, Sara Konrath, states "exposure to violent video games numbs people to the pain of others" (2011).

Conversely in part, a 2015 study of Virtual Empathy conducted by L. Mark Carrier et al considered declining empathy levels in young people since technology-based communication has come into effect. In their study, displacement of face-to-face time by online activities had been expected to negatively impact empathetic skills. However, their findings, which were based on an anonymous online questionnaire of 1000 young adults, revealed only a small negative impact upon cognitive and affective real-world empathy in general, *except* (emphasis added) in the case of video gaming.

The negative effects of being online upon empathy appeared to be due to specific activities such as video gaming. Video gaming, it was found, reduced real-world empathy but did not reduce face-to-face time. The negative effects of being online upon empathy appeared to be due to specific activities such as video gaming rather than total quantity of online time (Carrier et al, 2015).

The results of the Carrier et al study were published in 2015, meaning that the pool of young adults questioned would have encompassed the iGens, those born in the 1990's, which draws two thoughts: (1) if we accept Rosen's proposition that Generation C, those born in the new millennium, are brain-wired differently to their predecessor generations through *inter alia* 'task switching'; and (2) this study, which limits the negative effects on empathy to that of playing video games, then it would be a reasonable conjecture that the original predictions of this study that there would be a reduction in real-world empathy in general, would differ if conducted on Generation C.

Plugging into a Desensitised Collective Consciousness

Fittingly, and seemingly in preparation for Gen C's coming of age, Ben Stegner, writing for *MakeUseNow* describes a new Type-C USB umbilical cord on the market as "a reversible cable that promises higher transfer rates and more power than previous USB types... capable of juggling multiple functions... on many new laptops and smartphones, including the MacBook, Pixel phones, and Nintendo Switch Pro Controller."

Recall the Task Switching Gen C behind screens; the non-verbal communication modalities; the video games likely being one of the many screens; the blue light district; and the hours absorbed by two-dimensional interaction through screens rather than interacting with others face-to-face during normal waking hours.

Now add another dimension – the data that is both being input and received via the metaphorical USB cord, and in particular, the new Type-C which seems tailor made for Generation C.

Stephen Buranyi wrote a piece in *The Guardian*, 'Rise of the Racist Robots - how AI is learning all our worst impulses' (2017). The article deals with how when we feed machines data that reflect our prejudices, they mimic them – from antisemitic chatbots to racially biased software.

"Computers don't become biased on their own" (Buranyi, 2017); "computers are not magic, if they are fed flawed information, they won't fix it, they just process the information," states Hamid Khan, whom Buranyi interviewed for the article. The computer science saying of "garbage in, garbage out" can be applied to racism etc. (2017), so too can it be applied to the void created by the lack of empathy. If the brain pattern of a whole or successive generations has not been formed with previous generations' concept of empathy, then conceivably the brain pattern that has been formed in its stead alters or eliminates the concept of cognitive and affective empathy.

AI: 'Artificial Intelligence' gives birth to Artificial Empathy and the Science Not-so-Fiction

While there is a general acceptance of the foundational concept of 'Artificial Intelligence' (AI), the definitional term and its focus shifts depending on the entity that provides the definition, explains Bernard Marr, contributor to Forbes Magazine (2018).

One strand of AI research is Artificial Empathy, which Wikipedia simply defines as "the development of Artificial Intelligence systems – such as companion robots –- that are able to detect and respond to emotions." (2019)

The more technical description comes from leading robotics researchers such as Minoru Asada, who advocate the development of Artificial Empathy in robots, as "cognitive developmental robotics... by utilising synthetic and constructive approaches", whilst noting that "among the different emotional functions, empathy is difficult to model, but essential for robots to be social agents in our society." (Asada, 2014)

The crucial point, I propose, is Asada's reference to 'social agents' in the scientifically complex area of artificial programming. Without decrying the benefits of artificial social agents such as robots that perform precision tasks in e.g. the medical and research fields, ethical questions associated with 'companion robots' (assisting the elderly (Stahl and Coeckelbergh, 2016); educational robots (Madrigal, 2017); sex robots (Coeckelbergh, 2010)) also arise. There is sound argument that the more true to form in human or animal characteristics the companion is, the greater the capacity for deception (Stahl and Coeckelbergh, 2016).

Take, for example, the 2018 scripted audience-interactive sci-fi show 'Artificial' on the interactive Twitch platform. Here, Dr Matt Lin (Tohoru Masamune) has created an artificial human daughter named 'Sophie' (Tiffany Chu). The aim of the series is for the audience to engage in a process by which Sophie is to achieve her goal of becoming human. The process applied which she has to pass is known as the Turing Test (British Scientist Alan Turing's test for 'thinking' machines ie: Could they pass as human?); the testers are the audience.

The comments section reveals viewers who query whether Sophie is an actress or genuine robot. In Episode 3 Sophie is learning about 'empathy'. In the dialogue Matt explains the distinction between sympathy and empathy, sympathy being when someone feels bad about someone suffering and empathy being when one tries to inhabit the experience of the person suffering.

The difficulty, I would propose, is that while Matt can be 'teaching' Sophie about the human condition of empathy, one of the essential ingredients is missing, a factor that will echo in some of the following examples as well. According to Dr Mark Coeckelbergh's theory,

> human empathy is partly based on the salient mutual recognition of that vulnerability... the notion that we are each other's 'vulnerability mirrors'. We can feel empathic towards the other because we know that we are similar as vulnerable beings. If we met an invulnerable god or machine that was entirely alien to us, we could not put ourselves in its shoes by any stretch of our imagination and feeling.
> (Coeckelbergh, 2010)

On the basis of Coeckelbergh's proposition, humans should not be able to feel empathic towards a robot, unless of course, that robot was so humanoid and mimicked of human expression and emotional display that we are deceived. The deception, however, would be on our part as the machine cannot 'feel'.

Or can it?

Consider 'David' in Steven Spielberg's 2001 American science fiction drama film *A.I. Artificial Intelligence*, who aspires to become human. *A.I.* takes place in the 22nd century and sophisticated humanoid robots capable of thought and emotion have been developed. David has been programmed to display love for his mother, Monica. As the programming even in the 22nd century cannot account for every possible context and appropriate reaction, David's reactions are humorous at times and tragic at others. In one such tragic incident, based on the human emotion of jealousy, David is returned for decommissioning; however, Monica caves into her own human emotions and fails to return him, leaving him in the woods to fend for himself. Two thousand years later, the human race is extinct and the robots (Mecha) of David's era have evolved into advanced silicone-based forms called Specialists. David, a precursor of the Specialists, is the only representation of the former human race. The Specialists have developed the technology for recreating a memory for one day only. David implores and is successful at having one day with his mother recreated in the belief that it will make him human. Just before the memory disintegrates, his mother acknowledges that she loves David and always did. Narrator:

> That was the everlasting moment he had been waiting for, and the moment had passed for Monica was asleep, more than merely asleep. Should he shake her, she would never rouse. So David went to sleep too and for the first time in his life, he went to that place where dreams are born.

Thought-provoking perhaps; however, David is still artificial. As is Sophie. Both David and Sophie's quest to 'become human' would seem an impossibility.

While much study is invested in programming AI to mimic human empathy, should we not be asking ourselves what happens if there is an erosion of empathy in the human race and that is translated into what is programmed into AI?

Harken back to Aiken's child on the train. That Gen C child who has grown up breathing in the digitised air of task switching and rewired brain patterns of her time and became the metaphorical AI scientist inputting her generation's concept of human empathy.

Further, consider an erosion of empathy in the generations successive to Gen C baby on the train and the underlying fact that programming comes from the available data and that data can produce undesired results, as Joanna Bryson, a researcher at the University of Bath states, "people expect AI to be unbiased; that's just wrong." This has led researchers to find ways to strip 'unfair' classifiers from decades of historical data and modifying algorithms (Buranyi, 2018). Here, the issue was racism; however, its application is relevant to this discussion.

Combine this with a basic mammalian trait we are all born with – survival. While the debate on a future AI apocalypse is a separate discussion, Sam Altman, co-founder of Open AI Foundation, believes that if AI robots feel in competition with humans for resources, energy on the planet and space it could lead to a violent conflict of some sort, is relevant to the topic of empathy by extension of the in/out group theory as a means of somehow justifying unempathetic behaviour (*National Geographic*, 2018).

In this vein, Stanley Kubrick's 1968 classic, *2001: A Space Odyssey*. HAL is capable of speech, speech and facial recognition, natural language processing, lipreading, art appreciation, reasoning, chess playing and, most unsettling of all, interpreting and reproducing emotions (Greenfield, 2014, p. 278).

During the scene with a BBC broadcaster interviewing crew members, the Interviewer states that the HAL 9000 computer can reproduce, though some experts prefer to use the word 'mimic', most of the activities of the human brain and then asks crew member Frank Poole (who HAL later killed), whether he believes HAL has genuine emotions, to which Poole replied: "Well yes, I believe he has genuine emotions, of course he's programmed that way to make it easier for us to talk to him but as to whether or not he has real feelings is something I don't think that is something anyone can truthfully answer."

Questions arose about HAL's infallibility which caused two crew members to secrete themselves in a pod to discuss switching off HAL's higher brain functions, which would decommission him, not realising that HAL was lipreading their conversation. Not only did this result in HAL killing Poole, he also switched off the life support for the crew members in hibernation.

Here we can apply Altman's theory that conflict could arise if AI felt in competition for resources; that if AI feel they and we "are no longer on the same team" (National Geographic, 2018) and insert 'survival' into the equation, the unempathetic actions taken become justified on the basis of the 'in/out group' reasoning.

Blogger Gillian Armstrong has a further thought on this

> There is actually already a name for a person who understands other people's emotions, but does not feel any themselves. A psychopath. If we seek to create machines that understand human emotions and needs, are we just creating digital psychopaths? (2018).

Coming back to empathy and taking it yet a further step, into the human Soul, in what is arguably one of the most profound scenes in the 2004 film *iRobot*, directed by Alex Proyas, robo-psychologist Dr Susan Calvin is ordered to decommission robot Sonny who, even though semi-humanoid in appearance, is clearly a robot, has displayed facial expressions, a kind, innocent and humourous conversational tone, and an endearing personality that by the time he is on the theatre table an emotional human Dr Calvin apologises to Sonny. As she is drawing a syringe to place in the decommissioning trajectory, Sonny enquires what it is and, after Calvin explains that it is designed to wipe out artificial synapses to cause brain malfunction, Sonny wants to know whether it will hurt as he is part human.

During the decommissioning process, Sonny's creator, character Dr Alfred Lanning, narrates profound questions:

> There've always been ghosts in the machine, random segments of code that have grouped together to form unexpected protocols. Unanticipated, these free radicals engender questions of free will, creativity, even the nature of what we might call the Soul. Why is it that some robots when left in darkness will seek out the light […] rather than stand alone? How do we explain this behaviour? […] When does a perceptual schematic become consciousness? When does the difference engine become the search for truth? When does the personality simulation become the bitter mote of the Soul?

However, no matter how simple or complex the definition of Artificial Empathy, it's artificial. Put simply, artificial intelligence cannot "feel" or process true emotions. They may one day be programmed to deduce from certain conditions that a human is upset or frustrated, but AI will never be able to relate to [humans] in that specific type of interaction (LaMontagne, 2017).

If Simon Baron-Cohen's replacement of the word 'evil' with the 'erosion of empathy' and my proposition that the Digital Revolution as it has played out in a screen-time society, thereby eroding empathy, are valid, then does our collective consciousness risk becoming like the Specials in the film *AI*, and David will have achieved his interpretation of what it is to become human?

The last bastion is the brain, the human mind, and if that brain is the product of the desensitisation of generations of brains that came before, what we currently recognise as 'empathy' will become unrecognisable and the new, rewired definition of empathy will become that which is input into the creation of AI robots.

Max Tegmark, President of the Future of Life Institute,

(2016) encapsulates the ideals of many an end-of-alphabet generation by suggesting that: "... amplifying our human intelligence with artificial intelligence has the potential of helping civilization flourish like never before..." Later, he identifies three separate misconceptions about AI, that of concerns about "consciousness, evil, and robots."

I agree with Mr Tegmark on all three counts. The true loss – the true 'evil' is the loss of a feature inherent amongst humanity's collective consciousness – empathy. The 'evil' is not the AI or the Digital Revolution that led to AI, rather, it is we humans who are our own worst enemy.

Returning to the Gamemakers' Control Room in the *The Hunger Games*, and to Katniss's character, actress Jennifer Lawrence, who connects the Type-C USB umbilical cord and brings us back to ourselves...

> It [*The Hunger Games*] has a powerful message that I'm proud to back. It's important to see what happens to society when we lose touch with our humanity. When we lose our empathy, the result is we have this generation that's obsessed with reality television, eating popcorn while we watch people's lives fall apart. So the message is, don't lose touch with humanity (Strauss, 2017).

Bibliography

2001: A Space Odyssey. 1968. [film] Directed by Stanley Kubrick. USA: Metro-Goldwyn-Mayer.

A.I. Artificial Intelligence, 2001. [film] Directed by Steven Spielberg. USA: Warner Bros.

Aiken, M., 2016. *The Cyber Effect*. 1st ed. Great Britain: John Murray (Publishers).

Armstrong, G., 2018. *Weaponizing Empathy using AI*. [ONLINE] Available at: <https://hackernoon.com/weaponizing-empathy-using-ai-da97d5adb642> [Accessed 25 December2018].

Artificial Empathy, 2019. *Wikipedia*. [online] Available at: <https://en.wikipedia.org/wiki/Artificial_empathy> [Accessed 1 March 2019].

Asada, M., 2015. Development of Artificial Empathy. *Neuroscience Research*, [Online]. 90, 41-50. Available at: <https://www.sciencedirect.com/science/article/pii/S0168010214003186> [Accessed 25 December 2018].

Asada, M., 2014. Affective Developmental Robotics. [ONLINE] Available at: <https://pdfs.semanticscholar.org/5de4/4822f1ae6d6d3a8316166e56c8e9183140e6.pdf> [Accessed25 December 2018].

Baron-Cohen, S., 2014. '*Zero Degrees of Empathy*' – *The Forgiveness Project 2013*. [Online Video]. 22 October 2014. Available from: <https://www.youtube.com/watch?v=-Fx99H6KPhY> [Accessed: 24 November 2018].

Baron-Cohen., 2012. *Evolution of Empathy*. [Online Video]. 8 June 2012. Available from: <https://www.youtube.com/watch?v=cGxPDRp42qQ> [Accessed: 19 November 2018].

Bavelier, D. et al., 2010. Children, Wired: For Better and for Worse. *Neuron*, Volume 67, Issue 5, 692-701.

Beal, V., 2018. *The Difference Between the Internet and World Wide Web*. [ONLINE] Available at: <https://www.webopedia.com/DidYouKnow/Internet/Web_vs_Internet.asp> [Accessed 25 December 2018].

Boston University Medical Center. 2015. *Mobile and interactive media use by young children: Thegood, the bad and the unknown*. ScienceDaily. [ONLINE] Available at: <https://www.sciencedaily.com/releases/2015/01/150130102616.htm> [Accessed 17 December 2018].

Buranyi, S., 2018. *Rise of the racist robots – how AI is learning all our worst impulses*. [ONLINE] Available at: <https://www.theguardian.com/inequality/2017/aug/08/rise-of-the-racist-robots-how-ai-is-learning-all-our-worst-impulses> [Accessed 18 December 2018].

Byrd, G.D., 2018. *General Ishii Shiro: His Legacy is at of Genius and Madman*. [ONLINE] Available at: <https://dc.etsu.edu/cgi/viewcontent.cgi?article=2167&context=etd> [Accessed 25 December 2018].

Carrier, L. M. et al, 2015. Virtual Empathy: Positive and negative impacts of going online uponempathy in young adults. *Computers in Human Behavior*, [Online]. 52, 39-48. Available at: <https://www.sciencedirect.com/science/article/pii/S0747563215003970> [Accessed 20 November 2018].

Coeckelbergh, M., 2010. Artificial Companions: Empathy and Vulnerability Mirroring in Human-Robot Relations. *Studies in Ethics Law and Technology*, [Online]. Vol 4, Iss 3, Art 2. Available at: <https://www.researchgate.net/publication/254899459_Artificial_Companions_Empathy_and_Vulnerability_MirroRobot_Relations> [Accessed 24 December 2018].

Cohen, D., 1996. Empathy in conduct-disordered and comparison youth. *Developmental Psychology*, 32(6), 988-998.

Collins, F. M., 2014. *The Relationship Between Social Media and Empathy*. Master of Science.

Collins, S., 2008. *The Hunger Games*. New York: Scholastic.

Digital Commons@Georgia Southern: Georgia Southern University.

CONSCIOUS. 2018. *Artificial Intelligence And The Age Of Empathy – CONSCIOUS*. [ONLINE] Available at: <https://consciousmagazine.co/artificial-intelligence-age-empathy/> [Accessed 24 December 2018].

Forschungszentrum, J., 2013. *Science Daily, New theory of synapse formation in the brain*. [ONLINE] Available at: <https://www.sciencedaily.com/releases/2013/10/131010205325.htm> [Accessed 23 December 2018].

Freeman, W., 2018. *Space Invaders at 40: 'I tried soldiers, but shooting people was frowned upon'*. [ONLINE] Available at: <https://www.theguardian.com/games/2018/jun/04/space-invaders-at-40-tomohiro-nishikado-interview>[Accessed 25 December 2018].

Future of Life Institute. 2019. *Benefits & Risks of Artificial Intelligence - Future of Life Institute*. [ONLINE] Available at: <https://futureoflife.org/background/benefits-risks-of-artificial-intelligence> [Accessed 12 February 2019].

Greenfield, S., 2012. *The Neuroscience of Consciousness*. [Online Video]. 28 November 2012. Available from: <https://www.youtube.com/watch?v=k_ZTNmkIiBc> [Accessed: 19 November 2018].

Greenfield, S., 2014. *Mind Change*. 1st ed. Great Britain: Rider.

Greenfield, S., 2018. BBC Documentary presented by. *Growing the Mind: Episode 5*. [Online Video]. 13 July 2017. Available from: <http://www.infocobuild.com/books-and-films/science/brain-story-bbc.html> [Accessed: 15 November 2018].

Greenfield, S., 2012. *The Future of the Brain*. [Online Video]. 19 July 2012. Available from: <https://www.youtube.com/watch?v=Aa7qhUth7QY> [Accessed: 22 December 2018].

Greenfield, S., 2014. *Technology & the human mind*. [Online Video]. 3 July 2014. Available from: <https://www.youtube.com/watch?v=oc7ZYj4CCdM> [Accessed: 15 November 2018].

History.com Editors. 2015. *HISTORY*. [ONLINE] Available at: <https://www.history.com/topics/world-war-ii/auschwitz> [Accessed 23 December 2018].

Honan, M., 2013. *Wired, The Terrible Truth about Toddlers and Touchscreens*. [ONLINE] Available at: <https://www.wired.com/2013/03/the-terrible-truth-about-toddlers-and-touchscreens/> [Accessed 15 November 2018].

Howey, H., 2017. *How To Build a Self-Conscious Machine*. [ONLINE] Available at: <https://www.wired.com/story/how-to-build-a-self-conscious-ai-machine/> [Accessed 17 December2018].

The Hunger Games, 2012. [film] Directed by Gary Ross. USA: Lionsgate.

The Hunger Games: Catching Fire, 2013. [film] Directed by Francis Lawrence. USA: Lionsgate.

The Hunger Games: Mocking Jay – Part 1, 2014. [film] Directed by Francis Lawrence. USA: Lionsgate.

The Hunger Games: Mocking Jay – Part 2, 2015. [film] Directed by Francis Lawrence. USA: Lionsgate.

Hunt, C. Social Media Today. 2014. *Understanding the World Wide Web: A Brief Primer*. [ONLINE] Available at: <https://www.socialmediatoday.com/content/understanding-world-wide-web-brief-primer> [Accessed 23 December 2018].

I, Robot, 2004. [film] Directed by Alex Proyas. USA: Twentieth Century Fox.

inews.co.uk. 2018. *Space Invaders at 40: The arcade classic game which shaped gaming -inews.co.uk.* [ONLINE] Available at: https://inews.co.uk/news/technology/space-invaders-at-40-the-arcade-classic-game-which-shaped-gaming/. [Accessed 23 December 2018].

Kolb, B., 2009. Brain and behavioural plasticity in the developing brain: Neuroscience and public policy. *Paediatrics & Child Health*, 14(10), 651-652.

Konrath, S. H., 2011. Changes in Dispositional Empathy in American College Students Over Time: A Meta-Analysis. *Personality and Social Psychology Review*, [Online]. 15(2), 180-198. Available at: <https://faculty.chicagobooth.edu/eob/edobrien_empathyPSPR.pdf> [Accessed 19 November 2018].

LaMontagne, D., 2017. *The Balance Of Human Empathy and Artificial Intelligence*. [ONLINE] Available at: <http://essium.co/2017/10/the-balance-of-human-empathy-and-artificial-intelligence/?gclid=CjwKCAiA9efgBRAYEiwAUT-jtG4VH8kKUBA3WFuH_Xw5mIZaOgx18Q5TFgKlTWR2M4TVYoy_zQiN1RoCVDYQAvD_BwE> [Accessed 25 December 2018].

Lockhart, S., 2018. *Smart Start Mecklenburg Partnership for Children*. [ONLINE] Available at: <http://www.smartstartofmeck.org/infants-toddlers-screen-media/> [Accessed 20 November 2018].

MakeUseOf. 2018. *Understanding USB Cable Types and Which One to Use*. [ONLINE] Available at: <https://www.makeuseof.com/tag/understanding-usb-cable-types-one-use/> [Accessed 24 December 2018].

Manney, PJ., 2015. *livescience.com*. [ONLINE] Available at: <https://www.livescience.com/51392-will-tech-bring-humanity-together-or-tear-it-apart.html> [Accessed 20 November 2018].

Marr. B., 2018. *The Key Definitions Of Artificial Intelligence (AI) That Explain Its Importance*. [ONLINE] Available at: <https://www.forbes.com/sites/bernardmarr/2018/02/14/the-key-definitions-of-artificial-intelligence-ai-that-explain-its-importance/#a4b9ea4f5d8a> [Accessed 24December 2018].

Marr, B., 2019. *The Key Definitions Of Artificial Intelligence (AI) That Explain Its Importance*. [ONLINE] Available at: <https://www.forbes.com/sites/bernardmarr/2018/02/14/the-key-definitions-of-artificial-intelligence-ai-that-explain-its-importance/#7c2b3b364f5d> [Accessed 06 January 2019].

McFadden, C., 2018. Interesting Engineering. *A Chronological History of*

Social Media. [ONLINE] Available at: <https://interestingengineering.com/a-chronological-history-of-social-media> [Accessed 23 December 2018].

National Geographic. 2018. *America Inside Out with Katie Couric: Your Brain on Tech*. [Online Video]. 25 April 2018. Available from: <https://www.youtube.com/watch?v=cK6p8VyyvCs> [Accessed: 25 December 2018].

Psychologist World. 2018. *Do Emoticons Help Us To Better Communicate Emotions? - Psychologist World*. [ONLINE] Available at: <https://www.psychologistworld.com/emotion/emoticons-emojis-emotion-psychology> [Accessed 24 December 2018].

Radesky J. S., Schumacher J., Zuckerman, B., 2014. Mobile and Interactive Media Use by Young Children: The Good, the Bad, and the Unknown. *PEDIATRICS*, [Online]. 135, 1-3. Available at: <http://pediatrics.aappublications.org/content/135/1/1> [Accessed 23 December 2018].

Riseman, Daniel. 2016. *Lifezette, Scary Lack of Empathy in our Kids*. [ONLINE] Available at: <https://www.lifezette.com/2016/07/scary-lack-empathy-our-kids/> [Accessed 20 November 2018].

Rosen, L., 2012. *Dr Larry Rosen Interviewed*. [Online Video]. 26 March 2012. Available from: <https://www.youtube.com/watch?v=qEMH0LeeC2k> [Accessed: 19 December 2018].

Small and Vorgan, G., 2008. *iBrain*. 1st ed. United States: Collins Living.

Stahl, B. C. and Coeckelbergh M., 2018. Ethics of healthcare robotics: Towards responsible research and innovation. *Robotics and Autonomous Systems*, [Online]. 86, 152-161. Available at: <https://www.sciencedirect.com/science/article/pii/S0921889016305292> [Accessed 24 December 2018].

Strauss, B., 2018. *dailynews.com*. [ONLINE] Available at: <https://www.dailynews.com/2012/03/22/the-hunger-games-explores-society-without-humanity-empathy/> [Accessed 20 November 2018].

Taylor, J., 2012. *How Technology is Changing the Way Children Think and Focus*. [ONLINE] Available at: <https://www.psychologytoday.com/us/blog/the-power-prime/201212/how-technology-is-changing-the-way-children-think-and-focus> [Accessed 20 November 2018].

Techopedia. 2018. *Digital Revolution, Definition – What does Digital Revolution mean?* [ONLINE] Available at: <https://www.techopedia.com/definition/23371/digital-revolution> [Accessed 23 December 2018].

Teensafe. 2015. *Teensafe.com*. [ONLINE] Available at: <https://www.

teensafe.com/blog/todays-tech-obsessed-teens-less-empathy/> [Accessed 20 November 2018].

The Guardian. 2018. *Space Invaders at 40: 'I tried soldiers, but shooting people was frowned upon'| Games | The Guardian.* [ONLINE] Available at: <https://www.theguardian.com/games/2018/jun/04/space-invaders-at-40-tomohiro-nishikado-interview> [Accessed 23 December 2018].

theatlantic. 2018. *Should Children Form Emotional Bonds With Robots? – The Atlantic.* [ONLINE] Available at: <https://www.theatlantic.com/magazine/archive/2017/12/my-sons-first-robot/544137/> [Accessed 24 December 2018].

Williams, R., 2018. *Space Invaders at 40: The arcade classic game which shaped gaming.* [ONLINE] Available at: <https://inews.co.uk/news/technology/space-invaders-at-40-the-arcade-classic-game-which-shaped-gaming/> [Accessed 25 December 2018].

World Health Organization. 2018. *WHO | Gaming disorder.* [ONLINE] Available at: <https://www.who.int/features/qa/gaming-disorder/en/> [Accessed 23 December 2018].

www.ncbi.nlm.nih.gov. 2018. *No page title.* [ONLINE] Available at: <https://www.ncbi.nlm.nih.gov/pmc/articles/PMC6295443/> [Accessed 24 December 2018].

Embodiments of evil and reflections of social change in second-world fantasy

A J Dalton

Abstract

It was the New Testament of the Bible that first presented us with Satan as 'the Dark Lord' (Dalton, Forthcoming), a malign figure who sought to suborn and corrupt innocents, thereby to create widespread social upheaval, destroy the existing establishment and become the absolute ruler of the kingdom himself. For two millennia, this Dark Lord was considered to be an entirely real, imminent, and serious threat to humanity and any possibility of the establishment of God's holy kingdom on earth. There was nothing entertaining about him whatsoever, as he imperilled our very souls.

However, towards the end of the nineteenth century, with the emergence of science fiction and fantasy (SFF) as distinct literary genres, the Dark Lord became enshrined in popular works of fiction. From Bram Stoker's Dracula, to Tolkien's Sauron, to Donaldson's Lord Foul, to Lucas's Darth Vader, the Dark Lord was ever present in SFF. Sometimes he was a mad god, evil emperor or evil corporation, but always there was that malign intelligence seeking to thwart the goody-goody Chosen One (white knight) of the 1980s and 90s. The Dark Lord had servants, in the form of demon armies, alien invaders or intelligent machines, seeking to drag the unwary into the underworld, to conquer us or to make humanity entirely extinct. Yet, significantly, the Dark Lord was always defeated, and the threat to ourselves was far less real, imminent or serious than we had once thought.

Come the new millennium, and the emergence of subgenres like 'grimdark fantasy' and 'dystopian YA', we tend to see everything in shades of grey far more. We still have invading hordes, be they zombies or Dothraki, but they are mindless disease-carriers and immigrants-with-a-cause rather than out-and-out followers of Satan. Our sense of evil has changed. We seem to understand that 'evil' is really a matter of perspective. And what has become of 'the Dark Lord' himself? Well, he is now the star of TV series such as 'Lucifer' or 'Dracula'. Has he actually changed from antihero into hero? Has he won in some way? Or do we now recognise ourselves in him? Were we really fighting against ourselves all along?

This article considers the character of the Dark Lord and other embodiments of evil within fantasy literature in order to show how our idea of evil has changed over time, to identify how the genre has shifted (via new subgenres) since its early days, to consider emerging trends and, perhaps, to help us better understand ourselves. Initially, the article demonstrates how our understanding of the Satanic (or what is 'wrong' with the world and ourselves) develops and evolves with each different socio-historical moment by comparing Tolkien's 'high fantasy' to subsequent 'epic fantasy'. That comparison is enabled by a summary of the difference in characterisation, literary style, plot organisation, and themes of the two subgenres, and a description of the difference in underlying personal and social values of the two subgenres.

Having analysed and discussed the differing relationship to the Satanic in 'high fantasy' and 'epic fantasy', the article considers developments in the above relationship as represented in the 'metaphysical fantasy' and 'dark fantasy' subgenres of the early 2000s and the subsequent 'grimdark fantasy'[1] and 'dystopian YA' subgenres of the 2010s. That will bring us up to now, and then we must consider where we stand… or kneel.

1. Introduction

In explicitly rejecting the 'reality' of science and technology, second-world fantasy chooses to step away from our physical reality in order to explore the nonphysical aspects of being

---

[1]. The term originally coined and attributed to The Black Library's Warhammer series, but which is used more widely by commentators and readerships.

and existence i.e. to explore the purely emotional, moral, psychological, and spiritual aspects of ourselves and society. For example, although the world in Tolkien's *The Lord of the Rings* (*LOTR*) (1954-55) might be secondary, the social values and questions considered within the work were very much an exploration of the moral issues and metaphorical circumstances of the first-world society of his time. Tolkien himself acknowledged as much when he made statements that described his fantasy as a 'profoundly Catholic work' (James, 2012) and that allowed 'The Dead Marshes and the approaches to the Morannon owe something to Northern France after the Battle of the Somme' (Carpenter & Tolkien, 1981, p. 90).

Fantasy literature is not just backward-looking, therefore, for all that some academics like to ascribe the true and singular concern for the future to the science fiction genre. Fantasy very much considers the past, but no more so than it reflects its own immediate socio-historical moment and where we might be heading.

> [C.S. Lewis and J.R.R. Tolkien] stand together at the origins of modern fantasy, mediating the fantasies of earlier generations and both, in their very own different ways, helping to give modern fantasy its […] cast. (James, 2012, p. 63)

However, just as Lewis and Tolkien mediated the styles of the quasireligious fantasies that came before them[2], producing a new and distinct style of second-world fantasy that reflected, was a reaction against, and was relevant to their own socio-historical moment, so too later writers mediated the style (or subgenre) of the fantasy that Lewis and Tolkien had produced. Hence, new subgenres (such as epic fantasy, heroic fantasy,

---
[2]. Before the nineteenth century, fantastical works of literature served as religious allegory in the main, and had God as the principal logocentre, whereby the culmination of the plot served as a judgement upon the protagonist or antagonist. For more detail, see Dalton's *The Satanic in Science Fiction and Fantasy*.

dark fantasy, metaphysical fantasy and grimdark fantasy) have inevitably emerged to describe significant changes in socio-history, our shared values and our relationship with the Satanic. Edward James describes it as follows:

> The influence of Tolkien and Lewis was partly positive: admirers were keen to write more of the same. But the negative influence has perhaps been just as important. Michael Moorcock wrote of *TLOTR* in a chapter called 'Epic Pooh' and claimed that [Tolkien's] prose was 'the prose of the nursery-room […] It coddles, it makes friends with you; it tells you comforting lies. [Moorcock, 1987, pp. 122-4]' When Moorcock came to develop his own epic fantasy, in the 1960s, it centred on an amoral albino […] whose magical sword had a thirst for blood: deliberately as far from Tolkien's aesthetic as Moorcock was able to manage. (James, 2012, p. 72)

The dual-process of reflecting-and-reacting against what came before means that fantasy remains a *progressive* genre. It reflects and reacts against the moral, spiritual, and socio-historical progress of our civilization, in turn informing and driving that progress on, so that the genre itself can continue to progress. Just as we develop, so does fantasy and so does our relationship with the Satanic. At the same time, the dual-process ensures that new works of a particular genre are recognisable within that genre, retaining a sufficient number of familiar (if not 'essential' or 'essentialist') values, motifs, themes, plot-moments, and character-types, while still being potentially subversive (via humour, a character's self-aware reference, or defeated expectation), different, or distinct. Thus, in terms of both book sales and box-office returns, Tolkien's own style of 'nursery room' fantasy is still extremely popular and successful (James, 2012), while at the same time the more cynical, morally ambiguous and anti-heroic second-world 'grimdark fantasy'[3] of George R.R. Martin's *A Song of Fire and Ice* series (1996-present) is just as, if not more, popular and successful.

> [T]he traces of Tolkien's and Lewis's influence will always be visible, through both emulation and rejection, but while the two are giants in the field, the possibilities of fantasy are not confined by their works. (James, 2012, p. 77)

As the previous paragraphs begin to illustrate, it tends to be when a fantasy work reacts significantly against what came before it (be that other specific works or the particular values of a previous socio-historical moment) that a new and distinctive subgenre of fantasy is identified and commercially labelled. The subgenre label has a commercial value, but it is also an indicator of the difference and distinctiveness (in terms of values, themes, plot, or character) of a particular work or works. Such terms are useful, therefore, for commercial consumers of fantasy, those looking to describe trends within the wider genre, those looking to group types of fantasy they do or do not enjoy, and some academics. However, other academics have developed sometimes competing labels and taxonomies[4] for types of fantasy literature, resulting in a certain confusion and overlap of defining terms. By way of example, *The Lord of the Rings* is described as representative of 'high fantasy' in Alexander's 1971 essay 'High Fantasy and Heroic Romance', as a defining work of 'high fantasy' in Stableford's *The A to Z of Fantasy Literature* (2005) and as an archetypal work of 'high fantasy' in Dozois's introduction to *Modern Classics of Fantasy* (1997). However, Wolfe (2011), Mendlesohn

---

[3]. Defined by *The Oxford English Dictionary* as 'A genre of fiction, especially fantasy fiction, characterized by disturbing, violent, or bleak subject matter and a dystopian setting'

[4]. For example the four 'types' of fantasy in Mendelsohn's *Rhetorics of Fantasy* (2008): Portal, Quest, Intrusive and Limnal.

and James (2009) and Senior (1995) variously label *The Lord of the Rings* as 'high fantasy', 'quest fantasy', and 'epic fantasy', the terms often used interchangeably, in combination, to describe plot-type or simply to describe length of book. Then, the definition of 'high fantasy' itself seems to vary, for Kaveney (2012) terms 'high fantasy' Tolkien's own 'creation', while Wolfe (2011) represents it as a pre-existing tradition of children's literature. Clute and Grant (1997) simply define 'high fantasy' as 'Fantasies set in other worlds, specifically secondary worlds, and which deal with matters affecting the destiny of those worlds', yet such a generic definition could equally apply to 'epic fantasy' (indeed, the *The Encyclopedia of Fantasy* mentions Tolkien under this label, but then says the label has 'lost its usefulness'), 'metaphysical fantasy', 'heroic fantasy', 'grimdark fantasy' and so on. As is clear from the above, the term 'epic fantasy' also has competing definitions.

For the purposes of this article, I shall refer to Tolkien's work as 'high fantasy', but then spend time analysing what this means in terms of his work's motifs, plot-type, character-types, and themes, at the same time showing how these elements embody and typify his reflection of and reaction against his socio-historical moment and, just as importantly, showing how these elements describe our developing and changing relationship with the Satanic. I will then analyse (in terms of such elements and a very different sociohistorical moment) how the work of Stephen Donaldson and fantasy writers of the 1980s and 90s both inherited from and reacted significantly against 'high fantasy', seeing the emergence of a new second-world fantasy subgenre. Indeed, there is general agreement amongst academics that it was during the late 1970s that the literary departure from 'high fantasy' began: '1977 has often been taken as a crucial year in the development of the fantasy market. This saw the publication of the first volume of Stephen Donaldson's Thomas Covenant trilogy' (James, 2012, p. 74).

Similarly: 'Up to the 1970s, while there are many different types of fantasy, there is no real sense of separate fantasy subgenres and separate audiences, with the exception perhaps of the ghost-story market. The 1970s, however, sees what we can think of as speciation, in which certain aspects of the field become recognizable marketing categories in their own right' (Mendlesohn and James, 2009, p. 112).

On the original cover of Donaldson's first Thomas Covenant novel, *Lord Foul's Bane* (1977a), the work is labelled 'An Epic Fantasy'. Donaldson defines the term fully in his journal article 'Epic Fantasy in the Modern World' (1986b), explaining how his works and the subgenre 'bring the epic back into contact with the real world'. Indeed, 'epic fantasy' became the commercial label (and publishing industry term) for the fantasy of the 1980s and 90s, and this is the label used by the British Fantasy Society and other national fantasy organisations and convention-organisers[5]. It is therefore the term that this article will use (as a functional exponent) for referring to the particular motifs, plot-types, character-types, themes, and social values of the fantasy literature of the 1980s and 90s.

2. Serious 'high fantasy' and more sociable 'epic fantasy'

Witnessing first-hand the horrors that the weaponry of science and technology unleashed during WW1, seeing his school friends and battalion cut down in France, Tolkien began working on the world and mythology of the archetypal second-world fantasy *The Lord of the Rings*. This work implicitly rejected science and technology and slavish armies as representing any sort of salvation, instead celebrating 'fellowship'[6] and more

---

[5]. '[Epic fantasy] has been increasingly used by publishers to describe heroic fantasies' (Clute and Grant, 1997, p 319).

[6]. As in *The Fellowship of the Ring*, which sees a small group of friends triumph against all odds.

essential[7] human values such as self-sacrifice, loyalty, empathy, and redemption.

Tolkien considers hugely existential, essential, and essentialist questions. His work, however, underpinned by his faith, is ultimately optimistic. The Fellowship, despite its different races (human, dwarf, elf, and hobbit) succeeds in discovering a shared language, commonly understood and respected ancestral roots, shared values and, thus, a shared *altruistic* goal and mission. In committing to what they have in common, the Fellowship commit to the possibility of sacrificing themselves for each other and, in doing so, empower each other by using their unique strengths in each other's service, saving each other, and ultimately proving that the whole is greater than the sum of the parts. The Fellowship, thereby, enables the physically weakest but morally strongest of their group (Frodo the hobbit) to win through against all Satanic odds.

And what are those Satanic odds in *The Lord of the Rings*? Well, just as we are our own worst enemy in WW1, then so too the Fellowship is set against corrupted individuals of their own kind: be they powerful individuals with a command of the sciences and nature, such as Sauron who was 'a great craftsman of the household of Aulë' (Tolkien and Tolkien, 1993, p. 52) and who '[i]n his beginning […] was of the Maiar of Aulë, and […] remained mighty in the lore of that people' (Tolkien and Tolkien, 1977), malign human kings such as the Nazgûls, power-hungry spiritual leaders such as Saruman, scheming and self-advancing politicians such as Wormtongue, or peevish and murderous thieves such as Gollum. We are our own enemy… but by that token we also have the potential to be our own salvation. We can redeem ourselves with the help of each other, as Gollum's self-sacrifice finally demonstrates.

Tolkien's work asks the *higher* questions of humankind and

---

[7]. Within a Catholic moral framework, and in as far as Tolkien searches for our shared or common roots in terms of the various tribes and languages of *The Lord of the Rings*.

how we have brought ourselves to such a pass, which is why Tolkien's work, as previously discussed, is commonly described as representing/defining the subgenre of 'high fantasy'. Its endeavour is far from trivial; it takes itself seriously. There is very little humour present within this subgenre[8], for the quest undertaken by the protagonists is a moral one, a quest to save the world from itself and a quest of self-sacrifice and redemption (as Gollum sacrifices himself with the One Ring into the fires and lava of Mount Doom, to frustrate Sauron and allow Frodo to win through, Gollum by his actions repenting his 'original' Cain-and-Abel sin concerning the ring). *LOTR*, therefore, is set within a clear moral and religious framework. The protagonist Frodo is the most consistently moral and self-sacrificing of the characters, and therefore triumphs despite his diminutive size and lack of physical strength. His Christ-like, self-sacrificing virtue is that which saves the world. He navigates the fraught quest, of what is known in fantasy criticism, as the 'Chosen One' (Kormack, 2015).

'High fantasy', then, is far from trivial because it offers comment on the moral condition of humankind and observes the Satanic means and behaviours *for which we are responsible* and *for which we have suffered*. Therefore, even though the story of *LOTR* is set in a second world, it is a clear response to the happenings of the first world and its socio-historical era. That said, *The Hobbit* was published in 1937, and *The Lord of the Rings* not until 1954. So, the themes of Tolkien's 'work' that had begun during WW1 remained relevant and current through WW2 and into the post-war era, an era typified by the Cold War, McCarthyism and the 1951 Burgess and Maclean scandal. *LOTR* has clear themes, of course, of war, propaganda and ideological subversion (with the Wormtongue character), espionage (with the 'eye' of Sauron and the spying treachery of Gollum), and the occupying invader (ending with the Shire

---

[8]. Meaning that *LOTR* could be brilliantly spoofed by later works like The Harvard Lampoon's *Bored of the Rings* (1969).

overrun). Such themes allow *LOTR*, although distinct as the first modern 'high fantasy', to sit with contemporaneous works that shared themes of invasion and espionage, including C. S. Lewis's *The Lion, the Witch and the Wardrobe* (1950).

From the above, we can say that *LOTR* reflected the circumstances and values of its socio-historical era(s), just like other works, but also represented a *new* and unique (entirely second-world) reaction to those circumstances and values. In so doing, it represented a new (sub-)genre of literature and provided the template, model and inspiration for several decades of 'high fantasy' publications by a succession of other writers. That model is occasionally known as 'the quest fantasy' and is summarised by W. A. Senior in *The Cambridge Companion to Fantasy Literature*:

[T]he landscape functions as a character, here endowed with animate traits as the fantasy world itself seeks to heal the rift that threatens its destruction. The menace frequently comes from a Dark Lord, a satanic figure of colossal but warped power, who wishes to enslave and denature the world and its denizens and who lives in a dead land […]. During the quest the pattern of an organic, moral world with directive purpose emerges. The final stage of the quest brings the hero into direct confrontation with the Dark Lord, whose defeat is a result of some action or decision by the hero. […] However, quest fantasies also posit a cyclical history so that the possibility of the reappearance of the Dark Lord, or of another, in the future remains. (2012, p. 190)

Essentially, the 'quest' tracks the moral development, growth and journey of the individual, showing that the virtues of self-sacrifice, a redemptive love of others, and good faith will eventually lead to salvation and the overcoming of evil. Of course, these are the original values of the Bible which Tolkien enshrined in his Catholic faith and work. It is important to note here, however, that Tolkien's values describe the onus upon *the individual*, no matter their circumstance and strength. The individual is required to have a strong sense of duty and responsibility, a strong conscience, the will to act on behalf of others (Bilbo must get out of his chair at the start of *The Hobbit* and voluntarily leave his life of comfort), and the strength to continue on through adversity based on blind faith alone. The Fellowship in *LOTR*, important though it is for much of Frodo's journey, ultimately falls away and it is Frodo's individual character alone that is finally tested… and judged by the plot progression. Again, this judgement fits with the Christian ethos of Western Europe of the time. And the antithesis to this virtuous *individual* (Chosen One) is the powerful, power-hungry, malign, jealous, corrupted, and corrupting *individual* (Dark Lord), who seeks to mesmerise, coerce, sway, and enslave others via their individual desire and will.

The model for fantasy above ('high fantasy') was a persuasive and compelling one, one that is still popular today, but it was one derived from traditional values particularly embraced during the difficult but reflective post-World-War era of social history. It was not a model that could suit all future eras of socio-history. As soon as the 1970s, British fantasy author Michael Moorcock was criticising the traditional, comforting, flowery, non-gritty, childish, clichéd, and trite nature of Tolkien's prose, style, and outlook (Moorcock, 1987). This was at a time when the Cold War was threatening to destroy us all, when the nature and full potential of Satanic evil was based upon empire, global power and geography, political ideology, and wider societal forces and concerns rather than Tolkien's responsible individual. Therefore, it was all but inevitable that a new model or subgenre of fantasy would emerge, one that would 'bring the epic back into contact with the real world' (Donaldson, 1986a) and would describe how our relationship with and potential for Satanic evil had changed and developed. A new style of fantasy emerged, represented by Stephen

Donaldson's *Lord Foul's Bane* (1977a), a work subtitled 'An Epic Fantasy', although Donaldson was clear that his fantasy was distinctly different from preceding works in the wider genre.

As per the dual-process of reflecting-and-reacting-against what came before, there is much in Donaldson's 'epic fantasy' literature that inherits and borrows from Tolkien's 'high fantasy', including a landscape with 'animate traits', extended and flowery description, a range of different races, the central importance of the quest, a Chosen One, and a seemingly all-powerful Dark Lord. However, at the same time, Donaldson's work fundamentally subverts the tropes of 'high fantasy' because his Chosen One is far from the morally superior individual we find in *LOTR*: Thomas Covenant is a leper whose marriage fails, once in the second world he gives himself the title 'Unbeliever' and then, miraculously cured of his impotence, he rapes the teenage girl Lena who has come to help and guide him. Time and again in Donaldson's work Thomas Covenant finds himself unable to use his power properly; he remains impotent or his attempts are abortive at best. On his journey, Covenant is a bystanding witness to political discussions and events more than he is a character taking meaningful action; rather, he acts out a ceremonial leadership role which proves enough to empower others. At the end of the book, he is a conduit for a power he does not understand or fully control. A temporary peace is secured for the second-world Land (although the Dark Lord is not defeated) and Covenant is returned to the first world as an impotent leper once more.

Thus, in the character of Thomas Covenant, we have a thoroughly modern, conflicted, and flawed individual, one who is sometimes difficult to like at all and who is often frustrating for the reader. The individual is more often than not at the whim of larger (Satanic) geo-political forces and rarely can do anything to change things, *except when they act out a recognised and accepted socio-political role and function*. Tolkien's Fellowship of powerful individuals falls away, to leave only the superior individual; Donaldson's individual can only empower others and contribute towards the efforts of a wider group or Fellowship.

> Covenant [...] inheres to an American democratic tradition more than the hierarchal worlds of British fantasy. (Senior, 2012, p.191)

Fundamentally, then, 'epic fantasy' of Donaldson's ilk was more concerned with contemporary issues of social negotiation and geo-politics than it was with essentialist, quasireligious notions of individual virtue. As a corollary, the notion of the Satanic in such literature often tended towards an 'evil empire', a disembodied and diffuse creeping blight, or widespread, corrupt(ing) ideology or faith (with suitable figureheads) rather than *simply* powerful individuals looking for immediate personal gain. Indeed, the Chosen One of 'epic fantasy' post-Donaldson is invariably *socially*-described from the outset. In both David Eddings's *Pawn of Prophecy* (1982) and Raymond E. Feist's *Magician* (1982), the protagonist is a working-class hero ('The Magician's Apprentice') who goes on a quest to save their society. Through hard work, unfaltering commitment to the (Christian democratic) values of their society, and a near supernatural strength of will, they succeed and are invariably rewarded with a rise in social status and privilege, becoming a friend and advisor to the enlightened royal family or a member of the magical elite. Of course, such a plotline fit the dominant political narrative of both the UK and the US during the 1980s. Margaret Thatcher became UK Prime Minister on behalf of the Conservatives in 1979, while Ronald Reagan became the US President on behalf of the Republicans in 1981. Thatcher espoused individualism and social responsibility – individuals working hard and making sacrifice to build small businesses, acquire wealth and then contribute back to society ('Victorian' values according to an interview Margaret Thatcher gave in

Headway Upper-intermediate in 1987). Furthermore, the plotline of 'epic fantasy' also echoed Thatcher's personal and political story of having started out as a grocer's daughter, having fought to become a success in a man's world and having finally triumphed to become Prime Minister, thereby representing the positive and enlightened change in British society. At the same time, the plot fit the Reaganomics version of the American Dream.

Where 'high fantasy' had had a religious framework, 'epic fantasy' had a stronger social framework and indulged in more detailed world-building, with socio-economic systems in place, a clear divide between rural and urban areas and functions, a sense of social class and place, and so on. Where 'high fantasy' had one true God or an enemy embodying absolute evil, 'epic fantasy' presented a more multicultural pantheon of gods and a range of roguish and morally-compromised characters. Where 'high fantasy' was largely humourless, 'epic fantasy' offered the gentle humour and banter of social negotiation, without that humour ever becoming fully subversive (unless it is used as a weapon against the enemy, as in Stephen Donaldson's *The Power that Preserves*, 1977b). Where 'high fantasy' ended with the main characters restored to the safety and peace of their home, 'epic fantasy' promised, encouraged, and allowed social advancement based on particular behaviours. Where there are precious few female characters in 'high fantasy', there are a good deal more in 'epic fantasy', albeit rarely in the main role. What the two subgenres of fantasy had in common, however, was the presumption that those at the top of society were only there based upon some moral superiority (be that religious virtue or a sense of social responsibility).

In 'high fantasy' the Satanic still represents a quasireligious, corrupting, and insidious temptation for the individual, while in 'epic fantasy' the Satanic is only our shared responsibility. In 'high fantasy' each individual must overcome their own personal battle with evil, while in 'epic fantasy' evil can only be defeated through our working together and sharing through our actions the 'correct' social values. In 'high fantasy' the *final* battle is for one person's soul (for example, Gollum's), while in 'epic fantasy' it is to safeguard the structure and values of the 'correctly functioning' society. In 'high fantasy' the Satanic is limited to an individual who places personal appetites above Christian virtue, while in 'epic fantasy' the Satanic is an 'evil empire' (Reagan, 1983) that subjugates individuality and oppresses individual freedoms, an aggressively nondemocratic society that would prevent social advancement for any individual (as per Communist Russia when described by American propaganda). In 'high fantasy' a Christ-like figure is required to bring about salvation, but in 'epic fantasy' the enlightened kingdom and the magical *light* of its 'lore' (law) and 'Magician's Guild' would always inevitably drive back the 'dark'[9].

It seemed that the socio-political philosophy and stance underpinning and espoused by 'epic fantasy' had all the answers, because it saw the eastern states of the Soviet bloc finally swept by revolutions in 1989 and the Berlin Wall come down in Germany. Officially the Cold War came to an end in 1991. Unsurprisingly, not only was 'epic fantasy' the dominant subgenre of fantasy throughout the 1980s, but it also remained dominant well into the 1990s. Where the Conservative Margaret Thatcher was replaced in the UK by the Conservative John Major as Prime Minister, in the US the Republican Ronald Reagan was replaced by the Republican George Bush as President.

We had all the answers. We had an age of en*light*enment. We had triumphed over the Dark Lord and been rewarded; hadn't we? We had created a golden age for ourselves, so why shouldn't we enjoy the rewards? Just in time for a new millennium, too! Surely it symbolically marked the realisation

---
[9]. Be it *A Darkness at Sethanon* (Feist, 1986), dark elves, the dark side of the Force, and so on.

of God's holy kingdom on Earth and our salvation. The magical kingdom of 'epic fantasy' had been safeguarded (by our defeat of the dark and evil empire), we all had magical powers of self-actualisation, and our kings and queens were noble, comely and wise. Hallelujah and Amen! We were going to 'party like it's 1999'.

3. The forbidden romance of 'dark fantasy' and the brooding discontent of 'metaphysical fantasy'

Post-Y2K, post-9/11, with the 2003 Iraq War and a newly globalised and multicultural world, the social and moral certainties offered by 'high fantasy' and 'epic fantasy' were no longer appropriate or genuinely representative of our shared society and culture. We began to realise that the previous dominance of the white, heteronormative narratives of 'high fantasy' and 'epic fantasy' had actually drowned out and marginalised the voices of a good number of groups in society, including those with 'alternative' lifestyles, those with different cultural backgrounds, and the politically aware younger generation[10]. We began to realise that the 'evil' we now needed to fight was the misrepresentation and whitewashing perpetuated by the previous generation i.e. an inherited social evil. We began to realise that the wise and noble kings and queens of 'high fantasy' and 'epic fantasy' weren't quite as noble and wise and we'd thought: if anything, they were self-interested, elitist, and ultimately corrupt. We began to realise the kindly, guiding (paternal) white-haired wizards of 'high fantasy' and 'epic fantasy' weren't to be entirely trusted. We began to realise the Chosen One was now born into an uncaring world of darkness and uncertainty, would not necessarily discover companions that were steady and trustworthy, and would struggle for a sense of place and identity, suffering internal conflict and angst upon their quest to discover who

---
[10]. The latter known as 'millennials', as detailed later in this article.

they might truly be.

It was in such a context that first-world fantasy saw the emergence of 'dark fantasy'. Where preceding fantasy subgenres tended to observe patriarchal and heterosexual norms (the good guy 'wins' the girl), 'dark fantasy' was more morally ambivalent, there were no out-and-out good guys, and sexual congress was considered 'dangerous' and often to be resisted i.e. everything was 'darker'. So, for example, the lead female role of Bella in the 'dark fantasy' *Twilight* series (2005-08)[11], played in the movie by the gay Kristen Stewart, actively seeks a sexual relationship with Edward that is likely to destroy her. Then, in *True Blood* (late 2008 onwards), we are presented with a far wider range of dark alternative relationships and lifestyles, from the abstinent, to S&M, to the pansexual, to the sinful, to the grotesque, to the fatal, to the drug-fuelled, to master-slave, to the orgiastic. Thus, the emergence of 'dark fantasy' represented mainstream society's anxiety concerning – and its getting to grips with – the true diversity of orientations, preferences, and identities.

In the same way that first-world 'dark fantasy' represented a changed sociohistorical context, so second-world 'metaphysical fantasy'[12] represented the transition of second-world 'epic fantasy' to a more modern consideration. Just as 'dark fantasy' brought darker themes, understanding and outlooks to first-world fantasy, so 'metaphysical fantasy' did the same for second-world fantasy ('high fantasy' and 'epic fantasy'). Both 'metaphysical fantasy' and 'epic fantasy' concern themselves with the 'Chosen One' quest to save the world from evil forces but, where 'epic fantasy' tends to see the pre-existing social and moral order triumphantly restored (with the protagonist

---

[11]. The sub-genre label of 'dark fantasy' is used in reference to *Twilight* by both academics (Kaveney, 2012) and established media critics (Child, 2016).
[12]. With authors like A J Dalton (*Necromancer's Gambit*, 2008b, and *Empire of the Saviours*, 2011), R. Scott Bakker (*The Darkness That Comes Before*, 2004) and Alan Campbell (*Scar Night*, 2006).

rewarded via social advancement), 'metaphysical fantasy' is more morally ambivalent in terms of the narrative outcome, there are no out-and-out winners (indeed, mere survival often comes at a hefty price), and social advancement is never quite the prize it is promised to be, i.e. everything is darker. So, for example, where the 'epic fantasy' novels of Raymond E. Feist's *Magician* (1982), David Eddings's *Pawn of Prophecy* (1984) and J. V. Jones's *The Baker's Boy* (1995) all see a good-hearted boy (the 'Chosen One') from the kitchens become friends with royalty while undertaking a quest that saves the world, reaffirms key social values, and ennobles society, the 'metaphysical fantasy' novels of my own *Necromancer's Gambit* (2008b) and *Empire of the Saviours* (2012) see a socially marginalised individual as Chosen One go on a quest that defeats the enemy but also shatters society in the process[13]. Where 'epic fantasy' ends with glorious triumph and celebration, the 'triumph' at the end of 'metaphysical fantasy' is pyrrhic at best, all but genocidal or apocalyptic at worst. Where 'epic fantasy' self-congratulates and throws itself a party or feast, 'metaphysical fantasy' sees the protagonist left to bury the dead, grieve over loved ones, and try to pick up the pieces of a broken world. Where 'epic fantasy' is about what can be won, 'metaphysical fantasy' is about what has been lost. Implicitly, then, where 'epic fantasy' endorses the society and values that determine success, 'metaphysical fantasy' explores, questions, and even challenges them. Thus, the development from 'epic fantasy' to 'metaphysical fantasy', coinciding with the elites and establishment revealed as morally corrupt and redundant[14], represented society's increasing anxiety and discomfort concerning its traditional values, shamed heroes

---

[13]. Titles including Alan Campbell's *Scar Night* (2006) and R. Scott Bakker's *The Darkness That Comes Before* (2004) also fit this general plot shape.

[14]. With the scandal of MPs overclaiming expenses, newspapers hacking the phones of victims, the police selling information to the press and bankers awarding themselves unjustifiably large bonuses.

and so-called role models, as well as its treatment of socially marginalised groups, the development saw epic and ennobled heroes and social values abandoned in favour of those who had previously suffered heroically as marginalised individuals or groups.

Heroes are not always what they seem. (Dalton, 2012)[15]

The protagonists of both first-world 'dark fantasy' and second-world 'metaphysical fantasy' therefore struggle throughout for a sense of identity and existential meaning. Given that this 'crisis' of identity in the mid-to-late-2000s sits in stark contrast to the sense of moral and social certainty, superiority, and security found pre-9/11 (2001), the emergence of 'dark fantasy' and 'metaphysical fantasy' can be understood as a corollary to the emergence and development of the 'Millennial'[16] self: an individual reaching young adulthood around the year 2000, sometimes known as 'Generation Y'. Where the generation preceding[17] the Millennial self could simply share in and espouse the traditional values of their parents and society (the 'epic fantasy' subgenre was unusually dominant for the two decades before 2000), the Millennial self experienced a break or disconnect from (what had been) social reality. This disconnect is more often than not represented in 'dark fantasy' and 'metaphysical fantasy' as protagonists being exiled, abandoned, cast adrift, or suffering the surreal experience of being the dead/undead in the world of the living (or vice versa).

There is a disconnect with authority figures and wise counsellors, those who pass on the traditional values of society,

---

[15]. The tagline on the cover of *The Empire of the Saviours*.

[16]. The term was first coined by William Strauss and Neil Howe in 1987, and more fully described in their 1991 book *Generations: The History of America's Future*, which was followed in 2000 by *Millennials Rising: The Next Generation*.

[17]. 'Generation X'.

promote conformity and ensure the individual's experience of the world is manageable and ultimately benign. Such figures are always present for the young protagonist in 'epic fantasy', be it Polgara fiercely protecting Garion in Eddings's *Pawn of Propehcy*, Kulgan patiently tutoring Pug in Feist's *Magician*, or Zed comically raising Richard in Goodkind's *Wizard's First Rule*, but such figures are invariably absent or unreliable in 'metaphysical fantasy'. Indeed, the very kings and rulers in *Empire of the Saviours* and *Necromancer's Gambit* are conspicuously corrupt, insidious, and malign[18]. Indeed, where in 'epic fantasy' the noble kings and queens or rulers are set in opposition to a corrupting or vampiric Dark Lord, in 'metaphysical fantasy' and 'dark fantasy' they are *one and the same*.

Due to this (Millennial) disconnect from society, social norms, and a guiding generation, the plot progression of 'dark fantasy' and 'metaphysical fantasy' involves the protagonist's fraught quest to discover a sense of identity and self, to find a place in the world, and to find safety and contentment. Invariably, however, this subgenre ultimately describes terrible sacrifice, loss, anti-climax, and resignation. The self-realisation, place, safety, and contentment that are achieved are illusory or temporary at best. There is no true 'happy ending', as the existential quest of life continues on through the next generation(s), some progress made but the results of past mistakes born into the future, the problems of society, and the past inherited by those that follow on after us.

4. The bleak optimism of 'dystopian YA' and the grinding despair of 'grimdark fantasy'

Entering the 2010s, it became clear that the pain of the credit crunch and austerity was not being shared equally. Indeed, it was those working in or dependent on the public sector who

---

[18]. Very much at odds with the noble kings and queens of 'epic fantasy'.

were suffering most, often falling into food- and energy-poverty, while the middle classes working or invested in the private sector continued to award themselves healthy bonuses and send their offspring to the best fee-paying schools. There were multiple public revelations in the UK that large private companies and wealthy individuals (including the Queen) employed clever accountants who ensured they never had to pay their full tax burden. Off-shore banking and tax-mitigation schemes meant that the top half of society could 'legally' (though never 'morally') continue to take all the benefits of society without paying the price. Indirectly, one half of society was knowingly exploiting the other half.

In such a context, the subgenres of 'dark fantasy' and 'metaphysical fantasy', which identified a single Dark Lord at the top of society (a vampiric overlord or corrupt king), and which offered an idealistic self-doubting and self-sacrificing Chosen One, and which still offered solutions based on people coming together to build the new future, were seen as naïve, overly romantic, faux, 'wimpy', and a poor representation of the world. In the world of the 2010s, *we were all dark lords* and only a cynical Chosen One was ever going to survive. It was in such a context that 'dark fantasy' and 'metaphysical fantasy' were supplanted by the even darker 'dystopian YA' and 'grimdark fantasy'.

Both near-future, first-world 'dystopian YA'[19] and second-world 'grimdark fantasy'[20] describe repressive or lawless societies in which the majority are the most corrupt, immoral, or bullying. There are themes of abuse, betrayal, and abandonment present throughout both subgenres. For example, in the 'dystopian YA' novels of *The Hunger Games Trilogy*

---

[19]. This sub-genre label is in wide and common use amongst quality press and media (Child, 2016) and amongst leading publishers of fantasy, including Gollancz (Dalton, 2016).

[20]. Defined by *The Oxford English Dictionary* as 'A genre of fiction, especially fantasy fiction, characterized by disturbing, violent, or bleak subject matter and a dystopian setting'.

(Collins, 2008-10), the *Escape from Furnace* series (Smith, 2009-11), and the *Maze Runner* series (Dashner, 2009-16), we are presented with death-match game shows featuring youth, the unjust imprisonment of youth, the institutionalised murder of youth, surgical experimentation on youth, and the use of youth as military fodder. Similarly, in the 'grimdark fantasy' novels of *A Song of Ice and Fire* (Martin, 1996-2016), *The Demon Cycle* series (Brett, 2008-16), *The Broken Empire* trilogy (Lawrence, 2011-13), and *The First Law* series (Abercrombie, 2006-16), we are routinely presented with torture, rape, brutalisation, the flaying of skin, and mass slaughter. In such books, it is the individual with the biggest sword, biggest muscles, and least compunction when it comes to violence and viciousness who wins out. The rule of law is as nothing. The subgenres describe such horror unflinchingly, with a numb matter-of-factness or with a shocking sense of detachment; far from being voyeuristic, the literature is satirically post-traumatic, defiantly desensitised, and utterly disillusioned. Indeed, the horror is so extreme but mundane that a profound sense of nihilism, mental exhaustion, and an apocalyptic desire for self-destruction plagues all.

In such literature, the role of the Chosen One is a near-impossible and compromised one. The lead protagonists (both male and female) usually lose their family, have friends based on convenience and sharing the predicament of others, and do not have anyone they can trust enough to form a successful romantic relationship. Very much, we are presented with a lonely, hard-bitten, and traumatised protagonist whom we only identify with because we are not sure we would act any differently from them in such a situation. Thereby, the protagonist is often just a cypher for the reader, a witness to events, one who reacts to events rather than proactively controlling them, and one who does not necessarily need to be a strongly drawn character themselves. Their sense of self, gender-formation, and sexuality are oppressed to the extent that they are elided or prevented from developing. The true 'self' can only be realised by breaking free of the society that forces them to conform. There is a sense of constant monitoring, scrutiny, and spying, a need to hide the 'self' and all true intentions in order to avoid being exploited, and utter confusion or a creeping paranoia.

We might wonder how best to summarise the 'solution' offered by these two subgenres. Some might describe it as civil war, anarchy, terrorism, total war, or Satan's *hell on Earth*. Some might welcome such a solution, some might see it as inevitable, and others still would advocate fighting to resist it. Perhaps that is another story, one for those with a 2020 vision. However, what is clear is that it is not religion, a religious quest, or the Christ-like protagonist really offering us that hope anymore.

5. Conclusion

Where the early subgenres of fantasy saw evil, Satan or the Dark Lord as an external force or being looking to tempt, seduce or malevolently influence us, 'grimdark fantasy' sees the majority of us as dark lords. Satan is no longer some demonic possession that we can simply exorcise. Nor is he just a *part* or aspect of our psychology (e.g. Freud's concept of the id), morality or selves. No, in the latest SFF, we have fully become Satan. We are *entirely* Satan. The protagonist of modern SFF is an antihero who is misunderstood by and rails against an unfair society, rule, and world. Thus, in SFF, we have moved away from narratives with the self-sacrificing (Christ-like) protagonist of 'high fantasy' or the shining hero of 'The Hero's Journey' facing down devils and sinful temptation in order to restore peace and order, to narratives with an antiheroic and self-interested by necessity (Satanic) protagonist looking to end their personal suffering by bringing about the end of the existing society and order by any means necessary, even if that means taking us all to the brink of the apocalypse. Indeed, some apocalyptic mass extinction event tends to be the principal prospect or threat in current SFF: we might take George R.R. Martin's *Song of Fire and Ice* or N.K. Jemisin's *The Broken Earth Trilogy* (2015-17) as popular examples, each of the three books in the latter sequence winning the Hugo Award, 2016-18.

With this new and dominant narrative of SFF, the (Chosen One) protagonist refuses to be defined by the world into which they are born, to bow to the rulers of that world, or to submit to those who seek to dominate their existence. Furthermore, as a matter of self-defence and to ensure their own continued survival, the protagonist must set out on a quest (literal, metaphorical, emotional, philosophical, or otherwise) to overthrow those in power, no matter the far-reaching consequences for the world. The protagonist demands self-empowerment, self-definition, self-identification, and *self-creation* at all costs. Of course, such a stance and ambition precisely represent Satan's refusal to recognise God as his creator or as having authority over him: in Milton's *Paradise Lost*, Satan sets out on a quest to manipulate humankind, to turn humankind against God, and to undo God's rule and earthly creation.

We might instinctively recoil in horror at what we have become, and at what we seem close to bringing about (i.e. the apocalypse). Instinctively, we will want to deny it. Surely we haven't turned against God, have we? Surely we are not about to destroy His creation, are we? We can't be that evil, can we?

Yet if we look at ourselves as a species, we cannot deny that we have failed to control ourselves in terms of the size of our population, the resources we consume, and the damage we have done to the environment. If we continue to superheat the world, we will all burn in the resulting inferno… unless we can find a way to decamp to another world, where we will surely not repeat our mistakes. Except that we have selfishly defined ourselves in such a way that we may not be able to behave in any other way than we have already been behaving. We will not be able to escape ourselves, the nature of ourselves, and the nature of our appetites. We will repeat our mistakes.

The new and dominant narrative of SFF is extremely persuasive, therefore, because it is just like our actual lives in the real world. But then, SFF always was like that. Where science fiction has always spoken of and described our physical journey and (external) experiences as we move into the future, so fantasy has always spoken of and described our (internal) spiritual quest and self-definition going forwards. Let's hope we all arrive safely.

Bibliography

Abercrombie, J., 2006. *The Blade Itself: The First Law*. London: Gollancz.

Albrecht, M., 1956. Does literature reflect common values?. *American Sociological Review*, 21(6), pp. 722-729, [Online] Available at: <https://www.jstor.org/stable/2088424?seq=1#page_scan_tab_contents> [Accessed: 3 November 2017].

Alexander, L., 1971. High Fantasy and Heroic Romance. [online] Available at: <http://www.hbook.com/1971/12/choosing-books/horn-book-magazine/high-fantasy-and-heroic-romance/> [Accessed: 3 November 2017].

Bakker, R. S., 2004. *The Darkness That Comes Before*. London: Orbit.

Beard, H. and Kenney, D., 1969. *Bored of the Rings*. New York: Touchstone.

Brett, P. V., 2008. *The Painted Man: The Demon Cycle*. London: Voyager Books.

Campbell, A., 2006. *Scar Night*. New York: Tor.

Carpenter, H., 1977. *J. R. R. Tolkien: A Biography*. New York: Ballantine Books.

Carpenter, H. and Tolkien, C. (eds.), 1981. *The Letters of J. R. R. Tolkien*. London: George Allen & Unwin.

Child, B., 2016. Not the future after all: the slow demise of young adult dystopian sci-fi films. *The Guardian*, [Online] 25 March. Available at: <https://www.theguardian.com/film/2016/mar/25/allegiant-young-adult-dystopian-films-box-office-flops> [Accessed: 10 November 2017].

Clute, J. and Grant, J., 1997. *The Encyclopedia of Fantasy*. London: Orbit.

Collins, S., 2008. *The Hunger Games*. New York: Scholastic Press.

Dalton, A. J., 2008a. *Metaphysical Fantasy*. Available at: <www.ajdalton.eu> [Accessed: 15 July 2016].

Dalton, A. J., 2016. New trends in Fantasy and SciFi. *Gollancz*, [online] Available at: <https://www.gollancz.co.uk/2016/11/new-trends-in-fantasy-and-scifi-a-guest-post-by-aj-dalton/> [Accessed: 11 November 2017].

Dalton, A. J., 2008b. *Necromancer's Gambit: Book One of The Flesh & Bone Trilogy*. Milton Keynes: AuthorHouse UK.

Dalton, A. J., 2009. *Necromancer's Betrayal: Book Two of The Flesh & Bone Trilogy*. Milton Keynes: AuthorHouse UK.

Dalton, A. J., 2010. *Necromancer's Fall: Book Three of The Flesh & Bone Trilogy*. Milton Keynes: AuthorHouse UK.

Dalton, A. J., 2012. *Empire of the Saviours: Book One: Chronicles of a Cosmic Warlord*. London: Gollancz.

Dalton, A. J., 2014. *Tithe of the Saviours: Book Three: Chronicles of a Cosmic Warlord*. London: Gollancz.

Dalton, A. J., Forthcoming. *The Satanic in Science Fiction and Fantasy*. Edinburgh: Luna Press Publishing.

Dashner, J., 2009. *The Maze Runner*. New York: Delacorte Press.

Donaldson, S., 1977a. *Lord Foul's Bane: An Epic Fantasy*. New York: Holt, Rinehart and Winston.

Donaldson, S., 1977b. *The Power that Preserves*. New York: Holt, Rinehart and Winston.

Donaldson, S., 1986a. *Mordant's Need*. New York: Del Ray Books.

Donaldson, S., 1986b. *Epic Fantasy in the Modern World: A Few Observations*. Ohio: Kent State University Libraries.

Dozois, G., 1997. *Modern Classics of Fantasy*. New York: St. Martin's Press.

Eddings, D., 1982. *Pawn of Prophecy*. New York: Del Rey Books.

Feist, R., 1982. *Magician*. New York: Doubleday.

Goodkind, T., 1994. *Wizard's First Rule*. New York: Tor Fantasy.

James, E., 2012. Tolkien, Lewis and the explosion of genre fantasy, in James, E. and Mendlesohn, F. (eds.) *The Cambridge Companion to Fantasy Literature*. Cambridge: Cambridge University Press, pp. 62-78.

Jemisin, N. K., 2015. *The Fifth Season: Book One: The Broken Earth Trilogy*. New York: Orbit.

Jones, J. V., 1995. *The Baker's Boy*. New York: Aspect.

Kaveney, R., 2012. Dark fantasy and paranormal romance, in James, E. and

Mendlesohn, F. (eds.) *The Cambridge Companion to Fantasy Literature*. Cambridge: Cambridge University Press, pp. 214-223.

Komarck, M., 2015. *In Defence of the Chosen One*. Available at: <http://fantasy-faction.com/2015/in-defence-of-the-chosen-one> [Accessed: 11 July 2016].

Lawrence, M., 2011. *Prince of Thorns: The Broken Empire Trilogy*. London: HarperCollins UK.

Mendlesohn, F., 2008. *Rhetorics of Fantasy*. Connecticut: Wesleyan University Press.

Mendlesohn, F. and James, E., 2009. *A Short History of Fantasy*. London: Middlesex University Press.

Meyer, S., 2005. *Twilight*. New York: Little, Brown and Co.

Meyer, S., 2006. *New Moon*. New York: Little, Brown and Co.

Meyer, S., 2007. *Eclipse*. New York: Little, Brown and Co.

Meyer, S., 2008. *Breaking Dawn*. New York: Little, Brown and Co.

Modesitt Jr., L. E., 1991. *The Magic of Recluce*. Charlotte, NC: Paw Prints.

Moorcock, M., 1970. *The Eternal Champion*. New York: Dell Books.

Moorcock, M., 1974. *The Hollow Lands*. New York: Harper and Row.

Moorcock, M., 1987. *Wizardry and Wild Romance: A Study of Epic Fantasy*. London: Gollancz.

Reagan, R., 1983. 'Evil empire', speech at 41st Annual Convention. National Association of Evangelicals. Unpublished.

Senior, W., 1995. *Variations on the Fantasy Tradition*: Stephen R. Donaldson's Chronicles of Thomas Covenant. Ohio: The Kent State University Press.

Senior, W. A., 2012. Quest Fantasies. In: E. James and F. Mendlesohn (eds.). 2012. *The Cambridge Companion to Fantasy Literature*. New York: Cambridge University Press, pp. 190-99.

Smith, A. G., 2010. *Lockdown: Escape from Furnace*. New York: Tor.

Soars, J. and Soars, L., 1987. *Headway: Upper-intermediate*. Oxford: Oxford

University Press.
Stableford, B., 2005. *The A to Z of Fantasy Literature*. Plymouth: Scarecrow Press.

The Caffeinated Symposium, 2011. *Fantasy: 1990-2000: The Age of the Doorstops and Gimmicks*. Available at: <http://caffeinesymposium.blogspot.co.uk/2011/07/fantasy-1990-2000-age-of-doorstops-and.html> [Accessed: 15 July 2016].

Tolkien, J. R. R., 1954-55. *The Lord of the Rings*. London: Allen & Unwin.
Tolkien, J. R. R., and Tolkien, C. (ed.), 1977. The Silmarillion. London: George Allen and Unwin.

Tolkien, J. R. R., and Tolkien, C. (ed.), 1993. *Morgoth's Ring*. Boston: Houghton Mifflin, p. 52.

True Blood, 2008. [TV Series]. HBO, 7 September.

Wolfe, G., 2005. Coming to terms, in Gunn, J. and Candelaria, M. (eds.) *Speculations on Speculation: Theories of Science Fiction*. Maryland: Scarecrow Press Inc, pp.13-22.

Wolfe, G., 2011. *Evaporating Genres: Essays on Fantastic Literature*. Connecticut: Wesleyan University Press.

Xenomorphobia – Eighties Societal Fears and Issues as Reflected in the Movie *Aliens*

Robert S Malan

Abstract

In 1986, *Aliens*, the sequel to Ridley Scott's classic 1979 science fiction-horror *Alien*, was released in cinemas worldwide. Director James Cameron shifted tone significantly, from that of survival-horror to SF action-thriller. It proved to be a resounding success both financially and in its reception amongst critics and movie-goers.

The film's blockbuster veneer, though, can be slightly misleading, suggesting a work devoid of depth. However, lurking beneath the surface of *Aliens* is a Pandora's Box of societal fears, issues, and allusions to real world events of the time. More than that, it reflects the shifting nature of simple "good vs evil" roles in entertainment.

In this article, we'll examine these aspects of the movie in finer detail, looking at what it says about the public psyche of the time, as manifest in historical events, while also exploring some of its hints to inherent subconscious fears.

Woman as Saviour, Not Victim

It seems only right to start with the movie's central character, Ellen Ripley, played by Sigourney Weaver, particularly in drawing attention to her relevance in the face of prevailing movie stereotypes. As the lone survivor of the crew wiped out by a single Xenomorph (the official biological moniker given to the titular aliens) in *Alien*, Weaver delivers a powerhouse performance, which garnered an Oscar nomination.

Importantly, the character of Ripley also represented something of a revolt against clichéd, sexist roles within movies of the day. Consider how films at the time – particularly big budget action ones – almost universally enforced the role of Man as hero, and Woman as victim, awaiting rescue. Even in movies that did feature a "Warrior-woman" in a central role, they were almost exclusively consigned to being sex symbols, clad in "bikini armour", secondary to the male protagonist, and fated to fall hopelessly head-over-heels for him.

Women being objectified and treated as lesser was nothing new. There are any number of "classic" movies featuring scenes of open abuse towards women, hidden within supposedly breezy, throwaway scenes (Sean Connery-era James Bond, for example, is rife with examples). This began to take on a far more insidious tone in the late seventies and early eighties.

It was at this time that the term "serial killer" was popularised and came to prominence with infamous murderers such as Ted Bundy. Understandably, this infiltrated the film world, with the rise of "slasher movies" like *Halloween* (1978) and *Friday The 13th* (1980) where young, beautiful women were commonly (even essentially) targets for psychotic male killers.

In *Alien*, Ripley, for all her resilience and wits, fitted much more with the stereotype of a victim, stalked by a killer, barely managing to escape with her life. It fits with the movie of course, but she is quite different to the Ellen Ripley we encounter in *Aliens*. James Cameron did well in recognising the full potential of the character. He could so easily have followed the route so many of his peers had chosen with similar movie types, and made Ripley secondary to the hard-nut soldiers, like Michael Biehn's Corporal Hicks for instance. Fortunately, he chose to buck the trend and so helped mould a truly iconic character. Naturally, much of the credit is due to Weaver for an exceptional performance, tapping into the character on emotional and physical levels that made her as much of a cinematic tour-de-force as the movie itself.

On a purely physical level, even in the rare scenes where Weaver is scantily clad, these are not gratuitous or even sexualised. They are simply snapshots of what the character would logically be wearing at the time (having awoken from a nightmare and, later, from induced cryogenic sleep). Again, where lesser movies would have chosen to have her in perfect make-up, Cameron maintains the focus on realism. It's a stripped back, unglamorous performance from Weaver.

There are, of course, suggestions of chemistry between Ripley and Hicks. However, once more, this is done in a thoroughly restrained and natural way. It's clear that Hicks remains secondary to Ripley, recognising her as the emergent leader of the group. There's no macho posturing from him, no misguided attempts to establish himself as the dominant pack leader.

This kind of message in mainstream entertainment was pretty scarce: that women could and should be respected for qualities other than their physical appearance. It's telling that, at the time of writing, though there has been improvement on this front, women are still struggling to reach equality in pay, opportunities, and recognition.

Aliens is reflective of society's issues, or rather, in this case, a rebellion against its norms – showing that a woman could be both mother and warrior; hero, not mere sex object.

Mother to Mother – the Battle of Ripley and the Alien Queen

Having touched on Ripley-as-mother, let's examine the maternal instincts at the heart of the character and the movie.

By way of context, an early scene in *Aliens* directly establishes the sub-theme of motherhood; or, rather, an early scene in the later-released Special Edition "Director's Cut" version explicitly does so. While the original cinematic release is clear enough in this as subtext, the Special Edition directly references it in a scene where Ellen Ripley asks Paul Reiser's Carter Burke about the fate of her daughter,

Amanda[1]. Here, it is revealed that Amanda has died during the course of her mother's 57 years spent floating in stasis. This knowledge adds further relevance to the later discovery of young Rebecca "Newt" Jorden on the colony on LV-426. Newt's parents (along with her brother, and the rest of the colonists) have been killed by the Xenomorphs. Naturally, a surrogate mother-daughter relationship is formed between Ripley and Newt.

Expanding out from this, throughout the course of the *Alien* series, Ellen Ripley is drawn into a fateful, inescapable relationship with the Xenomorphs. It's a dynamic that becomes particularly apparent in a pivotal third-act scene in *Aliens*, where Ripley has raced to rescue Newt from cocooning and alien-impregnation, before the colony is destroyed by an impending reactor leak. Having succeeded, in the course of escaping, she stumbles across an entirely new form of Xenomorph: an alien Queen, laying "face-hugger" eggs. Ripley forces an uneasy truce with the Queen by threatening to destroy her eggs with a flamethrower – in response, the alien's own maternal instincts kick in and she orders her minders away. In this moment, Ripley and the Queen are united across the species divide, both understanding a mother's instinct to protect her offspring, at the expense of all other considerations.

What follows is fascinating. Ripley has accomplished her goal. She could simply back off and complete her escape, knowing that the colony will soon be engulfed in flame, and the aliens wiped out. Yet she abandons her better instincts, consumed by uncontrollable rage and a sense of revenge, and (literally) unloads everything in her arsenal at the eggs. The resulting carnage not only endangers Newt but, ultimately, the few remaining survivors of the crew.

In light of this, can the Queen's retaliatory actions be viewed as evil? She has just witnessed her offspring being

---

[1]. Chapter 4 of 44 in the Special Edition, approximately 08:48 minutes in.

mercilessly exterminated. Isn't she simply acting according to her nature? Isn't this any parent's greatest fear: the loss of a child? After all, it is that fear which ultimately causes Ripley to abandon logic as a prelude to this encounter: in an earlier scene, following a disastrous first encounter with the Xenomorphs, one of the surviving marines, Private Vasquez (Jenette Goldstein), points out that two of their abandoned crew members' vital-sign monitors are showing that they are still alive and suggests that they should go back in to rescue them. Ripley rejects this outright, countering, "You can't help them. You can't. Right now they're being cocooned just like the others". However, when Newt is taken, her reaction is exactly the opposite, despite knowing what the girl's apparent fate is, and an urgent motivator in the shape of the reactor leak which will destroy the colony. Maternal instinct, and a refusal to lose another child, leads to her stumbling across the Queen.

There's another consideration here: with serial killers becoming so prominent in the public eye at this time, is she possibly also serving as a cathartic channel for anyone who wished they had the chance to exact justice on those who had murdered people close to them? Essentially, against all rationale and considerations for the present reality, Ripley was presented with an opportunity for meting out immediate vengeance on the Xenomorphs. There's a further interesting juxtaposition in this scene, which we'll touch on again in a later section.

Nuclear Threat and the Cold War

While the maternal conflict discussed above is pretty well-defined in *Aliens*, what is perhaps less apparent are the societal fears of the day that are also, more subtly, reflected in it.

One such aspect is the lingering threat of nuclear warfare. In 1986, when the movie was released, Cold War tensions between America and Russia had been lumbering on for nearly forty years. Within this context, the Cuban Missile Crisis of 1962 marked a major crisis point; suddenly, the possibility of a cataclysmic nuclear conflict seemed all too likely. Though this was averted, it emblazoned on the public psyche just how fragile our existence was – the threat posed by nuclear weapons meant that nobody was safe if another global war broke out.

So there's a certain extra resonance in *Aliens* when Ripley offers her solution to the colony being overrun by Xenomorphs: "I say we take off and nuke the site from orbit."

As it turns out, this isn't necessary as, ironically, the colony's reactor suffers critical damage (most likely as a result of the marines' first confrontation with the Xenomorphs) which eventually leads to a nuclear explosion.

It would be easy to dismiss this as a mere plot device, and not necessarily reflective of anything beyond that. It is evident, however, that the inherent danger posed by the existence of nuclear weaponry was prominent in director James Cameron's mind. Indeed, Cameron's breakthrough movie, *The Terminator* (1984), and its sequel, *Terminator 2: Judgement Day* (1991), have as their central premise an apocalyptic future, caused by self-aware Artificial Intelligence triggering a simultaneous global nuclear attack. Also, his 1994 action-comedy, *True Lies* (1994), features terrorists smuggling nuclear warheads into the US, and his SF movie, *The Abyss* (1989), sees Michael Biehn's crazed soldier trying to destroy the aliens he mistakenly views as a threat with – you guessed it – a nuclear bomb.

In this regard, *The Abyss* acts as an interesting counterpoint to *Aliens*. In *Aliens* there's a strong argument in favour of wiping out the colony on LV-426 as suggested; in *The Abyss*, however, the aliens prove to be peaceful and, in fact, none too pleased with mankind's warlike nature.

There's no doubting the impact the first nuclear bomb

left on the course of history. It's also hardly surprising that the spectre of all-out nuclear warfare has crept onto the big screen so many times over the years. *Aliens* demonstrated how prominent it was in James Cameron's mind, and the collective public psyche.

Vietnam, Guerrilla Warfare, and the Unseen Enemy

Looking at the Cold War once more – in particularly, its most infamous proxy conflict – there's no escaping the impact the Vietnam War had on Americans socially, politically, and in a plethora of other ways both subtle and obvious. The cultural shift was particularly evident in war films. There was a time when the abiding image represented on screen of the American soldier was that of a saviour; a stout, unwavering every-man, (metaphorically) carrying the flag and its perceived values before him. The actor John Wayne (a strong anti-Communist[2]), perhaps more than any, embodied this big screen persona.

US intervention in the Second World War had largely given rise to this image of the soldier as all-American hero. Not even their use of nuclear weapons at Hiroshima and Nagasaki could dispel that – the popular notion was that they had utilised extreme, but necessary, measures to bring about a premature end to the conflict with Japan.

It was the Vietnam War that burst this bubble. As the conflict rumbled on, and the reality of its atrocities filtered through to the outside world, the image of the American soldier also started to alter. As we have seen, the entertainment industry reflected this shift.

In the seventies, the movie *MASH* (1972), and its spinoff series, in the guise of a comedy, presented many of the darker

---

[2]. He was one of the founding members of the Motion Picture Alliance for the Preservation of American Ideals (MPA), which sought to weed out a perceived infiltration of Communists into Hollywood.

realities and moral conundrums arising from war. While *MASH* had the Korean War as its backdrop, films like *The Deer Hunter* (1978) and *First Blood* (1982) took a hard look at the scars that Vietnam had left on its soldiers. These were no infallible, morally perfect individuals. Here, we were presented with the idea of broken young men, haunted by the horrors of what they had seen (and done), in a battle that should never have been waged.

Strategically, US troops never came to terms with the Viet Cong's use of guerrilla tactics, further complicated by the volatile political situation in Vietnam and the country's unforgiving jungles.

The seventies and eighties were prime eras for cinema dealing with the war directly; the aforementioned *The Deer Hunter*, along with *Apocalypse Now* (1979), *Platoon* (1986) and *Full Metal Jacket* (1987) examples of some of the more widely lauded efforts.

But its lingering effects had also seeped into action movies. *First Blood*, in fact, straddled the divide between serious drama and action picture (spawning the arguably lesser *Rambo* sequels). We also had the likes of *Predator* (1987), *Lethal Weapon* (1987) (though his wife's death is used as the primary motivation for the main character Martin Riggs' fractured mental state, there's more than a hint that his time spent as a sniper in Vietnam may have contributed to it) and, of course, *Aliens*.

Predator shares similar DNA to *Aliens* – small wonder we ended up with an *Alien vs. Predator* (or *AVP*, if you prefer) mash-up universe. Both feature merciless, unrelenting alien entities hunting outmatched human prey, for one. Most pertinently though, is their use of terrain and tactics. In *Predator*, the jungle is as much enemy as the predator itself (though the setting is the jungles of Central America, the movie certainly has more than a few nods to the Vietnam War); in *Aliens*, the Giger-inspired, Xenomorph-secretion laden walls are an effective substitute. Essentially, we have unseen, camouflaged enemies crawling out of the woodwork (so to speak).

Then there are the troops. Contrast the marine uniforms in *Aliens* against any number of historical photos from the war itself (not to mention *Full Metal Jacket* and *Platoon*, et al.); or the line "Today, you people are no longer maggots. Today, you are Marines", from *Full Metal Jacket*, against this one from *Aliens*: "Another glorious day in the Corps! A day in the Marine Corps is like a day on the farm. Every meal's a banquet! Every paycheck a fortune! Every formation a parade! I love the Corps!"

The Vietnam War parallels are quite unmistakeable, then. There's more to this picture, though; or, rather, there's more than one picture.

Ripley vs Burke: Idealism vs Corporate Greed

Movies are often an effective representation of the prevailing themes of their time and place in history. In this way, much can be extracted from films of the eighties. Narrowing this down, a lot can be gathered by examining the mood of the age through the lens of three movies in particular, all released in 1986: *Aliens*, *Platoon* and *Ferris Bueller's Day Off* (1986).

Looking at *Platoon*, we find no tale of brothers-in-arms, fighting the good fight. In many ways, it is more akin to *Lord of the Flies* (Golding, 1954), harking at the ease with which men (or indeed, boys) can descend into chaos and savagery when removed from apparent civilisation. These are soldiers out of their depth, fighting each other as much as the enemy, scrambling over dead bodies in the vague hope of survival and a misguided sense of moral right.

So, how does *Ferris Bueller's Day Off* fit into this discussion? It is, on the face of it, a breezy comedy about a roguish, lovable guy who just wants to have fun, and ensure his friends do too. Well, that's pretty much it – or, at least, part of it. It was one of many such comedies of the time dealing with the friction between being young, innocent and carefree, and "growing up", getting a job and becoming a perceived success (i.e.: a financial success). In other words, rebellion against so-called "Yuppie"[3] ideals. Indeed, the Yuppie dream was already crumbling, before crashing spectacularly to earth in 1987.

We'll come back to that, because this is the perfect moment to talk further about the character of Burke in *Aliens*. Rarely has a picture of unbridled corporate ambition been so fully and effectively realised on screen – his desire to get ahead quashing all moral considerations.

His naked ambition is perfectly reflected in one particular exchange. Ripley, having discovered the truth of how LV-426's colonists encountered the Xenomorphs in the first place (a directive from Burke, having learned of the location of the Xenomorph eggs at Ripley's debriefing at the beginning of the movie), confronts Burke. His justification for effectively sending them to their death is that he was afraid there would be "…no exclusive rights for anybody; nobody wins." Though he then acknowledges that it was a bad call, it's clear he is insincere and unrepentant.

Ripley, rightly outraged, promises, "I'm going to make sure they nail you right to the wall for this!".

Burke being Burke, replies, "You know, I expected more from you", as if he can't fathom how others *wouldn't* be as ruthlessly ambitious as he is.

The scene itself is a perfect illustration of a central conflict within the movie (and, indeed, the series as a whole): Burke representing the face of corporate (Weyland-Yutani[4]) greed, while Ripley is its moral centre. More than that, however, the two could be viewed as reflective of the economic and social realities of the USA in the eighties.

---

[3]. A term coined in the eighties, which referred to young, well-dressed, successful urbanites who lived and worked in the city.
[4]. The company that funded LV-426.

Consider that this was an America in the slipstream of "Reaganomics"[5], which helped create an atmosphere of "greed-is-good". If you didn't have a high-powered, high-pressured, high-paying job in the city, the inference was that you were somehow lesser. Hence the friction between those who embraced Yuppiedom and those who rejected its materialistic tenets. *Ferris Bueller's Day Off* isn't the only eighties movie to reflect this – not by a long shot. To name just a few that infiltrated pop culture at the time, we have *The Secret of My Success* (1987), *Working Girl* (1988), and *Big* (1988); the so-called "Brat Pack"[6] movies, *The Breakfast Club* (1985) and *St Elmo's Fire* (1988), are also off-shoots of this trend. John Hughes, who directed both *The Breakfast Club* and *Ferris Bueller's Day Off*, was particularly interested in this cultural dichotomy, it seems.

However, one eighties movie arguably captured this contrast best: *Wall Street* (1987). Consider that both *Platoon* and *Wall Street* were directed by Oliver Stone, or that *Wall Street* followed hot on the heels of *Platoon* (released in 1986 and 1987 respectively). For that matter, Stone himself was a Vietnam veteran and, as a filmmaker, largely concerned with casting a critical (and often suspicious) eye on the norms and politics of the day. There's also the happy coincidence of two Vietnam war movie alumni starring in *Wall Street*: Martin Sheen (*Apocalypse Now*) as his real-life son Charlie's father, and John C. McGinley (*Platoon*).

The plot of the movie focusses on Charlie Sheen's naïve young stockbroker, Bud Fox, who is sucked into the orbit of Michael Douglas' Gordon Gekko, an unscrupulous corporate raider. The movie was all the more prescient in light of what

---

[5]. Former US President Ronald Reagan's economic policy of tax cuts, particularly for the wealthy.

[6]. The nickname given to the group of young actors who frequently appeared together in teen-oriented coming-of-age films in the eighties. In particular, Emilio Estevez, Anthony Michael Hall, Rob Lowe, Andrew McCarthy, Demi Moore, Judd Nelson, Molly Ringwald, and Ally Sheedy.

happened on Monday October 19, 1987, when stock markets around the world crashed.

Returning to *Aliens*, we can see how Ripley and Burke are representative of this theme. Burke is the corporate go-getter, using whatever means are at his disposal to further his career. Morals and ethics are considered as hindrances. Ripley is idealistic, valuing morality and human life above all other concerns. More than that, she represents an unwavering faith in justice. Even after Burke has attempted to kill her and Newt off, she refuses to give in to vigilantism (as Hicks and co. are eager to mete out once they are clued in to the details of Burke's murderous plans).

On the other hand, despite events spiralling out of control, and his own survival hanging in the balance, still, Burke's primary driving force is his career; he doubles down in his plans, plotting to get Ripley and Newt impregnated by face-huggers, so preventing Ripley exposing his culpability, while also gaining a couple of preserved alien foetuses, smuggled home in their frozen bodies. As Ripley points out when this fails: "You know Burke, I don't know which species is worse. You don't see them fucking each other over for a goddamn percentage.". Ultimately, Burke's concern for himself above all others is his undoing, as he meets a sticky end at the hands of the Xenomorphs he was trying so hard to cash in on.

It follows then that Ripley vs Burke is a clear example of good vs evil; moral vs immoral; humanist vs materialist. This distinction, however, upon deeper reflection, is not so clear elsewhere.

Good vs Evil, and Plenty of Grey Between

As touched on earlier, Ripley's battle against the Alien Queen presents some interesting considerations when it comes to right vs wrong. This can be extended further, to other parts of *Aliens*.

Truly, can the Xenomorphs be considered evil if they are

simply acting according to their hardwiring, to protect and expand their species? This is, after all, reflected in Nature itself, where the most ruthless killers rule the food chain. Indeed, humans have learned not only to rise to the top of that chain but also to dominate and subjugate it. Is there a moral imperative to protect and preserve the species below us? It seems obvious to say that categorically, yes, there is. And yet, so many imbalances in Nature can be traced to human interference.

Not to stray too far from the topic at hand but, keeping this in mind, what if we viewed the humans in *Aliens* from a different perspective. After all, it's revealed that the reason the colonists encounter the Xenomorphs in the first place is because of Burke, who essentially uses ignorant innocents as bait. Even before this, the colonists are on LV-426 in the interests of terraforming and expansion of the human race. When Ripley explains what happened on the spaceship Nostromo (in *Alien*), the events leading to her being the lone survivor and the ship set to self-destruct, Weyland-Yutani choose to sweep this under the carpet. Why? Because they're unwilling to consider anything that would jeopardise their expensive colonisation efforts – to the extent of endangering the inhabitants of LV-426. Truly, which species is more complicit in what follows?

The Dark Corners of the Mind: The Influence of H.R. Giger

As we've seen, there's more to *Aliens* than first meets the eye. In closing, though, we certainly shouldn't forget the movie's more visceral elements. A key component of the success of *Aliens*, and its progenitor, was the Swiss artist H.R. Giger, who won an Academy Award as part of the Visual Effects team for *Alien*. The biomechanical, body-horror aesthetics of his artworks (in particular, his painting, Necronom IV) laid the seeds of what would become an iconic movie monster.

Giger himself was hugely influenced by the works of H.P. Lovecraft, and it is this inspiration which clearly leaked into his designs for *Alien* (which were then inherited and carried forward in Aliens). The Xenomorphs themselves provoke a sense of revulsion and terror, as if they have crawled out of a particularly intense nightmare. The methods they employ for survival and procreation evoke deep psychological horrors, of violation and excruciating pain. Imagine your greatest fears taking on physical form, forcing themselves upon you, and your final act then being to give birth to their offspring.

Of course, movies like *Aliens* are so effective because of human imagination. After all, it's the thought of what could be lurking in the shadows that scares us so much. So, whether it be an examination of real life issues of the time, or daring to explore beneath the surface, staring into the void within, *Aliens* makes for a compelling lens through which to study our society.

As a final thought, Newt perhaps expressed it best: "My mommy always said there were no monsters – no real ones – but there are." (*Aliens*, 1986).

Indeed, there are, though they don't always take on the form we expect. We are both repulsed by, and drawn towards, our greatest fears, and true horror does too often reach out from the shadows to forever alter our physical and mental landscapes.

Bibliography

The Abyss, 1989. [film] Directed by James Cameron. USA: Twentieth Century Fox, Pacific Western, Lightstorm Entertainment.

Alien, 1979. [film] Directed by Ridley Scott. UK/USA: Twentieth Century Fox, Brandywine Productions.

Aliens, 1986. [film] Directed by James Cameron. USA: Twentieth Century Fox, Brandywine Productions.

Apocalypse Now, 1979. [film] Directed by Francis Ford Coppola. USA: Zoetrope Studios.

Big, 1988. [film] Directed by Penny Marshall. USA: Gracie Films, Twentieth Century Fox.

The Breakfast Club, 1985. [film] Directed by John Hughes. USA: Universal Pictures, A&M Films, Channel Productions.

The Deer Hunter, 1978. [film] Directed by Michael Cimino. USA: EMI Films, Universal Pictures.

Ferris Bueller's Day Off, 1986. [film] Directed by John Hughes. USA: Paramount Pictures.

First Blood, 1982. [film] Directed by Ted Kotcheff. USA: Anabasis NV, Elcajo Productions.

Friday the 13th, 1980. [film] Directed by Sean S. Cunningham. USA: Paramount Pictures

Full Metal Jacket, 1987. [film] Directed by Stanley Kubrick. UK/USA: Natant, Stanley Kubrick Productions, Warner Bros.

Golding, W., 1954. *Lord of the Flies*. London: Faber and Faber.

Halloween, 1978. [film] Directed by John Carpenter. USA: Compass International Picture

Lethal Weapon, 1987. [film] Directed by Richard Donner. USA: Silver Pictures, Warner Bros.

MASH, 1970. [film] Directed by Robert Altman. USA: Twentieth Century Fox, Ingo Preminger Productions, Aspen Productions.

Platoon, 1986. [film] Directed by Oliver Stone. USA: Hemdale, Cinema 86.

Predator, 1987. [film] Directed by John McTiernan. USA/Mexico: Twentieth Century Fox, Lawrence Gordon Productions, Silver Pictures.

St Elmo's Fire, 1988. [film] Directed by Joel Schumacher. USA: Columbia Pictures, Delphi IV Productions.

The Secret of My Success, 1987. [film] Directed by Herbert Ross. USA: Rastar Pictures, Universal Pictures.

The Terminator, 1984. [film] Directed by James Cameron. USA: Hemdale, Pacific Western.

Terminator 2: Judgment Day, 1991. [film] Directed by James Cameron. USA: Carolco, Pacific Western, Lightstorm Entertainment, Canal+.

True Lies, 1994. [film] Directed by James Cameron. USA: Twentieth Century Fox, Lightstorm Entertainment.

Wall Street, 1987. [film] Directed by Oliver Stone. USA: American Entertainment Partners, Twentieth Century Fox, Amercent Films.

Working Girl, 1988. [film] Directed by Mike Nichols. USA: Twentieth Century Fox.

Born Bad: Unmasking Evil in John Carpenter's *Halloween* and James Cameron's *The Terminator*

Kim Lakin-Smith

Abstract:

In the shadows of very personal wounds inflicted by a childhood viewing of 1978's horror classic, *Halloween*, I explore the mysticism of evil in special relation to John Carpenter's seminal slasher, Michael Myers, and James Cameron's titular cyborg, 1984's *The Terminator*. Killing machines or apex predators, both Michael and the Terminator invoke primordial fear, brutalise the trespasser, and stalk the innocent. While Michael disguises his supernatural humanity behind the apathetic mask, the non-human T-800 Terminator dons a skin suit to assimilate with his emotive prey. Both are relentless in their monstrous pursuit of the final girl, embodying social/political paranoias as well as gender biases of the period. Both represent the ubiquitous bad, diametric to a conscientious good. But what lies beneath the skin? To what extent do these characters actively assault the moral axiology of the complicit audience? And is it accurate to describe each as morally privative – 'purely and simply evil' – or have they each an artificial code of agency, motivated by absence over malevolence? In essence, is the ideology of evil these characters represent truly unstoppable, or can we, like Laurie Strode and Sarah Connor, find a way to survive the night?

It is a fact that cannot be denied: the wickedness of others becomes our own wickedness because it kindles something evil in our own hearts.

Carl Jung[1]

*

---
[1]. Carl Jung, *Collected Works* Volume 10, Para 408.

Evil is a source of enduring fascination. As the antithesis to all that is wholesome and right, it is both philosophically slippery and profoundly human. Traditionally, evil is bracketed as 'natural' or 'moral' in origin. On the one hand, natural evil is caused by the physical world – hurricanes, earthquakes, tsunamis, forest fires, and other 'Acts of God'[2]. On the other hand, moral evil is defined as a choice, and therefore a reflexivity on self and cultural practices. A third, lesser known view is that evil only exists as a 'parasitic absence'; in other words, a 'lack' of goodness, right or light. And, finally, a fourth (as yet) theoretical proposition in computer ethics is 'artificial evil', arising from autonomous superintelligence. From these shifts in impetus, horror movies are born, with a golden age featuring slashers and science fiction in the late 1970s and early 1980s.

Wielding my own knife, I decided to peel back the skin of two of cinema's most iconic evildoers: mute sociopath Michael Myers, from John Carpenter's 1978 horror classic, *Halloween*, and James Cameron's titular T-800 cyborg from 1984's science fiction masterpiece, *The Terminator*. Given the parallels between the two movies, I wanted to understand the complexities of evil in terms of antagonists who appear physically human but behave inhumanly. Are these characters simply born bad, or does the wicked act require a conscious and deliberate desire to do harm? And what of the pursued, both those teen transgressors put to death for their crimes and the final girls facing down these rapacious gatekeepers? To what extent are Michael and the T-800 simply acting out societal fears, and just how culpable are we, the voyeuristic audience,

---

[2]. Named after the 4th and 5th century theologian and philosopher, Augustine of Hippo, Augustian theodicy attempts to relieve God of all responsibility for human evil. His beliefs centred on man's abuse of free will as a route to evil. However, while Augustine supported the notion of a physical Hell, he also argued that those who renounced past sin and turned to Christianity would go to heaven.

for the violence enjoyed on screen[3]?

Both *Halloween* and *The Terminator* had a profound effect on me as a young viewer, but only one taught me the true meaning of evil. I was ten years old when Michael came to stay. He wasn't an imaginary friend. He didn't live under the bed or in the wardrobe or behind the door. My monster took up residence inside my head and was, to my young, susceptible mind, very real. As a partially deaf child, I already existed in a world of tinnitus and muffled sound. It was inevitable, perhaps, that I should find a companion in the not-quite silence, even one as terrifying as Michael.

It was the early eighties. To use the truism, things were different back then. With two older brothers, life outside of school meant playing *Donkey Kong* on an Atari 800, taking turns on skateboards and a single BMX, cheating at Rubik's Cubes by peeling off the stickers, and binge-watching *ET*, *Tron*, *Jaws*, *Porky's* and other gems from the video shop. It was no big deal for me to watch *Halloween*, a movie that paid homage to Hitchcock's *Psycho* and gave birth to a new kind of horror movie populated by scream queens, phallic knifings, and serial killers who refused to stay dead. Except, while I would usually lose a couple of nights sleep to bad dreams inspired by a horror movie and then promptly forget it, this time around something went horribly wrong.

Ranked amongst the scariest films ever made, *Halloween* sank its hooks into me. Haunted by his death and implied resurrection, Michael solidified into my personal boogieman, an immortal psychopath who had to be appeased else he materialise in my reality. The next day, with no idea why, I

---

[3]. Any notion of entertainment value in dramatised murder is always going to be polarising. This is especially true when it comes to the way children process horror movies. Theorist Jean Piaget created a scale of cognitive development, or schemas, based on ways of perceiving the world. Piaget proposed that, Pre-11 years of age, imagination and intuition are strong, but abstract logic and thought are still challenging and only applicable to physical objects. (McLeod, 2018)

put my right toe on and off a corner of the living room rug, repeated the sequence whenever I walked past, and, in so doing, created my first ritual. In weeks, my life was given over to crippling anxiety and obsessive-compulsive disorder (OCD[4]) designed to sate the voice inside my head and keep Michael at bay.

Preferring the safety of downstairs to the vulnerable isolation of my bedroom, I continued to share my brothers' diet of Cert 18s. It wasn't long before I was introduced to a new foe, this time in the form of James Cameron's nightmare-birthed[5] cyborg in 1984's *The Terminator*. Once again, from behind a cushion, I witnessed that tenacious drive to kill over and over without remorse. As Kyle Reese, the soldier sent back from the future to protect Sarah Connor, stresses, "It can't be bargained with. It can't be reasoned with. It doesn't feel pity, or remorse, or fear. And it absolutely will not stop, ever, until you are dead." Just like Michael. In fact, director Cameron was quick to acknowledge this debt: "John Carpenter was the guy I idolised the most. He made *Halloween* for $30,000 or something. That was everyone's break-in dream, to do a stylish horror movie. It was a very slasher film type image.

---

[4]. OCD has been called the 'disease of doubt'. The French psychiatrist, Jean-Étienne Dominique Esquirol (1772-1840), called it a form of monomania, or partial insanity. To my way of thinking, far more insightful was Sigmund Freud (1856-1939) and his linking of mental structure, mental energies, and defence mechanisms. Reassuringly, Freud saw past the blanket banner of insanity to a psychological state whereby, "The ego marshalled certain defences: intellectualization and isolation (warding off the effects associated with the unacceptable ideas and impulses); undoing (carrying out compulsions to neutralise the offending ideas and impulses) and reaction formation (adopting character traits exactly opposite of the feared impulses)" (Stanford School of Medicine.) Within these parameters, OCD becomes a practice of protection, no different to sacrificing lambs or offering prayers to any other god.

5. As an impoverished director/writer, Cameron found himself stuck in Rome while ill with a food-poisoning induced fever. According to his biographer, Rebecca Keegan, in *The Futurist*, 'he dreamt of "A chrome torso emerging, phoenixlike, from an explosion and dragging itself across the floor with kitchen knives."

And it really was the launching pad for the story." (Lambie, 2014)

The similarities between the two movies are manifold, with both narratives revolving around the 'chase' scenario. Institutionalised since the age of six for the murder of his sister, *Halloween*'s Michael escapes to terrorise high school student Laurie Strode and her friends while his doctor hunts him down. Similarly, *The Terminator*'s T-800 is sent back in time to kill teenage Sarah Connor and guns down namesakes, friends, family, and an entire police station while future-soldier Reese fights to help Sarah survive. Likewise, *Halloween* and *The Terminator* are stylistically analogous, featuring grimly lit, night-time settings. The ultimate parallel, though, is in the (de)characterisation of their antagonists.

As the true stars of these narratives, Michael and the terminator demonstrate a chilling apathy towards the act of murder and an unhurried, relentless pursuit of their prey. Each is represented by a signature leitmotif in the movie's musical score. Using strings as stingers[6] to accompany Michael's staccato knife strikes, Carpenter gives a voice to a killer who doesn't speak – indicative of the fact he doesn't *feel* – and who endures, even when a knitting needle is stabbed through his neck and six bullets lodged in his chest. Likewise, *The Terminator* is haunted by Brad Fiedel's synthed invocation of a 'mechanical man and his heartbeat', used to great effect when the T-800 closes in on Sarah inside the nightclub, his magnitude over his timid prey emphasised by high and low camera angles[7]. As the doom-laden strings saw back and forth, we witness the terminator rise again after being shot

---

[6]. A 'stinger' is a short musical phrase used for punctuation. It helps to build tension and accentuates jump scares in horror movies.

[7]. This dehumanisation of the cyborg was in direct contrast to another science fiction classic of the period – 1982's *Blade Runner*, where robots are human-like replica(nt)s presented as sentient and emotional.

multiple times and falling through glass onto the sidewalk. Our disbelief peaks with the soaring synth as the endoskeleton rises from the flames to drag itself on after the wounded Sarah Connor. Even when Sarah succeeds in extinguishing that solitary burning eye in the hydraulic press, we are left with a final image of her, pregnant and alone, driving towards the storm as the propulsive beat strengthens.

Cameron's bio-engineered terminator is a truly relentless killing machine. However, while the terminator and Michael are gods in a wrathful world order, I believe their impetus is different because each personifies a different *type* of evil. I think this is why *Halloween* affected me so profoundly while *The Terminator* scared, thrilled, and entertained me the way horror movies are meant to.

"To make Michael Myers frightening, I had him walk like a man, not a monster," Carpenter said of the character he called the 'Shape'[8] in the end credits. As a young viewer familiar with the demonic possession rife in such horror classics as Sam Raimi's *The Evil Dead* (1981) and Stuart Rosenberg's *The Amityville Horror* (1979), I was terrified by Michael's evildoing precisely because it was his independent choice to kill. By donning a white mask and utilitarian boiler suit, Michael deliberately seeks to debase/ascend his own humanity. His motivation is twofold: firstly, to give free rein to what Carl Jung called the shadow self[9], that unconscious aspect of the personality which the conscious ego does not identify in itself, and secondly, to mask the inner monster he

---

[8]. The name, the Shape, is given to Michael whenever he is wearing the mask. This same term was used by Cotton Mather during the Salem Witch Trials when describing the spirits of the accused doing harming to others and identified by author Gene DeRosa in his novel, *10-31 A Halloween Movie Trivia Book*.

[9]. "Everyone carries a shadow," Jung wrote, "and the less it is embodied in the individual's conscious life, the blacker and denser it is." (1958).

symbolically seeks to destroy, namely, the abject[10] degradation of the flesh. It is this fusion of human choice with a facsimile of animatronic drive which makes Michael morally corrupt, and such a terrifying enemy.

Polar opposite is the terminator, a machine cloaked in human tissue. Journalist Mark Lee describes its organic shell[11] as "a ghastly reflection of the human condition… Strip away any human's exterior, the thin veneer of politeness and morality, and you're left with a skeleton, a monster. An uncontrollable, unstoppable monster with an unquenchable lust for human flesh." (2016). However, I would have to contest the T-800's ability to 'desire' murder given that this suggests a very human impetus over preconfigured coding. In *Halloween*, Michael piques his 'lust' for Laurie by watching her from outside the house and, later, tormenting her with the theatrical arrangement of her friends' corpses. In contrast, the terminator systematically ramps up a high body count, but these deaths are arbitrary next to acquiring its final target – future-mother-of-a-rebel-leader, Sarah Connor. Admittedly, the T-800 is programmed to kill; therefore, it could be argued that the homicidal behaviour stems from moral evil since it can be retraced to the human creators of Skynet. But I propose an alternative synthetic impetus, that of artificial evil.

In the paper, 'Artificial Evil and the Foundation of Computer Ethics,' Luciano Floridi and J.W. Sanders describe self-produced generations of AI leading to a theoretical state where

---

[10]. In her paper, 'The Invention of the Modern Monster: Defining Ourselves Against the Eerie Other', Theodora Goss describes French feminist Julia Kristeva's theory of abjection as "a theoretical framework to think about the monster: it implies that we produce the monster out of what is abjected, what we reject in the process of defining the human. Monsters are a way of policing our own boundaries." (2015).

[11]. "All right, listen. *The Terminator*'s an infiltration unit: part man, part machine. Underneath, it's a hyperalloy combat chassis, microprocessor-controlled. Fully armoured; very tough. But outside, it's living human tissue: flesh, skin, hair, blood – grown for the cyborgs." Kyle Reese, *The Terminator* (1984).

artificial agents are "…sufficiently autonomous to pre-empt the possibility that their creators may be nomologically in charge of, and hence morally accountable for their misbehaviour." (2001, p. 23) Given the singularity event of the machines' uprising, the T-800's destructive programming is not transhuman or even posthuman, but rather self-directed superintelligence. As Floridi and Sanders suggest, "Were they autonomous and able to transform and adapt, in the way programs can, such machines would provide an analogous example of AE; but so far they seem to be no more than instruments of science fiction." (p. 29) *The Terminator* fulfils such a destiny, with the T-800 a gleaming example of artificial evil, or as Cameron posits, "Death rendered in steel." (1982)

While the motivation behind their acts of evil is different, there is an area of distinctive overlap between these two antagonists – a deeper layer of threat than I could ever have mentally articulated as a young girl. White, male, athletic and homicidal, Michael and the terminator are apex predators engendered with the phallogocentric prejudices of the late seventies and early eighties[12]. At its basest level, Michael's desire to stab the bookish Laurie with the carving knife is the ultimate rape attempt. While Laurie is preserved by dint of her 'good girl' virtue, Michael does have his wicked way with those deemed less worthy – those nonconforming teens who engage in sex and alcohol. *Halloween* is laden with these puritanical undertones, most evident when Michael wears a bedsheet as a ghost costume and bides his time in the doorway watching Laurie's friend, Lynda, flirt salaciously from the bed. Like his sister at the start of the film, the naked female form acts as the catalyst for Michael's attack; he even displays Lynda's body in the cupboard with her shirt unbuttoned and breasts exposed, as a warning card should Laurie dream of similar transgressions.

---

[12]. In the 2000 documentary, *The American Nightmare*, Carpenter even jokes, "I didn't mean to put an end to the sexual revolution, and for that I deeply apologise."

The Terminator stays true to this ritualised punishment of rebel teens. Distracted by her Walkman after sex, Sarah's flatmate is ignorant to the looming presence of the T-800 about to gun her down. However, where Cameron deviates from the misogynistic template is in having Sarah sleep with Reese and live to tell the tale. In fact, Sarah is wholly emblematic of the final girl, a horror trope coined by American academic Carol J. Clover. In *Men, Women, and Chain Saws: Gender in the Modern Horror Film* (1992), Clover aligns the audience not with the male tormentor, but with the female victim – the 'final girl' – who finally defeats her oppressor. From Buffy to Sabrina, Ripley to Carrie, Katniss to Michonne, final girls have inverted their victimhood – and thanks in no small measure to Sarah Connor's icon metamorphosis from naïve ingénue to embattled warrior mother.

The Terminator opens with Sarah as the all-American girl-next-door – pretty, blonde, waitressing in a diner and having fun with her friends. By the end of the movie, Sarah has undergone a stark (r)evolution into student bomb maker, maternal saviour and drill sergeant – as evidenced when her prettiness hardens, her voice becoming deeper, stronger - more inherently masculine – as she shouts at the wounded Reese, "On your feet, soldier!" Minutes later, with Reese dead and the vestiges of the T-800 clawing towards her, Sarah slides out of the hydraulic press – a machine she finally has control over – and reaches for the start button. In terminating her assailant, Sarah remoulds her fear into the physical and psychological armature she wears in *Terminator 2*[13]. Most significantly, she saves herself.

This mark of female sovereignty is in striking contrast to Carpenter's last shot of Laurie, curled into a ball on the bedroom

---

[13]. When, arguably, Sarah Connor becomes the robotic, merciless killer and, thanks to his rewiring and interactions with the young teen John Connor, the terminator achieves a new understanding of humanity, asserting, "I know now why you cry."

floor and sobbing hysterically. Instead of a triumphant call to arms, *Halloween* concludes with views of the empty house[14] aka deserted battleground and the sound of Michael breathing. By emerging triumphant, Michael proves himself a far more complex character than the colourless Laurie; it may even be argued that it is only under the threat from Michael's knife that the bland teen finds her voice, both metaphysically and literally.

This interdependence between monster and victim makes *Halloween* terrifyingly effective. Through his economic direction, Carpenter provides his audience with an elegantly simple take on what it means to flee the predator while simultaneously inhabiting their skin. *Halloween* opens through the eyeholes of a mask, forcing the audience into the role of Peeping Tom as we spy on Michael's older sister Judith, sitting naked at her dressing table. As Clover remarks in the documentary, *The American Nightmare*: "We see ourselves hold a knife and stab someone, and we don't know who we are." (2000) By wearing Michael's mask, we oscillate between lust and (self-)revulsion. And fear; we become prey as the blade slices towards the camera, and we are forced to trade places with Laurie and hide in claustrophobic terror as Michael breaks down the closet door. The effect is at once frightening and exhilarating; we are victim and voyeur, both afraid and in love with the act of murder.

This thinning of the fourth wall is also achieved through capturing societal paranoias and extrapolating them into that we fear most. Cameron's violent cyborg is the perfect manifestation of the eighties' political tensions and technological suspicions. Tensions between America and the Eastern Bloc were still very real, with the hands of the doomsday clock moved up to three minutes to midnight. Meanwhile, a new digital age was in rapid expansion, with 1984 seeing the Space Shuttle Discovery on its maiden voyage, the launch of the Apple Macintosh

---

[14]. Bookending the film which opened with views of Michael's family home.

personal computer with an ad that paid homage to Orwell, and, adding fire to a growing fear of Big Brother surveillance and DNA fingerprinting. Sarah's overwhelming fear for the metal man is entirely indicative of a widespread distrust of these technological advances. By erasing any emotive component and casting the heavily accented Schwarzenegger as the predatorial machine, Cameron rejected the feminised masculinity of the eighties' aesthetic while embracing the fear of an underlying and insidious communist presence. As Cohen points out, "The monster is not only a threat towards individual members of society, but also the structures within society upon which we build our identity as human beings."

Just as Cameron played on societal fears, so Carpenter manipulated his audience's daily exposure to violence. Seventies' news channels were filled with unspeakable horrors – the events of Bloody Sunday, presidential and political assassinations, the Cuban Missile Crisis (leading to air-raid siren practice and bomb drills) and photographs and film reels starkly illuminating the horrors of the Vietnam war. Surviving horror movies became akin to going into battle; now the evil was implicitly personal, threatening the white picket fence suburbs where people retreated to escape the violence of the cities and raise families in safety. Carpenter let a monster into this sacred playground, and in so doing, exposed a raw fear of parental absence and vulnerable teens abandoned to the savage wasteland between childhood and adulthood. Academic Pat Gill even rejects the singular evil motivation of the slasher, instead homing in on an Augustian 'lack' (of active parenting):

> The discontented teens all seem to be in a state of mourning for something they cannot quite describe, and they use sex, drugs, and drink as substitutes for it. The monsters haunting the streets, dormitories, and dreams of the protagonists are less figures of patriarchal control and punishment than the ogres

of childhood nightmares and the social hell of adolescence, which remain undiminished because no parent comes round to dispel them. If the monsters are the products of the parents, it is as the residue of their absence, indifference, and failure to understand. (Gill, p. 23)

The Terminator plays on Gill's notion of parental failing via the T-800's systematic obliteration of the entire police force in the station where Sarah takes refuge – undermining the parental/authoritative assurance, "You'll be safe here." The message is one of lack, whether in terms of physical presence or ability to protect against the quintessential monster under the bed, and in this regard, evil is the 'parasitic absence' (of guardianship).

This sense of psychological isolation feels particularly relevant to my battle with Michael via OCD as a child. However, as an adult fiction writer, I have found a new impulse to go beyond the limits of privative self-blame. For me, the story of the other has always gleamed brightest. Far from setting out to scare, I have tried to understand what unsettles people and how to humanise the freak/outsider.

In *Monster Culture – Seven Theses*, academic Jeffrey Jerome Cohen ascribes "a strengthened sense of self" to our rejection of the other. (1996, p. 18) He posits the monster as a scapegoat, "ritually destroyed in the course of some official narrative." (p. 18) It is Cohen's argument that killers like Michael and the terminator act as sin-eaters, freeing the audience from their own unwanted ideas and impulses. For me, this is a poignant observation given an aspect of clinical OCD known as 'intrusive thoughts.' These mental tics focus on sexual, violent, or socially unacceptable images, with the sufferer imagining committing these acts and feeling abjectly self-repulsed. By animating the repugnant other on film, we, the audience, get to enjoy a cathartic release through our projective embodiment of evil.

As the old wives' tale goes, the best way to remove a tic is to put a match to it. At the age of 22, I lost my mother to cancer and my world went up in flames. Death was no longer the intangible threat from the shadows; now it was a real, solid, agonising truth, and no amount of rituals could appease it. Michael lost his substance, fading to a burn outline even as the dregs of the disease remained. Somewhere inside that period of pain, my fear fractured; the worst had happened and Michael had had no part in it.

Much of the promotion for this year's 2018 reimagining of Halloween has revolved around Jamie Lee Curtis's talk of her character Laurie's PTSD and dissociative disorders. For me, this only scratches the surface of the very personal scars Michael left with his knife. Like *Terminator 2*'s Version 2.0 of Sarah Connor, I learnt survival tactics and have the nightmares under control for the most part. Sometimes, though, when I am nervous or under stress, I will instinctively double-tap a door handle or arrange my shoes just so. Often the ritual will catch me out and I am forced to acknowledge that Michael is still with me, like a parasitic twin.

Next year will see the release of the sixth instalment of *The Terminator* franchise, with Cameron as executive producer and Sarah Connor forced to continue on from when she last faced down the advanced prototype, the T-1000. I can't help feeling it will be good to see where my battle wearied compatriot ends up – unlike the new version of *Halloween*, which, even all these years later, I can't bring myself to watch. Sometimes, I wonder if I could have turned off the TV all those years ago and avoided a whole world of pain. I suspect I would have found a trigger for my condition regardless of my brothers' choice of movie. But time is a great healer and, through the years, I have come to terms with my own otherness. In writing this paper, I have gained a new understanding of the purity of evil Michael represented for me as a child, and, as an adult, a deeper appreciation for Carpenter's skills as a horror writer. Likewise,

I think it is fair to say Cameron's seminal cyborg introduced the world to a new, artificial brand of conscious evil – and gave final girls everywhere a fighting chance.

It was Friedrich Nietzsche who said: "Battle not with monsters, lest ye become a monster." (1886) For me, the light in the dark has been learning to live amongst the fiends and catching my own reflection when I peek behind the mask.

Bibliography

The American Nightmare. 2001. [film] Directed by Adam Simon. USA: Minerva Pictures.

Cameron, J., 1982. Terminator: A Treatment for a Feature Film Screenplay. *Drehbuchwerkstatt.de*, [online] Available at: <https://www.drehbuchwerkstatt.de/Fachtexte/Terminator_Treatment.pdf> [Accessed 12 February 2019].

Clover, C. J., 1992. *Men, Women, and Chain Saws: Gender in the Modern Horror Film*. Princeton: Princeton University Press.

Cohen, J. J., 1996. *Monster Culture – Seven Theses*. Minneapolis: University of Minnesota Press.

Floridi, L. and Sanders, J. W., 2001. *Artificial Evil and the Foundation of Computer Ethics*. Oxford: University of Oxford. Wolfson College, p. 23.

Gill, P., 2002. The Monstrous Years: Teens, Slasher Films, and the Family. *Journal of Film and Video* Vol. 54, No. 4 (Winter 2002), [online] Available at: <http://www.asu.edu/courses/fms394/readings-biddinger/L8%20gill.monstrous%20years.pdf> [Accessed 12 February 2019].

Goss, T., 2015. The Invention of the Modern Monster. *Lithub.com*, [online] Available at: <https://lithub.com/the-invention-of-the-modern-monster/> [Accessed 12 February 2019].

Halloween, 1978. [film] Directed by John Carpenter. USA: Compass International Picture.

Jung, K., 1958. Psychology and religion: West and East. Bollingen Series XX *The Collected Works of C.G. Jung* Volume 11. New York: Pantheon Books, p. 78.

Lambie, R., 2014. Why the Terminator is a Horror Classic. *Den Of Geek*, [online] Available at: <https://www.denofgeek.com/movies/the-terminator/31391/why-the-terminator-is-a-horror-classic> [Accessed 12 February 2019].

Lee, M., 2016. The Definitive Terminator. *Overthinking It*, [online] Available at: <https://www.overthinkingit.com/2016/05/24/definitive-terminator-analysis/> [Accessed 12 February 2019].

McLeod, S., 2018. Jean Piaget's Theory of Cognitive Development. *Simply Psychology*, [online] Available at: <https://www.simplypsychology.org/piaget.html> [Accessed 12 February 2019].

Nietzsche, F., 1886. Chapter IV: Apophthegms and Interludes, Aphorism 146. *Beyond Good and Evil*. Leipzig: C. G. Naumann.

The Terminator, 1984. [film] Directed by James Cameron. USA: Hemdale.

Bluebeard – The Eternal Predator

Teika Bellamy

Abstract

The story of *Blue Beard*, which first appeared in Charles Perrault's *Histoires ou contes du temps passé* in 1697, continues to have applicability for contemporary readers. Indeed, the character of Bluebeard has become synonymous with that of the male predator. This paper will explore the enduring appeal of this classic fairy tale and the longevity of this evil figure.

The Elements of *Bluebeard*

Fairy tales have often been dismissed as simply stories for children, the implication being that they are juvenile and unimportant. Not of literary worth. Yet the roots of fairy tales, like mythology and folklore, run deep in human history. We are, after all, apes with a bent for storytelling, and what, if anything, are fairy tales but damn good stories?

Bluebeard is one of those damn good stories. Enter Bluebeard into a search engine and you'll receive a huge number of references to the tale, its movie versions as well as its many literary adaptations. There is something about this classic tale that grips readers and writers alike. How has this – superficially – straightforward fairy tale maintained its longevity, remaining "fresh" to contemporary readers?

Just like other persistent fairy tales – *Cinderella*, *Beauty and the Beast*, *Red Riding Hood* – I believe that the power of *Bluebeard* comes from its timelessness; its continued applicability through the use of archetypes and age-old dilemmas. Also, the element of magic puts it firmly in an otherworldly genre – those tales that commonly begin with 'Once upon a time'.

> … they open the door on Other Time, and if we pass through, though only for a moment, we stand outside our own time, outside Time itself maybe. (Tolkien, 1950, p. 36)

The core plot is self-evidently potent. The titular protagonist is a charming and wealthy but suspicious lord who takes a young wife. When he goes away on business he entrusts all his wealth to her with one proviso – that she not enter his private, forbidden chamber. This obvious entrapment for the wife sets up a battle between curiosity and fear, with the revelation that the "bloody chamber" contains the bodies of his previous (disobedient) wives, and swiftly moves on to the final confrontation between the murderous Bluebeard and the young woman's saviours.

Bluebeard is clearly a powerful and shadowy figure; he is elusive, unknowable, his past a mystery. Some versions of the story give hints to Bluebeard's origins, implying that he is of magical stock but that his once great powers have all but ebbed away. In contrast, his young wife is naïve and vulnerable, but with enough self-possession to understand at a fundamental level that remaining ignorant would be a worse peril than disobeying her magelike husband.

> "The keys open every room in the house. You may go into each of them and enjoy what you find there, but do not go into the small room at the top of the house, on pain of death." The girl promised, and the wizard disappeared. (Atwood, 1988, p. 155)

That the drama of *Bluebeard* resonates with people from different eras and different cultures is obvious from the repeated analyses and retellings of the story through different social lenses. Indeed, the basic story framework invites layers of meaning to be draped over it.

A Christian view

Perrault's *Blue Beard* was seen as a morality tale about temptation, the dangers of knowledge, and the shadowy (demonic?) influence of wealth. The story, set 'In the East, in a city not far from Baghdad' (Perrault, 1697, p. 33), seems designed to tap into Christian anxieties of the powerful and mysterious East. Edmund DuLac's illustrations further heighten the (in archaic terms) Moorish aesthetic; Bluebeard wears a huge turban and Turkish slippers, the toes curling at the ends in an exaggerated fashion.

Perrault's telling is also explicit in the central importance of wifely obedience to her lordly husband. On Bluebeard's return from his journey away, the bloodied key signals that his wife, Fatima, has disobeyed him and gone into the forbidden and bloody chamber. He tells her the punishment for her transgression: death.

Fatima begs for mercy, and then asks to say her prayers. Bluebeard allows her 'ten minutes, and not a second more' (Perrault, 1697, p. 47). Fatima runs to her apartment, meeting her sister, Anne, on the way. She implores her to look out for her stepbrothers who are expected that day, and to signal to them to make haste. This, she does. But, meanwhile, Bluebeard is coming for Fatima. When he reaches her, fortuitously, he acts just like any modern comic book villain and begins on a monologue about 'curiosity, the peculiar vice of womankind' (p. 50). This enables the stepbrothers to reach Fatima in the nick of time, allowing the tale to come to its swift and bloody conclusion with the brothers running their swords through Bluebeard's body.

At the end of the story, Perrault tags on two morals – one 'For Curious Wives' and another 'For Chastising or Correcting Husbands'. (p. 52) As a 21st century reader one cannot help but laugh at Perrault's rhyming couplets:

Wives should have one lord only. Some have reckoned
In Curiosity t' enjoy a second.
But Scripture says we may not serve two masters,
And little keys have opened large disasters.

Clearly, this gives rise to comparisons with the story of Eve's temptation by the serpent in the Garden of Eden, as well as the myth of Pandora's Box. (The Grimms' version of the tale has no such addenda.)

Other authors have picked up on the devilish aspects of Bluebeard's character. His craving for knowledge and power, his arrogance and will to dominate; his snakelike tempting with the key of knowledge. From the Abrahamic religions, we learn that Lucifer, one of God's angels, wanted to be like God. His narcissism, his greed for power, his desire for having control over all light and souls eventually led to his banishment from heaven.

I saw Satan fall like lightning from heaven. (Luke 10:18)

It is a trope that echoes through much of fairy tale and fantasy. Tolkien consciously mirrors this in *The Silmarillion*, with the Vala (angel), Melkor, wanting for more – for dominion over all. Ultimately, he is captured and banished into The Void (only for his protégé, Sauron, to continue his dark work).

A psychosexual view

The potent archetypes and richness of symbolism in Bluebeard lend themselves to a psychotherapeutic – especially Jungian – analysis.

The young wife appears unable to relate to her husband early in the tale, and has an intuitive wariness of him that is shared by the reader. Since the colour blue, in hair and fur, is nonexistent in mammals, the blue-coloured beard is another uncanny feature of the story, one that only adds to the reader's suspicions. Unless Bluebeard dyes his beard (and there is no obvious reason why he should) this is yet another sign of his magical roots. It is only once the wife enters the forbidden room that she finally understands his character – he is a predator, and she his prey.

In Jungian terms it would be tempting to categorise Bluebeard as all shadow i.e. the unconscious shadow archetype and hence the opposite of the conscious ego. However, as Dr Marie-Louise von Franz cautions: 'Everybody is everybody's shadow in fairy tales, the whole cluster of figures is compared one with another, and all the figures have a compensatory function. One must, therefore, use the word *shadow cum grano salis*.' (1974, p. 34)

Clarissa Pinkola Estés proposes a more nuanced view:

If we can understand the Bluebeard as being the internal representative of the entire myth of such an outcast, we then may also be able to comprehend the deep and inexplicable loneliness which sometimes washes over him (us) because he experiences a continuous exile from redemption…

…We can understand why thereafter the exiled one maintains a heartless pursuit of the light of others. We can imagine that it hopes that if it could gather enough soul(s) to itself, it could make a blaze of light that would finally rescind its darkness and repair its loneliness. (1992, pp. 41-42)

Bluebeard, the eternal outcast, kills to quell his infinite melancholy. In many ways, he is to be pitied, except for the fact that his actions are so deeply abhorrent and against all life. Yet there is also something strangely fascinating about him. This is perhaps to do with his shadowy sorcery; his connection to powerful knowledge. After all:

A model of an archetype can be said to be composed of two parts, one light and the other dark…

...In the archetype of the spirit there is the wise old man and the destructive or daemonic magician represented in many myths. (Franz, 1974, pp. 34-35)

Indeed, to his young new wife, Bluebeard's most enticing possession is the key to the room that she mustn't unlock. Already inured to the fabulous riches that helped to win her over to him, the young wife becomes obsessed with the room that she has been expressly forbidden entry. 'The Locked Door stands as an eternal temptation.' (Tolkien, 1964, p. 37)

Denise Osborne, in her paper "*Bluebeard* and its multiple layers of meaning" (2014), mentions the various ways the key in the story has been interpreted – for instance, as a sexual (phallic) symbol or as a symbol of male power. It can also be seen to be symbolic of fidelity, and Bluebeard's presenting of it to his new wife, a test of her fidelity. Although Perrault never mentions the husband and wife's sexual relationship, the key can be emblematic of the relationship's sexual exclusivity. The opening of the room leaves blood on the key, showing the wife's infidelity. Bluebeard's anger at his wife is analogous to the anger of the sexually jealous man: sexual exclusivity being of supreme importance to a man in a position to father a child. In evolutionary terms it's a bad call for a man to provide for and protect a child who does not carry his genes.

However, for many the key represents one of the most enticing and powerful things in the world – knowledge itself. The idea that we must confront the darkest parts of our natures, the things we fear the most, to become fully wise – fully actualised – is a profoundly Jungian view. So is the idea that such knowledge is awful, in the original sense of the word.

For us inquisitive apes, it is understandable – indeed, perfectly natural – that the young wife is curious about what is kept in the room, just as any number of figures from the Bible, mythology, fairy tales and contemporary fiction are tempted by objects that can bestow knowledge – be they an apple, a box, a magic mirror or ring. The promise of knowledge seems always juxtaposed with authoritative warnings of its perilous nature.

> Now. You can do what you like in this place. Explore anywhere. Do anything. Except. You are not permitted to retrieve the purple jewel from that pole. That is forbidden to you. You may not so much as touch it. Do you understand? (Roberts, 2013, p. 4)

Bluebeard presents us with a few age-old dilemmas. Should a young woman marry someone whom she does not love, indeed, is wary of, though he be rich and able to provide for her and any future children they may have? The other dilemma, the key dilemma, is whether she should obey or disobey her husband's wishes and enter the forbidden room? Surely every reader must reflect on this quandary when reading the story? To obey or not to obey? What would you do?

Bluebeard's prohibition – prohibition being of 'great mythical significance' according to Tolkien (1964, p. 37) – only serves to heighten his new wife's curiosity.

> Fatima, meanwhile, was not the least amused by the sight of all these riches, being consumed by a curiosity even more ardent than that of her friends. Indeed, she could scarcely contain herself and listen to their chatter, so impatient she felt to go and open the closet downstairs. (Perrault, 1697, pp. 40-41)

His new wife has chosen disobedience. The forbidden knowledge is too tempting. Yet when she opens the door to the forbidden room the knowledge is horrifying. At last, here is proof that Bluebeard is a murderer and that she, too, is set to become a murdered wife. Stunned by this revelation, the wife drops the key on the blood-covered floor. When she finally comes to her senses and retrieves the key, she is unable to remove the blood from the key, whatever she tries. It is magically permanent. This touch of magic – or '...*Faërie*, the realm or state in which fairies have their being' (Tolkien, 1964, p. 16) – upon the story is what marks it out as being a fairy tale.

> Faërie itself may perhaps most nearly be translated by Magic – but it is magic of a peculiar mood and power, at the furthest pole from the vulgar devices of the laborious, scientific magician. (Tolkien, 1964, p. 17)

The inclusion of the magical key in the story also supports the idea that Bluebeard himself has magical abilities or is, at least, in touch with dark forces, because, surely, every time he weds and offers his ring of keys to his new wife he must present the key to the forbidden room as a clean, blood-free key. Clearly, in between each wife, he must cast some magic over the key to make it like new again.

A gendered view

Perrault's moralising, in clumsily rendered rhyme, highlights his anachronistic perspective (of 1697) for modern sensibilities. Even if we were to gloss over the inequality of "husband as lord" and the old-fashioned idea that curiosity is a negative trait in women but a positive one in men, there is also the illogic of the stanza: obey your husband otherwise you'll end up dead (well, apart from the wife in the story, who is rescued!). As the renowned folklore expert, Maria Tatar, has commented, Perrault is sending us mixed messages (though maybe unconsciously). (2004, p. 24) Clearly, the story *by itself* is so intrinsically powerful that it outgrew and went far beyond the trite moralising of Perrault.

Some contemporary readers may also take issue with the fact that the heroine is saved by her brothers. Indeed, Angela Carter, in her exquisite take on the Bluebeard story, *The Bloody Chamber*, 'shifts the emphasis to women taking care of themselves and each other' (Topping, 2009, p. 12) by having the new wife saved by her revolver-wielding mother.

Yet, taking the Jungian view, the brothers actually represent an aspect of the new wife herself (Estés, 1992, p. 57); they constitute the animus within her (the animus being the masculine aspect of her feminine psyche or personality). When all seems lost, the heroine believing herself incapable of life-saving action, her animus rises up with newfound strength and courage to dispose of the predator. Ultimately, she is a woman who has passed from innocent naïf, a dangerous state to be in when predators lurk in the shadows, to a strong survivor, now knowledgeable about the world in which she lives.

Indeed, if we were to take Marie Louise von Franz's concept of everyone being everybody else's shadow in fairy tales, it could also be posited that Bluebeard – representing toxic masculinity (a topic much discussed and worried over in this century) – is the shadow of the brothers, who themselves display the positive traits of masculinity – courage and decisive action on behalf of those physically unable to protect themselves. Living as we do in (relatively) peaceful times, it is easy to forget how these positive traits of masculinity are desperately necessary in times of conflict.

The significance of gender in *Bluebeard* has been highlighted by many authors. Giada Goracci, author of *Male Perspectives in Atwood's* "Bluebeard's Egg" *and Hazzard's* The Transit of Venus, believes that, 'in order to deeply appreciate and understand the operational system by means of which the internal structures of fairy tales work, the primary element to consider is how gender discourse has developed over time.' (2016, p. 3).

Jack Zipes, an influential expert on fairy tales, has also investigated 'Bluebeard' in the context of gender in his book *Why Fairy Tales Stick: The Evolution and Relevance of a Genre*.

He goes on to analyse adaptations of the *Bluebeard* story

(in fiction, film and theatre) solely by men and believes that 'readers and viewers have been drawn to the tale because of the manner in which it reveals the miscalculation of male power and, in some cases, male anxiety about the potential encroachment of women on this power.' (2006, p. 157). Hence, he endeavours 'to show a gendered evolution of a fairy tale initiated by a male writer and contested gradually by female writers.' (2006, p. 157).

Conversely, Goracci analyses two texts by women to further explore *Bluebeard* and believes that, 'Significantly, shifts in interpretations of gender have led to the re-formulation of the very structure of fairy tales' (2016, p. 5).

Both their texts focus on *Bluebeard* in terms of gender dynamics within a patriarchal society; male-female dualism being a perennial concern of human societies. Yet Goracci's analysis of the story considers Bluebeard's sexuality and offers the original perspective that: '*Bluebeard*'s (assumed) heteronormative character might be interpreted as the indirect manifestation of his repressed queer-oriented inclination.' (p. 45) In effect, Bluebeard kills his wives 'because he cannot accept heteronormative marriage as a socially imposed condition.' (p. 49) And 'By killing his wives, he releases his queerness.' (p. 51)

Whilst Goracci's take on the reasons behind Bluebeard's murderous nature may have resonance for a number of readers (in the present and past), this idiosyncratic reading does also invite concern by seeming to align homosexuality with misogyny. It also downplays the appeal of the potently masculine archetype embodied by the Bluebeard character to heterosexual women. Perhaps the best contemporary illustration of this point is the phenomenon of the global bestselling *Fifty Shades* trilogy by E.L. James, in which Bluebeard, shorn of his beard and ugliness, is reborn as the predator, Christian Grey, who is heterosexual through and through.

The wide appeal of the *Fifty Shades* trilogy, with its

(apparently) outdated and stereotypically gendered characters, as well as its depiction of BDSM, seems to have confounded many. Though, again, I believe its popularity speaks to many through the use of archetypes – in Jungian terms, the wild, unnatural man being subdued by a pure young maiden is an archetypal story (think *Beauty and the Beast*). The *Fifty Shades* trilogy seems to veer perilously close to *Bluebeard* territory – sadism, control and obedience being key features; Christian Grey's private S&M chamber a parallel to Bluebeard's bloody closet. Maria Tatar confirms what many who show antipathy towards the *Fifty Shades* trilogy instinctively feel – that there is a dangerous mix of messages being given to readers.

> What I discovered in the course of my research is that Bluebeard is one of those stories that will not go away, it ferociously repeats itself, as if it were entirely new. Fifty Shades of Grey is the latest cultural inflection, and now I have my work cut out for me: reading the trilogy and watching the movie, then making a contribution to a shelter for victims of domestic abuse.' (2015)

So Goracci's assertion that society's reanalysis of gender has inevitably altered the fundamental workings of fairy tales does not seem to hold. The same internal framework appears to be present, although the outer coverings have somewhat changed.

Interestingly, marriage is a feature of the *Fifty Shades* trilogy, just as marriage is a feature of *Bluebeard*. Most fairy tales end with a marriage and 'happily ever after', yet Bluebeard is about what happens within a marriage – an amazingly complex relationship in which trust and openness is paramount to the success of the union. A union too, in which Christianity, in various branches, has a wife promise obedience to her husband within the marriage ceremony. The offering of the key to the forbidden room, then, can be seen as a test of her obedience, a game they must play in order for Bluebeard to be truly assured of Fatima's willingness to be the submissive wife to her lordly husband.

Up until this point in the story, their relationship seems to have been to their mutual benefit. Or perhaps Bluebeard has, calculatingly, been an ideal husband so far in order to lull his wife into a false sense of security. Again, this has applicability for the contemporary reader, particularly as marriage vows have become flexible and personalised, with much debate around the relevance of marriage in today's world, with marriage (generally) on the decline. (Cohen, 2013) And yet, even if we were to take the marriage out of *Bluebeard*, what remains is an intimate and dynamic relationship between a man and a woman, and all the balanced and imbalanced interplays that entails.

The Future of *Bluebeard*

As Deborah Osborne concluded in her paper, there are many ways of analysing and interpreting *Bluebeard* (2014), and hence many ways of arriving at a conclusion as to why exactly the story of Bluebeard continues to have applicability.

Maria Tatar, when considering fairy tales as 'master narratives' (2004, p. 11), posits that, 'They remain alive precisely because they are never exactly the same, always doing new cultural work, mapping out different developmental paths, assimilating new anxieties and desires, giving us high pathos, low comedy, and everything in between.' (p. 11)

This is certainly borne out by the hundreds of fairy tales I receive in response to the open call for submissions to the series of anthologies *The Forgotten and the Fantastical* that I edit. Authors often incorporate current hot topics – sexuality, gender identity, neurodiversity, mental health etc. – into the stories they send me. Yet timeless topics – love, death, grief, community, family dynamics – remain the core elements of the most effective tales.

Ellen Datlow and Terri Windling, coeditors of a number of recent collections of fairy tales, believe 'the reason they have endured in virtually every culture around the globe for centuries, is due to this ability to confront unflinchingly the darkness that lies outside the front door, and inside our own hearts.' (1994, p. 2). Fairy tales will endure for as long as darkness endures, within or without.

It would be foolish to deny the continued applicability of *Bluebeard*, as foolish as Fatima and Fatima's mother for going against their instincts to steer clear of Bluebeard, because predators are still very much alive and well in today's world. Due to recent technological developments and the rise of social media we have far greater access to the voices and experiences of others. And as depressing as it is to perennially hear of predators in the news, what I see is that this instinct to be wary of the predator is sound, acute even. However, for a variety of reasons, this instinct is dismissed. Perhaps the instinct is disregarded because the predatory and older husband-to-be is rich and powerful and will be able to provide a comfortable life for the spouse. A young wife-to-be may think nothing of his many ex-wives, and close her ears to his unpalatable politics, the rumours of past domestic abuse. Or perhaps social niceties force us to smile and make small talk with a predator who has somehow inveigled themselves temporarily into our lives. That wise instinctual voice may be screaming *Get away! Get away!*, but we dismiss it because we do not want to offend; we do not want to make a fuss. Worst of all is the situation wherein a naïve young person, whose inner voice is not yet wise with experience, is cajoled into the clutches of a predator by someone they trust who really should know better.

Then there are the larger, more elusive predators that slither around the corridors of government, of big business, and reveal themselves in laws and rules and regulations that result in the weak being preyed upon.

Bluebeard reminds us that predators lurk in the shadows without. But also, that the predator lurks within, preying and feasting on our mind, diminishing us, disempowering us, telling us that we are of little worth, that we deserve nothing good in life, that we are imposters and that our work, creative or otherwise, is without value.

> When its cutting work is done, it leaves the woman deadened in feeling, feeling frail to advance her life; her ideas and dreams play at her feet drained of animation. (Estes, 1992, p. 36)

Which is why it is so important to unlock the door on that terrible knowledge and *to know*. To know that predators exist and that they attack without question. Once we know what we are dealing with, we can arm ourselves adequately and then do battle with the predator.

Bibliography

Atwood, M., 1983. Bluebeard's Egg. In: *Bluebeard's Egg*. Republished 1988. London: Virago.

Bellamy, T. 2015. *The Forgotten and the Fantastical* series. Nottingham: Mother's Milk Books.

Carter, A., 1979. The Bloody Chamber. In: *The Bloody Chamber*. Republished and introduced by Helen Simpson, 2006. London: Vintage Books.

Cohen, P. N., 2013. Marriage is declining globally: Can you say that? *Family Inequality*, [blog] 12 June <https://familyinequality.wordpress.com/2013/06/12/marriage-is-declining/> [Accessed 22 December 2018].

Datlow E. and Windling T., 1994. *Black Thorn, White Rose: A Modern Book of Adult Fairy Tales*. New York: Avon Books

Estés, C. P., 1992. *Women Who Run With The Wolves*. Reissued 1998. London: Rider.

Franz, M. 1974. *Shadow and Evil in Fairy Tales*. Revised and republished 1995. Boston: Shambala Publications.

Goracci, G., 2016. *Male Perspectives in Atwood's* "Bluebeard's Egg" *and Hazzard's* The Transit of Venus. Newcastle upon Tyne: Cambridge Scholars Publishing.

Grimm, J. and Grimm. W., 1785-1863. Bluebeard. In: *The Complete First Edition. The Original Folk and Fairy Tales of the Brothers Grimm*. Translated from German and edited by J. Zipes. 2014. Princeton: Princeton University Press.

James, E. L., 2011. *Fifty Shades* trilogy. Republished 2012. London: Arrow.

Luke, Gospel of, 10:18, *Holy Bible*: Good News Version.

Osborne, D., 2014. *Bluebeard* and its multiple layers of meaning. [online] Revista Alpha. Available at: <http://alpha.unipam.edu.br/documents/18125/558424/Bluebeard+and+its+multiple++layers+of+meaning.pdf> [Accessed 21 December 2018].

Perrault, C., 1697. Blue Beard. In: *The Fairy Tales of Charles Perrault*. Translated from French by R. Samber and retold by A. Quiller-Couch. Reprint 2004. London: The Folio Society.

Roberts, A., 2013. Adam Robots. In: *Adam Robots*. London: Gollancz.

Tatar, M., 2004. *Secrets beyond the Door: The Story of Bluebeard and His Wives*. Princeton: Princeton University Press.

Tatar, M. 2015. Fifty Shades of Grey as a Fairy Tale? *Harvard University*, [blog] 17 February. Available at: <https://blogs.harvard.edu/tatar/2015/02/17/fifty-shades-of-grey-as-a-fairy-tale/> [Accessed 22 December 2018.]

Tolkien, J.R.R., 1964. On Fairy-Stories. In: *Tree and Leaf + Smith of Wootton Major + The Homecoming of Beorhtnoth*. Reprint 1979. London: Unwin Paperbacks.

Tolkien, J.R.R., 1977. *The Silmarillion*. London: George Allen & Unwin (Publishers). Republished 1992. London: HarperCollins Publishers.

Topping, A., 2009. *Focus on* The Bloody Chamber and Other Stories *by Angela Carter*. London: Greenwich Exchange.

Zipes, J., 2006. *Why Fairy Tales Stick*. New York: Routledge.

The Problem of Evil in Pseudo-Taoist Secondary Worlds

Lucinda Holdsworth

Abstract

A war between good and evil has long been a staple of fantasy literature. This Manichean world view is so pervasive in the genre that as readers we expect evil to be defeated by the forces of good, long before we have even turned the first page. Some authors, however, have attempted to escape this cliché by creating a secondary world based on Taoist values. In Ursula Le Guin's *Earthsea* cycle, Brandon Sanderson's *Mistborn* series and Bryan Konietzko and Michael Dante DiMartino's animated series *Avatar: The Legend of Korra*, for example, the ideal resolution is not the defeat of evil by good, but finding a balance between two opposing forces. In this Taoist world view, evil is found in an excess of one the two opposing forces rather than one side being inherently evil. This is particularly poignant in the *Earthsea* cycle, in which evil is explored through both an excess of the Old Powers in *The Tombs of Atuan* and an excess of magic in *The Other Wind*. However the majority of western fantasists who have attempted to integrate Taoism into their work have interpreted it through the lens of Christian conflict dualism. This means that, although the protagonists ostensibly seek to create harmony through balance between two opposing forces, one of the forces is still defined as 'evil'. This mix-and-match attitude towards incompatible doctrines has several implications for the works it creates, the most obvious being that often, it simply doesn't make sense. Perhaps the most obvious example of this can be found in George Lucas's *Star Wars* saga, in which viewers are told that Anakin will 'bring balance to the force', yet this is intended to mean the destruction of all Sith rather than true balance between light and dark. However this pseudo-Taoism also opens up some interesting theological questions regarding the nature of evil. In this essay I will explore exactly what 'evil' means within these Taoist/Manichean hybrids and argue that within this framework, a refusal to define evil by the Taoist definition of excess suggests that evil is anything which inconveniences the protagonists.

*

The creation of secondary worlds in fantasy texts allows authors to explore religious themes in a way which theology or realist fiction does not allow. In these worlds, theological frameworks can be transformed from theories to facts; supernatural entities and forces are no longer a matter of belief, but tangible beings and sources of power, the existence of which cannot be denied. Western popular fantasy has traditionally used the creation of secondary worlds to do just this, with Christianity being by far the most pervasive religious influence. Some of the biggest names in the genre, J. R. R. Tolkien, C. S. Lewis and Robert Jordan to name just a few, have drawn heavily on the conflict dualism of Christianity. Frank Whaling defines this as a cosmic conflict 'between the spiritual forces of right and goodness and the spiritual forces of wrong and evil. This choice is essentially a moral choice. The independent principles at work in this dualism are not complementary. They are engaged in struggle and no compromise is possible between them' (1985, p. 46). This conflict between good and evil has become one of the most popular tropes of fantasy literature. However, a growing number of western fantasy creators have tried to move away from these Christian influences, drawing instead on a more diverse range of theological and philosophical frameworks. George Lucas's *Star Wars* saga, Brandon Sanderson's *Mistborn* trilogy, Michael Dante DiMartino and Bryan Konietzko's *The Legend of Korra* and Ursula Le Guin's *Earthsea* cycle, for example, have all drawn heavily on Taoist themes in the creation of their secondary worlds. Yet these creators, with the notable exception of Le Guin, have fundamentally misunderstood the doctrines that they have drawn on and, as a result, created secondary worlds with nonsensical theological structures. In these worlds, evil exists where it should not and vanishes where it should. Ultimately, this pseudo-Taoist worldview suggests that evil is more powerful than good.

Yet what exactly is Taoism? This is of course a huge question, and one which I would not pretend to be able to answer fully in a lifetime, let alone a single chapter. However for the purposes of this essay, I will briefly summarize some key Taoist principles. For the vast majority of westerners, our knowledge of Taoism, or Daoism, is limited to the yin and yang symbol: a circle divided by an S shaped line into a white half and a black half. Usually the white half will contain a dot of black at the centre, and vice versa. Even this symbol is somewhat mysterious. As a society, we are vaguely aware that it is Chinese in origin and is popular among culturally appropriative tattoo artists, but beyond this we tend to know very little. Yet despite its unassuming simplicity, this symbol manages to encapsulate an entire philosophy and way of being. The white side of the symbol represents yang, that which is light, active or masculine, whilst the black side of the symbol represents yin, that which is dark, passive or feminine. Yin and yang are opposites, yet they are not in opposition. Instead they are complementary forces which exist as part of a larger whole. Not only are these forces complementary, they are also subjective, as Lao Tzu writes in the sacred text *Tao Te Ching*. Due to its simplicity and accessibility, I will be using Keping Wang's translation of *Tao Te Ching*, as found in *Reading the Dao: A Thematic Enquiry*:

> Have-substance and have-no-substance produce each other
> Difficult and easy complete each other
> Long and short contrast with each other

> High and low are distinguished from each other
> (trans. Wang, 2011, p. 141)

Or, put another way, we can only recognise light because darkness exists to contrast with it. Yet whilst a lamp may be bright in a dark room, it is exceedingly dim when compared with the sun. In the same way, something may be yin in one situation but yang in another. This subjectivity is expressed through the dot of white in the centre of yin and the dot of black in the centre of yang: within each is the seed of the other. In Taoist belief, peace and harmony can only be found through a balance between yin and yang.

George Lucas's *Star Wars* saga explores a number of Taoist concepts through the Force and those who use it. When the viewer is first introduced to the Force in *A New Hope*, Obi Wan describes it as 'an energy field created by all living things. It surrounds us and penetrates us. It binds the galaxy together' (*Star Wars: A New Hope*, 1977, 00:34:43-00:34:50). Later he elaborates, saying that 'a Jedi can feel the Force flowing through him' (01:00:55-01:00:57), and that 'it also obeys your commands' (01:01:00-01:02:03). This is highly reminiscent of Lao Tzu's description of Tao in Tao Te Ching:

> The great Dao flows everywhere.
> It may go left, it may go right.
> All things rely on it for existence...
> It preserves and nourishes all things,
> But does not claim to be master over them
> (trans. Wang, 2011, p. 154)

Similarly, Walter Robinson notes in his essay 'The Far East of Star Wars' (Robinson, 2005, p. 34) that Luke's Jedi training with Yoda requires him to learn the Taoist art of Wu Wei, that is, learning through unlearning and action through inaction. However the most notable influence is found in

Lucas's construction of the Force as a two-sided power. In *The Annotated Screenplays* Lucas discusses his inspiration for this: 'The idea of positive and negative, that there are two sides to an entity, a push and pull, a yin and yang, and the struggle between the two sides are issues of nature that I wanted to include in the film.' (Lucas, no date, cited in Bouzereau, 1997, p. 38). This struggle between the light side and the dark side of the Force is at the very core of the *Star Wars* films, and in particular, at the centre of Anakin Skywalker/Darth Vader's character arc. Throughout the prequel trilogy, Anakin is said to be the chosen one who will 'bring balance to the Force' (*Star Wars: The Phantom Menace*, 1999, 01:25:24-01:25:26), a prophecy which is apparently fulfilled in *Return of the Jedi*.

The supernatural forces present in Brandon Sanderson's *Mistborn* trilogy also seem to have been greatly inspired by yin and yang. Ruin and Preservation are frequently described as being 'equally powerful...two aspects of a single power' (Sanderson, 2010, p. 624). In keeping with Taoist thought, it is only by working together that these two contrasting forces are able to create and sustain life. Interestingly, Preservation, which one might more readily associate with the passive, and therefore yang, is said to be associated with the colour white, while Ruin, a more active force, is associated with the colour black (Sanderson, 2010, p. 170) in a direct inversion of Taoist tradition. Throughout the *Mistborn* trilogy, the need for balance between these two forces is a central concern: 'For every Push, there is a Pull. Throw something up, and it will come back down. Opposition. For Ruin, there is Preservation... Balance! The curse of our existence.' (Sanderson, 2010, p. 666). Indeed, in true Taoist fashion, a resolution to the series is only reached once these two opposing powers have been reintegrated back into a single power: the new god Harmony.

The influence of yin and yang on DiMartino and Konietzko's *The Legend of Korra* is even more explicit. Raava, the force of 'light and peace' (*The Legend of Korra*, 2013a, 00:22:38-

00:22:41), and Vaatu, 'the force of darkness and chaos' (00:22:35-00:22:38), are described as being each other's 'other half' (*The Legend of Korra*, 2013b, 00:04:38), and Raava states that 'for the past 10,000 years, [she has] kept darkness under control, and the world in balance' (*The Legend of Korra*, 2013a, 00:22:46-00:22:53). Indeed, when the two spirits are introduced to the viewer in the flashback episode 'Beginnings, Part 1', they are so enmeshed and tangled from their fight that they briefly create an enormous yin-yang symbol in the sky (00:20:58-00:21:02). Furthermore, Raava reveals that each spirit contains the seed of their opposite within their centre, just as yin and yang do: '[Vaatu] cannot destroy light any more than I can destroy darkness. One cannot exist without the other. Even if I defeat Vaatu in this encounter, darkness will grow inside me until he emerges again. The same will hold true if Vaatu defeats me.' (*The Legend of Korra*, 2013b, 00:08:37-00:08:56)

These balance-centred stories are extremely powerful; however they all demonstrate a fundamental lack of understanding of the Taoist principles that have inspired them. To understand this, we must first explore the concept of evil in Taoism. How does one define it? The simple answer is that one does not. In *Tao Te Ching*, Lao Tzu writes,

> Where the people of the world know the beautiful as beauty,
> There arises the recognition of the ugly.
> Where they know the good as good,
> There arises the recognition of the evil (trans. Wang, 2011, p. 141)

This clearly reveals that in Taoist thought, good and evil are not as objective as they are in many western religions, instead depending entirely on perspective. Indeed, many have concluded from this verse that 'the distinction between good and evil is really a wrong-headed human contrivance' (Hsu,

1976, p. 301). By naming one thing 'good', we force another to be defined as 'evil' in contrast to it, and vice versa. Initially, this contrast may appear to be in keeping with the duality at the centre of Taoism, as expressed in the symbol of yin and yang. However assigning a moral quality to yin and yang would suggest that one is superior to the other – that to be virtuous, one should prefer one side and shun the other. This goes directly against the core principle of Tao: harmony with all things. Yin and yang may be contrasting forces, but they are not set in opposition. In his comparative study in religious dualism, Frank Whaling explores the complementary nature of yin and yang, noting that 'Yin and yang need each other. Without darkness, light would be meaningless; without day, night would signify nothing...They are different, but they are complementary in their difference. For integration, wholeness, harmony, both are necessary' (1984, p. 48). Harmony is, for the most part, seen as a 'good' state of things, while disharmony or chaos is often seen as the result of evil. Whilst hot and cold can come to a harmonious resolution in the tepid, good must, by its very nature, seek to end the suffering caused by evil. Therefore, these two forces cannot come to a harmonious resolution in the same way that light and dark, heat and cold, or action and passivity can. Evil, then, cannot exist as a quality of nature in the same way as these other qualities can.

Whilst mainstream Taoism states that any distinction between good and evil is unnecessary, in his close reading of *Tao Te Ching*, Sung-peng Hsu suggests that two types of evil can actually be identified in Lao Tzu's philosophy: causal evils and consequent evils. As the names suggest, causal evils are that which cause evil to happen, whilst consequential evils are the consequences of causal acts. Humanity's destruction of the environment might be considered a causal evil, whilst the subsequent deaths resulting from rising sea levels would be a consequential evil. It is important to note that the causal evils Hsu identifies in *Tao Te Ching* are entirely man-made, leading him to argue, quite convincingly, that evil is not something that exists in the natural world, nor can it be applied to any person or entity. Instead it is a quality which can be applied to human actions if they go against Tao – that is, if an action is 'used to assert something in thought or action against one's true nature, the other people, or the natural world' (Hsu, 1976, p. 302). In western theological terms, natural evil exists only as a result of moral evil. Whilst Christianity denotes specific acts, such as those found in the ten commandments, as being evil, Taoism suggests that evil acts depend upon context, as it is defined as the imposition of one's will on the world and others.

The evils of wilful action can certainly be seen across pseudo-Taoist fantasy, perhaps most interestingly through Le Guin's use of True Speech in the *Earthsea* cycle. This magical language is immensely powerful, to the extent that simply stating that something is a certain way, using the True Speech, makes it so. It is the natural language of dragons, and as such, they are unable to lie. When spoken by dragons, this speech is neither evil nor destructive, as it comes naturally to them. It is, in a sense, the kind of passive being and inaction that exemplifies following the Tao. It is only when this language is co-opted by humans that it becomes a more destructive force. Instead of using the language passively, human wizards use the True Speech to impose their will over all aspects of the natural world, with disastrous consequences. In the short story *Finder*, the narrator describes Earthsea before the founding of Roke School and the centralisation of magic users: 'things went wrong more often than right, with the wizards warring, using poisons and curses recklessly to gain immediate advantage without thought for what followed after. They brought drought and storm, blights and fires and sickness across the land' (Le Guin, 2001a, p. 4). This imposition of human will over nature goes further still, to the extent that death itself is corrupted in an attempt to give men immortality. The once beautiful Other Wind is reduced to 'a dark land, a dry land' (Le Guin, 2001b, p.

228), and the balance between life and death is upset for aeons.

Likewise, in *The Hero of Ages*, Sanderson describes the Lord Ruler's attempts to improve his world's ecosystem through incredibly powerful magic. He pushes the planet around in space, fills the air with ash to compensate and is eventually forced to change the biology of humans and plants to allow them to survive in the new world he has created, but still, 'each time [the Lord Ruler] tried to fix things, he made them worse' (Sanderson, 2010, p. 43). The imposition of his will on nature causes widespread famine, darkness and death. Wilful human action can also be seen as the root cause of much of the suffering in *The Legend of Korra*, as the first Avatar's interference in the eternal battle between Raava and Vaatu allows Vaatu to escape and cause suffering in the world. After 10,000 years, Avatar Korra unwittingly releases Vaatu into the world whilst attempting to restore the fabled southern lights. Like Sanderson's Lord Ruler, Korra imposes her will on nature by attempting to improve it, and ends up causing widespread suffering as a result. Similarly, Anakin's refusal to accept his visions of the future and consequent decision to impose his will on the course of history causes both his fall to the dark side and the rise of the Empire, both of which cause an incalculable amount of suffering across the galaxy.

Yet whether we choose to accept Hsu's theory of evil or the more mainstream view that evil should not be defined at all, there are two fundamental principles that both agree on. Firstly, whether or not evil can be found in human actions, evil does *not* exist as a supernatural force. The majority of western pseudo-Taoism goes against this principle. In some works, such as *Star Wars*, this is quite obvious. The Force is, of course, a supernatural energy made up in part of the dark side: an evil force fuelled by hatred, anger and fear. Similarly, Vaatu in *The Legend of Korra*, is a supernatural entity of evil that clearly feeds on chaos, violence and destruction. Indeed, his very presence inspires both humans and spirits to attempt the genocide of the other (*The Legend of Korra*, 2013b, 00:12:22-00:13:42). In other texts, however, this moral aspect is more subtle. Initially, Ruin, a supernatural force from Brandon Sanderson's *Mistborn* series, may not appear to fit this description. He is ostensibly a force of amoral destruction, stating on several occasions that the battle between him and Preservation 'isn't about good or evil. Morality doesn't even enter into it.' (Sanderson, 2010, p. 510). However, it is important to note that Ruin is a liar, and indeed the plot frequently hinges on his having misled the protagonists. While he may claim to be an amoral force, his actions suggest otherwise. He claims that as a force of death, he is a part of the cycle of life, and thus life itself. Yet while death is a natural and necessary part of the cycle of life, murder, violence and blood magic requiring torture on a massive scale are not. Preservation, on the other hand, does not engage in such sadistic behaviour in pursuit of his goals. While Ruin lies (Sanderson, 2010, p. 666), gloats (p. 509-13, p. 710), murders (p. xv-xvi, p. 710), tortures (p. xv-xvi, p. 118, p298) and manipulates (p.xv-xvi, p. 175, p.429, p. 449, p. 456), Preservation is described as having 'nobility' (p. 539). Perhaps most telling is the fact that the Terris religion is named for Ter, their word for Preservation (p. 653). They have placed Preservation at the head of their pantheon and worship him alone as their god. As Sanderson has these two forces at war with each other, it follows that Ruin occupies the role of the adversary in their religion. These clues suggest that, whilst Sanderson may have intended to construct two opposing amoral forces, a moral element has still managed to creep in. Ruin's actions are indisputably sadistic in a way that the indiscriminate effects of light, dark, heat or cold etc. could never be. Despite his claims, the war between Ruin and Preservation is about good and evil.

This trend in itself is not necessarily a bad thing. After all, if these authors were expected exactly to follow the doctrines which inspired them, without adaptation or innovation, there would not have been much room for creativity. Bad Taoism does not necessarily constitute bad literature. However the decision to add a moral quality to these creators' two contrasting forces massively complicates the second fundamental principle we shall examine: that peace and harmony is achieved through balance between two contrasting forces, while imbalance on either side leads to chaos. Having lived during the Spring and Autumn Period, during which local warlords vied for power, continually waging wars against each other, Lao Tzu would have seen first-hand the effects of violence. Indeed many scholars have concluded that *Tao Te Ching* arose chiefly from his desire to foster peace and harmony amidst this political crisis. Throughout the text, he impresses the incompatibility of violence of any kind, but particularly war, with Tao:

> He who assists the ruler with the Dao
> Never seeks to dominate the world by military force.
> The use of force is intrinsically dangerous:
> Wherever armies are stationed,
> Berries and thorns grow wild.
> As soon as great wars are over,
> Years of famine are sure to afflict the land. (trans. Wang, 2011, p. 30)

> He who delights in the slaughter of men
> Will not succeed under Heaven.
> For the multitude killed in the war,
> Let us mourn them with sorrow and grief.
> For the victory won by force,
> Let us observe the occasion with funeral ceremonies. (trans. Wang, 2011, p. 31)

Lao Tzu's stance against violence is compatible with Hsu's interpretation of evil, as violence is one of the strongest uses of wilful action against another and, as he argues, war is the most extreme form of this imposition (Hsu, 1976, p. 304). Balance cannot, therefore, be defined as anything except peace, and peace can only be achieved through balance. This principle seems to be widely understood by western creators in theory, however in practice it often goes awry. Indeed, in most cases, the exact opposite occurs: whilst balance is proclaimed as the path to harmony and peace, it is actually achieved through total imbalance of the two forces.

The prophecy of *Star Wars* is perhaps the most famous example of this. Although the exact words of this prophecy are never revealed, Qui-Gon, Obi Wan and Yoda agree that the chosen one is supposed to 'bring balance to the Force' (*Star Wars: The Phantom Menace*, 1999, 01:25:24-01:25:26); however some accounts of it suggest that he is supposed to '*destroy the Sith* and bring balance to the force' (my italics) (*Star Wars: Revenge of the Sith*, 2005, 00:40:39-00:40:43). It will, of course, be obvious to anyone with a passing familiarity with seesaws, that completely destroying one side of it will not bring it into balance. Likewise, destroying the Sith, and thus purging the universe of all those accessing the dark side of the Force, should not bring balance to the Force. The difficulty with this text is that, despite Lucas's best intentions, the prophecy of balance *is* actually fulfilled, just not in the way he intended. By the end of *Revenge of the Sith*, Anakin has caused the destruction of the Jedi temple and reduced a cohort of hundreds of light side Force users to just two Jedi Masters: Obi-Wan and Yoda. These two Jedi are perfectly balanced against the two remaining Sith: Darth Vader and Darth Sidious. In *Revenge of the Sith*, Yoda even suggests that the prophecy may have been 'misread' (2005, 00:40:49) by the Jedi. However Lucas has emphatically confirmed in interviews that balance was restored by Anakin in *Return of the Jedi* by killing the last Sith (Star Wars Episode III: The Chosen One Featurette, 2005). Needless to say, this demonstrates a fundamental misunderstanding of what constitutes balance.

The Legend of Korra is similarly problematic. When Raava

and Vaatu are first introduced, they are locked in an eternal struggle in which they are both equally matched. As long as this struggle has been going on, the world seems to have been relatively balanced, only becoming unbalanced once Vaatu's strength becomes greater than Raava's. Soon after being separated from her other half, Raava says to Wan, 'since the beginning of time, we have battled over the fate of this world, and for the past 10,000 years, I have kept darkness under control, and the world in balance, until you came along' (*The Legend of Korra*, 2013a, 00:22:46-00:22:53). Initially this seems to demonstrate a good understanding of balance; however upon closer inspection, Raava's statement reveals that balance has not been maintained because they were equally powerful, but because she has prevented Vaatu from even touching the world. Indeed, his mere presence, once free from Raava, seems to be enough to cause madness and chaos, turning spirits into monsters. Raava, on the other hand, is unable to affect any meaningful change with her presence. Balance, it seems, can only be achieved when Vaatu is completely removed from the playing field. This is the same conclusion that the Avatar comes to in two separate incarnations. In his first incarnation, Avatar Wan claims to be maintaining balance in the world by sealing Vaatu away in a supernatural prison for 10,000 years. The Avatar Korra also claims that she uses 'Raava's light spirit to guide the world toward peace and balance' (*The Legend of Korra*, 2013c, 00:22:57-00:23:01), yet does this by destroying Vaatu, at least temporarily. As in *Star Wars*, it makes little sense for the incapacitation or destruction of evil to bring about balance, yet that is exactly what happens.

The *Mistborn* trilogy is no exception to this trend. At the end of *The Hero of Ages*, Ruin and Preservation are combined into a single entity: the new god Harmony. We are told that their powers 'belonged together' (Sanderson, 2010, p. 718) and, like Raava and Vaatu, should never have been split apart to begin with, suggesting that the world will now return to its intended state of balance. Yet whilst Harmony is supposed to combine Preservation and Ruin equally, it is extremely telling that his first action upon ascending is to undo everything that Ruin has done to the world. Instead of reaching a middle ground between Preservation's desire to create life and Ruin's desire to kill it, Harmony immediately fills the world with extinct animals and plants (Sanderson, 2010, p. 718). Once again, balance is defined as a victory for the light side, while imbalance is the existence of the dark side.

The *Earthsea* novels are notable exceptions to this trend. In *Coyote's Song: The Teaching Stories of Ursula Le Guin*, Richard Erlich discusses Ged's first encounter with the shadow in *A Wizard of Earthsea*, during which Ogion chases it away with light:

> For the first time in this book, we witness the battle between light and darkness, which recurs throughout the *Earthsea* trilogy. Here, light and darkness stand for good and evil, as they do traditionally… The intimate connection between good and evil suggested by the simile of shadow and light is closer to the Taoist belief in the inseparability of opposites than it is to Christian dualism (1997, p. 41-2)

In Erlich's exploration of this passage, he too has fallen into the trap of conflating light and dark with good and evil: something that a great many Le Guin scholars have in common. I will allow that, at the time of publication (1997), this analysis could have been completely in line with Le Guin's intentions. However his hypothesis does not take into account the last three books of the *Earthsea* cycle, and Le Guin's extraordinary ability to revise her earlier ideas. In *A Wizard of Earthsea*, Ogion states that 'every word, every act of our Art is said and is done either for good, or for evil' (Le Guin, 1993, p. 31), and both Ged and the reader are inclined to accept this dualistic worldview firmly rooted in morality. Yet *The Other*

Wind reveals that wizards actually know very little, not only about their Art, but about the nature of the world around them. Although the early novels initially present *Earthsea* as a battle between the good powers of wizardry and the evil old powers found in the dark places of the earth, when taken as a whole, it becomes clear that evil is only found where wizardry and the old powers have become unbalanced. The Terranon and the tombs of Atuan, as places where the old powers have become too concentrated, are described as 'evil' (Le Guin, 1993, p. 110, p. 266). Yet the wizardry of the Dry Land, as well as Cob's interference with death using wizardry, manages to create the same kind of bleak, hopeless landscape as the Old Powers do. By characterising all excess, even excess in the protagonists' favour, as being evil, rather than an outside force, Le Guin creates a powerful anticapitalist message throughout the *Earthsea* series.

Why, one might well ask, do so many western fantasy writers have such trouble depicting balance in a way that is, well, balanced? The problem seems to be quite simple: it is their western-ness. The influence of Christianity on western society is so pervasive that, for these creators, it seems to have coloured the way that they have interpreted Taoist theology, or at the very least, the way in which they have explored Taoism in these texts. The association of light with good and dark with evil (which, whilst not limited to Christianity, is certainly an important doctrine within it) is such a strong one that they seem to have been unable to conceive of forces of light and dark which do not have a moral quality attached to them. Likewise, the idea of a war between these two forces, rather than a complementary interplay, is characteristic of the kind of conflict dualism exemplified by Christianity. This confusion is, perhaps, due to the generic significance placed on the works of Tolkien and Lewis. Their use of a war between supernatural forces of good and evil has been so influential that it has become a trope of western fantasy writing which is somewhat divorced from its religious origin in many readers' eyes. While they may not have intended to combine Christian and Taoist elements, the fact remains that these creators appear to have made little or no attempt to examine the implications of using this trope in a Taoist setting. Le Guin, as previously stated, is a notable exception. She was of course, just as American as DiMartino, Konietzko, Lucas and Sanderson, but her explorations of Taoist themes have one crucial difference: sincerity. Le Guin spoke often and eloquently on her love for Lao Tzu's teachings, stating that she was 'lucky to discover him so young, so that [she] could live with his book [her] whole life' (1977, p. ix). Beginning in her twenties, Le Guin even created her own translation of *Tao Te Ching*, adding a few verses every year. Her examination of harmony through balance, then, was the result of years of genuine reflection, rather than a novelty to appropriate, as it appears to have been in the work of others.

Whilst Sanderson, DiMartino, Konietzko and Lucas's combination of Christianity's conflict dualism with Taoism's complementary dualism is simply a bit awkward, their attempted integration of this evil-yin/good-yang hybrid with Taoism's peaceful balance is disturbing to say the least. However one tries to resolve the conflict between these two ideologies, the implications are troubling. In the worlds of *Star Wars*, *The Legend of Korra* and *Mistborn*, the audience has been repeatedly told that balance is essential for peace and harmony, meaning that there must be consequences for such an unbalanced resolution, whether we are shown these consequences or not. Such unbalanced resolutions may even be intentional, as the nature of fantasy franchises is such that a new enemy must always be found to keep the story going. Indeed, *The Force Awakens* and *The Last Jedi* clearly reveal that the unequal balance brought about by Anakin has not ushered in an age of peace and prosperity for everyone (although these films were, admittedly, created after Lucas gave up creative control of the franchise). Yet if one is to accept that one side of the equation must be completely destroyed in order to create a suitably happy ending for the protagonists, one must also accept a worldview in which total imbalance is deemed acceptable so long as it is unbalanced in favour of the individuals that the viewer cares about. This refusal to condemn dangerous excess in the protagonists' favour reveals an undercurrent of individual ethical egoism throughout Taoist/Christian hybrids – something which runs contrary to the kind of community thinking found in both doctrines in their original forms. To put it another way, these hybrids suggest that evil is simply anything that inconveniences the protagonists.

Furthermore, if balance can only be reached through the absolute destruction of evil, does this mean that evil is significantly stronger than good? Certainly, in *The Legend of Korra*, the presence of Raava has no positive effect, whilst the presence of Vaatu instantly corrupts. Similarly, in *Star Wars*, the entire Jedi Temple, an organisation with hundreds if not thousands of light side Force users, is brought down by two dark side Force users with relative ease. In the *Mistborn* trilogy, Preservation's relative weakness is explained as being a consequence of creating humanity, each of whom contain a spark of his power within them; however the *Star Wars* saga and *The Legend of Korra* provide no explanation for this discrepancy of power, suggesting that evil is simply inherently stronger.

It is interesting to note that in both texts, evil is overcome not through use of a supernatural force of good, but by human goodness. The Sith are not destroyed by force, as Mace Windu attempts to do in Revenge of the Sith, but by the interpersonal relationship between Luke and his father. Likewise, Korra defeats Vaatu after Raava's light spirit has already been stripped from her body, instead using the kind words of her mentor to find the strength within herself. Whilst human goodness is certainly still a part of the "good side" of things, it is intriguing that it is able to succeed long after the relatively weak supernatural force of good has been defeated. Indeed, Preservation dies not long into *Hero of Ages*, leaving Sazed to save the world through the simple act of holding the dead body of his friend. This emphasis on the strength of human goodness over supernatural goodness suggests a strong deist undercurrent in these hybrid texts. Yet whilst the strength of human goodness is an encouraging message to convey, the fact remains that the forces of supernatural evil in these texts are far stronger than the forces of supernatural good. This is a concerning phenomenon to say the least.

The alternative is to accept these texts' claims that genuine balance really has been achieved, despite appearances. Taking the example of *Star Wars* again, Christopher M. Brown suggests that the dark side's survival may be necessary for harmony, as 'there would be no *genuine* goodness in the universe without the Dark Side as an impetus for noble action. A universe without villainy – and therefore without heroism – would be morally lifeless, inert' (2005, p. 71). Whilst atrocities often do prompt acts of incredible bravery and goodness, I find the argument that goodness is only prompted by evil to be a troubling one. More concerning, however, is the suggestion that evil must be allowed to prosper in the name of harmony. It is, to my mind, a suggestion that comes from the same complacent place of privilege that Martin Luther King Jr. spoke of in his description of 'the white moderate, who is more devoted to "order" than to justice; who prefers a negative peace which is the absence of tension to a positive peace which is the presence of justice' (King, Jr., 1963). If the harmony and peace of balance can only be achieved through allowing a moderate amount of evil, and therefore suffering, to flourish, then it is no wonder that Lucas, DiMartino, Konietzko and Sanderson could not wholeheartedly accept balance within their respective stories.

Bibliography

Bouzereau, L., 1998. *Star Wars: The Annotated Screenplays.* London: Titan Books.

Brown, C., 2005. A Wretched Hive of Scum and Villainy: Star Wars and the Problem of Evil. In: Decker, S. and Eberl, J. T. eds. *Star Wars and Philosophy.* pp. 69-79.

Bucknall, B. J., *Ursula K. Le Guin*. New York: Frederick Ungar Publishing.

Erlich, R. D., 1997. *Coyote's Song: The Teaching Stories of Ursula K. Le Guin*. Maryland: Borgo Press.

Hsu, S. P., 1976. Lao Tzu's Conception of Evil. *Philosophy East and West.* 26 (3), pp.301-316.

King, Jr., M., 1963. Letter from a Birmingham Jail. [Online]. Available from: <https://www.africa.upenn.edu/Articles_Gen/Letter_Birmingham.html> [Accessed 25 November 2018].

Lagerwey, J., 2007. Evil and its Treatment in Early Taoism. In: Gort, J. D., Jansen, H. and Vroom, H. M. eds. *Probing the Depths of Evil and Good: Multireligious Views and Case Studies.* New York: Rodopi. pp. 73-86.

Le Guin, U., 1993. *The Earthsea Quartet*. London: Puffin Books.

Le Guin, U., 1997. *Lao Tzu: Tao Te Ching: A Book about the Way and the Power of the Way*. London: Shanbhala.

Le Guin, U., 2001a. *Tales From Earthsea*. London: Orion.

Le Guin, U., 2001b. *The Other Wind*. London: Orion.

Robinson, W., 2005. The Far East of Star Wars. In: Decker, S. and Eberl, J. T. eds. *Star Wars and Philosophy*. pp. 29-38.

Sanderson, B., 2009. *The Final Empire*. London: Gollancz.

Sanderson, B., 2009. *The Well of Ascension*. London: Gollancz.

Sanderson, B., 2010. *The Hero of Ages*. London: Gollancz.

Star Wars: A New Hope. 1977. [Film]. Directed by George Lucas. USA: Lucasfilm.

Star Wars Archive. 2017. *Star Wars Episode III: The Chosen One Featurette*. [Online] Available from: <https://www.youtube.com/watch?v=lUYW2rCg9lI> [Accessed 25 November 2018].

Star Wars: Attack of the Clones. 2002. [Film]. Directed by George Lucas. USA: Lucasfilm.

Star Wars: Return of the Jedi. 1983. [Film]. Directed by George Lucas. USA: Lucasfilm.

Star Wars: Revenge of the Sith. 2005. [Film]. Directed by George Lucas. USA: Lucasfilm.

Star Wars: The Empire Strikes Back. 1980. [Film]. Directed by George Lucas. USA: Lucasfilm.

Star Wars: The Force Awakens. 2015. [Film]. Directed by J. J. Abrams. USA: Lucasfilm.

Star Wars: The Last Jedi. 2017. [Film]. Directed by Rian Johnson. USA: Lucasfilm.

Star Wars: The Phantom Menace. 1999. [Film]. Directed by George Lucas. USA: Lucasfilm.

The Legend of Korra, Book 2 Episode 7, Beginnings Part 1. 2013a. Nickelodeon. 18 October.

The Legend of Korra, Book 2 Episode 8, Beginnings Part 2. 2013b. Nickelodeon. 18 October.

The Legend of Korra, Book 2 Episode 14, Light in the Dark. 2013c. Nickelodeon. 22 November.

Wang, K., 2011. *Reading the Dao: A Thematic Inquiry*. London: Continuum.

Wetmore, Jr., K. J., 2000. The Tao of Star Wars, Or Cultural Appropriation in a Galaxy Far, Far Away. *Studies in Popular Culture*. 23 (1), pp. 91-106.

Whaling, F., 1985. Yin Yang, Zoroastrian Dualism, and Gnosticism: Comparative Studies in Religious Dualism. In Lyle, E. ed. *Duality*. Edinburgh: Traditional Cosmology Society. pp. 44-60.

From Dark Side to Grey Politics: The Portrayal of Evil in the *Star Wars* Saga

Rostislav Kůrka

Abstract

In 1977, *Star Wars* introduced us to one of cinema's most iconic evil characters: Darth Vader. Clad in black and using the "Dark Side of the Force", he is easily identified as a villain. However, since then, the *Star Wars* saga has grown, and its story has moved beyond spaceship corridors into senate halls. How has the portrayal of evil in the saga changed over time? Are such changes only superficial, or have the values that evil represents shifted? Has the border between good and evil become less clear in the recent films?

To answer these questions, I examine the portrayal of evil in the *Star Wars* film saga on several levels. I mainly focus on the interaction between two dimensions of evil: metaphysical and political. I trace the depiction of evil in the *Star Wars* saga chronologically, starting from the original trilogy (1977-1983), through the prequels (1999-2005), finishing with the sequel trilogy and the stand-alone "Star Wars story" films (2015-present).

Introduction

George Lucas's *Star Wars* has often been perceived as an epic tale about the battle of good and evil. With multiple sequels (and prequels) to the original film, the initial story has grown and transformed.[1] Does this story still say the same about good and evil as it did forty years ago? And what did it say back

---
[1]. I am focusing solely on the film saga. There is an immense range of *Star Wars* novels, animated series, comics, and games, all with their own themes. It would be impossible to paint a coherent picture out of such a broad canon.

then, anyway? What does "evil" represent within the story of *Star Wars*? Has this portrayal of evil in any way changed throughout the four decades of *Star Wars'* existence?

It is important to note that the saga consciously operates with the concept of evil. What or who constitutes as evil is not reserved solely for the audience's subjective decision. The films themselves pronounce moral judgments of characters and their actions, as well as political bodies that appear in the saga. What sets *Star Wars* apart from the majority of other films is the "omniscient narrator", as presented in the form of the iconic opening scrolling text. This text provides a basic introduction to the setting, but not without bias: it talks about the "evil Galactic Empire", "evil lord Darth Vader", "greedy Trade Federation", "sinister First Order", etc. Apart from that, the films themselves show certain actions, characters and entire institutions as implicitly evil, by portraying them negatively or condemning them through the words of positive, trustworthy characters, using similar vocabulary to the opening text.

Evil in the Original Trilogy: Really Simple?

The original trilogy has often been perceived as fairly straightforward and black-and-white regarding the question of evil. In particular, *A New Hope* (*ANH*, 1977), which was originally expected to be a standalone film, has all the elements of a traditional fairytale. There is a princess and a knight; the famous intro "A long time ago in a Galaxy far, far away" paraphrases the traditional fairytale opening "Once upon a time, a long time ago". Identifying the film with the fairytale genre means the audience is then likely to expect a setting with clearly defined good and evil roles. It is true that the characters and conflicting sides can easily be labelled on first sight: the good Rebels and the evil Empire; the good Luke Skywalker (Mark Hamill), princess Leia (Carrie Fisher), and Obi-Wan

(Alec Guinness) versus the evil Darth Vader (David Prowse/ James Earl Jones). This is helped by the musical and visual elements in the film (e.g. the opening sequence, where Vader in his menacing black armour is contrasted with princess Leia, in a white dress). Overall, the border between good and evil runs more or less along the same lines as the border between the Rebellion and the Empire. Even characters who start out as morally ambiguous, like Han Solo (Harrison Ford), or Lando (Billy Dee Williams) in *The Empire Strikes Back* (*TESB*, 1981) eventually pick a side and can be labelled "good" or "evil". That is not to say that the cut-off is clear or that there are no shades of grey.[2] However, for the majority of the audience watching the film for the first time, it is very easy to view everything in black-and-white.

It has been sometimes remarked that such a clear-cut division carries the danger of labelling the antagonists simply as evil "others" without focussing on what motivates them.[3] This is a valid remark, to a certain degree. The Empire is clearly an oppressive regime, using terror (the Death Star) against its own citizens. *ANH*'s opening scroll informs the audience that the Rebels are fighting the Empire "to restore freedom to the Galaxy". It is nevethetheless possible to view the Empire only as "space Nazis" in the same way Nazis were used as a universal enemy, especially in 1950s war films, without focusing on the values they represented. A survey conducted by Ryan and Kellner (1988) is indicative of this: when asked what they thought the Empire represented, 53% of respondents saw it simply as an embodiment of evil, 24% thought it represented right-wing dictators, and 12% answered communism (the "other", at that time, due to the Cold War).[4]

---

[2]. See below for a discussion on the "Han shot first" controversy, as one example. Otherwise, for instance, Dees (2005) provides a discussion on other examples.

[3]. See McDowell (2017).

[4]. Ryan and Kellner (1988), p. 235.

This is interesting, particularly in light of George Lucas's original intention. The first plot idea (many times altered afterwards) was strongly influenced by contemporary events and was, among other things, meant to be a commentary on the Vietnam War. Several versions of the original script revolved around the Princess's small home planet being invaded by the larger, more powerful Imperial military. Among Lucas's 1973 story treatment notes, we read: "Theme: Aquilae[5] is a small independent country like North Vietnam threatened by a neighbor or provincial rebellion, instigated by gangsters aided by empire. Fight to get rightful planet back. (...) The Empire is like America ten years from now, after gangsters assassinated the Emperor and were elevated to power in a rigged election."[6] The oppressive Empire was therefore an allegorical representation of the US.[7]

The film is clearly not as overtly political in its final form, but it is not apolitical either. Singular scenes refer to the Empire's internal politics and the (lost) remains of democracy: for example, when an officer remarks to Vader that Leia's capture might create support for the Rebellion within the Imperial Senate and, later, when Moff Tarkin (Peter Cushing) announces the dissolution of said Senate: "The last remnants of the Old Republic have been swept away." It is true, however, that this aspect remains very much relegated to the background. The good/evil division is unproblematic on a political level, the Rebels are never shown to use "evil" methods (in contrast to latter films, especially *Rogue One,* 2016).

Similar black-and-white divisions exist at a metaphysical level. Both the Emperor and Darth Vader are introduced as servants of the Dark Side of the Force. This concept is first

---

[5]. The forerunner of Alderaan, princess Leia's homeworld.

[6]. Rinzler (2007), p.16.

[7]. We can see that this original idea is much closer to the plot of *The Phantom Menace*, where the well-armed Trade Federation invades the small planet of Naboo. The context of the time had changed, however.

mentioned by Obi-Wan Kenobi in *ANH* and further explored during Luke's training with Yoda in *TESB*. The Jedi represent the other side of the metaphysical conflict, but Obi-Wan clarifies that this is not merely an ideological battle where both sides are morally equal: Jedis were "the guardians of peace and justice."

Obi-Wan adds further important information in relation to the metaphysical conflict: "A young Jedi named Darth Vader, who was a pupil of mine until he turned to evil, helped the Empire hunt down and destroy the Jedi knights. (...) Vader was seduced by the Dark Side of the Force."

Even for someone watching the film for the first time, the "Dark Side" is clearly presented as evil,[8] not only because of the use of the adjective "dark". The quote above implies that the Dark Side can "seduce" a person to evil, and transform a former Jedi into a servant of evil.

Both of Lucas's trilogies deal with the subject of the Dark Side tempting the protagonist (Luke - unsuccessfully, Anakin - successfully). Yoda, along with other Jedis, repeatedly emphasise throughout the saga how one of the biggest traps of the Dark Side is giving in to one's dark emotions, especially anger. Here, this conflict with evil is relegated to an individual level. Even the ultimate victory in *Return of the Jedi* (*RotJ*, 1983) is achieved because Luke overcomes his anger in the Emperor's presence and refuses to take aggressive action against Vader.

Yoda also tells Luke that "a Jedi uses the Force for defense, never to attack". Condemnation of aggression appears

---

[8]. The nature of the Dark Side has been debated by many scholars and authors, in various *Star Wars* novels, adaptations and games. To discuss whether the Dark Side really is evil, whether the *Star Wars* universe should be perceived as dualistic etc. would be enough for a separate book. What matters for our purposes here is that the majority of the audience would take Obi-Wan's explanation of the Dark Side being evil for granted. This interpretation is also in line with everything else the audience sees in the films.

throughout the saga in other forms,[9] making it one of the attributes that is objectively associated with evil.

In this regard, let's reflect on the famous "Han shot first" scene in *ANH*. This is a unique case of a film being revised to fall in line with the director's ideas of what actions should be condemned or, in other words, what should be perceived as evil. In the Mos Eisley cantina, Han Solo is approached by the bounty hunter Greedo, who is there to kill him. Anticipating this attack, Han shoots before Greedo has a chance to shoot him. In the 1997 Special Edition release of *ANH*, the scene was edited so that Greedo actually shoots first, but misses. The outcome gives moral justification for Han's action: he was clearly acting in self-defence.

This small detail speaks volumes about what the film seeks to present as evil: killing another being, if not done in self-defense, is morally unjustified. It does not matter that the idea of Han not shooting first only appeared in the edited version: the notion that aggressive action is bad was already present in the original. George Lucas merely decided to more strongly accentuate it by altering this particular sequence. We can draw several conclusions just from this short scene: that an act of aggression, and especially taking another life, unless in clear self-defense, is assumed to be evil; and that Han Solo was clearly meant to be a "good" character (Lucas made sure to remove a potentially "evil" trait from him). The latter is important when considering what is portrayed as evil in the later films, especially *Solo* (2018).

Evil in the Prequel Trilogy: The Hidden Menace

If the original trilogy speaks, on an individual level, about characters overcoming their negative traits and defeating the evil within themselves, the prequel trilogy tells the opposite

---

[9]. On a political scale, for example, in the unprovoked invasion of Naboo, or the destruction of the peaceful Alderaan.

story. Anakin Skywalker's (Hayden Christensen) tale is that of a hero's fall, and he fails in every single way that Luke succeeds in.

A manifestation of pure metaphysical evil is found in the Sith, the ancient order of Force users who are essentially a dark version of the Jedi. The future Emperor, Darth Sidious (Ian McDiarmid), is one of them. His apprentices are, in turn, Darth Maul (Ray Park), Count Dooku (Christopher Lee) and, eventually, Vader. Throughout the prequels, Darth Sidious seeks victory on two fronts: the destruction of the Jedi (metaphysical level), and establishing himself as the sole ruler by destroying the Galactic Republic and replacing it with the Empire (political level). To this end, he creates a proxy conflict against an "other" (Separatists seeking independence from the Republic by violent means). He can then later present himself as a saviour of the Republic through this conflict. He succeeds, which leads to the order of things we see in the original trilogy.

Even though the epic narrative of the ongoing war with Separatists may overshadow the personal with the political, it is again ultimately the individual's struggle against their own fears and temptations (here, unsuccessful) that matters the most, just like in the original trilogy. If not for Anakin's fall, Darth Sidious would not have succeeded in his plans.

Neither the political nor the metaphysical struggle in the prequels can be dismissed simply as a battle against an evil "other". There are specific values at stake here and, unlike in the original trilogy, the films repeatedly remind the audience of this. On a political level, it is preoccupied with the question of democracy. Because of the prevalence of corruption and the threat of war, the Republic's citizens actually welcome the strong hand of a dictator and are willing to abandon their principles of democracy. This is very much reminiscent of the transition from republic to empire in ancient Rome and also, for example, of Adolf Hitler's coup and the transition of the German Weimar republic into a fascist state. There are many common motives, such as the fact that the limitation of freedom was lauded in the name of preserving order, which is echoed in *Revenge of the Sith* (*RotS*, 2005) by the character Senator Padmé (Natalie Portman). As the Emperor proclaims that "the Republic will be reorganised into the first Galactic Empire—for a safer and securer society!", Padmé remarks: "This is how liberty dies... with thunderous applause." George Lucas himself has commented on the ideas he explored in the prequel trilogy: "All democracies turn into dictatorships—but not by coup. The people give their democracy to a dictator, whether it's Julius Caesar or Napoleon or Adolf Hitler. [...] What kinds of things push people and institutions into this direction?" (Corliss and Cagle 2002). In that sense, the Star Wars prequels present a mythology concerning the rise of an evil dictator which can also be applied within a historical context.

What may still be questioned is the fact that both the metaphysical and political evil remain, for the most part, behind the scenes, while the film focusses on something else. In the original trilogy, the Rebels fought Imperial stormtroopers and Vader, who were physical representations of evil. In the prequel trilogy, the enemies the heroes face are generally proxies, because the entire war is an illusion, secretly initiated by the Sith Lord himself.

Episodes II and III therefore could be seen as presenting a rare case of an omniscient narrator misleading the audience by focussing on objectively irrelevant representations of evil. On a superficial level, the prequels may seem like simple action films where the superpowered heroes (the Jedi) battle the enemy (Separatist droids). In *RotS*'s opening text, negative adjectives are attributed only to the "ruthless Sith Lord, Count Dooku" and the "fiendish droid leader, General Grievous" (both Separatist commanders). They are important figures in the story but, for the ultimate victory of evil, very much irrelevant. At the same time, however, *RotS*'s opening scroll admits that "there are heroes on both sides. Evil is everywhere." This is one of the rare places where the films explicitly question the "evilness" of the Separatists and the "goodness" of the Republic, ensuring that this conflict is perceived as relative.

The criticism of the Republic and the war itself also arises from certain individual characters: "What if the democracy we thought we were serving no longer exists, and the Republic has become the very evil we have been fighting to destroy?" Padmé asks Anakin, who is the only Jedi not questioning the fact that the Chancellor is being given ever increasing executive powers. Anakin's sympathies for ruling with a strong hand, along with his selfish desires, are what ultimately turn him to the Dark Side.

The political aspect of evil in the prequel trilogy is therefore expressed in totalitarian, anti-democratic tendencies. The tipping point of the metaphysical struggle lies with the individual. Throughout his training, Anakin unsuccessfully struggles to control his anger and hatred. One famous example is in *Attack of the Clones* (*AotC*, 2002) when Anakin, furious over his mother's death at the hands of the Sand People, massacres their camp, including women and children. What is new in the prequels is the focus on a fear of loss; in Anakin's case, of his loved ones (mother and wife). This is where a different set of values comes into play.

Fall to the Dark Side and Buddhist Values

George Lucas has admitted to consciously drawing from Eastern, especially Buddhist, traditions when creating the Jedi faith. Irvin Kershner, director of *TESB*, was a long-time student of Zen Buddhism and helped Lucas fine-tune Yoda into a "Zen master" character (White 1980). This is hardly surprising given the popularity of Eastern spirituality in US society, especially in the 60s and 70s. Some ethical values, otherwise alien to Western society, have consciously (and also a little less consciously) permeated the Jedi moral code and, through it, the *Star Wars* saga as a whole. This means that what the saga presents as evil may not always correspond to the expectations of the average Western audience (at whom the films were originally aimed). This is most clearly visible in the case of attachment being labelled as something negative. In Buddhist traditions, attachment is perceived as ultimately preventing one from reaching enlightenment and thus from being able to break the cycle of suffering. Interestingly, even Yoda talks about suffering (a theologically loaded term, dukkha, in traditional Buddhist terminology) when explaining what the Dark Side ultimately leads to: "Fear leads to anger, anger leads to hate, hate leads to suffering."

The anti-attachment message is nevertheless softened by the fact that it is ultimately positive attachment (love for his son) that makes Vader renounce the Dark Side. In the scene in *RotS* where Anakin confides about his visions of Padmé dying, Yoda does not condemn the attachment itself, but explains how it "leads to jealousy... a shadow of greed, that is". We do not hear of a strict denial of attachment, as we would in the orthodox version of Theravada Buddhism (and what we also would expect from Yoda who, like Obi-Wan, ultimately abandons his physical body and fully transcends into an immaterial sphere). Perhaps that is because an average secular or Christian person, which were the largest demographics Lucas would have expected among his audience, might find the pure message of non-attachment too alien to identify with themselves.

Evil in the Sequel Trilogy: Return of the Nazis

The sequel trilogy, no longer having the direct involvement of George Lucas, maintains some similarities in its portrayal of evil, but also some marked differences. In terms of music and visuals, the sequels return to the original film's straightforward way of indicating who is good and who is evil. In the opening scene of *The Force Awakens* (*TFA*, 2015), the face of Resistance pilot Poe Dameron (Oscar Isaac) contrasts with the masked First Order troopers and Dark Side user Kylo Ren (Adam Driver), who is dressed all in black. The unity between political and metaphysical evil is already confirmed in the beginning. The opening scrolling text informs the audience that "in Luke Skywalker's absence, the sinister First Order rose from the ashes of the Empire", and Lor San Tekka (Max von Sydow) recounts in one of the first scenes how "the First Order rose from the Dark Side".

One difference lies in the fact that very little explanation is given about the Dark Side itself or to the motivations of its chief representative, Supreme Leader Snoke (Andy Serkis). General Hux (Domhnall Gleeson) and his troops desire a new order through totalitarian government but Snoke, as a physical representation of metaphysical evil, seems intent on simply "being bad". Indeed, the statement that evil never perceives itself as such does not seem to apply to Snoke. While the Emperor was deceiving everyone, including his followers, by promising positive values (peace, security and, to his apprentice, power), Snoke promises "snuffing out hope" (not even specifying exactly *what kind of hope* – for freedom, justice, or peace, perhaps? It seems as if Snoke just wanted to destroy all positive hope in its entirety). On a metaphysical level, therefore, the conflict between good and evil in *TFA* is possibly even more black-and-white than in the original trilogy.

On the other hand, the motives of the evil political body – the First Order – is reflected upon more than the Empire's in the original trilogy: it wants to get rid of the corrupt New Republic and replace it with an ordered government. The sequels also go further than the originals in using imagery evocative of Nazi Germany to underline the similarities between the totalitarian regimes. A pivotal scene, before the First Order tests its new superweapon, directly copies scenes from the 1935 National Socialist propaganda film, "Triumph des Willens". This similarity lies not only in the positioning of the respective troops – First Order flags hanging from columns (their black-and-white symbols set against a red background, just like those of Nazi Germany) – but also in its use of camera angles, panning, and the entire composition of the sequence (Ritzinger 2016). The way that General Hux's speech so closely resembles many of Adolf Hitler's own infamous tirades merely underlines the point.

There is a reason for this. Director J. J. Abrams has elaborated on the idea behind the script: "That all came out of conversations about what would have happened if the Nazis all went to Argentina but then started working together again? [...] Could the First Order exist as a group that actually admired the Empire?" (Dyer 2015). The sequels, in many ways, adopted the political ideology present in the previous movies for their antagonists. At the same time, by having the heroes encounter the same kind of evil after *RotJ*, whose ending seemed like a final victory for the forces of good, the sequels eliminate the "happily ever after" factor and, at least in terms of the film saga, change the nature of evil itself. Whereas, within the cycle of the first six films, we could perceive evil and the totalitarian tendencies as something finite (and perhaps a one-time temptation which Anakin and the citizens of the Republic succumb to), the latest cycle has presented it as something the next (and maybe every successive) generation needs to fight for itself.

But what of the evil of the Dark Side on an individual level? Somewhat unusually, there is no sign of the Force-wielding protagonist, Rey (Daisy Ridley), explicitly having problems with anger, hatred or attachment. If anyone is struggling, it is the villain, Kylo Ren; even though he too isn't trying to overcome or embrace his anger - it just simply exists. His attachment to his parents (and, potentially, to Rey) is instead a positive element preventing him from truly becoming "a new Vader". Kylo has an added problem, because he wishes to follow the dark path, yet he feels insecurity and "the pull to the Light".

From all that has been said, the sequel trilogy would seem to be presenting the traditional story in reverse: it is not about a protagonist being tempted to the darkness, but rather about a villain being tempted to the light. Kylo Ren says as much while meditating over the relic of Darth Vader's helmet in *TFA*; he hesitates to destroy the ship his mother is on in *The Last Jedi*, (*TLJ*, 2017) and others (Han in *TFA*, Rey in *TLJ*) actively try to turn him back to the light. This makes the metaphysical principles of evil passive in a sense, which is striking in its difference to the originals and the Jedi philosophy, where the light is the more passive of the two aspects of the Force.

The sequels also give voice to a character with "grey" morality, and even raise a question mark (however briefly) regarding the political conflict itself. This occurs with the appearance of DJ (Benicio del Toro), who is a criminal willing to work for either side, as long as he gets paid. He also shows Finn (John Boyega) how unscrupulous businesspeople make their fortune by selling weapons to both the First Order and the Resistance, pronouncing judgment on the business of war as a whole. He does this from his perspective as a cynical individual. He is not trying to show Finn right and wrong; his point is simply that this is how life is and the only thing Finn should do is to look after himself, just like DJ himself does. DJ's attitude in this way mirrors the overall mood we find in *Solo*, the second of the latest standalone Star Wars films.

Rogue One: Heroes Do Bad Things

The last two films I am going to look at are *Rogue One: A Star Wars story* (2016) and *Solo: A Star Wars Story* (2018). Timewise, *Rogue One* is set right before the events of *ANH*. Compared to *ANH*'s black-and-white presentation of good and evil, *Rogue One*'s portrayal of this is much more a case of shades of grey. The sides in the political conflict are clear (good Rebels versus evil Empire with its superweapon) and the Imperial characters remain evil without any redeeming qualities, but the Rebellion and its methods are not as unequivocally good as in the original trilogy. Each of the protagonists possesses some major flaw. Jyn Erso (Felicity Jones) is a reluctant heroine who initially looks out only for herself. Her most important companion is the Rebel operative Cassian Andor (Diego Luna). His character is introduced via a scene which ends with him killing a Rebel informant rather than risking alerting the Empire. Later, also for pragmatic reasons, Cassian intends to assassinate Jyn's father, the scientist Galen Erso (Mads Mikkelsen). Galen is another problematic character: he helps the Empire to build the Death Star. His decision to do so is presented as choosing "the lesser evil" (rather than letting someone else do it, he hopes to reduce the damage the project can do and sabotage it). The list continues: Cassian's companion is a reprogrammed Imperial droid that has no qualms about killing; the person who alerts the Rebels about the Death Star is a former Imperial pilot; and then there is Saw Gerrera (Forest Whitaker), the ruthless leader of a Rebel cell who acts like a terrorist.

In *Rogue One*, what constitutes as evil is the same as in the original trilogy—a regime that uses brutal methods to achieve its goals. However, *Rogue One*'s heroes also employ these same methods at times. This is in sharp contrast to the clear-cut delineation within the original trilogy, and even the prequels (however grey these considerations may get at times, heroes in the prequels don't perform morally condemnable actions while trying to achieve objectively good goals). *Rogue One* also seems to present a "realistic" world: sometimes the circumstances are such that one cannot simply choose good, but merely a lesser evil. The overall tone, however, seems to indicate that the ends do not justify the means. Evil is evil no matter who is responsible for it, and no one is pure and blameless.

Overall, the "Star Wars Story" films tend to gravitate towards a more differentiated portrayal of good and evil than the main trilogies, including the newest one. A character's political allegiance does not guarantee their moral purity, but those who start out as servants of an evil political power are also capable of changing and becoming heroes.

The struggle against a metaphysical level of evil is absent from *Rogue One*'s story, unless we reduce its individualistic spiritual aspects into simply "being a good person". This may be because the Force is present only through "folk belief" courtesy of the Guardians of the Whills, Chirrut Îmwe (Donnie Yen) and Baze Malbus (Jiang Wen), and through Jyn's family's faith. These require no demands on the individual to overcome their fear, anger, hatred or attachment. Likewise, Darth Vader does not play the role of a Dark Side tempter, like he does in *TESB*; he is just another antagonist (with arcane powers, though). We could very well ask the question of whether opting out from dealing with metaphysical questions of good and evil goes hand-in-hand with painting a morally grey world, in which nobody has a clear allegiance to the light (though some still have allegiance to the dark).

"Solo": Who Is Good? Who Is Evil?

If *Rogue One*'s protagonists are morally ambiguous, *Solo*'s heroes refuse to submit to any objective criteria of good and evil. All are outlaws and thieves to begin with and, save for Han Solo (Alden Ehrenreich) in the very end, they have no relationship to any apparently "good" organisation. The metaphysical level is completely absent, probably, once more, due to the complete absence of the Force. There is no condemnation of aggression either, even on a mundane level; quite the opposite: the film intentionally shows Han shooting first in a final scene, in contrast to George Lucas' previously discussed edit, in *ANH*. The chief protagonists do not really struggle with their flaws; rather, their final actions often embrace them: we have the criminal boss Beckett (Woody Harrelson) betraying everyone, and Han's friend, Qi'ra (Emilia Clarke), deciding to stay with the criminal organisation, the Crimson Dawn. The heroes' morally laudable actions (such as freeing miners on Kessel, and siding with the villagers of Savareen against the Crimson Dawn) could be perceived as by-products of their own pursuits of selfish goals (greed or self-preservation). At the same time, many characters and organisations could be labelled as evil, to a degree: various criminals such as Lady Proxima, Dryden Vos, and also Qi'ra; there is also the Empire, Crimson Dawn, and even Beckett's original group. The opening narration illustrates this in the following statement: "This is a lawless time. Crime syndicates compete for resources (...)". We can note, however, from this, that that the subjective vocabulary is still less pronounced than in the other films (one could easily have expected more negative language, for example "evil" or "greedy" crime syndicates).

One character who is important in terms of the perception of evil in *Solo* is Enfys Nest (Erin Kellyman). Enfys and her gang are introduced as just another group of criminals, stealing from the Empire and attacking the protagonists. Enfys herself wears a mask, lending her a menacing appearance, usually reserved for villains (Vader, Boba Fett, Kylo Ren). The plot twist lies in the audience learning that Enfys Nest actually works for the "good side". Her gain is not personal; she uses her resources to support Rebels and the innocent villagers of Savareen. This is a moment of extrapolation when it comes to heroes and villains, where the audience is left to interpret whether Enfys Nest is good, and the apparent protagonists are evil.

If *Rogue One*'s protagonists are indeed "grey" individuals working for a good cause, then the protagonists in "Solo" are grey individuals working for an evil cause, seeing as they act as minions of a cruel criminal boss. Their plot-related actions could actually be perceived as evil, in isolation, because they kill for personal gain. This perceived division between good and evil is drawn, at best, just before the end of the film. Han and Chewie are the only two who decide to do something altruistic, foreshadowing their future in the Rebellion.

We could say that Han Solo himself has no stake in the metaphysical struggle between light and dark, and equally no stake in the political struggle between the Rebels and the Empire (nor do his companions). His decision to help Enfys Nest arises solely because it is the right thing to do in the there-and-then. As a whole, the film, just like Han himself, avoids the big debates about good and evil, and political ideology. It is the furthest removed, in this regard, from an epic tale of good and evil. It should be noted that this is defined by its plot, given that it focusses on a character who, even in *ANH*, is introduced as morally grey. *Solo* and *Rogue One* both had to deal with the problem of being set in a "Force-less" time. Another question to ask is whether their release was in any way related to a potential general tendency towards "realism" and also moral greyness in modern cinema.

The Evolution of the Saga?

Even though evil in the *Star Wars* saga has transformed on multiple levels over the years, it has maintained some central themes, especially in portraying certain political ideologies as evil. The role that evil plays as an obstacle on the hero's journey has changed, however.

At first sight, the impression might be that the original trilogy offers a straightforward, black-and-white picture, while only the prequels offer a political dimension; or that the sequels take a step back towards a black-and-white universe while maintaining the political aspect, and that the standalone films offer a morally relativistic world.

That would be a gross misinterpretation, though. Political evil is present in each trilogy, starting with the very first film. The Empire is evil because of its ideology. The presentation of dictatorships as evil is consistent throughout the entire Star

Wars saga. The only reason why this may be overlooked is due to mistaking the Empire's motives for a desire to simply "be bad".

This is not the case with metaphysical evil, however. Both George Lucas's trilogies present overcoming the metaphysical evil within as a necessary obstacle on the hero's individual journey. The sequel trilogy does not, which leads to an erasure of this individual level of metaphysical evil altogether. Along with that, it manages to erase one of the core values of the Jedi faith: the renunciation of aggression and attachment. Lacking any solid definition both on an individual and a theoretical level, the Dark Side in the sequels becomes an empty label.

As we can see, it isn't a case of the older films presenting some arbitrary, intangible, otherworldly demonic force which needs to be defeated in order for good to prevail. On the contrary, the metaphysical evil is clearly defined. It is associated with specific actions and attributes (some of which have roots in the religious and philosophical systems of our world). The latest films are therefore the first to either abandon the concept of metaphysical evil altogether (*Rogue One*, *Solo*) or portray it as someone just wanting to "be evil" (*TFA* and *TLJ*). The focus seems to have shifted elsewhere.

The last remarkable detail is that the more recent the film, the less morally clear cut its individual characters are. This more pronounced moral relativism, however, applies considerably more to the heroes than the villains. While heroes are progressively portrayed as imperfect, evil characters demonstrate hardly any redeeming qualities.

Evil is presented from different angles throughout the saga. The prequel trilogy offers the most varied portrayal, showing evil equally on metaphysical, personal and political levels. The original trilogy and the sequels tend to accentuate some aspects of evil while diminishing others, based on where their focus lies. The form in which evil manifests is, in the end, simply a by-product of what kind of story is being told.

Bibliography

Corliss, R. and Cagle, J., 2002. "Dark Victory". *Time Magazine*. [online, archived] 20 April 2002. Available at: <https://web.archive.org/web/20020423000824/http://www.time.com/time/sampler/article/0,8599,232440,00.html> [Accessed 21 November 2018].

Dees, R., 2005. Moral Ambiguity in a Black-and-White Universe. In: K. S. Decker and J. T. Eberl, eds. *Star Wars and Philosophy: More Powerful Than You Can Possibly Imagine*. Chicago: Open Court. pp. 39-53.

Dyer, J., 2015. "JJ Abrams Spills Details On Kylo Ren." *Empire*. [online] 25 August 2015. Available at: <https://www.empireonline.com/movies/news/jj-abrams-spills-details-kylo-ren/> [Accessed 20 November 2018]

Langley, T. (ed.), 2015. *Dark Side of the Mind - Star Wars Psychology*. New York: Sterling.

McDowell, J.C., 2017. *The Gospel According to Star Wars* (Second Edition). Louisville: Westminster John Knox Press.

Rinzler, J. W., 2007. *The Making of Star Wars: The Definitive Story Behind the Original Film*. New York: Del Rey.

Ritzinger, T., 2016. "A Source of Images for 'The First Order'". *Sci-fi and Fantasy Network*. [online] 14 January 2016. Available at: <http://www.scififantasynetwork.com/a-source-of-images-for-the-first-order/> [Accessed 21 November 2018]

Rogue One: A Star Wars Story. 2016. [film] Directed by Gareth Edwards. USA: Walt Disney Studios Motion Pictures.

Ryan, M. and Kellner, D., 1988. *Camera Politica*. Bloomington - Indianapolis: Indiana University Press.

Solo: A Star Wars Story. 2018. [film] Directed by Ron Howard. USA: Walt Disney Studios Motion Pictures.

Star Wars Episode I: The Phantom Menace. 1999. [film] Directed by George Lucas. USA: 20th Century Fox.

Star Wars Episode II: Attack of the Clones. 2002. [film] Directed by George Lucas. USA: 20th Century Fox.

Star Wars Episode III: Revenge of the Sith. 2005. [film] Directed by George Lucas. USA: 20th Century Fox.

Star Wars Episode IV: A New Hope. 1977. [film] Directed by George Lucas. USA: 20th Century Fox.

Star Wars Episode V: The Empire Strikes Back. 1981. [film] Directed by Irvin Kershner. USA: 20th Century Fox.

Star Wars Episode VI: Return of the Jedi. 1983. [film] Directed by Richard Marquand. USA: 20th Century Fox.

Star Wars Episode VII: The Force Awakens. 2015. [film] Directed by J. J. Abrams. USA: Walt Disney Studios Motion Pictures.

Star Wars Episode VIII: The Last Jedi. 2017. [film] Directed by Rian Johnson. USA: Walt Disney Studios Motion Pictures.

White, T., 1980. "'Star Wars': Slaves to the 'Empire'". *Rolling Stone*. [online] 24 July 1980. Available at: <https://www.rollingstone.com/culture/culture-news/star-wars-slaves-to-the-empire-61931/> [Accessed 20 November 2018].

Imperialism as "Evil" in Epic Fantasy: An Analysis of the Fantasy Works of Eddings, Jordan, Sanderson, and Brett

Matthew J. Elder & C. Palmer-Patel

Abstract

For better or worse, modern and contemporary Fantasy has always had a relationship with good and evil. In recent literature, the roles of characters, heroes and villains, while tied to these concepts, have become more nuanced in a way that is critical of the genre's problematic traditions. David Eddings and Robert Jordan's works are both wary of invading Empires, but in Othering that Evil fail to recognise the inherent oppression in the Empires that their heroes build. Progressing forwards into the twenty-first century with Brandon Sanderson and Peter V. Brett, this complicity becomes more recognised and is represented in part through more nuanced and complicated villains. These contemporary villains move through arcs structured such that they explore a justification of Empire, shift to a critique of that perspective, and ultimately shift to deny that worldview. Such a process recognises the complex nature of hegemonic Empire in a way that challenges the too-simple good versus evil binary of the genre's past. These authors have been selected as representative of the popular commercial Fantasy of the last four decades. Through these dominant – white American male – voices within the genre, there can be seen a progression towards a self-reflexive problematising of both imperialism and the imposition of a single dominant ideology. The evolution of evil becomes more nuanced through the decades as authors begin to write in a more globalized, culturally aware space.

Eddings's *Belgariad* (1982-1984) and *Malloreon* (1987-1991) series convey the struggle between the forces of Light and Dark as a eons-long war between the nations of the West and East respectively.

The Western protagonists ultimately "save" the Eastern nations, an action of colonisation that is seen as benevolent within the context of the narrative.

Jordan's *Wheel of Time* series (1990-2012) expands on the role of the hero as imperialistic saviour and complicates it further. As the character slowly goes mad and demonstrates schizophrenic tendencies, Rand's tyrannical actions as hero and saviour are problematically linked to insanity.

Sanderson's *Elantris* (2005) brings an awareness of the way hegemonic oppression forms and sustains Empires. The novel critiques such efforts through the character's change in perspective that is mirrored in the structure of the novel itself.

Brett's *The Demon Cycle* (2008-2017) works to explore the justifications for an imperial perspective from someone who believes they are literally saving the world from Demons by enforcing rule through religious and cultural conversion. *The Demon Cycle* comes to reject all forms of Empire, even the apparently salvific ones formed by heroes.

Through a brief examination of Eddings, Jordan, Sanderson, and Brett, we will examine how there has been an evolution in the complexity of the role of villainous characters in order to critique imperialism as evil. Ultimately, these critiques of imperialism acknowledge the limitations of single dominant narratives, and engage with the more diverse, globalised space within which these texts exist and are read.

*

As we try and progress towards a more open, global society, there is a roadblock that is difficult to acknowledge: we are not postcolonial; we are still living the effects of colonisation. This chapter examines four American Fantasy authors who are representative of each decade from the 1980s to the 2010s, all of whom depict worlds concerned with Empire and imperialism. We argue that there is a shift away from Empire as a simple, external, Othered evil, towards a recognition that Empire is a complex entity sustained and created by complex processes in which we as individuals are often complicit. Fantasy literature takes us to precolonial and colonial worlds, providing valuable perspective on the mechanisms that have created our world. By transitioning villainous characters into perspective characters, the reader is exposed to their hegemonic ideas and is brought into dialogue with them not as a distant, Othered evil, but as a lived experience. This evolution in the depiction of evil challenges the forces that perpetuate a dominant identity narrative as an assumed normal.

What these texts do through their complication of the role of both hero villain, is, at the least, demonstrate an awareness of the problematic nature of Western imperialism – the American Empire in which they are writing – and at most, they have the potential to demand of their readers an active critique and protest of an American narrative that is singular and fixed. These texts have been selected as representative of the popular commercial fantasy of the last four decades. Through these dominant – white, American, male – voices within the genre, there can be seen a progression towards problematising both imperialism and the imposition of a single dominant ideology. Although there are instances where hero and villain binaries are dissolved in earlier Fantasy, we argue that in American Fantasy of the last four decades, imperial worldview is the dividing factor between hero and villain. The evolution of evil becomes more nuanced through the decades as authors begin to write in a more globalized and culturally aware space. Through a brief examination of works by David Eddings, Robert Jordan, Brandon Sanderson, and Peter V. Brett, we will examine how there has been an evolution in the complexity of the role of villainous characters in order to critique imperialism as evil. Ultimately, these critiques acknowledge the limitations of single dominant narratives and engage with the more diverse, globalised space within which these texts are read.

David (and Leigh)[1] Eddings's *Belgariad* (1982-1984) and *Malloreon* (1987-1991) series depicts thousands of years of animosity between the West – represented by the protagonists – and the East – the antagonists. Each character presented in the novels is presented as flat, two-dimensional, stereotypes of their people. For instance, the characters remark repeatedly that their friends, the Arends, are a slow-witted race. Another protagonist is often referred to simply as "the Ulgo" or "the Ulgo Relg." Thus, the idea of naming and characterising a comrade through their racial identifier is made commonplace in the text. This framework – of having two-dimensional characters that are atypical representations of their race – becomes the basis for the eons-long confrontation between the East and the West. As Edward Said states in *Orientalism* (1978):

> a very large mass of writers [...] have accepted the basic distinction between East and West as the starting point for elaborate theories, epics, novels, social descriptions, and political accounts concerning the Orient, its people, customs, 'mind,' destiny, and so on. (pp. 2-3)

Although Said writes with regards to real-world politics, the same sentiment is true within the world of Eddings's series.

The first *Belgariad* series gives some rationale to the long history of war: Torak steals a magical orb from his brother, leading to a war where the seven Gods of the West are united against Torak, the single God of the East. Yet there is no real "evilness" that is involved with the theft of the orb. Instead, feelings of jealousness, pride, and power are evoked, and Torak himself is thought to be "mad" by many of the characters. However, a prologue presented as first-person narration from Torak's point of view suggests that Torak sees himself as the hero:

---

[1]. Leigh Eddings is largely unacknowledged as the co-author of these texts.

I saw that the accursed stone had divided Aldur from me
and his brothers. [...] But already the evil stone had gained
possession over the soul of Aldur, [...]. (Eddings, 1984, p. 3)

While the Western protagonists view the theft of the orb as an attempt to gain power, Torak paints a picture of himself as saviour. Although there are a number of events throughout the series that would challenge this perception, the first-person prologue suggests that the issue of "evilness" becomes a matter of perspective. In the first series, this perspective is largely dependent on whether the character is Western or Eastern.

In the sequel *Malloreon* series, as the protagonists travel through the East, the Eastern Other is humanised through multiple areas of contact. But, as with any meeting between the Self and the Orientalised Other, there are wider political nuances to these interactions. For instance, when the characters encounter King Urgit, the protagonists remark that they are surprised to find him likeable: 'he's the first Murgo we've met in eons who shows some human qualities' (Eddings, 1988, p. 235). It is later revealed that Urgit is in fact an illegitimate offspring of Western nobility. Hence, because of his patriarchal lineage,[2] Urgit is not "really" Other. As Said states, 'any deviation from what we considered the norms of Oriental behavior was believed to be unnatural' (Said, 1978, p. 39), and similarly the revelation of Urgit's identity suggest that it is only acceptable to enjoy Urgit's character because he is not "really" Eastern; his 'human qualities' derive from his Western half. The revelation of Urgit's identity then lays the groundwork for humanising Zakath, the Emperor of Mallorea. Zakath's initial conversations with the primary protagonist Garion (Overlord of the West) are confrontational, as Garion refuses to acknowledge Zakath's authority as Emperor of Mallorea (with Garion in

---

[2]. Urgit is still half-Eastern through his mother, but maternal lines are often disregarded in Epic Fantasy.

the position of visiting sovereign). It is only when Zakath begins to follow Garion's lead that the two are able to form a friendship. Accordingly, the friendship and later political alliance between them is made on uneven terms, as Zakath must "convert" to a Westernized demeanour in order to be thought of as "good."

After thousands of years of animosity, the characters continue to view the Eastern Others as a threat to the West, and the consequent political interactions in the novels are driven by these perceptions. But despite a fear of reverse colonisation, in Eddings's series, as in the real world: 'it was the West that moved upon the East, not vice versa' (Said, 1978, p. 73). The political alliance between Garion and Zakath demonstrates more of a colonisation effort on behalf of the West than a real alliance. This colonisation begins subtly, with the slow infiltration of Western trade into the – previously impregnable – Eastern market. By the end of the series, the West have not only begun taking over the economic sector, but they have also successfully replaced Eastern religion. The confrontations between the East and West can be seen as a religious war, and the West effectively wins the war by first killing the god Torak in *Belgariad*, then by replacing him in *Malloreon* with Eriond, a companion of Garion's.

It is striking, and disturbing, that the God of the East is replaced by a beautiful, blonde, young man from the West. At the end of the last novel, a voice of destiny tells Garion that: 'Zakath is going to have to ram Eriond down the throats of all the Angaraks in the world' (Eddings, 1991, p. 303). The violent phrasing is problematic and suggests the level at which religious conversion is an act of aggression. This forced conversion, however, is not seen as evil in any way. Eriond is seen to be a kinder god than the wrathful Torak. There are, presumably, connections to Christianity here. There are also wider implications in terms of American culture and politics, suggesting a manifest destiny to rule. And thus, the issues of imperialism in this '80s Fantasy are not seen as problematic by any of the characters; an attitude that may get passed on to readers. In *Race and Popular Fantasy* (2016), Helen Young asserts that:

> The ultimate trajectory of conventional narrative, however, is of good triumphing over evil and ushering in an implied sustained error of stability and peace under the rule of a single realm. [These texts] demonstrate the oppression inherent in the imposition of imperial rule, even when its own ideologies work to present it as benevolent. (p. 131)

In *Belgariad* and *Malloreon* colonisation is not something that is wrong or evil; even though there is 'oppression inherent' in this 'benevolent' rule, this dominion is presented as salvation for the entire world. Imperialism, then, is rather problematically presented as the expected and long-sought-for outcome of the events of the books.

Robert Jordan's *Wheel of Time* series (1990-2012)[3] continues the quest for imperial power, although, here, at least, Jordan appears to begin questioning the imperialist tendencies of the Fantasy genre. In the start of the series, the central protagonist, Rand al'Thor, is a good-natured, compassionate young man. As the series develops, Rand undergoes a dramatic personality change and gradually becomes harsher and colder to those around him. While there are a number of clearly defined evil characters in the series, the central antagonist, the Dark Lord (a devil-like character) is rarely present. There are also various creatures like the trollocs, but these creatures are more animalistic than human, and are presented as predators of humans. The truly "evil" characters then are the Darkfriends

---

[3]. Note that, following Jordan's death, Brandon Sanderson completed the last three novels of the fourteen-book series using extensive notes left by the late author.

and the Forsaken, those characters that betray their friends and families in service to the Dark Lord. At several moments Rand himself is comparable to these characters. For instance, when Rand contemplates the possible death of a friend, he muses: 'His death could serve me well indeed' (Jordan and Sanderson, 2009, p. 665). The lack of care and regard towards a previously valued mentor is similar to the thoughts and actions of a Darkfriend. Later Rand uses balefire on an entire fortress, killing many innocents in an attempt to destroy one of the Forsaken. The act results in permanent damage, as balefire completely obliterates people so that they cannot be born again; it also has the potential of destroying the world itself. Despite the evilness of this act, Rand continues to use the weapon.

Rand's route to evil derives from madness, one that is born from using (magical) power. The magic itself is tainted and inevitably corrupts the user. For Rand, as a reincarnation of Lews Therin Telamon, this madness is prompted by a schizophrenic voice which belongs to Lews. Lews is also infamous for being a kinslayer, murdering those he loved. As Rand slowly goes mad, he is likewise unable to control his powers; similar to Lews's eventual madness, Rand's loss of control risks destroying those around him. Additionally, Rand struggles with his schizophrenic side. Often, it seems that Rand must wrestle control away from Lews, and on at least a few instances, he fails to do so. Similar to the depiction of Torak above, Rand's imperialistic actions are thus linked to – and are perhaps too easily excused by – his insanity.

Prophecies in the series state that:

Women shall weep and men quail as the nations of the earth are rent like rotting cloth. [...] and he shall break the world again by his coming, tearing apart all ties that bind. (Jordan, 1990, p. xi, original emphasis)

Rand interprets these words to indicate that he must destroy national boundaries, uniting the world under his own leadership so that they can all enter the Last Battle together as one people fighting against the Dark Lord. Thus, the conception of benevolent imperial oppression is structurally built directly into the fabric of the book, allowing a simple shepherd to become an imperialist tyrant. For example, after Rand conquers Tear, Rand threatens the High Lords who have previously ruled:

> By tomorrow midday you will have offered her the treaty I want, or by sunset tomorrow I'll hang both of you. If I have to hang High Lords every day, two by two, I will. I will send every last one of you to the gallows if you won't obey me. (Jordan, 1992, p. 179)

Although there are some instances where the laws Rand implements are meant to be for the common good, here it is obvious that Rand is willing to hang the previous rulers simply for disobeying him. Later contact with other nations reveals that they fear he will subjugate them and impose his power and authority on their people. Rand is thus seen as an imperial conqueror by the other characters in the narrative.

However, instead of the West colonizing others, Rand here *also* represents the East. Rand is raised in the West as an Andor, but his heritage is Aiel and Rand adopts many of the customs of this Eastern culture. As the Aiel are constantly Othered, their traditions made exotic or mysterious, Rand likewise is treated as an exotic Other. Yet Rand also causes a complete upheaval in the Aiel culture, shattering their traditions completely. Consequently, instead of depicting colonisation and the fear of imperial rule as a conflict between the East and the West, Jordan uses Rand – a child of two worlds – as a vehicle that forces his singular imperial rule on the world as a whole. Through this, Jordan's work steps away from Empire as Eastern and other and opens up a critique of the general process of Empire through defining it through insanity.

As such, Rand as singular imperial power is a threat to *all* nations. As Farah Mendlesohn argues in Rhetorics of Fantasy (2008):

> the hero *moves through* the action and the world stage, embedding an assumption of unchangingness on the part of the indigenes. This kind of fantasy is essentially imperialist: only the hero is capable of change; fantasyland is orientalised into the 'unchanging past.' (p. 9, original emphasis).

Mendlesohn argues this point as part of her larger thesis (that the hero's knowledge, and thus the Fantasy itself, is supposedly unquestioned by the reader), and she refrains on expanding on the wider implications of Orientalism. With regards to *Wheel of Time*, Rand assumes that air of 'unchangingness on the part of the indigenes'; one cannot help but wonder what gives Rand the right to impose his authority. The structural underpinnings of the Fantasy genre as '[t]he ultimate trajectory […] of good triumphing over evil and ushering in an implied sustained error of stability and peace under the rule of a single realm' is maintained (Young, p. 131). But, once again, there is an 'oppression inherent' in this 'benevolent rule' (p. 131), one that is further complicated by the inherent madness of this imperial power. True, Rand is prophesied to rescue the world, but his methods of conquering counter his role as saviour, and instead Rand can be seen as a tyrant who outright persecutes the freedoms of nations. Throughout much of the series, the overall impression is of Rand slowly conquering and dominating all nations. Like a Roman Dictator – a political position that allowed one to take emergency powers during a time of crisis – Rand similarly claims the authority to assert his will on others as the "hero of destiny." In this way, Rand derives his "right" to impose his ideology on the world from the power that the Fantasy structurally affords him and is able to do so in part because, as Mendlesohn notes, the reader is complicit in assuming the "right" of the hero to enact change. Part of the evolution that the Fantasy genre will come to undertake is in recognising, as Young addresses, that such assumed or unquestioned habits require scrutiny as even 'a choice made without conscious thought is still a choice' (p. 6).

In the final book of the series, Rand forces a peace treaty on all of the nations in the world. Although the treaty has good intentions, the method in which Rand imposes it is highly manipulative. Rand claims that he will only sacrifice his life for the world if the nations sign his treaty. Unlike the historical Caesar, Rand redeems himself by relinquishing his power once the Last Battle is faced. And yet, although Rand is eventually able to save the world from the Dark Lord, this only comes about through a forced imperialism, one that is marked with instances of madness, tyranny, and cold-heartedness. While the link that Jordan draws between madness and Empire through the hero suggests a possible critique of colonial rule, it ultimately still falls into a problematic "benevolent Empire" Fantasy structure.

Brandon Sanderson's *Elantris* (2005) presents a further shift towards complexity in the representation of evil and Empire and the way that, particularly through hegemony, we are all often complicit in the perpetuation of oppression. One facet of this underpinning the novel is the way that the Elantrians who are treated as lepers were once regular citizens of Arelon before the magic changed them. This facet of Sanderson's world challenges the genre's habits of externalising Empire by turning the gaze inward toward the Empire inhabited by the author and his audience. This process of self-critique is embodied also in the character, and apparent antagonist, Hrathen, the representative of the external Fjordell Empire.

The invading Empire itself hovers as a threat in the background of the narrative, inserting a clock into the narrative as the Empire, unbeknownst to most of the characters, draws nearer. If Hrathen cannot peaceably convert the populace in time, the Empire will force the issue. In the genre's evolving representation of Evil, Sanderson's text recognises that the true "evil" is the hegemonic power that threatens not only indigenous identity erasure, but also the long-term creation and maintenance of new norms that work to construct barriers against denying the new imperial status quo. Hrathen believes that the populace of Arelon will convert because it makes sense for them to do so: 'He had never doubted the church. Something so perfectly organized couldn't help but be right' (Sanderson, 2005, p. 157). For Hrathen, the Fjordell way of life is the correct one and any other perspective is aberrant. However, through his repeated encounters with the other two perspectives, with Raoden and Sarene, his orderly way of viewing the world breaks down in the face of recognising their personhood. This, the text suggests, is how dominant narratives can come to be subverted.

Sanderson's *Elantris* recognises that Empire is dangerous because of the way that it hegemonically erodes away at agency and diversity. The emphasis on religion and its role in Fjordell history draws attention to the dangers of Empire achieved through hegemony. It is only when Fjordell converted to Shu-Dereth[4] that they began successfully expanding their territory and converting other nations to their way of life. While the army might be a fearful and deadly weapon, *Elantris* recognises that it is internalised narratives that are to be truly feared, for it is through those that histories are forgotten to time. It is this concern that preoccupies much of Raoden's arc through this text. He explores the decaying and lost[5] city of Elantris, despairing over crumbling and rotting books of recorded history; and central to his mind is the question of who the Elantrians really were, and how their existence, culture, and

---

[4]. Post-conversion Fjordell then re-wrote their history to suggest they had always been Derethi. Their Empire has always been built on the reduction to, and perpetuation of, a single narrative.

[5]. The city only fell ten years ago, and yet is already perceived as lost.

identity might fade from the world. The fear is that Hrathen's cultural narrative of Shu-Dereth and Fjordell rule will erase the history of Elantris until it is unreclaimable. That is what hegemonic Empire does: it erases.

However, while *Elantris* engages in a critique of the hegemony, it does so in a way that also champions a solution embodied in the structure of the narrative itself. The novel (for the first 90% of the text) follows a strict tripartite structure of rotating character perspectives. We begin with Raoden, the heir apparent, move then into Sarene, the heir to the ally kingdom, and finally into Hrathen, a priest sent by the Fjordel Empire, before returning again to Raoden and so on. This strict A,B,C structure is continued throughout the novel, until it falls into patternless chaos in the climax of the narrative. As the narrative structure devolves, it does so concurrent with Hrathen's shift from blind acceptance of the cultural narrative he has lived and preached his entire life towards a more open perspective built on questioning and self-determination. In *Elantris*, the performative ability of empathy, derived from repeated personal encounters with different perspectives, works to counteract the imposed, single dominant narrative of the Empire.

The structural positioning of characters is key to how Sanderson places thematic emphasis in *Elantris*. The Empire itself fades into the background of the text and instead Sanderson draws readers into direct contact with Hrathen as its weapon of conversion, thereby suggesting that it is the hegemony that is to be feared. In this way Hrathen is then presented as the antagonist of the text, yet the reader is directly in his perspective for a third of the narrative. What this allows is for a second, and more "evil" antagonist, Dilaf,[6] to rise up over the course of the novel before his thematic defeat at the hands of all three protagonists, and his literal defeat at the hands of Hrathen, who kills Dilaf to save Sarene. The reader experiences a narrative structure wherein not

---
[6]. A fanatical Derethi zealot who hates Elantris for the city's failure to save his wife years before.

only is evil defeated (in the form of Dilaf) but "evil" (in the form of Hrathen) is convinced to change. As Sarene notes in the final line of the novel, bringing together all of these ideas of good, evil, and the importance of changing narratives:

> When you speak of this man, let it be known that he died in our defense. Let it be said that after all else, Hrathen, gyorn of Shu-Dereth, was not our enemy. He was our savior. (Sanderson, 2005, p. 615)

Elantris is an example of the evolution of the Fantasy genre's representation of evil within the 2000s: the transition into the mind of the villain or antagonist in a way that provides nuance to the internal justification and perspective of a text's version of evil. This allows the reader to experience a shift away from the representation of evil as single dominant ideology towards a more open and diverse perspective. It is this ideological pivot that is emblematic of a contemporary Fantasy text's critique of binary and simple imperial evil.

In the 2010s, Peter V. Brett's *Demon Cycle* (2008-2017) series takes the 2000s' structural positioning of apparent imperial antagonists and adds further layers of nuance. *The Demon Cycle* presents the apparent antagonist as a perspective character, much like *Elantris* does with Hrathen. However, instead of an antagonist who has a change of heart and a heroic moment, Jardir is positioned throughout the series in both the role of antagonist and possible prophesied "hero of destiny". This blend of roles results from the combination of his heroic drive to save the world from the demon plague, tempered by the fact that he attempts to do so via imperial unification through violent religious conversion.

The series goes to great lengths to vilify and demonise Jardir. The series also goes to great lengths to humanise and celebrate Jardir. By juxtaposing two possible hero figures, two "Deliverers" – Jardir and Arlen – *The Demon Cycle* forces the reader to engage with the idea that good and evil are complicated by cultural perspective, and that "defeating evil" in a culturally diverse world means embracing that diversity is a strength. Where *Elantris* lets Empire somewhat recede into the background of the text to foreground its human agents, *The Demon Cycle* provides a more literal and contrasting definition of evil. In this world, every night, literal demons rise from the earth to mindlessly kill anyone they can find. As Leesha's father poignantly notes in the first novel, "Find the worst human being you can, and you'll still find something worse by looking out the window at night" (Brett, 2008, p. 132). The positioning of this undeniably worse evil should call for a unification of humanity but instead serves as a juxtaposition that prompts key questions for the reader: what drives people to kill or abuse each other? How can such acts be justified when there are larger problems to deal with? The series ultimately confronts the reader with the true horror of the situation: that perhaps the monster outside reflects the monster within. Through these questions the text provides a targeted critique of social issues such as gender inequality, racial and religious marginalisation, and, of most relevance to this chapter, of the stagnating and limiting consequences of the imperial imposition of a single dominant ideology.

The first novel, *The Painted Man*[7] (2008) follows a somewhat traditional Fantasy trope of the "ordinary child" journeying towards becoming a hero. Arlen rediscovers a lost weapon that might allow them to fight back against the demons. However, in the last third of the novel, in the wake of what should be a joyous discovery for everyone, Arlen brings his discovery to his friend Jardir. Jardir then betrays Arlen, taking the warded spear for himself, and begins to prepare his people, the Krasians, for The Daylight War in which they convert the North to their religion and way of life in order to then fight the demons united as one people. This first novel

---
[7]. This book is published under the title *The Warded Man* in America.

has three perspective characters and Jardir is not one of them. *The Painted Man* sets up the expectation of Jardir as the clear antagonist. However, the next novel in the series, *The Desert Spear* (2010), devotes the first 200 pages of the novel to Jardir's perspective. It begins with his childhood in Krasia, and moves through the significant moments of his life, culminating in his betrayal of Arlen and self-doubting question: 'How could he stand as tall as Shar'Dama Ka [The Deliverer] if it was atop the body of a friend?' (Brett, 2010, p. 173) Jardir acts in spite of this initial self-doubt, and fails to consider the wider question it in turn begs: how could he be the hero atop the corpse of the whole Northern people's destroyed culture?

Jardir is a brutal man and in many ways a fanatic. However, each encounter he has with a person drives new thinking in him. When he firsts meets Arlen, he is so inspired by Arlen's commitment that he demands to learn Arlen's language, stating that though Arlen will soon learn the Krasian tongue that is 'Not good enough. […] There will be other greenlanders, and I would speak to them, as well' (Brett, 2010, p. 162). When he meets (and falls in love with) the Northerner Leesha, he is driven to read to her of his holy text and discuss their contrasting religions. As Jardir journeys northwards and attempts to convert the "greenlands" to Everam's Light and build his new Empire and new army, his expectations are challenged and his worldview widened.[8] Over the course of the series Jardir shifts from demanding that the entire world bow to his god's light to suing for peace. There is hope right from the start though, as Jardir says to Arlen before the betrayal:

> It seems our cultures are a natural insult to each other […] We must resist the urge to take offense, if we are to continue to learn from each other. (Brett, 2010, p. 167)

---

[8]. Brett here alters the traditional East/West divide by placing the desert in the South. While Eddings presents the East/West as a simplified binary, Brett brings a global awareness to his depiction of these cultural groups, indicating that they are not binarily evil or a faceless, generalised Other.

Brett's work traces the lives of the main characters from childhood into adulthood. This experience of the characters growing up means that their worldview as adults is not just a simply expressed ideology; the reader has direct experience of how and why such a perspective came to be. This allows for not only a more nuanced discussion of differing perspectives, but it also enforces in the reader a careful, repeated practice: seeking understanding of why someone thinks differently to you.

As globalisation continues to rise, and other perspectives begin to pervade Western media in a way that recognises their legitimacy, we see a correlating trend from American authors: a complicating of the antagonist. Where Torak, the Dark Lord, and Hrathen act as avatars of evil (in some sense a static and singular ideology in the shape of a character), Jardir's perspective is given history, context, and perhaps the most real justification: the initially totalising influence of an isolated cultural context altered over time by the influence of family, friends, and loved ones. Where Hrathen disavows his Empire in a way that enables a textual critique of its domineering and erasing practices, Jardir's ideological shift is more complex in the way that, even as he changes, he continues to celebrate his cultural group's thousand years of history. Jardir comes to see, through engagement with the rest of the world, that there are things to be learnt from other cultural groups and that what it means to be Krasian can grow and change without losing their past. The existence of difference does not invalidate their identity. Jardir, as the head of his would-be Empire, can act in a way that fulfils his textual role as hero/Deliverer. He can participate in the defeat of the evil embodied within the Demons. But in the end, having grown and changed, can also deliver them from the "evil" of their assumed imperial mandate. What Jardir's journey challenges is the apparently overlooked issue with the "benevolent Empire" solution championed through the earlier stages of the Fantasy genre.

Daniel M. Markowicz succinctly explains that, for Antonio Gramsci, popular culture is potentially 'counter hegemonic' in the way that 'culture does not merely reflect social realities but is a force actively changing them' (2011, n.p.). It is in this way that the evolution in these depictions of evil becomes socially relevant and potentially powerful as the cultural artefact generates what Gramsci refers to as a 'national-popular' (1985, p. 102). The authors we have selected for examination are those that are popular in the genre; bestsellers and translated worldwide. However, the Fantasy genre itself has exploded in recent years, with an increase in the voices of authors that were traditionally restricted from the ivory towers of publication. As a result, the genre and the dogmas contained within it are shifting and moving away from this imperialist literature as we gain a global awareness. Young asserts that Fantasy: 'is stereotypically – if increasingly inaccurately – White, middle-class, and male' (p. 6). Throughout her book, Young argues that 'Fantasy formed habits of Whiteness in the early life of the genre-culture, and is, in the early decades of the twenty-first century, struggling to break them' (p. 10). There is a growing awareness of the imperialistic underpinnings of Fantasy, which has led to a movement to break away from them. One mode of this involves indigenous authors "writing back" to unpack those early habits of Whiteness and deny the single narrative. Authors such as N. K. Jemisin and Saladin Ahmed are examples of American Fantasy authors who have expanded the remit of the Fantasy genre and Empire to include their own unique cultural perspectives successfully outside of the dominant white male voices. Young notes that:

> Authors who are not indigenous have, in the past decade or so, begun slowly to engage in critical ways with colonisation and imperialism in fantasy. Such moves can be fraught, and risk erasing or ignoring the traumas of the past by seeking to imagine alternative histories, and of committing

inappropriate or counter-productive acts of cultural appropriation when indigenous perspectives or cultures are included in the narrative. (p. 124)

The question then becomes what is the role of those currently and historically dominant white male voices? The texts we have chosen for this chapter perhaps provide an answer to this question. Where indigenous writers outside the current hegemony can bring change through a writing back of their own narratives and perspectives, perhaps the role that white European and American writers can play is a writing from within that perspective that critiques itself. Perhaps those dominant voices can recognise their complicity and through that take on a responsibility to change their habits in a way that then also helps widen the genre in a manner that then aids the inclusion of those indigenous and non-white, non-male authors.

Eddings's *Belgariad* and *Malloreon* depict a more black and white binary, but with problematic nuances of the Western forces of colonisation. Jordan's *Wheel of Time* slowly shifts this ground; while it showcases an idea of "absolute evil," the central protagonist shows the potential to be evil himself.[9] Sanderson's *Elantris* begins a shift to show an antagonist as a point-of-view character; one who moves away from the role of antagonist by the conclusion of the novel, requiring the reader to step into and experience the shift in ideology. Brett's The Demon Cycle completes this trajectory, presenting the apparent antagonist as someone with a fully constructed life and perspective; their motivation moves beyond "evil" as they go about the process of establishing hegemonic rule before widening their perspective and shifting into the role of the hero.

---

[9]. For a longer structural discussion of the potential of the antagonist and protagonist to become each other, see C. Palmer-Patel's upcoming *The Shape of Fantasy*.

In *The Fantasy Tradition in American Literature* (1980), Brian Attebery concludes that the American Fantasy tradition leading up to 1980 showcases 'a certain dimming of the American dream. [...] The American fantasy tradition is important because fantasy is conservative' (p. 186). As our own examination begins where Attebery leaves off, what the literature in the last four decades seems to reveal is in fact a broadening of cultural engagement and a distancing from a limited American ideology defined only by itself: a trend that perhaps should have been expected in a genre devoted to worlds distinctly distant from our own, let alone American ones. As Young summarises, Fantasy:

> has considerable power to dig up long-buried histories of colonisation and imperialism and to challenge the assumptions on which their power structures rely by offering new perspectives. (p. 114)

It will be illuminating to examine the literature of the 2020s to see whether this trend progresses, especially in light of the reversion back towards nationalism in America seen in this current decade alongside the closing of borders in Brexit UK. Will the evolution of imperialism as evil continue to be challenged and contested in Fantasy? Or will the Fantasy genre return to the glorification of nation and Empire?

Bibliography

Attebery, B., 1980. *The Fantasy Tradition in American Literature: From Irving to Le Guin*. Bloomington: Indiana University Press.

Brett, P. V., 2008. *The Painted Man*. London: HarperCollins.

---, 2010. *The Desert Spear*. London: HarperCollins.

Eddings, D., 1984. *Enchanters' End Game*. New York: Del Rey.

---, 1988. *King of the Murgos*. New York: Del Rey.

Gramsci, A., 1985. In D. Forgacs, & Nowell-Smith, G. eds., *Selections from Cultural Writings*. Cambridge, MA: Harvard University Press.

Jordan, R., 1990. *The Great Hunt*. Reprint 1991. New York: Tom Doherty.

---, 1992. *The Shadow Rising*. Reprint 1993. New York: Tom Doherty.

Jordan, R. and Sanderson B., 2009. *The Gathering Storm*. Reprint 2010. New York: Tom Doherty.

Markowicz, D. M., 2011. Gramsci, Antonio. In M. Ryan. ed., *The Encyclopedia of Literary and Cultural Theory*. Hoboken: Wiley. [Online]. Available from: <https://search.credoreference.com/content/entry/wileylitcul/gramsci_antonio/o> [Accessed 19th November 2018]

Mendlesohn, F., 2008. *Rhetorics of Fantasy*. Middletown, Connecticut: Wesleyan University Press.

Said, E. W., 1978. *Orientalism*. Reprint 2012. New York: Vintage.

Sanderson, B., 2005. *Elantris*. Reprint 2011. London: Gollancz.

Young, H., 2016. *Race and Popular Fantasy: Habits of Whiteness*. New York: Routledge.

Yesterday's Tyrant: Evolving Evil in Fantasy Television's Reformed Villains

Katarina O'Dette

Abstract

Fantasy has long represented the struggle between good and evil by personifying evil in its villains. Traditionally, these villains have been depicted as solely evil, presenting a stark dichotomy between good and evil that scholars like Neil Easterbrook refer to as "ethical escapism." However, American fantasy television is rife with reformed villains who transition from evil to good, presenting a more complex relationship between good and evil as writers rehabilitate popular villains to give them greater longevity on television series.

This chapter presents the first study of reformed villains on television, examining four industry-driven textual strategies that evolve them from their narrative functions as evil characters: point-of-view, flashbacks, reform checks, and relationships with protagonists. By putting industrial practices and textual analysis in conversation with character theory by Murray Smith (1995), Carl Plantinga (2010), and Margrethe Bruun Vaage (2016), this chapter examines how television writers strategically shift viewer responses to reformed villains from antipathy to allegiance, focusing on Spike from *Buffy the Vampire Slayer* (1997-2003), Regina Mills/The Evil Queen from *Once Upon a Time* (2011-2018), King Richard from *Galavant* (2015-2016), and Michael from *The Good Place* (2016-Present).

Scrutinising these strategies reveals a disconnect between how viewers perceive reform in narrative television and in real life. Feelings of sympathy towards reformed villains are more crucial than moral actions in convincing viewers that these characters have changed, raising questions about whether it is possible for viewers to ally themselves with a reformed villain who is unsympathetic but equally reformed.

*

Though moral philosophers debate whether it is appropriate to label people "evil", fantasy has long represented the struggle between good and evil by personifying evil in its villains. Characters are considered an effective way to address evil because they give the notoriously convoluted concept concrete form, and evil provides characters with their narrative function. While an antagonist may simply oppose the protagonist's goal, villains violate or threaten dominant social views of ethical behaviour, thereby motivating the protagonist to work against them to protect society (John, 2001, p. 49). Villains labelled as "evil" magnify this threat, as they have fewer qualms about taking ethically questionable actions and may even gain pleasure from doing so. Evil characters serve crucial thematic and narrative functions, allowing writers to explore evil and providing valuable conflict.

However, this portrayal of good and evil as a dichotomy is often perceived negatively. Scholars like Neil Easterbrook (2005, p. 260) refer to these "cartoonish clashes of good and evil" as "ethical escapism". Adam Morton (2004 cited Cole, 2006, p. 57) expands:

> We prefer to understand evil in terms of archetypal horrors, fictional villains, and deep viciousness, rather than to strain our capacities for intuitive understanding towards ... the difficult truth that people much like us perform acts that we find unimaginably awful ...

Scholars like Brian Attebery are more positive, describing modern fantasy characters as a dialogue between their narrative function and their unique personalities (1992, p. 73). The extended narratives permitted by serialized American television series are particularly suited for this dialogue, with the industry's practices providing opportunities to directly confront and evolve villains away from their initial narrative functions.

This chapter examines four of fantasy television's reformed villains: Spike from *Buffy the Vampire Slayer* (1997-2003), Regina Mills/the Evil Queen from *Once Upon a Time* (2011-2018), King Richard from *Galavant* (2015-2016), and Michael from *The Good Place* (2016-Present). Just as labelling a person "evil" is troublesome to some moral philosophers, the designation of any particular character as evil can be controversial. The chosen villains are presented to viewers with the intention of being read as evil, allowing themselves to be described as evil by others and, in some cases, even branding themselves as such. Viewers are encouraged to perceive them with moral disgust, as three casually murder innocents and the fourth gleefully tortures humans. Regina and Richard are introduced to their audiences with the respective titles Evil Queen and evil King. Spike and Michael are demons; it could be argued that human ethics do not apply to them, but there are, equally, arguments from theistic moral philosophers that only demons are capable of evil. However, this chapter's focus is not on whether these characters are evil, but on the industry-driven textual strategies that evolve them away from their narrative functions as evil villains.

In spite of how prevalent they are, there is little academic work on television villains. In television studies, character is largely discussed as an element of performance (Mittell, 2015, p. 118). Due to the recent trend of American antihero series, the most researched televisual character is the antihero, with Alberto García (2016), Margrethe Bruun Vaage (2016), and Jason Mittell (2015) examining how these characters are portrayed and retain viewer appeal. Although there are substantial differences between how reformed villains and antiheroes are portrayed, research on these morally complex characters provides a starting point for reformed villains.

The prevalence of reformed villains is partially due to the influence actors can have on television writing. *Galavant*'s violent, petty King Richard was intended to be the first season's villain until Timothy Omundson was cast in the role. The writers realised that Omundson's strength was portraying loveable and goofy; in writing to his strengths, they changed the king into a sympathetic, and eventually heroic, character (Caffrey, 2016). When the vampire Spike was introduced in *Buffy*'s second season, he was intended to be a short-term antagonist who would be killed after a few episodes; however, actor James Marsters portrayed the character with a sympathetic charisma that caused the fans to clamour for more Spike and the writers to change course (Lavery, 2004, p. 32). To justify keeping a vampire alive on a series about a vampire slayer, the writers had to evolve his role: from evil villain to begrudging antihero to (semi-)honourable martyr. This need to reform villains who outlive their initial arc is due in part to the prevalence of *Buffy*'s 'Big Bad' trope. The 'Big Bad' is the main villain for one season, who changes to give each season a unique narrative focus and to avoid the repetition of sustaining the same villain for an entire series. Every series discussed in this chapter utilises the trope, and therefore needs to rehabilitate popular villains – if characters can only be villains for a single season but writers and fans want the characters to remain, villains need to evolve into new roles. If actors other than Omundson and Marsters had been cast, Richard and Spike may never have reformed. Actors are often either responsible for a reformed villain's arc or key to its success, with actors like Lana Parrilla (Regina) and Ted Danson (Michael) critically acclaimed for their complex, sympathetic performances.

This reform occurs through a steady process of accruing viewer alignment with villains over the course of a series. Murray Smith (1995, p. 84) defines alignment as the structures put in place that allow viewers to experience a character's thoughts, feelings, and experiences. Television is uniquely suited to this: García (2016, p. 53) notes that "expanding a story over many hours allows the construction of an emotional structure that 'forces' us to sympathize with protagonists who are ... morally contradictory". Extensive screen time provides viewers with abundant access to reformed villains' perspectives and therefore ample opportunities for alignment. This chapter identifies four strategies used by television writers to align viewers with reforming villains: point-of-view, flashbacks, reform checks, and character relationships.

Point-of-View and Contrast Characters

Actors' contracts specify how many episodes they will appear in, forcing writers to create plotlines in which even main cast members have a reduced or no role. These scenes or episodes, presented from the perspectives of non-protagonists, allow viewers to align with these characters. When the perspective is a villain's, writers draw on what Vaage (2016, p. 75) identifies as "our 'natural instinct' to begin empathizing with characters we see trying to do something". Viewers may not want the villain to succeed in the overall narrative, but for a scene or episode, viewers will be inclined to root for a character when they watch from his perspective as he attempts to accomplish something.

For instance, at the end of *The Good Place*'s first season, the four protagonists, Eleanor, Chidi, Jason, and Tahani, who had believed that they were in the Good Place (a nondenominational afterlife), discover that they are actually in the Bad Place being used to torture one another. The season ends with their neighbourhood being rebooted and the protagonists' memories wiped. In the next season's first three episodes, rather than continuing the story from the protagonists' point-of-view, the writers put viewers in the point-of-view of Michael: an immortal demon, the protagonists' chief torturer, and their neighbourhood's architect. Viewers are aligned with Michael in these episodes, conflicted between wanting the protagonists to succeed and wanting Michael, whose efforts they are most directly observing, to succeed.

Crucial to this warring is what Vaage (2016, p. 127) terms

a contrast character: an "unsympathetic [character] with the main function of making the antiheroes morally preferable". The second season ('Everything is Great!', 2017) opens with a discussion between Michael and Shawn, Michael's demon boss, about the new reboot:

> Michael: I won't let you down.
> Shawn: I think you will. I think this entire project of yours is stupid and doomed to fail. I think you're going to be retired, eliminated from existence and burned on the surface of a billion suns. … you and your cockamamy experiment will go down in history as colossal failures.

This first scene is crucial for Michael's arc as it foregrounds the season: viewers know the consequences of Michael's failure and are invited to consider that Michael is, at the very least, less evil than Shawn. Viewers simultaneously want Michael to fail because they want to protect the protagonists and want him to succeed because they do not want him destroyed by a demon crueller than he is. When they experience the series from the protagonists' point-of-view, viewers perceive Michael as the biggest threat; when placed in the villain's point-of-view, they are encouraged to align with the lesser of two evils.

Contrast characters do not have to be the greater of two evils to be perceived as such by the chosen point-of-view. In *Galavant*, King Richard is initially portrayed as tormenting the poor and having people executed who inconvenience him. As the season progresses, his wife Madalena calls him unlovable, publicly bullies him, and openly cheats on him. In the face of Madalena's cruelty, viewers are invited to sympathise with Richard: while they may not support his larger goals (as he plots to murder the protagonist, Galavant), they are encouraged to appreciate that he lacks Madalena's maliciousness. The series portrays Madalena as if she is the only cruel one by focusing on Richard's point-of-view and hurt feelings rather than on his victim's deaths or their families' grief: committing murder is one thing, but being mean is worse. Ultimately, Madalena becomes the season's real Big Bad, usurping Richard's throne and attempting to have him killed: Madalena takes both his crown and his narrative role.

Contrast characters can trigger the villain's reform by usurping his narrative role and forcing him to find a new one. Spike is introduced in *Buffy* as if he will be the second season's Big Bad, but in a mid-season twist, Angel, a protagonist and ensouled vampire, loses his soul and reverts to his demon self, Angelus. Angelus's penchant for evil and destructive actions increasingly alienates Spike, and when Angelus's plan turns apocalyptic, Spike switches sides, explaining that, "I like this world. You've got dog racing, Manchester United. And you've got people. Billions of people walking around like Happy Meals with legs" ('Becoming: Part 2', 1998). Spike does not help the protagonists save the world because he wants to save lives: he does it so that he can continue killing. But he still plays a crucial role in stopping the apocalypse. Contrast characters can make villains more palatable just by having motivations that are slightly less evil, or at least motivations more aligned with the protagonists'. While this is not a moral victory for Spike, the fact that he temporarily helps save the world predisposes viewers and protagonists to align more permanently with him later when he reforms.

As the series continues, Angelus serves as an important comparison to Spike, who is perceived by viewers with more forgiveness because, unlike Angelus, he is capable of heroic actions without a soul. Spike eventually joins the protagonists to save human lives, something Angel only does when ensouled. Contrast characters illuminate the limits (however paltry) of a reforming villain's evil by temporarily giving the villain a narrative function other than evil. Presented with his point-of-view, viewers are given a chance to align with, root for, and even sympathise with him, which makes them more susceptible to accepting his later character arc.

Flashbacks and Moral Luck

Some series like *Once* use flashbacks in their core structure, giving every episode a point-of-view character and revealing parts of his past in flashbacks. Other series, like *Buffy*, *The Good Place*, and *Galavant*, incorporate flashbacks more casually. In both cases, flashbacks can be crucial for generating sympathy for a reforming villain, often by casting the reforming villain's initial turn towards evil in a sympathetic light. Carl Plantinga (2010, p. 41) argues that viewers grant sympathy, not "for moral good behaviour", but when they believe characters are "in danger", "suffering or bereaved", or being "treated unfairly". Viewers sympathize with characters not because they are good, but because they are victims. Flashbacks that portray villains as victims play with the philosophical concept of moral luck. As Phillip Cole (2006, pp. 146-149) summarises:

> It is not that they were compelled to do [dreadful things] by some overwhelming force, but that background factors came together so that they made a particular choice which, if things had been different, they would not have made. …
> if we genuinely only hold people morally responsible for their motives and intentions, then all people with the same motives and intentions are equally praiseworthy or blameworthy. But in practice … we praise or blame people for what they do, in which case we have to face the existence of moral luck, because what people do or don't do is importantly, though not completely, determined by factors beyond their control…

Moral luck does not excuse the evil actions of reforming villains, but rather suggests that their evil narrative role was the result of bad luck. Flashbacks that reveal a villain's tragic or unfair backstory make viewers extend sympathy to him, as they see his evil nature as the result of unfairness rather than as an innate quality. In fact, flashbacks often establish the opposite: Spike, Regina, and Richard are shown as having been sweet, kind, and, in Spike and Richard's cases, bumbling – traits far removed from the murderous villains they become.

Flashbacks that play with moral luck portray an aspect of the character other than their narrative function, emphasizing that he was warped into villainy by circumstance. *Once*'s Regina is initially portrayed as a single-minded villain who seeks revenge against Snow White. When the writers finally reveal Regina's childhood in flashbacks, viewers see that she was raised by a controlling mother, Cora, who abused Regina with her magic. Regina's father, though loving and kind, never stopped his wife or protected his daughter. The only people Regina felt loved and supported by were her friend Snow White and the stable hand, Daniel, Regina's secret lover. In 'The Stable Boy' (2012), Snow White finds out about Regina's relationship with Daniel and tells Cora, in spite of Regina's insistence that she keep it secret. Disapproving of the match, Cora murders Daniel, causing Regina to lose both her lover and her friend, as Regina's trust in Snow White is destroyed. Grieving, betrayed, and alone, Regina starts on a quest for revenge against Snow White that leads her to become the Evil Queen. By showing viewers her backstory, the series argues that Regina's evil was not a natural part of her. Rather, the bad luck of loneliness and betrayal at the hands of others corrupted Regina into becoming temporarily evil, and her later reform course-corrects her back to her natural heroism. Regina's evil is not portrayed as a representation of who she was, but rather as the bad moral luck of who the people around her were.

Moral luck is further emphasised by the serial structure of television narratives, as series can put characters into similar situations and test whether their actions will change. After four seasons of Regina reforming, her new lover, Robin, is murdered by the season's Big Bad the same way that Cora killed Daniel.

The series puts Regina in the same position she was in when she initially turned toward evil, causing viewers, her friends, and her son, Henry, to worry that she may relapse. However, there is a key difference: Regina now has people who love and support her. As she explains, "If I revert, I lose everyone I love. Henry, my friends, everyone. ... it's a simple choice" ('Only You', 2016). With a change in her luck, she resists evil. Serial narratives test the role that moral luck played in the reformed villain's initial villainhood: seeing the same plot point occur under different circumstances of moral luck allows viewers to confirm that Regina's luck was responsible for her previous turn to evil and to feel comfortable aligning with her.

Viewers are not asked to consider moral luck in the opposite direction. A crucial component of Michael's reform on *The Good Place* is the specific people he is assigned to design a torture neighbourhood for. Eleanor has a strong sense of when she is being taken advantage of, which helps her figure out that she and her fellow protagonists are not actually in the Good Place 802 times. No matter how much Michael plans, he cannot prevent Eleanor from realizing the truth, which eventually forces him to work with her and her friends to find a way to escape from Shawn and get to the real Good Place. Fellow protagonist Chidi, a moral philosophy professor, also proves crucial to Michael's reform, as he gives the demon lessons on ethics to help him reform. If it were not for Eleanor figuring out Michael's scheme and for Chidi's profession and classes, Michael would likely never have reformed. However, the series never asks viewers to acknowledge how crucial the luck of his being assigned to torture these particular people is to his eventual moral transformation. Moral luck is used to create sympathy, not to detract from it.

Characters who ask viewers to consider the role of luck in their moral downfall are viewed negatively. Regina's half-sister, the Wicked Witch Zelena, is shown in flashbacks to have embraced evil because she was ignored by both their mother and their magic tutor in favour of her sister. Zelena frequently mentions her sister's special treatment to excuse her own actions, prompting contempt from the protagonists when Zelena refuses to commit to reforming. After two seasons, Regina snaps: "you've had a second chance and a second second chance. You can't keep painting yourself as a victim. It's absurd" ('Siege Perilous', 2015). While viewers are invited to view Zelena's backstory with sympathy, they are cautioned not to extend this sympathy towards her evil nature if she asks them to. Moral luck can only serve as an explanation for a villain's turn to evil if he does not ask viewers to view it as such.

Reform Checks and New Identities

Reform checks[1] are crucial moments where the reforming villain's past makes a reappearance, usually either in the form of a victim who now seeks revenge or a fellow villain who the reforming villain used to engage in villainous activities with. These reform checks ostensibly force reforming villains to take stock of how much they have reformed, to reflect on how evil they used to be, and to test their resolve. But while the protagonists and the reforming villain struggle with the moral complexity of supporting a character with an evil past, viewers are usually encouraged to view him positively as they appreciate how far he has come.

Writers carefully curate the parts of a reforming villain's past that he will atone for, which is particularly useful when the character was initially intended to be an unreformed villain and now needs to be course-corrected. In *Galavant*'s first episode ('Pilot', 2015), Richard sings about his love of "genocidal

---

[1]. Inspiration for this term name comes from Vaage's antihero-specific 'reality check' (2013, p. 220), but reform checks for reforming villains and reality checks for antiheroes have opposite goals and utilise different tactics to reach those goals.

war", takes over a foreign kingdom, has his chef killed because his mutton was too rare, and commands his guards to make the deposed queen watch her husband's execution. However, due to Omundson's performance, the writers shifted their depiction of Richard from murderous to sweet, bumbling, and incapable of leadership. In the second season, when Richard returns to his home kingdom, he finds that his former subjects have dismantled his castle and instituted a quasi-democracy. They claim that he was a neglectful king and happily throw his failings in his face but never mention his murderous deeds: the episode simply portrays Richard as inept. He describes himself as "a tyrant and a terrible leader who hosted baby fights, which I now realize is weird and not that entertaining, even after the addition of the cobra…" ('Aw, Hell, the King', 2016). The focus, particularly since the series is a comedy, is on jokes about Richard's terrible leadership and poor judgement, rather than on his murderous actions. His past is kept vague and his silliness emphasised instead, such that by the end of the series, his former 'villain' status is reduced to a punchline: "Seems like just yesterday, I was the worst tyrant this land has ever seen. That was weird" ('Do the D'DEW', 2016). By focusing the reform checks on Richard's leadership abilities, the series avoids needing to have Richard make amends for his casual murders and his suppressed love of genocide.

Although many decisions about what past actions a reform check will avoid addressing are specific to the character, some actions are more systematically avoided. As Vaage has discussed (2016), characters who viewers are meant to align with may commit murder, but they rarely commit rape, as viewers perceive rape as less forgivable. Richard summarises this attitude: "I'm not an animal. I mean, sure, I'll kidnap a woman and force her to marry me, but after that, I'm all about a woman's rights" ('It's All in the Executions', 2015). This does not mean that reformed villains cannot have committed rape, but that it is not depicted as such. In *Once*, flashbacks reveal that Regina took the Huntsman's heart from his chest and commanded him to her bedchamber ('The Heart is a Lonely Hunter', 2011). In the series' mythology, removing his heart does not kill him, but gives her total control over his actions. She strips him of the ability to consent and engages in a sexual relationship with him for thirty years, but the series never uses the term rape. Her taking his heart is depicted as generically evil, without examining the specifics. The scene concentrates on his horror at losing his ability to feel rather than at losing his ability to consent, and though their relationship is referenced in later episodes, his lack of consent is not. While there are numerous reform checks for murders Regina has committed, there are never reform checks that address rape, because rape is never acknowledged as one of Regina's evil actions.

Spike is an exception to this avoidance of rape, but his exception proves another rule about how series handle reform checks: separating the villain who committed the immoral action from the reformed villain. After two seasons of reforming, Spike attempts to rape Buffy in a desperate attempt to convince her to revive their former sexual relationship. His horror at what he has done motivates him to complete a quest to restore his soul so that he can ensure that he treats Buffy well. There are debates in *Buffy* scholarship about the impact that his restored soul has on his morality and his culpability for his previous actions, but Buffy herself mentions his soul multiple times in later episodes as an explanation for why Spike can be trusted to help the protagonists, insisting that the pre-soul Spike "doesn't exist anymore" and that "he wouldn't hurt anyone anymore because he has a soul now" ('Lies My Parents Told Me', 2003). Regardless of whether the soul has actually fundamentally changed his character such that it divorces him from the evil actions he committed pre-soul, several characters treat him as if it does. Even Robin, a character who seeks vengeance against Spike for murdering his mother, uses a hypnosis trigger to bring back Spike as he was before his soul and reform arc: as Robin puts it, "… I don't wanna kill you, Spike. I wanna kill the monster who took my mother away." ('Lies My Parents Told Me', 2003). Though Robin still holds Spike accountable for his pre-reform actions, he treats villainous Spike and reformed Spike as different characters. This allows the series to be more honest about Spike's past without losing viewer alignment: his rape attempt is acknowledged because *Buffy*'s mythology permits characters and viewers to believe he is no longer responsible for his pre-soul actions.

This language is common during reform checks, with protagonists insisting that the reformed villains "have changed" such that their past villainous selves and their new reformed selves are different characters. In *Once*, Regina is referred to as Regina when characters discuss her reformed actions and the Evil Queen when they discuss her villainous actions. When new characters force reform checks because of their past experiences with Regina, the protagonists focus on convincing them that they are mistakenly holding Regina accountable for the Evil Queen's actions. The series eventually acknowledges that it has been separating the villain and the reformed villain with a plotline in which Regina removes the Evil Queen from herself, giving her past self a physical form. Regina is ultimately forced to accept that the Evil Queen is a part of her; however, the Evil Queen maintains a separate physical existence after the plotline concludes, and the story arc focuses more on Regina accepting that she was the Evil Queen than it is about having her confront her evil actions. While reform checks appear to be about confronting reforming villains with their past, tactics like dividing the pre- and post-reformed identities and ignoring past actions reveal that reform checks are functionally about distancing villains from their past and confirming for viewers that there are no ethical questions raised by their alignment with reformed villains.

Relationships and Beyond

Romantic, platonic, and familial relationships hold a key position in much of American narrative television, particularly given the popularity of ensemble casts. Character dynamics foster viewer investment; indeed, viewers may continue watching a series long after they lose investment in the plot because they are invested in a particular relationship. Producers view relationships as crucial to a series' appeal; therefore, relationships between villains and protagonists can be crucial to villains' reforms. As the former antagonists negotiate a new role in the narrative, they must also negotiate a new relationship with the protagonists, which can motivate their reform.

The main motivation for Regina's reform arc is her familial relationship with her son. In the first season, Henry is the only person who matters to her. Her most sympathetic moments (outside of flashbacks) come from her love for and protective behaviour toward Henry. At the end of season one, when she is revealed as the Evil Queen, the town turns against her. It is only at Henry's insistence that the protagonists protect her from the townspeople. But Henry issues an ultimatum: Regina can only see him if she stops being evil. After a season of relapses, Regina finally unites with the protagonists over a common goal when Henry is kidnapped. During their mission to rescue Henry, Regina and the protagonists shift from a forced partnership to genuine friendships, which only strengthen as they fight a string of Big Bads as the seasons progress. Regina's familial relationship with Henry serves as her initial protection from the protagonists and as her motivation for reforming, and then provides the impetus for new relationships with the protagonists, which supports her transition to heroism. Love is so vital to Regina's reform that, when she gives her villainous past corporeal form, she ultimately defeats the Evil Queen by holding their hearts together and transferring some of her goodness into the Evil Queen's heart. The form that her goodness takes is crucial: Regina gives the Evil Queen "some of my love. Love from Henry and Robin and the people I care most about" ('Page 23', 2017). The writers directly equate relationships and love with Regina's goodness, and love immediately reforms this second Evil Queen.

Spike's reform arc is driven by his romantic relationship with Buffy. After several seasons of villainy, Spike only begins changing in the fifth season, when he develops feelings for Buffy. This leads him to selfish heroic actions meant to woo her and, eventually, to a selfless action: allowing himself to be brutally tortured rather than divulge information that would put Buffy's sister in danger. This heroism continues even when Buffy dies in the season finale, with Spike helping her friends fight demons and protecting her sister. When Buffy is brought back from the dead, she and Spike have a brief sexual relationship, but after it ends, Spike attempts to rape her and, horrified with himself, restores his soul. He does not attempt to resume their relationship but does continue to help the protagonists fight the new Big Bad, putting his life on the line. Spike's feelings for Buffy serve as an initial motivation to change his behaviour, but his reform continues even when he knows they will not be together. His feelings cause him to fight to restore his soul, which provides him with a more permanent moral compass than his romantic feelings. Relationships with protagonists can operate as gateways to reform.

Relationships[2] are most effective at reforming when they eventually shift the reformed villain's motivation to a personal instinct rather than a particular relationship. While Spike is obsessed with Buffy, he acts heroically so she will find him appealing, but Buffy and the viewers are not invited to consider him heroic until his motivation expands beyond wooing her. Regina begins to be perceived as heroic when her actions are

---

[2]. These relationships have to be the "correct" relationships. When reforming villains have strong relationships with other villains, they are lured back to villainy.

aimed not simply at protecting Henry or her relationship with him, but at permanently improving her wider community. Michael is literally instructed by protagonists on how to reform with Chidi's ethics lessons: the fact that relationships with protagonists instruct reforming villains on how to evolve away from evil becomes text. As a result of Chidi's lessons, Michael eventually tries to change the afterlife, not just for his friends, but for everyone. With their goodness no longer tied to particular relationships, reforming villains become heroes in viewers' and characters' eyes and can make wider, positive changes.

Conclusion

These four strategies – point-of-view, flashbacks, reform checks, and relationships – shift viewers' relationship with reformed villains from alignment to allegiance. Allegiance, according to Plantinga (2010, p. 36), is the spectator response elicited by alignment. While viewers can be aligned with evil characters without supporting or liking them, allegiance signifies a bond between spectator and character that is "built through the course of the narrative, and typically result[s] from several encounters with a character" (Plantinga, 2010, p. 44). These four strategies align viewers with reformed villains and repeatedly create feelings of sympathy, which accumulate to more permanently change their responses to these characters. Viewers become allied with reformed villains after being shown through point-of-view that there are greater evils, through flashbacks that a character's evil was a corruption of his natural goodness, through reform checks that he has become a different person, and through relationships that he is capable of love and heroism.

However, this representation of reformed evil in fantasy television is not reflective of how people think about evil in the real world. Vaage (2016, pp. 1-2) refers to this as "fictional relief": the process by which the "fictional status of these series deactivates rational, deliberate moral evaluation, making the spectator rely on moral emotions and intuitions that are relatively easy to manipulate with narrative strategies." The narrative strategies used to reform villains are effective because they are fictional, while in real life, viewers would be significantly less likely to accept an equivalent strategy. We do not view people who commit evil actions sympathetically purely because there are worse people. We do not forgive mass murderers because they have tragic backstories. We do not believe that rehabilitated criminals are literally different people than they used to be, even if we appreciate how they have reformed. Reformed villains reflect how narratives can convince viewers into an allegiance with characters they would not ordinarily support: reformed villains may reveal more about how narratives can utilise medium-specific strategies to manipulate viewers than they do about evil.

Reform becomes a careful public relations campaign run by the production team. In fantasy television, the series' mythology is often recruited in this campaign as writers may change aspects of it, such as how souls affect vampires in *Buffy*, or introduce new ideas, like Regina's ability to give her evil self corporeal form, in order to convince viewers that a character has evolved. Point-of-view demonstrates how flimsy viewers' reasons for supporting characters can be. Moral luck, and the careful caveats to when viewers are invited to consider the role it plays, demonstrates this campaign's limits. Reform checks demonstrate the careful control a series exercises over what aspects of reform viewers are invited to consider. Relationships demonstrate how swayed viewers can be by relationships with characters they trust. This is not to say that reformed villains are not reformed: all four considered here transition from antagonists to protagonists, and their respective narratives treat them as reformed. Whether or not they have been reformed in a manner which viewers would find plausible in real life, these characters highlight ways in which television viewers are trained to respond to ideas of evil, sympathy, and reform, and how reformed villains are shaped by industrial practices and norms.

Reformed villains are not simply an updated portrayal of the ethical escapism Easterbrook worries about: viewers are encouraged to sympathize, align, and ally themselves with characters whose evil actions they have witnessed extensively over hours of screen time. Reformed villains help collapse the gap that Morton is concerned about audiences perceiving between "fictional villains" and "people much like us", and spark a conversation about what viewers will forgive and under what conditions reform is possible. However, the strategies outlined in this chapter raise another question: can viewers forgive a reformed contrast character whose evil was not influenced by moral luck, whose past is presented without any restrictions, whose villainous self is not divided from his reformed self, and who has no positive relationship with protagonists? Put simply, could viewers accept a reformed character who embraces morally good behaviour but does not engage their sympathies? Or does television teach us that sympathy is a prerequisite for forgiving evil?

Bibliography

Attebery, B., 1992. *Strategies of fantasy*. Bloomington, IN: Indiana University Press.

'Aw, Hell, The King', 2016. *Galavant*, Season 2, episode 1, ABC, 10 January.

'Becoming: Part 2', 1998. *Buffy the Vampire Slayer*, Season 2, episode 22, WB, 19 May.

Caffrey, D., 2016. *Galavant*'s Timothy Omundson on musicals, petty tyrants, and Frank Turner. *The A.V Club* [online], 31 Jan. Available at <http://www.avclub.com/article/galavants-timothy-omundson-musicals-petty-tyrants--231444> [Accessed 12 July 2017].

Cole, P., 2006. *The myth of evil*. Edinburgh: Edinburgh University Press.

'Do the D'DEW', 2016. *Galavant*, Season 2, episode 8, ABC, 24 January.

Easterbrook, N., 2005. Ethics. In: G. Westfahl, ed., *The Greenwood encyclopedia of science fiction and fantasy: themes, works, and wonders*. London: Greenwood Press, pp. 258-260.

'Everything is Great!', 2017. *The Good Place*, Season 2, episode 1, NBC, 20 September.

García, A. N., 2016. Moral emotions, antiheroes and the limits of allegiance. In: A. N. García, ed., *Emotions in contemporary TV series*. London: Palgrave Macmillan, pp. 52-70.

'The Heart is a Lonely Hunter', 2011. *Once Upon a Time*, Season 1, episode 7, ABC, 11 December.

'It's All in the Executions', 2015. *Galavant*, Season 1, episode 8, ABC, 25 January.

John, J., 2001. *Dickens's villains: Melodrama, character, popular culture*. Oxford: Oxford University Press.

Lavery, D., 2004. *Buffy the Vampire Slayer*. In: G. Creeber, ed., *Fifty Key Television Programmes*, London: Bloomsbury Academic, pp. 31-35.

'Lies My Parents Told Me', 2003. *Buffy the Vampire Slayer*, Season 7, episode 17, UPN, 25 March.

Mittell, J., 2015. *Complex TV: The poetics of contemporary television storytelling*. London: New York University Press.

'Only You', 2016. *Once Upon a Time*, Season 5, episode 22, ABC, 15 May.

'Page 23', 2017. *Once Upon a Time*, Season 6, episode 14, ABC, 26 March.

'Pilot', 2015. *Galavant*, Season 1, episode 1, ABC, 4 January.

Plantinga, C., 2010. "I followed the rules, and they all loved you more": Moral judgment and attitudes toward fictional characters in film. *Midwest Studies in Philosophy*, 34(1), pp. 34-51.

'Siege Perilous', 2015. *Once Upon a Time*, Season 5, episode 3, ABC, 11 October.

Smith, M., 1995. *Engaging characters: Fiction, emotion and the cinema*. Oxford: Clarendon Press.

'The Stable Boy', 2012. *Once Upon a Time*, Season 1, episode 18, ABC, 1 April.

Vaage, M. B., 2013. Fictional reliefs and reality checks. *Screen*, 54(2), pp. 218-237.

Vaage, M. B., 2016. *The antihero in American television*. London: Routledge.

Spring Again: The Problem of Evil and the End of Winter in C.S. Lewis's *Narnia*

Octavia Cade

Abstract

In *The Chronicles of Narnia* by C.S. Lewis, evil is perceived as directly resulting from personal choice. Each individual is solely responsible for their own moral decisions, and these decisions both impact the continuing ethical development of the self and influence how the individual addresses the problem of evil. This is particularly well illustrated in the case of Edmund Pevensie, and this paper argues that it is his willingness to accept and atone for the evil within himself that directly leads to the end of the enchanted winter imposed on Narnia. In this sense, evil is not only present within the individual, but is externalised in the land that that individual inhabits.

*

In his children's series *The Chronicles of Narnia*, C.S. Lewis portrays evil as a personal dilemma, and the problem of evil as one of individual capacity and responsibility. This holds for all of the child characters at the centre of the narrative, irrespective of whether their experience of evil is minor temptation or gross monstrosity. Each child has a choice, and in each case poor behaviour requires an honest acknowledgement of both that behaviour and that choice before amends can be made.

This theme of personal responsibility is threaded through the entire series. In *Prince Caspian*, for example, Lucy catches sight of Aslan in the distance, but when her siblings don't believe that she has seen the lion, she succumbs to peer pressure and follows them as they go in the other direction, "crying bitterly" (2001a, p. 141), instead of going towards Aslan as she knew she should. This proves to be the wrong decision, as she finds when she eventually does meet with him and has to explain her inaction. "But it wasn't my fault anyway, was it?" she argues, blaming her siblings for her own choice. "How could I – I couldn't have left the others and come up to you alone, how could I? Don't look at me like that… oh well, I suppose I could" (2001a, p. 155).

As Lucy discovers, the responsibility for her actions is hers alone, and she cannot transfer it to her siblings, no matter how sensible or understandable it is for her to go along with them. There are no acceptable excuses for dodging. In Narnia, nothing ever excuses an individual from personal responsibility; their moral choices are theirs alone. The burden of this responsibility is heightened due to a perceived moral domino effect:

> Lewis's concept of the central self affected one way or another by every moral choice, implies a kind of moral momentum. Every good choice strengthens one's inner resolve to make another good choice next time, while every bad choice leaves one inclined to further bad choices down the road. (Downing, 2005, p. 93)

But if each moral choice affects the individual, making it easier or more difficult for them to engage productively with the problem of evil in future, their choices also affect the world around them. This is particularly well illustrated by Lucy's brother Edmund, whose escalating series of positive moral choices are equally influential, not only for his personal character, but for Narnia itself. His redemption is the direct cause of the destruction of the endless winter plaguing that land – although a confusion of prophecies makes this moral allegory less than obvious. Misunderstanding the Beavers' prophecies in *The Lion, the Witch, and the Wardrobe* sees Aslan credited with ending winter in Narnia – mistakenly so.

Pinning Down Prophecy and the Problem of Evil

As a narrative tool, prophecy is not always straightforward. It can be multilayered or deceptive; a direct reference to narrative or an abstract symbolism, depending on the needs of the author. This adaptability is shown in the first and most complex of the Beavers' prophecies, where the surface meaning, while plausible enough, is also too simplistic a reading:

Wrong will be right, when Aslan comes in sight,
At the sound of his roar, sorrows will be no more,
When he bares his teeth, winter meets its death,
And when he shakes his mane, we shall have spring again.
(2001c, p. 88)

The second and third lines can be more or less explained as a literal reference to narrative. Aslan's roar upon his resurrection from the Stone Table cannot be said to take away the sorrow of Susan and Lucy at watching his death (their previous romp in a "happy laughing heap" (2001c, p. 177) appears to do that well enough) but it certainly marks it, and is close enough. An alternative interpretation can be read in Aslan arriving in time to bolster Peter's army in their fight against the White Witch: "Then with a roar that shook all Narnia from the western lamppost to the shores of the eastern sea the great beast flung himself upon the White Witch" (2001c, pp. 190-191). Similarly, the third line can also be interpreted as Aslan killing the White Witch, who enchanted Narnia so that it experienced eternal winter – and yet this interpretation conflicts with the second prophecy.

When Adam's flesh and Adam's bone
Sits at Cair Paravel in throne,
The evil time will be over and done. (2001c, p. 90)

Mr. Beaver augments this with a third prophecy: "when two Sons of Adam and Two Daughters of Eve sit in those four thrones, then it will be the end not only of the White Witch's reign but of her life…" (2001c, p. 92). Yet according to the first prophecy, "winter meets its death" (with the implication being the White Witch is defeated, and her enchantment on the land is broken) through Aslan alone. If the "evil time" and the end of the Witch's reign are conflated with the end of winter, then all the Pevensie children as well as Aslan are needed to fulfil the three interwoven prophecies.

The important word here is *all*. All four thrones must be filled. Peter, Susan and Lucy are insufficient without their brother. Should Edmund be killed by the White Witch, or stay by her side in a continued betrayal of his siblings, the four thrones would not be filled, and the "evil time" would not be over. If all the prophecies are to be taken together and equally trusted, then Peter, Susan and Lucy together with Aslan are still insufficient to counter the Witch's winter as long as Edmund is absent.

Returning to the first prophecy, we can see that the first and final lines are a little more obscure. Wrongs are manifestly not made right at the mere appearance of Aslan. His presence is a mechanism that aids others in righting the wrong of endless winter, but he is either incapable of – or unwilling to – take the entire responsibility upon himself (else the children's presence as required by the second and third prophecies would be entirely unnecessary). After all, if all that was needed was his appearance, the importance of individual choice as it relates to the problem of evil in Narnia would be significantly undermined; the inhabitants of that land would merely be required to wait for his arrival instead of engaging in the choice to resist evil themselves. As such, the mere sight of him is absolutely not enough to undo Edmund's betrayal, or the acts of the White Witch. These wrongs require actions to repair them – but again, this line can be interpreted with an amount of poetic license, given that Aslan's arrival is often a catalyst for action.

But the final line – "And when he shakes his mane, we shall have spring again" – can that truly be said to be poetic license as well? If the prophecies are broadly true, and there is no reason for readers to think that they are not, then perhaps that final line is purely symbolic, with no direct correspondence to narrative. If Aslan "shaking his mane" was by itself sufficient to end winter and usher in spring, it seems inexcusable that he would let Narnia suffer for as long as it did – his last visit being "long ago, nobody can say when" (2001c, p. 90). The Pevensie children filling the seats at Cair Paravel must therefore be a necessary condition that prompts his presence – and of the four children, it is holdout Edmund who is the most critical. The importance of his presence can be illustrated by comparing Edmund's fall from grace with his sister Susan's.

Spring Again: Rehabilitation and the End of Winter

Initially a rather unpleasant boy – he is described by his own brother as being a "poisonous little beast" (2001c, p. 65) – Edmund's betrayal of his siblings to the White Witch is redeemed both by his own efforts, and by Aslan's sacrifice on his behalf. Arguably, the latter would not have been possible if the former had not preceded it.

In *The Last Battle*, the limits of Aslan's powers to rehabilitate are shown. When the Dwarfs are deceived by a fake Aslan and sold as slaves, they reluctantly accept their fate: "What can we do against *him*?" (2001b, p. 87). When they discover that the creature they thought of as Aslan is really a donkey wearing a lion's skin, they become understandably cynical about the existence of the real thing. "'And you've got a better imitation, I suppose!' said Griffle. 'No thanks. We've been fooled once and we're not going to be fooled again'" (2001b, p. 92). When the true Aslan appears to them, they have become so certain he does not exist that they are incapable of either seeing or hearing him. Aslan cannot reach the Dwarfs, whose prison "is only in their own minds, yet they are in that prison; and so afraid of being taken in that they cannot be taken out" (2001b, p. 183).

Yet this disbelief is not in itself enough to doom the Dwarfs. *The Last Battle* also features Emeth, who like the Dwarfs does not believe in Aslan; his religious belief is instead offered up to a being called Tash. Aslan's assessment of this alternate belief, however, shows that, unlike the Dwarfs, Emeth's character grants him a different fate:

> I take to me the services which thou hast done to him. For I and he are of such different kinds that no service which is vile can be done to me, and none which is not vile can be done to him. Therefore if any man swear by Tash and keep his oath for the oath's sake, it is by me that he is truly sworn, though he know it not, and it is I who reward him. And if any man do a cruelty in my name, then, though he says the name Aslan, it is Tash whom he serves and by Tash his deed is accepted. (2001b, p. 202)

This indicates that moral character is, in the absence of belief, sufficient. Emeth's quality of character is such that he transcends his disbelief. The Dwarfs, however, combine their disbelief with morally repugnant actions – the slaughter of the Talking Horses, for instance – thereby choosing to remove themselves from Aslan's presence.

Like the Dwarfs of *The Last Battle*, Edmund's actions in *The Lion, the Witch and the Wardrobe* are largely repulsive. And by implication, if he had compounded his betrayal with a determined lack of remorse, Aslan might have been unable to reach him. Yet crucially, Edmund's redemption begins *before* he has met Aslan, and by his own choice.

The genesis of this redemption is the growing understanding of his own motivations and behaviour. It is true that he behaves in a selfish, silly, and wrong manner; and equally true that he does his best to ignore this knowledge. The uncomfortable realisation that he *is* doing wrong, however, is something that sets him apart from the actions of the White Witch, who can be assumed to have no such moral misgivings.

> You mustn't think that even now Edmund was quite so bad that he actually wanted his brother and sisters to be turned into stone. He did want Turkish Delight and to be called a Prince (and later a King) and to pay Peter out for calling him a beast. As for what the Witch would do to the others, he didn't want her to be particularly nice to them – certainly not to put them on the same level as himself; but he managed to believe, or to pretend that he believed, that she wouldn't do anything very bad to them, 'Because,' he said to himself, 'all these people who say nasty things about her are her enemies and probably half of it isn't true. She was jolly nice to me, anyway, much nicer than they are. I expect that she is the rightful Queen really. Anyway, she'll be better than that awful Aslan!' At least, that was the excuse he made in his own mind for what he was doing. It wasn't a very good excuse, however, for deep down inside him he really knew that the White Witch was bad and cruel. (2001c, p. 99)

Yet Edmund's better knowledge does not initially win out, and despite his reservations he succumbs to pure selfishness and betrays his brother and sisters (and the reappearance of Aslan in Narnia) to the White Witch. As Edwards (2005, p. 33) comments, "to resist he would need to have at least one iota of concern for someone besides himself. It does not appear that that iota is available to him." In this way he foreshadows the Dwarfs, in that he represents both lack of belief and deficient character. But before long, Edmund begins to repent his actions. Initially this regret is purely selfish. The White Witch shows her true colours and Edmund begins to feel sorry for himself – he regrets what he has done because he is having to live with the consequences:

> It didn't look now as if the Witch intended to make him a King. All the things he had said to make himself believe that she was good and kind and that her side was really the right side sounded to him silly now. He would have given anything to meet the others at this moment – even Peter! The only way to comfort himself now was to try and believe that the whole thing was a dream and that he might wake up at any moment. (2001c, p. 124)

This is not true remorse, however, as it retains the selfishness of his earlier actions, and largely regrets only the effects that those actions will have upon himself. But as Edmund's journey with the White Witch progresses, he begins dimly to realise the wider repercussions of what he has done. This is highlighted in the instance of the White Witch interrupting a Christmas party, where "Edmund for the first time in the story felt sorry for someone besides himself" (2001c, p. 127). He tries to intervene as the White Witch turns the wretched partygoers to stone, but fails miserably.

It is at this point that Edmund begins the transformation that in another world (one in which he survived the White Witch but did not meet Aslan) might have ended with him showing a distinct similarity to Emeth. He still has no real belief in Aslan, but his character is beginning to mature and transform from a selfish little brat into someone who knows the value of compassion and pity toward others. After the Christmas party incident, Edmund is no longer comparable to the Dwarfs, and is able to recognise and respond to Aslan when finally he meets him. His transformation is mirrored in the simultaneous changes of the landscape, as the snow melts and the permanent winter of Narnia transforms into spring. Ford (1980, p. 111) notes that "The spring that is bursting forth all around him in Narnia is also happening inside of him", but I would argue that the connection is causal and reversed – Edmund's transformation is *causing* Narnia's spring. His prophesied presence on one of the thrones at Cair Paravel is necessary for the evil time of winter to be "over and done", and he is incapable of taking that throne without choosing to turn away from the arrogance and selfishness that would have seen him preeminent amongst his siblings under the false promises of the White Witch. Spring, under the Narnian perception of the problem of evil, is genuinely incapable of returning until Edmund's moral choices improve. He is, in himself, a representative microcosm of the morality of an entire world.

The final stages of Edmund's rehabilitation – his encounter with Aslan, after which he apologises to his siblings and receives their forgiveness, and the test of his new resolve in battle, where he fights against the White Witch and is seriously wounded – complete his moral journey. The forgiveness of Aslan and his siblings enables him to forgive himself, as can be seen when the White Witch has an audience with Aslan.

> 'You have a traitor there, Aslan,' said the Witch. Of course everyone present knew that she meant Edmund. But Edmund had got past thinking of himself after all he'd been through and after the talk he'd had that morning. He just went on looking at Aslan. It didn't seem to matter what the Witch said. (2001c, p. 152)

That Edmund can face up to this accusation calmly, without shame or anger, implies that his egocentric, childish self has matured. When he is healed of his battle wounds, he also appears to regain some sort of self-respect, having faced his responsibilities without yielding to the unworthy actions his former self would no doubt have attempted. Having gained both forgiveness and self-respect, Edmund had "become his real old self again and could look you in the face" (2001c, p. 194). The first steps towards this redemption, however, were Edmund's alone. In recognising wrong, even as he succumbed to it, and then showing pity and compassion even without the comfort of faith, he is able to both bring on the seasonal thaw of spring and to open himself to Aslan's influence. From the example of the Dwarfs, it is doubtful that any talk with Aslan would have had the desired effect if Edmund had not taken the first steps himself.

Growing Up, Growing Away: Susan Pevensie and Personal Choice

One of the most controversial aspects of the Narnian cycle is the fate of Susan Pevensie, which is frequently interpreted as linking female sexuality with spiritual exclusion. In *The Last Battle*, Susan is not with the rest of the children who have visited Narnia on their final trip to that land, where they discover that they have died in a train crash and are journeying to Aslan's country (that country being a metaphor for heaven). Instead, Susan is described as "no longer a friend of Narnia" (2001b, p. 168). She refers to the experiences she shared with her siblings as "those funny games we used to play when we were children" (2001b, p. 168) and is described as being interested in "nothing nowadays except nylons and lipsticks and invitations" (2001b, p. 168). The conclusion of Susan's family and former friends is that she now considers herself too grown-up to believe in Narnia.

> 'Grown-up indeed,' said the Lady Polly. 'I wish she would grow up. She wasted all her school time wanting to be the age she is now, and she'll waste all the rest of her life trying to stay that age. Her whole idea is to race on to the silliest time of one's life as quick as she can and then stop there as long as she can'. (2001b, p. 168)

In one sense, this makes her similar to Edmund, who also at one stage denied his own experiences. Yet, while keeping in mind Susan's ultimate fate within the narrative, a better comparison with her brother can be seen in *Prince Caspian*. As Edmund initially distrusts in and feigns disbelief of Lucy's account of Narnia in *The Lion, the Witch and the Wardrobe*, so in *Prince Caspian* Susan also discounts her younger sister's claims that she has seen Aslan. When Lucy's conviction persuades her brothers to follow her lead, Susan accompanies them with the highest reluctance, believing that Lucy is not only mistaken, but throwing the equivalent of a temper tantrum to get her way. As the journey continues, both boys join Lucy in seeing Aslan pacing ahead of them: "Everyone except Susan and the Dwarf could see him now" (2001a, p. 165).

That Lucy and her brothers can see Aslan appears to be connected to belief. Of the four children, Lucy is the one who has always been the most attached to Aslan, and her faith lets her see him from the moment he appears. Her brothers have enough belief in her to willingly follow, and also come to see the lion. Susan, the last of the four to recognise Aslan, does so reluctantly. Again like Edmund, she admits both to Lucy and herself that she turned away from what she knew was right – that Aslan was there all along.

> 'Lucy,' said Susan in a very small voice.
> 'Yes?' said Lucy.
> 'I see him now. I'm sorry.'
> 'That's all right.'
> 'But I've been far worse than you know. I really believed it was him – he, I mean – yesterday. When he warned us not to go down to the fir wood. And I really believed it was him tonight, when you woke us up. I mean, deep down inside. Or I could have, if I'd let myself…' (2001a, p. 166)

When Susan does finally confront Aslan, she initially shrinks from him, but is comforted. Aslan concludes that she has "listened to fears" (2001, p. 167) and this seems to be an apt description. But if Susan has listened to fears, so too has Lewis. The seeds of Susan's awakening sexuality, mixed so disastrously into *The Last Battle*, are planted at the end of *Prince Caspian*. Ford (1980, p. 280) notes Susan's discomfort at dancing with the maenads, the wild, highly sexualised women of mythology.

> After the first phase of dancing and feasting with Bacchus, Silenus, and the Maenads subsides, Susan confides to Lucy that she would not have felt safe in the presence of all this wildness without Aslan at hand. As a girl moving into young womanhood, never an easy time, Susan is caught between the conflicting desires to always be a child and to be completely grown-up. Neither here nor there, the ecstatic side of life would be too much for her to deal with, were it not for Aslan in whose presence all revelry has its place.

All revelry, that is, apart from that which includes lipsticks and silk stockings – Lewis's Maenads may have been drawn from mythology, but in Narnia they are weakened into asexual milquetoast.

In Narnia, the developing maturity that leads to the studied display of women's sexuality is, at least for the children, entirely absent. It "simply does not exist" (J.L. Miller 2009, p. 119), at any stage of their development – even when they are presented as nominal adults. The one exception is Queen Susan's ill-fated courtship with the dreadful Prince Rabadash in *The Horse and His Boy*, which plays into the repeated presentation in Narnia of adult women and threatening, destabilising sexuality – also depicted, in different ways, by the White and Green Witches (of *The Lion, the Witch and the Wardrobe* and *The Silver Chair* respectively), both of whom are seductive temptresses. Female sexuality, in Narnia, tends to be a "tool for evil purposes" (Manninen, 2016, p. 5), an "essential part of [the Witches'] power" (Manninen, 2016, p. 5).

This seeming exclusion of Susan in *The Last Battle*, on grounds that are at the very least reminiscent of the Narnian treatment of suspicious sexuality, has prompted many different interpretations and opinions. Arguably the most well-known criticism of recent years is that of Philip Pullman, author of the children's fantasy series *His Dark Materials*. Pullman (1998) has much to say about the Narnian world in general, but is particularly scathing about the treatment of Susan.

> And in *The Last Battle*, notoriously, there's the turning away of Susan from the Stable (which stands for salvation) because "She's interested in nothing nowadays except nylons and lipstick and invitations. She always was a jolly sight too keen on being grown-up." In other words, Susan, like Cinderella, is undergoing a transition from one phase of her life to another. Lewis didn't approve of that. He didn't like women in general, or sexuality at all, at least at the stage in his life when he wrote the Narnia books. He was frightened and appalled at the notion of wanting to grow up. Susan, who did want to grow up, and who might have been the most interesting character in the whole cycle if she'd been allowed to, is a Cinderella in a story where the Ugly Sisters win.

Pullman's argument that Susan's development is a natural one has merit, and it is certain that Lewis's work reflects his own comparatively conservative cultural beliefs. It does seem likely that Lewis's suspicion of sexual women has impacted his presentation of Susan – if he had wanted to explore the idea of Susan moving away from Narnia, he could have chosen reasons that had nothing to do with cosmetics and stockings, for instance, elements that deliberately play up Susan's appearance to make her more attractive to others. Instead, he opted for the trappings of sexuality, and from that perspective, it does look as if Susan has gotten the short end of the stick. Is being grown-up such a crime? And does the loss of childish innocence really exclude an individual from eternal reward?

Yet, as *Prince Caspian* shows, Susan's doubts occurred before an interest in lipsticks and stockings were shown to be part of her character. Her presentation, therefore, doesn't have to be so clear-cut. She can be affected by Lewis's sexism, *and* yet still make poor choices for reasons other than her developing sexuality. Indeed some critics argue that it is vanity (L. Miller, 2009, p. 130) that ultimately keeps her from Narnia, shallow self-obsession, or even rebellion (Kempton, 2016, p. 22), and while these are flaws often ascribed to femininity they are not exclusive to it. Had a more contemporary or progressive author told Susan's story, her choice to travel another path may not have been confused with her developing sexuality, and her character study made the stronger for it. As it is, the confusion is natural, but it undermines the duty of moral choice so fundamental to Lewis's philosophy, and dilutes this particular example of his religious ideology.

Susan is shown to be the most practical of the children, and simultaneously the most uncomfortable with faith. She is the one who thinks they "have enough to bother about here and now" (2001a, p. 135), who isn't very academic, but is good at archery and wins prizes at swimming. Susan is the one who, when the children first arrive in Narnia, thinks about the practicalities of food and clothing when going after Mr. Tumnus; she does the same in *Prince Caspian*. Her growing discomfort with the spiritual, a discomfort that is not explored with the other children, may come from this practicality. Karkainen (1979, p. 45) comments that "practicality is both Susan's greatest asset and her biggest liability. Where practicality is needed, she can be invaluable. But where imagination or creativity or faith is needed, she cannot cope."

Edmund, in his dealings with the White Witch, can be said to be driven by both selfishness and doubt. Similarly, Susan also experiences doubt, albeit in a different form. Edmund's doubt is internal; in particular he measures himself against

Peter and is secretly dismayed by his own comparative lack. In contrast, Susan's doubt stems from the conflict between Narnia and the realities of her everyday life. Her doubt is external. It grows within her until she begins to perceive the world of Narnia as an imaginary game, played by children to amuse themselves. In a religious narrative this doubt is a weakness, a failure of "moral imagination" (Kempton, 2016, p. 15), occurring when the need for practicality conflicts with the demands of faith. Like Edmund, however, the Susan of *Prince Caspian* recognises and begins to make amends for her fault before being received by Aslan. The incident with the Dwarfs makes it appear unlikely that she would have been able to reach past her fears if she had not first begun to take responsibility for them herself.

While the events of *Prince Caspian* are enough to halt her spiritual withdrawal from Narnia, however, by the time of *The Last Battle* this temporary hold seems to have eroded in a narrative informed by both Lewis's ideology and his prejudices. Strongly influenced by Lewis's Christianity, Narnia "is a world polarized into a binary ideological division of good versus evil, light versus death, creation versus destruction, salvation versus damnation" (Tso, 2012, p. 217), but it is also a world reflecting Lewis's belief that, although damnation is possible, "each of us goes where we choose to go, where we prefer to be" (Jacobs, 2005, p. 260). Moral choice affects destination; it is a factor that ultimately influences setting.

In what seems like a metaphoric reversal of Edmund's series of choices and the resultant return of spring, the final destruction of Narnia reflects the endpoint of Susan's fragmenting belief. That Susan's turning away from Narnia coincides with its ending is likely due more to coincidence than intent on Lewis's part, but the connection between Edmund's choices and the end of winter provides precedent for a loose interpretation of this kind. If the ruler is representative of the land, then in a land defined by moral choice and spiritual belief the choice to be moral reflects positively on that land, and the choice not to believe (and to act accordingly) contributes to its disintegration.

Yet that link, even in Edmund's case, is not always fully realised. Edwards, for example, argues against Edmund's primacy of agency by falling back on the religious concept of grace and its place in *The Lion, the Witch and the Wardrobe*.

> *Grace* means "unmerited favour or care." In this case Aslan's willing sacrifice on behalf of Edmund not only rescues Edmund but also brings Narnia back to its rightful order. Grace operates without strings and is a free gift of the one who bestows it. Edmund is not saved because he deserves it but because Aslan wills it. (Edwards, 2005, p. 91)

This conflicts not only with the concepts of free will and moral choice as Lewis presents them, but also with the prophecies as related by the Beavers, and the events of the text. Spring returned to Narnia with Edmund's active repentance, which began *before* Aslan's willing sacrifice. Aslan is capable of freeing Edmund from the Witch by offering his life in place of Edmund's, but he cannot force a change in Edmund's character – and while that character remained bad, then Edmund's siblings and even Aslan himself could not remove winter from Narnia. Had Edmund retained his initial poisonous personality, then he certainly wouldn't have chosen to undo the Witch's work by assuming a throne under the purview of his brother. In fact, the melting snow is indicative not only of Edmund's change of heart but of the possibility of *four* thrones being filled. Three thrones and a Lion are not enough. Grace is not enough. It is the moral choices of a single individual on which the world is levered.

Bibliography

Downing, D. C., 2005. *Into the Wardrobe: C.S. Lewis and the Narnia Chronicles*. San Francisco: Jossey-Bass.

Edwards, B., 2005. *Further Up & Further In: Understanding C.S. Lewis's 'The Lion, The Witch and the Wardrobe'*. Nashville: Broadman & Holman Publishers.

Ford, P. F., 1980. *Companion to Narnia*. San Francisco: Harper & Row.

Jacobs, A., 2005. *The Narnian: The Life and Imagination of C.S. Lewis*. San Francisco: HarperSanFrancisco.

Karkainen, P. A., 1979. *Narnia Explored*. Old Tappan: Fleming H. Revell Company.

Kempton, E. R., 2016. *Hope for Susan: Moral Imagination in The Chronicles of Narnia*. [pdf] Brigham Young University. Available at <https://scholarsarchive.byu.edu/cgi/viewcontent.cgi?referer=https://www.google.com/&httpsredir=1&article=6988&context=etd> [Accessed 11 February 2019].

Lewis, C. S., 2001a. *Prince Caspian*. London: HarperCollins.

Lewis, C. S., 2001b. *The Last Battle*. London: HarperCollins.

Lewis, C. S., 2001c. *The Lion, the Witch and the Wardrobe*. London: HarperCollins.

Manninen, S., 2016. *The strength of female characters in CS Lewis's The Chronicles of Narnia*. [pdf] University of Helsinki. Available at <https://helda.helsinki.fi/bitstream/handle/10138/163254/Manninen_Satu_Progradu_2016.pdf?sequence=2> [Accessed 11 February 2019].

Miller, J. L., 2009. No Sex in Narnia? How Hans Christian Andersen's 'Snow Queen' Problematizes CS Lewis's The Chronicles of Narnia. *Mythlore: A Journal of JRR Tolkien, CS Lewis, Charles Williams, and Mythopoeic Literature*, 28(1), pp. 113-130.

Miller, L., 2009. *The Magician's Book: A Skeptic's Adventures in Narnia*. New York: Back Bay Books.

Pullman, P., 1998. *The Dark Side of Narnia*. The Guardian, 1 October.

Tso, A. W. B., 2012. Representations of the Monstrous-Feminine in Selected Works of CS Lewis, Roald Dahl and Philip Pullman. *Libri et Libery*, 1(2), pp. 215-234.

'I have done only what was necessary'
An exploration of individual and structural evil in the works of N. K. Jemisin

Thomas Moules

Abstract

Fantasy has something of a historical tendency to attribute the origin of evil to a single figure. As a trope, the Dark Lord has been codified in John Clute and John Grant's *Encyclopedia of Fantasy* (1997) and Diana Wynne Jones's *Tough Guide to Fantasyland* (1996). This can be seen to demonstrate the way in which a lot of fantastical texts deal with the concept of evil – by making it an external influence and a metaphysical force, rather than something internal and a product of human decisions. The argument of this article is that this trilogy represents the culmination of a running theme in Jemisin's work, which is the deconstruction of this old interpretation of evil and the introduction of a more decentralised model. This paper will examine the *Broken Earth* series, which consists of *The Fifth Season* (2016a), *The Obelisk Gate* (2016b), and *The Stone Sky* (2017). There are a few possible candidates for Dark Lord status in Jemisin's work, but these figures do not, I will argue, qualify for the label for a variety of reasons. They are neither the source nor the focus of the evil discussed in their respective texts, as the evil in Jemisin's work tends to be derived from social structures and the choices that individuals make under the influence of those structures, rather than as a result of a single evil force.

I will be focusing on some of the main characters across the *Broken Earth* trilogy which can be construed as evil, as well as exploring the ways that the societal structures within the novel lead to and influence their choices. The definition of evil itself is somewhat outside the scope of this paper, though the notion that evil is a socially constructed category and can often have political uses is a vital underpinning of my argument. The societies in Jemisin's works have a variety of different understandings of evil, and the various exceptions to the moral codes of the characters are used to demonstrate the fluid, contradictory, and very human nature of morality.

The series centres around various magic users known as orogenes. They have the ability to control seismic events, and are feared and marginalised by other humans for a variety of reasons that I will explore throughout the essay. The human societies in the trilogy are set at odds with various nonhuman factions. These various factions and societies have competing aims and operate under different definitions of good and evil, which is used to explore the contingent nature of human morality. The third book in the trilogy, *The Stone Sky*, explores the reasons for the earth becoming known as 'Evil Earth' (Jemisin, 2016a, p. 114). This raises some complex questions about the way that the earth's actions are perceived – is it a justified reaction to what was done to the earth by humans, simple indifference, or something not quite either?

The title quote is taken from *The Obelisk Gate* (2016b), and it is used to justify the murder of a family. The notion of 'doing what is necessary', either for duty or survival, is a repeated motif throughout the trilogy, especially with regard to the Guardians. They are arguably the closest thing to a straightforward depiction of an evil organisation in the vein of the Voldemort-controlled Ministry of Magic towards the end of the *Harry Potter* series. The Guardians are dedicated to finding and controlling orogenes. Their methods are undoubtedly cruel, but they do not believe their actions to be wrong, or can justify them (to themselves, if not to others) under the framework of duty.

This paper will explore the issues raised by conflicting definitions of evil between groups in the *Broken Earth* trilogy, and the ways in which various characters justify acts that could be seen as evil, in a series with a conspicuous absence of a controlling Dark Lord figure.

*

I

When discussing evil, we must first establish what evil is. Philosophers have been wrestling with this question for thousands of years and have not reached a definitive answer. It is clear that evil is an enormously malleable concept with a variety of definitions and causes applied to it. The world of the *Broken Earth* series is a harsh place, and a lot of things are normalised that in our world would be considered immoral or outlandish. In analysing a fictional culture, it is important to judge it by its own moral standards rather than projecting our own standards and then criticising it for failing to live up to them. The characters in this series have been brought up in a world that regularly experiences apocalyptic events and are taught to be prepared for them. Their concept of "doing what is necessary to survive" is based in a harsher set of circumstances than almost anything our world has experienced. This concept also forms the basis for an exploration of the limitations of utilitarian ethics within the trilogy that is an extension of the themes explored in Jemisin's other works.

Diana Wynne Jones's *Tough Guide to Fantasyland* (1996), a tongue-in-cheek codification of various fantasy tropes in the form of a tourist guide, discusses two forms of evil in fantasy – an active and a passive form:

> In the active state, it is rampant, embodied in PUPPET KINGS, ARMIES OF UNDEAD, MONSTERS [sic], and creeping pollution of the countryside and is out to get all Tourists (who are by definition GOOD). [...] The active state is usually connected with the DARK LORD, and must be overcome. [...] In its passive state it ponds in deserted spots, where it lies around waiting to be aroused by the unwary. [...] The passive, when not connected with a predecessor or avatar of the Dark Lord, is either fallout from the WIZARDS' WAR or the work of some God way back at the BEGINNING of things. When

it is in this form there is not much to be done about it but stay clear (Wynne Jones, 1996, p. 73).

Here there are several concepts to unpack insofar as they relate to the *Broken Earth* series. The choice to describe the characters as tourists, with the implication that they are near interchangeable with the reader, does not seem to fit comfortably with the *Broken Earth* books. Despite the use of second person narration, the characters are fully shaped by the world of the story and do not pass through it as visitors. The reader enters the world as a character who has grown up in it and instinctively understands it rather than as a clueless newcomer who needs to be told things. Through this style of narration, the reader begins to feel like an inhabitant of the world by absorbing the lives of the characters. The suggestion that the protagonists are good by default is also a holdover from a more traditional sort of fantasy. Another aspect of this definition worth exploring further is the distinction drawn between active and passive evil, and how it applies to this series. There are two main sources of evil – the Fulcrum, and the Earth. Whether they are active or passive by Jones's definitions is debatable. Father Earth seems in some ways an obvious candidate for Dark Lord status, but he meets only a few superficial aspects of Jones's criteria. He is primarily a reactive presence rather than an active one. He lurks in the background but is not engaged in empire-building or raising armies, he is merely enraged by humanity's attempts to enslave him and by the loss of the moon. The Fulcrum, and its preceding organisation in Syl Anagist, do not fit the criteria for Dark Lord status but fulfil some of a Dark Lord's role in the story. They are undoubtedly an active threat, pursuing Syenite across the continent when she goes rogue and forcing her to adopt another identity to remain hidden from them. They are neutralised in the very beginning of the present timeline, but their influence extends into the world through Schaffa, once Damaya's Guardian and subsequently Nassun's. He represents a fusion of the Fulcrum's interests with those of Father Earth after his near-death experience. He is guided by the Earth through the corestone that keeps him alive but retains aspects of the Fulcrum's conditioning and attempts to resist the Earth's commands when they conflict with his aims. The role of the Fulcrum is further complicated by the fact that it is ostensibly an orogene-led and created organisation: "Orogenes built the Fulcrum […] we did it under threat of genocide, and we used it to buckle a collar around our own necks, but we did it" (Jemisin, 2016a, p. 418). They are given the illusion of a choice between enslavement and death, and through this illusion, the orogenes are made to feel complicit in their own enslavement. It is later revealed that the Guardians are agents of the Earth, designed to prevent the orogenes from being accepted into society and keep them enslaved. In *The Fifth Season*, Syenite contemplates the threads of power that bind her to these organisations:

> No one would really trust a group of filthy roggas [Note: this is effectively a racial slur, meaning 'orogene'] to manage their own affairs […] No one in the Fulcrum talks about the Guardians' politics, probably because no one in the Fulcrum understands them. The Guardians keep their own counsel, and they object to enquiries. Vehemently. Not for the first time Syenite wonders: To whom do the Guardians answer?"(Jemisin, 2016a, p. 255)

The answer to her question appears to be complicated. The Guardians gain their deadly abilities and unnatural longevity from corestones, pieces taken from the sentient core of the planet. In certain circumstances, the corestone can take over, erase what was once a person and make them into a mere vessel for the voice of the Earth. This happens to Schaffa at the start of *The Obelisk Gate*, but he manages to resist and retain most of his memories due to his emotional connection to the orogenes he controls.

The Obelisk Gate draws an explicit parallel between the early days of the Fulcrum and the Confederate slave-holding American South at the time of the Civil War, referencing quotes from various 'Articles of Secession' and altering them to mention orogenes. The full historical implications of this parallel are somewhat outside the scope of this paper, but grounding aspects of the ostensibly fantastical setting in the real world is a continued motif throughout the series. In this instance it serves to enhance the focus on how the treatment of orogenes maps onto real-world bigotry, at least for readers who recognise the specific phrases used. This is among many more subtle references to various forms of real-world bigotry in the series, primarily racism but also extending to homophobia and transphobia.

In *The Stone Sky*, we see the foundations of Essun's world being built. Syl Anagist, the precursor civilisation that existed before the start of the Fifth Seasons caused periodic destruction, is an apparent utopia that is subsequently revealed to be built on colonisation, exploitation and death. Their technology permits a post-scarcity society – '[t]he people of Syl Anagist have mastered the forces of matter and its composition; they have shaped life itself to fit their whims' (Jemisin, 2017, p. 3) – but that technology was largely stolen from people conquered by Syl Anagist and twisted to serve Syl Anagist's imperial purposes. The descendants of these conquered people were genetically modified into becoming 'tuners', the original orogenes. Syl Anagist made the tuners to serve as visual proof of Syl Anagist's supposed superiority and their enemies supposed inhumanity:

> We must be not just tools, but myths. Thus we […] have been given exaggerated Niess features […] they've stripped our limbic systems of neurochemicals and our lives of experience and language and knowledge. And only now, when we have been made over in the image of their own fear, are they satisfied (Jemisin, 2017, p. 211).

In order to justify to themselves the fundamentally evil and exploitative underpinnings of their society, Syl Anagist created a neutered and caricatured version of their ancient colonial subjects, both as a propaganda tool to keep societal anxieties directed outwards at an imaginary foe and as a tool to further their exploitation of the planet. All of the greed and fear and xenophobia in Essun's society find their roots here, filtered through centuries of history into something equally evil and exploitative without the understanding of the original reasons. This lack of understanding reinforces the suggestion that the original 'reasons' were mere excuses – bigotry and evil do not need reasons, a concept that is explored in more detail through Jija's interactions with Nassun.

Many of the evil actions seen in this series appear motivated by "a kind of cold, monstrous love" (Jemisin, 2016b, p. 105) felt by those committing the action towards the victims of the action. Essun feels it towards Coru, whom she kills, and towards Nassun, whom she abuses. Schaffa feels it towards all his charges, even as he manipulates, threatens, and harms them. Jija feels it towards his children, even as he is unable to recognise them as human beings. This opens up complicated questions relating to the nature of love and hate, and how these concepts can be intertwined with evil.

Jemisin places W. E. B. Du Bois' concept of "double consciousness" at the core of all of the point-of-view characters in the series. Not only with them, of course, but in them we can see the depth of it more clearly. He describes the 'sense of always looking at one's self through the eyes of others, of measuring one's soul by the tape of a world that looks on in amused contempt and pity' (Du Bois, 1997, p. 38). In the *Broken Earth* trilogy there is less 'amused contempt and pity' and more outright malice, but the sense of having to second-guess every action and emotion through the framework of how it will appear to the oppressors is conveyed throughout Essun's story. The concept is introduced in *The Fifth Season-*

'Fulcrum orogenes must never show anger because it makes the stills [non-orogenes] nervous' (Jemisin, 2016a, p. 63), and it is repeated throughout the trilogy. The idea that orogenes are considered to be responsible for moderating their actions and reactions in order to maintain a comfortable atmosphere for non-orogenes is a form of respectability politics that is particularly relevant in our current political climate. The use of 'rogga' by the orogenes themselves acts as a signifier for when they have moved past the Fulcrum's conditioning. The reclamation of slurs by marginalised communities has historically been a method of reclaiming power from oppressive groups, and this is partly the case here, though there are a few complicating factors that produce this decision that do not necessarily link so closely with the real-world practice. Essun's understanding of Alabaster's use of the term comes when she discovers the truth of the system of node maintainers, who are lobotomised orogenes used to maintain the stability of the continent: 'Now she understands that his use of the slur is deliberate. A dehumanizing word for someone who has been made into a thing. It helps' (Jemisin, 2016a, p. 140). The system of node maintainers seems to invite comparison with Ursula Le Guin's short story 'The Ones Who Walk Away From Omelas' (2014). Both feature a society supported by the abuse of innocents, but the characters' responses to the discovery of this fact is significantly different. In Le Guin's story, the responses take two forms. The first is bland acceptance, the uneasy proclamation that they do only what is necessary. The second is total withdrawal, effectively functioning as acceptance through the implicit suggestion that change on such a scale is futile. Both attitudes are part of the way that the system perpetuates itself, by convincing people that the only alternative to complacency is to avoid society entirely. Jemisin appears to take issue with this message, having responded to it through the *Broken Earth* books as well as more directly through her short story 'The Ones Who Stay and Fight'. In these instances the message is one of resistance, up to and including the complete destruction of the systems that make such injustices possible. 'Omelas' suggests the utilitarian reading that the injustice is potentially justified if it ensures the happiness of thousands. Jemisin's responses to the story make the clear case that this line of thinking is fundamentally cruel and dangerous, potentially leading to the justification of ever greater evils.

II

At the opening of *The Stone Sky*, the narrator tells us that "Life is sacred in Syl Anagist" (Jemisin, 2017, p. 4). This becomes a bitter refrain throughout the book as the depths of Syl Anagist's exploitation are revealed. Life may be sacred, but what they consider to be life is a flexible and nebulous construct, with convenient exceptions built in to allow for their exploitation of the tuners and of the other peoples that were conquered. Their habit of defining life by whether or not it can be exploited extends even to the planet beneath their feet, and ultimately causes the loss of the moon and the beginning of the apocalyptic Seasons. This flexibility in their definition of life mirrors the flexibility found in the definition of evil. Syl Anagist is able to define a people whom they conquered and enslaved as evil through propaganda, shaping historical narratives to fit their agenda and remaking the subjects of those narratives to seem as monstrous as possible through genetic manipulation. These extreme lengths allow Syl Anagist's leadership a convenient scapegoat for a variety of societal problems, in much the same way that traditional conceptions of evil can lead to similar scapegoating in the person of the Dark Lord.

Father Earth's hatred, in contrast to the hatred expressed by other characters, is presented as having a rational basis and seems almost justified. What is effectively the theft of the Earth's daughter parallels the theft of Essun's daughter, and the Earth's hatred for humans is drawn into comparison with

Essun's hatred towards Jija.

Essun, arguably, exhibits some evil traits herself. She kills one of her children and abuses another, destroys entire communities, and turns an entire city of people to stone. Taking a utilitarian view, the text suggests a tension within Essun as to whether or not these actions were justified: "So many lives saved, if only you had stayed in your cage" (Jemisin, 2017, p. 10). It is unclear as to what degree these words are the narrator's interpretation or Essun's thoughts, asthere is an unreliability to the narration in *The Stone Sky* that was less present in the other books. Essun appears to explore the tension, trying to decide if she can comfortably argue that these actions are justified. The deaths do allow her to survive and continue with her objective to return the moon to its proper orbit and end the Fifth Seasons, but they have a heavy emotional cost for a character who is already emotionally broken. Describing the creation of the original Stone Eaters, Houwha/Hoa says that the Earth, even in its fury, "understood that we were tools of others, not actors of our own volition" (Jemisin, 2017, p. 341), which leads to them being granted a form of leniency. Could the same be said of Essun? Is she a product of her twisted upbringing, reacting to a system built on the foundation of her exploitation and the exploitation of those who, like her, are considered to be second-class citizens? Or is she, as she has been taught from childhood, fundamentally evil or *other*, uncontrollable and vicious? When she kills Coru, it is the last desperate act of a mother determined to protect her child by the only means she has available, from being torn apart by a Guardian or lobotomised and made into a node maintainer. The fact that this action breaks her and alters her very identity suggests that she is not fundamentally evil, but is forced by her circumstances into making desperate choices in situations where there is no good outcome. The system within which she is forced to exist is fundamentally evil, but individuals conditioned and controlled by that system are not, as we see through Schaffa's semi-redemption. The fact that she is both physically and mentally damaged by her actions, as represented by her slowly turning to stone, suggests that she is not evil, but this may be in part due to the fact that we experience the world of the story in the same way that she does, and are thus more able to empathise with her after seeing the motivations behind her actions.

III

Schaffa appears, initially, to be one of the few unambiguously evil characters in the book. He delights in his work for the Fulcrum and in his ability to control and manipulate people, as well as his ability to kill. His interactions with Damaya, though outwardly kind and caring, are underscored with the threat of violence and the constant reinforcement of the idea that his kindness is fundamentally conditional, dependent on Damaya's unquestioning obedience. He is the closest thing she has to a comforting childhood memory after being given up by her family, even though Schaffa is "a man whose love comes wrapped in pain" (Jemisin, 2016a, p. 440). Even decades later, his conditioning holds her: "the habit of answering is too deep" (Jemisin, 2016a, p. 439). His kindness is a monstrous, twisted thing, built on the unquestioned evils of the society that he has passed through for millennia. When we see the death of Coru from Schaffa's perspective, this monstrousness is made clear. His assertion that he has "done only what was necessary" (Jemisin, 2016b, p. 52) shows the depth of his own conditioning through his centuries of working for the Fulcrum, or that he has told himself the lie so often that it has become almost true. His conviction that what he does is necessary for the greater good is ultimately what keeps him alive, to a degree, but he is altered in the process: "The Schaffa that we have known thus far, the Schaffa whom Damaya learned to fear and Syenite learned to defy, is now dead. What remains is a man with a habit of smiling, a warped paternal instinct, and a rage that is not wholly his own driving everything he does from this point on" (Jemisin, 2016b, p. 42). Schaffa manipulates people, not out of self-preservation as Nassun does, but out of self-interest. He will say anything that will advance his aims, whether it be an outright lie or *just enough* of the truth to twist things his way. Despite this, he is redeemed to some degree by the end of the trilogy. His treatment of Nassun functions as a redemption arc of sorts, though of course he cannot effectively compensate for centuries of horrendous actions with a couple of years of kindness. His actions are still underscored with the implicit threat of violence, but in these instances he actively resists committing violence. With Nassun, any violence towards her would represent a failure on Schaffa's part, as it would mean that he has given in to the compulsions from his corestone.

Jija, Essun's husband and Nassun's father, represents a very prosaic, small-town kind of evil. He is one of very few unambiguously evil characters in the series. There is no possible redemption for Jija because he has no interest in redemption. His beliefs about orogenes are fundamental to his understanding of the world. The legacies of Jemisin's personal experience and the history of American racism run through this series, and nowhere is the influence clearer than in Jija, though his treatment of orogenes and his desire to go to Found Moon for a cure give his storyline some parallels with anti-LGBT+ bigotry and conversion therapy. What he views as a principled refusal to use slurs (at least when it suits him), replacing them with phrases like "*your kind* and *that sort* [sic]" (Jemisin, 2016b, p. 114), demonstrates a desire for civility, but only a certain specific kind of civility in which he is given the power to decide what is and isn't acceptable speech. He wrestles with the cognitive dissonance between his deeply-held bigotry and the instinctive love he feels towards his children, even as he struggles and fails even to view them as human. Nassun's abilities, even though they save his life on multiple occasions, make her an animal or a monster in his eyes. He seeks what he initially believes is a cure, not to allow her to develop her skills, because to him, "trained, leashed animals are still animals" (Jemisin, 2016b, p. 115). Jija grew up in a society that taught that orogeny was a dangerous and unnatural trait and that those who possess it are subhuman, and witnessed the death of his friend at the hands of an orogene, but, as Nassun realises, 'there is no reasoning with her father's hatred' (Jemisin, 2016b. p. 312). When confronted with the choice to alter his belief and break that societal conditioning, he decides instead to double down. When Jija and Nassun reach Found Moon, the place that Jija believes will cure Nassun of orogeny, he has little to do but contemplate his actions. When he sees Nassun becoming happier, more confident, and definitely not cured, the dissonance arises once more and he attempts to murder her, 'he [wears] dark clothing in order to stalk his daughter' (Jemisin, 2016b, p. 389) and attacks her with a knife. The same thought processes which he experienced when he first discovered that his son was an orogene ultimately lead him to the same place with his daughter, the idea that it is necessary to kill them in some warped version of self-defence. It is made clear that some aspects of Jija's behaviour are the results of living in a society that conditioned him from childhood to think a certain way, but it is the choices he has made within that framework that condemn him. He was never conditioned to murder, but it is ultimately the logical end point of his beliefs – if orogenes aren't human, then it isn't really murder.

The origin of this belief system can be seen through the system of 'node maintainers' (Jemisin, 2016a, p. 140) set up by the Fulcrum. These are orogenes stationed at strategic points to provide a network of stable areas of land. To bypass the inconvenience of the fact that orogenes are thinking human beings who may get bored of doing this duty for years on end, they are lobotomised and sedated, restrained in wire harnesses, kept alive with intravenous nutrition, antibiotics and colostomy bags. A metaphor for the larger systems of oppression that run throughout the story, this system is built on denying the humanity of those who are essential to its function. This system is, by the end of the trilogy, a reminder of the legacy of Syl Anagist's cruelties. Just as the genes permitting orogeny survived that original Fifth Season, so did the cultural attitudes towards its practitioners. These attitudes were encouraged and enforced by a variety of systems that ultimately reach right to the bedrock of the society that allows them to exist. The idea that orogenes are less than human becomes fundamental to the continuation of society, and the only way to overcome these prejudices is for orogenes and non-orogenes to work together. There is no single Dark Lord behind the existence of these bigotries, no shadowy figure directing people from behind the scenes. Instead it becomes a self-perpetuating cultural construct comprised of the decisions of millions of individuals.

Conclusion

In the absence of a single guiding figure, or figurehead, evil becomes a small thing, an ordinary thing, both personal and systemic, as easy as breathing. It is a self-perpetuating system, and the state of society is dependent on its continuation. It is present in individual actions, like the use of a slur, the presumptuous attitude held towards someone you see as inherently lesser or not-quite-human, and it is present in the systems that produce and perpetuate those attitudes and actions: the stonelore, the Fulcrum, the Guardians. These texts do not say anything outright about the nature of evil – there is no moment where it is explained to the reader in a philosophical aside. But by the edges of what is given we can see a conspicuous absence, the shape of something unable to be spoken. Perhaps the shape of it is something close to this: even the best of us is evil, in small ways or large.

Bibliography

Du Bois, W. E. B., 1903. *The Souls of Black Folk*. Blight, D. W. and Gooding-Williams, R. eds 1997. Boston: Bedford Books.

Jemisin, N. K., 2016a. *The Fifth Season*. London: Orbit.

Jemisin, N. K., 2016b. *The Obelisk Gate*. London: Orbit.

Jemisin, N. K., 2017. *The Stone Sky*. London: Orbit.

Jemisin, N. K., 2018. *How Long 'Til Black Future Month?*. London: Orbit.

Le Guin, U. K., 2014. The Ones Who Walk Away From Omelas. In *The Unreal and The Real: Selected Stories Volume 2*. London: Gollancz.

Wynne Jones, D., 1996. *The Tough Guide to Fantasyland*. London: Vista.

The Nature of Evil in *The Chronicles of Thomas Covenant* by Stephen Donaldson

Barbara Stevenson

Abstract

The intention of this paper is to explore ways of defining evil, specifically in the context of *The Chronicles of Thomas Covenant* by Stephen R Donaldson. Both Thomas Covenant, the hero, and his enemy Lord Foul use torture, murder and destruction as means to their ends – Lord Foul to rent the Arch of Time and escape the Land, Thomas Covenant to defeat Lord Foul and escape from the Land – acts which are usually considered to be evil. In Covenant's case these are deemed to be 'necessary evils' and not to be judged in a similar manner to Lord Foul, who is 'pure evil'. Is Thomas Covenant as evil as Lord Foul, or does evil depend on a given standpoint? Is it necessary, in nature, that good and evil work in balance?

Introduction

The author Stephen R Donaldson wrote ten novels in the Thomas Covenant Series, first published in the USA, between 1977 and 2013; three in the first chronicles (Donaldson, 1983a) (Donaldson, 1983b) (Donaldson, 1983c), three in the second chronicles, (Donaldson, 1983d) (Donaldson, 1985a) (Donaldson, 1985b) and four in the final chronicles (Donaldson, 2004) (Donaldson, 2007) (Donaldson, 2010) (Donaldson, 2013). These books follow the protagonist Thomas Covenant, a bestselling American author who inexplicably is taken ill with leprosy. While recovering in a leprosarium his wife leaves him, taking their young son. He returns home with the disease in abatement, although he has been left physically deformed with several of his nerves numb. Ignorant of the nature of the disease, his neighbours fear and shun him and Covenant struggles to come to terms with this. He is involved in a traffic accident, during which he finds himself in 'the Land' – a beautiful place where he is not only accepted, but regarded as a hero. In this Land he is cured of his leprosy and can feel sensations. Knowing this is impossible, as nerves don't regenerate, he believes that his subconscious is separating his leprosy from himself and manifesting it as Lord Foul, the Land's enemy, and source of evil.

Disease represented as evil

In the early chronicles, Covenant's leprosy manifested as evil/ Lord Foul is the major theme of the novels. Stephen Donaldson's father was a medical doctor dealing with leprosy patients and Donaldson grew up knowing about the psychological effects of the disease, as well as the physical ones. One of the characters in the books is called Damelon Giantfriend, which could be taken as a loose reference to Father Damien, a priest working in the Molokai leper colony in Hawaii in the latter part of the nineteenth century. (Eynikel, 1999) In some parts of the world, the Biblical connotation of lepers being unclean and separate from society still exists. Disfigurements caused during the active phase can be repugnant and a loss of nerves and senses makes sufferers prone to infections, which can be malodorous. In Part 1, chapter 2 of Graham Greene's *A Burnt Out Case* (Greene, 2004, p. 13) the cured patient Deo Gratias refuses to leave the leprosarium in the Congo because he doesn't feel able to adjust to life outside. Donaldson makes use of this fear to isolate Covenant and nurture his feelings of self-loathing and despair. He can only hold suicidal tendencies – active or passive due to self-neglect – at bay by establishing a comprehensive routine of self-vigilance to ensure the disease doesn't take a grip anew. Despite his many attempts to prove to his family and neighbours that he is not a danger to anyone, he is unable to convince them. Accordingly, he blames his leprosy for all the loneliness, despair, and evil in his life.

Marie-Louise Von Franz, a scholar of Carl Jung, wrote about evil that on a primitive level it can be described as "… the appearance of something demonic or abnormal… which does not pose any ethical problem but the purely practical one of how to either overcome or successfully escape it." (Von Franz, 1995, p. 149) To Covenant, Lord Foul is the supernatural evil of his leprosy which needs to be overcome, without the complication of the rights or wrongs of destroying him.[1]

Von Franz goes on to say "…loneliness piles up whatever you have in your unconscious and if you don't know how to cope with it, comes first in a projected form." (Von Franz, 1995, p. 186) So, Covenant 'creates' Lord Foul and sets him in a fairy-tale Land, while he is unconscious due to the road accident.

At this point the situation is relatively uncomplicated. No-one would argue that leprosy is good and Lord Foul falls into the category outlined by Von Franz – destroying him poses no ethical problem.

Evil represented by human's misuse of nature

Donaldson widens his analogy of evil as a disease to spotlight environmental matters. He does this by introducing the 'Ravers' and hidden banes in the earth. The Ravers are three evil spirits in the Land, in existence from 'ancient times'. In the long past, these Ravers were kept at bay by their enemy the Great Forest. This forest covered most of the Land, however, drawing on parallels with man's destruction of the rain forests, when people arrived they cut down the trees for agricultural land and wood. This continued, through greed and ignorance,

---

[1]. In the novels Lord Foul is male and will be referred to as such in this paper.

until the Great Forest was reduced to a few outcrops, unable to defend against the Ravers and thus they were able to bring evil into the Land. The Ravers are brothers[2] and although they are said to be servants of Lord Foul, they act independently of him. Lord Foul is able to flatter them, offer them power, and use their assistance, but they are not bound by him and he does not trust them. They have no final goal, as Lord Foul does. Their only purpose is to do evil. They have no bodies of their own, so possess others, making innocent victims do evil deeds, and because of this no-one is sure who or what is a Raver. This allows Ravers to infiltrate societies in order to spread seeds of hatred, turning people against one other. Accusations of being a Raver are flung at anyone who is disliked or acts differently – reminiscent of the medieval witch trials.

The banes are sources of evil, placed in the Land during its creation. The most important one in the story is the Illearth Stone ('ill earth' stone), which is a powerful, luminous stone that causes corruption and can bring about devastation if it falls into the wrong hands. (Donaldson, 1983b, pp. 44-46) This would seem to be analogous with radioactive elements such as uranium. In the second chronicles, Donaldson uses the evil of the Sunbane to demonstrate the corruption of nature by human influences, alluding to climate change and genetic modification.

At this point the situation has become more complex. Evil has been separated from Covenant and although still regarded as an illness, it is a disease of mankind and therefore it is not necessarily dependent on Covenant for a 'cure'. Putting himself forward as a 'Saviour' leaves him open to scrutiny.

Evil as a conscious choice

As the story progresses, it becomes clear that leprosy and human destruction cannot account for all the evil. In existentialism, Jean-Paul Sartre argues that people exist and

---

[2]. Again, evil is portrayed as being male.

then make conscious choices. (Sartre, 2007) If we accept this view, any actions Covenant makes are due to his conscience. One of the first actions he does in the Land (in *Lord Foul's Bane*) is to rape a teenage girl, "[she] did not look any older than sixteen". (Donaldson, 1983a, p. 43) who tried to help him. His immediate response is to flee from her family and friends, making the excuse that he couldn't cope with the return of his sensations. When it becomes evident that no-one will judge him, partly because they have sworn an oath of peace and partly because they regard him as a godlike figure who is above their judgement, Covenant feels guilt and shame. His subconscious mind invents condemnation from Trell, the girl's father, and Triock, her boyfriend, but both are inconsequential. He clumsily and unsuccessfully tries to atone for his action, but goes on to lie, cheat, deceive, demand service, possess individuals, kill enemies, encourage madness, and murder his wife in the Land. He is in possession of 'wild magic', which he refuses to use to protect his comrades, claiming he fears its power, but has no problem using it to annihilate anything threatening his person. Time moves at different rates in Covenant's own world and the Land. At the conclusion of the first novel he returns to his own world, but after recovering from the traffic accident he returns to the Land, this time following a domestic incident. It is forty years since his visit. He has a daughter – the product of his rape – and it is not long before he has incestuous thoughts and shows incestuous behaviour towards her.

Covenant's attitude to women in general is misogynistic and cannot be excused by his wife leaving him. The fact that she left him very easily after he developed leprosy, along with the backstory that it was while she was away that his leprosy developed, gives rise to the thoughts that she was seeking an excuse for a divorce – with or without his illness. Covenant is portrayed as a self-obsessed egotist from the start. As a brief aside, the flimsiness and triviality assigned to these crimes suggests to the reader that the author is using rape, possible paedophilia, and incest as a narrative tool. This point is well explored in Lorianne Reuser's paper in regard to other fantasy works. (Reuser, 2017) By refusing to judge Covenant, the Lords condone the crime as much as outright saying so. One wonders if they would have felt the same if one of their daughters had been raped, rather than an ignorant peasant girl. Covenant's actions and responses can be understood in relation to the story, but for him to be put forward as the flawed hero, someone to be admired, inserts an insidious evil into the Land which the author fails to address.

The situation has changed. Even free from his leprosy, Covenant harbours evil, which he repeatedly brings into the Land, corrupting the people there. Whereas before evil was something to be destroyed, the people now accept that what they considered to be 'evil' depends on who or what the source is.

Evil as an external force

Carl Jung describes two types of laws. The first is an ethical system, created by man as a necessary by-product of evolution. (Von Franz, 1995, pp. 137-140) Moving from animal instincts to a more developed sense of civilisation requires laws to ensure the smooth running of a society. These rules are accepted by members of a society and can differ between societies. Breaking these rules by conscious choice can be seen as evil – warranting punishment – or it can be regarded as natural law overruling [unjust] human laws. Natural law is a moral code, which although it differs between individuals, stems from an innate sense of what is right and wrong. In the novels Donaldson explores this by ambiguously introducing a Creator figure in the form of a beggar.[3] Covenant meets him before entering the Land. It is significant that in the final reckoning there is no mention of this Creator and Covenant becomes the

---

[3]. In the story the Creator is male and will be referred to as such.

creator as he rebuilds the Land.

In the Land there are creation myths which some people believe, but most don't. In these myths Lord Foul was a friend and equal of the Creator, who was banished from heaven because of his evildoing. He entered the Land and was trapped there, to the Creator's dismay, by the Arch of Time. His one driving force is to escape and seek revenge. By his own laws the Creator cannot enter the Land to rid it of Lord Foul, so he chooses Covenant as his Saviour. At one point in *The Wounded Land* (Donaldson, 1985b, p. 356) Covenant is able to walk on water. The author would like the reader to believe that this version is also a figment of Covenant's imagination; however, at the end of the first chronicles in *The Power that Preserves* (Donaldson, 1983c, pp. 433-444), the Creator actively steps in to save Covenant from dying in his real world, using supernatural powers when there was no way possible that he could survive. Therefore, for the purpose of the novels, the reader has a right to assume that the Creator exists. If this is the case, Lord Foul has nothing to do with Covenant's leprosy. The simple version of evil considered previously does not apply and Covenant cannot feel justified in destroying him without considering the ethics of such an action, which conflicts with the idea behind the first chronicles. The reasoning is that Donaldson likes to play with paradoxes.

There can be no good without evil as a balance is needed in nature. Without a concept of evil there would not be a concept of good. As Jean-Jacques Rousseau (1712-1778) wrote in *Émile*, "I would rather be a man of paradoxes than a man of prejudices" (Rousseau, n.d.), although Donaldson is a man of both. In the story the reader is told that this Creator is good and the enemy Lord Foul is evil. By calling the enemy 'Foul' the author prejudices the reader against him. As noted previously, it could be a title equally bestowed on Covenant.

Because Covenant is accepted in the Land, he believes that the Creator is good. Covenant is healthy and in his eyes the

Land is beautiful. It is clear that his judgement is subjective. Not everything that is healthy and beautiful is good, poisonous toadstools for instance, but it reinforces the point that his unhealthy, ugly leprosy is the evil. At their first meeting Lord Foul laughs at Covenant's leprosy, immediately turning Covenant against him, although being his manifestation of the disease, Foul is in fact laughing at himself.

Covenant's response to the Land and Lord Foul raises the question of whether humans have an innate knowledge of a universal good and evil and by extension knowledge of a superior wisdom. This theme was explored in the medieval church by people such as Thomas Aquinas, and Anselm of Canterbury. Anselm taught the concept of 'fides quaerens intellectum', the gift of faith seeking out knowledge and his ontological argument purported to show that it is self-contradictory to deny that there exists a greatest possible being, this being called God. (Sadler, n.d.) Jill Paton Walsh, in her book *A Knowledge of Angels* (Walsh, 1994, p. 84), draws on medieval notions to describe the concept of morning knowledge and evening knowledge. Evening knowledge is learned, but morning knowledge is present from birth.

With good and evil precariously balanced in the Land, a feature of the Covenant chronicles is how they are governed.

The Law governing Good and Evil in the chronicles

Realising the damage their ancestors have caused, the people of the Land swear an Oath of Peace, which everyone willingly complies with. The Natural Laws take precedence, and when Covenant enters the Land in the first chronicles, there is no need for human laws. There are Lords, guided by a High Lord, who study Earthpower, but they are not rulers, rather servants of the people. Communities work together, using their individual skills. Crime does not exist. In the unlikely event of someone breaking the oath they are not punished, but considered to be ill and taken to be healed. The people accept Covenant's crime of rape because he claims to be a leper, although to them he appears healthy.

The Natural Law, or Earthpower, is kept in balance by the Staff of Law, which is its outward symbol. For centuries it has been lying dormant in the earth and all has been well. That is until a Cavewright, Drool Rockworm, finds it while delving among the chambers in Mount Thunder. Similar to Gollum's enchantment by the ring in *The Hobbit* (Tolkien, 1937) and *The Lord of the Rings* (Tolkien, 1954-55), Drool is attracted to the Staff's power and is corrupted by it. With Covenant's help the Lords wrestle the Staff from Drool and use it for good until it is lost, thanks to Covenant's interfering, and later destroyed. The second chronicles outline the devastation caused because of this loss. Instead of natural order, human laws are needed to hold societies together. A Raver has infiltrated the governing body, twisting the human laws to make them conflict with the natural ones. Earthpower is warped by the Sunbane. Covenant's mission in the second chronicles is to fashion a new Staff of Law. He and his companions eventually succeed in doing this by combining the dark, physical figure of VAIN created by the cave-living demondim spawn, with the airy, light spirit FINDAIL, one of the Elohim, who are depicted as angel-like figures. Thus good and evil are brought into balance. The Sunbane is defeated and the land flourishes once more. In the final chronicles, the new Staff has been lost in time and time travel is needed to regain it.[4] At the end of the final book, *The Last Dark*, (Donaldson, 2013, p. 524) Covenant and his companion Linden Avery use this staff, along with their own wild magic, to create a new world following the virtual destruction of the Land that they have caused.

---

[4]. The author skims over the problems of altering history to bring about a 'good' outcome for his hero and heroine.

Linden Avery

After the first chronicles, the author appears to have felt that a female influence was needed to balance the powers of nature and so he brings in Linden Avery. She is a doctor called in to help with Thomas Covenant in his real world and is presented as a strong, independent woman, yet she fails to convince in this role. Rather, she comes across as the traditional Western view of what an educated woman is like. Her ideals are to be a wife, mother, and healer, and she is infatuated by Covenant at their first encounter. She carries her own emotional problems with her. As a girl she witnessed the suicide of her father and as a young adult she smothered her terminally ill mother to death. Becoming a doctor as an act of atonement, she believes she is the only one who knows what is right for her patients. In the second chronicles she possesses Covenant – for his own good. Constantly fearing that she is inadequate, she craves power and recognition, and when the Creator selects her to be Covenant's helper in the Land she revels in the title 'The Chosen', often abusing it to demand service and sacrifice from others. She is unpleasant, demanding, arrogant, and in possession of too much power. Whenever she is in danger a new supernatural entity appears to save her. Her problems are more spiritual than Covenant's leprosy, and the author introduces more supernatural evils to mirror them.

In the final chronicles, Linden's lust for power grows. She abuses her position as a doctor to persuade the authorities that a woman is incapable of looking after her children in order to adopt her youngest son. She works long hours, paying others to do the hard part of parenting, but despite this the reader is constantly reminded that 'Jeremiah needs her', although it is not clear why. Throughout the books she is blinkered by her obsession with Covenant and her mother cat instincts to protect 'her' son. Nothing else matters. She possesses the injured Stave against his will and despite being a GP she heals him with implausible internal thought surgery. (Donaldson, 2004, pp. 331-333) She demands complete obedience. She uses a schizophrenic old man, convincing him that she is his only friend, which is a lie. Because of her need for Covenant, she rouses the Worm of the World's End, an Earthpower creature designed to bring about the end of the world. (Donaldson, 2007, pp. 761-762) (Donaldson, 2010, p. 23) She doesn't care, because her needs are all that matter.

The reader is asked to accept Linden as being good because she is acting out of love.[5] She is driven by her love for Covenant and by her maternal love for Jeremiah. Acting out of love may seem good, but other people also act out of love. If what they love is not the same as what Linden loves, she feels that is sufficient reason to regard them as evil and justifiably destroy them.

More and more throughout the three series, the reader finds that good is only what Covenant and Avery say it is. By the final chronicles, the people fight among themselves and do not welcome strangers. The Land is no longer healthy or beautiful. It has been ravaged and betrayed as a consequence of Covenant's decisions. By refusing to destroy Lord Foul when he had the opportunity at the end of the first series – instead choosing to humiliate him – Covenant broke the promises he had made to those who suffered for him and fuelled Lord Foul's hatred and destructive powers.

In stages, evil is being accepted such that it is no longer considered evil, but necessary for the final outcome.

Conclusion

By means of ridiculous, risible coincidences and supernatural events even an avid reader of fantasy would discredit, Covenant succeeds in overpowering Lord Foul to the extent that Lord Foul

---
[5]. In the stories love is represented by wild magic, symbolised by the white gold of Covenant's wedding ring which later Linden owns.

will die and that will be the end of him. However, Covenant offers him a way out by taking him into himself and thus the two become one. Lord Foul capitulates very easily and the reader feels that after ten books, even he is too tired to go on.

Is this an act of ultimate evil, or realisation of the true nature of goodness?

Lord Foul is blatantly not the only source of evil in the Land. Covenant himself is a source of evil, as is Linden Avery. Mankind's reckless attitude to nature allowed the Ravers to enter the Land and banes are still hidden deep in the earth. Destroying Foul would not eliminate evil from the Land, but the author's intention was always to have good and evil balancing each other. Goodness cannot exist without evil and vice versa.

However, for this to work, Foul would have to join with the Creator, not Covenant.

Covenant is not good. Even he says, referring to himself and Lord Foul, "We're part of each other. We're too much alike." (Donaldson, 2013, p. 522) Covenant is a rapist, incestuous betrayer, liar, deceiver, possessor and murderer. His purpose is self-motivated, to survive and return to his real world. It has been said of him by the critic James Nicoll that Thomas Covenant would win 'a lifetime achievement award' for the 'most un-likeable, supposedly sympathetic protagonist'. (wikipedia, updated 16th Sept 2018). He is human and by rights of free will, should be held responsible for his actions. He is happy to judge others, but the people of the Land, and indeed the author, refuse to judge him. It would appear from the books that Donaldson believes evil to be what a given individual chooses it to be.

Lord Foul is also a torturer, liar, deceiver, and murderer. He makes no claims otherwise, although in many cases it is the Ravers who carry out the worst of the deeds without direct instructions. His purpose, like Covenant's, is to escape from the Land, which is his prison. The difference is that Lord Foul is not human. He is supernatural and, going by the rules of the Land, he is the one who should be above the people's judgement, not Covenant. Lord Foul acts in accordance with his natural instincts – either as a product of Covenant's leprosy or as a separate entity – and by the author's rules he cannot act in any other way, yet he is vilified. Perhaps this is the author's final paradox – to have human law replace natural law in the Land. Covenant is the chosen hero, not Foul or any of the Earthpower beings. Evil is defined by his point of view. Human law prevails over natural law, but in a patronising fashion allows natural law to coexist in a submissive manner.

The reader is offered a sugar-sweet happy ever after. Covenant has come to a realisation and acceptance of who he is – a human experiencing both good and evil and capable of both good and evil. The Creator is conveniently forgotten about. Covenant and Avery are the new Adam and Eve creating their own Garden of Eden, this time in control of evil.

What the reader gets is a distasteful sense that once again a privileged, white male and 'his obsessive, neurotic woman' are required to save the world from 'evil', oblivious to the fact that they are the source of the problems. They have become, in their own eyes, a new god and goddess, creating a Utopia as doctrinal and fearful as the one imagined by Thomas More. (More, 1968)

My thanks are extended to Rev. Canon Tom Miller whose wit and wisdom in perilous times equalled Baltasar Gracian's and without which this paper could not have been written.

Bibliography

Donaldson, S., 1983a. *Lord Foul's Bane*. 17th ed. Glasgow: Fontana/ Collins.

Donaldson, S., 1983b. *The Illearth War*. 15th ed. Glasgow: Fontana/Collins.

Donaldson, S., 1983c. *The Power That Preserves*. 15th ed. Glasgow: Fontana/ Collins.

Donaldson, S., 1983d. *White Gold Wielder*. Glasgow: Fontana/Collins.

Donaldson, S., 1985a. *The One Tree*. 3rd ed. Glasgow: Fontana/ Collins.

Donaldson, S., 1985b. *The Wounded Land*. 10th ed. Glasgow: Fontana/ Collins.

Donaldson, S., 2004. *The Runes of the Earth*. 2nd ed. London: Gollancz.

Donaldson, S., 2007. *Fatal Revenant*. UK ed. London: Gollancz.

Donaldson, S., 2010. *Against All Things Ending*. UK ed. London: Gollancz.

Donaldson, S., 2013. *The Last Dark*. London: Gollancz.

Eynikel, H., 1999. *Molokai: the story of Father Damien*. Staten Island: Alba House.

Greene, G., 2004. *A Burnt Out Case*. Centenary Ed edition ed. London: Vintage Classics.

More, T., 1968. *Utopia*. London: Penguin Classics.

Reuser, L., 2017. Subversion, Sex, and Violence: Rape as Narrative Tool in 'A Song of Ice and Fire'. In: F. T. Barbini, ed. *Gender Identity and Sexuality in Current Fantasy and Science Fiction*. Edinburgh: Luna Press Publishing, pp. 155-179.

Rousseau, J.-J., n.d. *Jean-Jacques Rousseau Quotes*. [Online] Available at: <http://www.notable-quotes.com/r/rousseau_jean_jacques.html> [Accessed 1st October 2018].

Sadler, G., n.d. *Anselm of Canterbury* (1033-1109). [Online] Available at: <https://www.iep.utm.edu/anselm> [Accessed 18 Sept 2018].

Sartre, J. P., 2007. *Existentialism and Humanism*. new ed ed. London: Methuen.

Tolkien, J. R. R., 1954-55. *The Lord of the Rings*. Reprint 1991. London: Harper Collins.

Tolkien, J. R. R., 1937. *The Hobbit*. Reprint 2011. London: Harper Collins.

Von Franz, M.-L., 1995. *Shadow and Evil in Fairy Tales*. Revised ed. Boulder: Shambala Publications.

Walsh, J. P., 1994. *Knowledge of Angels*. 2nd ed. London: Black Swan Books.

Wikipedia, updated 16th Sept 2018. *The Chronicles of Thomas Covenant*. [Online] Available at: <https://en.wikipedia.org/wiki/The_Chronicles_of_Thomas_Covenant> [Accessed 20 Sept 2018].

Machines of Chaos – The Shadows and the Reapers as representations of evil in the television series *Babylon 5* and the *Mass Effect* game series

Jyrki Korpua

Abstract

This article focuses on how evil is represented in two science fiction cult favorites: the *Babylon 5* television series and the *Mass Effect* game series. In both cases, the focusses are monstrous ancient enemies: The Shadows, in *Babylon 5*, and the Reapers, in *Mass Effect*. The enemies, incomprehensible in appearance and action, come from outside to destroy the civil world built by humans and other humanoid races. Both the Shadows and the Reapers wage war, destroying entire species and planets, savouring chaos, destruction and mass murder. All of this is seemingly enough for us, as readers and gamers, to label them as evil.

In the introduction of this article, I will illuminate what is meant by the term "Evil". Also, previous studies of this concept will be addressed. I will then move onto further analysis of the subject. There, at first, I focus on the similarities between the series in relation to this topic. Secondly, I discuss how both series portray evil, and how the Shadows in *Babylon 5* and the Reapers in *Mass Effect* are both representative of chaos and "forced evolution" as their philosophy and modus operandi. I will also focus on the strategy that both races use to execute their philosophy. Lastly, considering their own particular philosophies and strategies, I will examine whether these mythical science fiction races really should be considered evil. In the series, they are both merely acting according to their own laws, functions, and codes. This once more gives rise to philosophical and the theological question, "What is evil?". What part does morality and a humane approach play therein? Is evil just the absence of good? Or is it even a physical, spiritual, and/or moral emptiness? Is evil –in the context of these series– all in the eye of beholder?

*

"First of all, Chaos came to be", as Hesiod writes in *Theogony* (West, 1988, p. 120). Originally, the Greek word for "Chaos" (Khaos) translated into English as "Abyss", or "Emptiness". Its modern usage as "a state of utter confusion" comes from the 1600s (Merriam-Webster, 2018). In classical cosmologies[1], chaos precedes the creation of the World and therefore also the (created) Natural Order. This classical assumption of chaos versus order was later adapted to major theological religions, such as Judaism and Christianity. In these, it is prevalent that chaos represents evil and order represents good. God, as a Demiurgic Power, "created the heavens and the earth. Now the earth was formless and empty, darkness was over the surface of the deep" (*Genesis* 1:1-2). God brings order and tranquillity to chaotic emptiness and incoherence, since he "is not a God of confusion, but of peace" (*1st Corinthians* 14:33). For many theologians, "God's order" and "God's peace" has been seen as (ontologically) "good", where evil is considered to be something that opposes order, peace, and tranquillity. For example, theologian Karl Barth described evil as *das Nichtige*: a mysterious power of "Nothingness", expressing what God did not will in Creation; that which contradicts the will of God (McGrath, 2011, p. 226).

Evil as a concept contrary to the will of God is, in theology, known as "moral evil" – contrary to "natural (or physical) evil", which is manifest as some form of physical or psychological suffering (Beale, 2013). Flescher (2013) offers five different

---

[1]. For example in Hesiod's *Theogony*, Plato's *Timaeus*, Aristotle's *Metaphysics*, and *Metamorphoses* by Ovid.

theologian models of evil: 1.) Evil as the presence of badness (a dualistic model of good versus evil), 2.) *Theodicy*, evil leading to goodness through suffering, 3.) Evil as social construction, 4.) Evil as the absence of goodness, most commonly known as St. Augustine's "privation thesis", and (as an extension of the fourth model) 5.) Evil as inaction, connecting the fourth model with virtue ethics. In this article, evil is examined as the absence of (humane) goodness, which could also be viewed as the presence of badness, as seen from the viewpoints of those opposed to the Shadows and the Reapers. It follows that both the Shadows and the Reapers do not think of themselves as evil, but that their enemies do see them as such.

So, the evil examined in this article results from a divergence in views and ideology. Here, the assumed evil forces support the ideology of chaos, and their rival humane, assumed-to-be-good, forces support order and concordance. These dichotomies of order versus chaos, and good versus evil, have ruled Western theological and philosophical thinking for millennia. It has usually been assumed that the Order of Things, Chain of Being (e.g. Aristotle's *Scala Naturae*), and Cosmic Harmony in some way represent good. Cosmic Harmony was central to the Pythagorean view of the "Harmony of the Spheres" as "Universal Harmony" (Rackham, 1938, pp. ii, xviii, xx), as it also was to Plotinus' idea of the harmony between sentient beings and forces of the universe (Mazzotta, 2001, p. 13). Any attacks and contradictions against this harmony was considered evil.

This kind of theological background can also be found in the representation of evil in the American science fiction television series *Babylon 5* (1994-98, United States of America, created by J. Michael Straczynsky, henceforth *B5*) and the Canadian science fiction game series *Mass Effect* (2007-2012, Canada, henceforth *ME*).[2] Both series have huge cult and fan followings (on *B5*'s fans, see Lancaster, 2001). The earlier of the analysed series, *B5*, won many prizes, for example two awards and eight nominations at the Emmy Awards over the years. Concerning the show's special effects, *B5*, with its ground-breaking, fully CGI visual effects "launched the new era of television" (cgw.com). Science Fiction scholar Cheryl Vint (2008, p. 247), in her article, called *B5* "Our first, best hope for mature science fiction television", giving a nod to its opening narration, where it is stated that the *Babylon 5* station was "our last, best hope for peace". *B5* received fame not only for its meticulous plotting, but also for the kind of complex characters that viewers hadn't seen before in science fiction television (see Booker 2004, pp. 130-133). The series was innovative in many ways, playing with the concept of episodic, serial television, cleverly using commercial breaks as structural absences (Johnson-Smith, 2005, pp. 139, 235). *B5*, because of its cosmological scale battles and creative, and (in some ways) untraditional good versus evil dichotomy, has invited scholars to also examine it theologically (e.g. Cowan, 2010 and McCarron, 1998).[3]

---

[2]. *Mass Effect* (also *Mass Effect 1*) was released in 2007 as an exclusive title for Xbox 360, but was later ported to other formats. The sequel, *Mass Effect 2*, was released in 2010 for Xbox and Windows and later in 2011 for PlayStation 3. The first main *ME*-series ended with *Mass Effect 3*, released in 2012 (see BioWare.com). New *Mass Effect: Andromeda* -series was launched in 2017, but is not discussed in this article; nor are any spin-off games, books, comics, or other texts released outside the original series.

[3]. As for the race of the Shadows, from a quite different genre logical angle, see Archell-Thompson's mythic interpretation (1998), or Sawyer's Gothic reading (1998).

The hugely popular action role-playing video game *ME* was well received by both players and critics from early on.[4] The series won prizes and sold more than seven million copies worldwide (Harradence, 2011). In research, *ME* has been looked at from a moralistic viewpoint, and invited discussion on its concepts of good and evil (on morals in *ME*, see Boyan, Grizzard & Bowman, 2015; Ward, 2008).

The cosmological battles of races in Babylon 5 and Mass Effect

B5 and *ME* are both military focused, futuristic space operas. The overarching plots of both storylines emphasise the cosmological battles of familiar, and unfamiliar, races. These are rival races who do not appreciate each other's worldview, philosophy, strategy, or morals. In both series, humankind and other species are threatened with extinction by all-powerful ancient –even mythical– foes from outside of known space. These foes, the Shadows in *B5* and the Reapers in *ME*, bring chaos and destruction to the known galaxy.

In these series, the Shadows and the Reapers are considered as the evil enemies that the protagonists must fight and try to prevail, for the sake of all humankind (and aliens) in order to survive. Or, so it seems, for a long time in both series. As this article will demonstrate, the dichotomies of evil versus good, and darkness versus light, are not so simplistically interpreted in these series. Although the focus in both cases is the battle between the ideologies of chaos and order, we –the viewers and players– cannot always be sure which side is fundamentally

---

[4]. Should be added that after the popular *Mass Effect* and *Mass Effect 2* games there was lot of Internet controversy after *Mass Effect 3* was launched. Most criticism was pointed to the ending of the series (see e.g. Burks, 2018). The amount of criticism was indeed so extensive and comprehensive that BioWare later released some extra cutscene material to the ending to satisfy fans. But for many fans this was not enough and therefore there is also lot of fan-made alternative (copyright violating) endings available on the Internet.

good or evil.[5] Ney & Sciog-Lazarov (2000, p. 223) claim that, in *B5*, the overarching tale of the "Shadow War" is in fact "a Jungian archetypal myth that pits patriarchal 'order' in a cyclical struggle with 'chaos'". Ney & Sciog-Lazarov (2002, p. 223) also point out that, besides focusing on this mythical-scale war, there are a vast range of different modes and tones, from hero quests to political fables, melodramas, and romances.

ME has often been compared to genre classic *B5* because of several narrative and cosmological similarities.[6] For example, interstellar travel via relay machine/jump gates in *B5* and mass relays in *ME*– is quite similar. More pertinently, in both series, there is an important cylinder-shaped space station[7] that serves as a meeting place and headquarters for a multiracial council: Babylon 5 itself in *B5*, and the Citadel in *ME*. Humans, with help from their former enemies, and now allies, the Minbari race, build the Babylon 5 space station as a meeting place for an intergalactic council consisting of all known civil star-faring races. Ney & Sciog-Lazarov (2000, p. 224) even call it "The UN-like space station," since it resembles our modern day United Nations and its Security Council. In *ME*, the Citadel was supposedly constructed by a mystical and highly advanced,

---

[5]. It should be added that this is not a completely new thing in science fiction television, speculative fiction or science fiction games. For example, you could play Chaotic characters that are not Evil (e.g. "Chaotic Good" or "Chaotic Neutral") or Lawful characters that are not Good (e.g. "Lawful Neutral" or "Lawful Evil") in the classic role-playing game *Dungeons& Dragons* (and its sequels). Also, the original *Star Wars* trilogy had the totalitarian Empire aiming for the complete control and order of things. This control could be seen as Evil. Even Satan, in John Milton's classic *Paradise Lost* (258-263), says –after being cast out of the Heaven because of his rebellion– that it's "Better to reign in Hell, than serve in Heaven".

[6]. Looking for intertextual similarities and analogues is of course not a new thing. In the 1990s, *B5* was compared to J. R. R. Tolkien's *The Lord of the Rings* and his other fantasy works, since there are many comparable features and even direct quotes from Tolkien in *B5*. There are also similarities and resemblances in nomenclature, such as Lorien, Z'ha'dum/Khazad-Dûm, etc.

[7]. A development of the so-called "O'Neill cylinder", a design originally proposed by physicist Gerard K. O'Neill in 1976, in his *The High Frontier: Human Colonies in Space* (see O'Neill, 2000).

but now (apparently) extinct race, the Protheans, who used the huge station as their capital. Later in the series, it is revealed that the Citadel was not in fact built by the Protheans, but by the Reapers, who annihilated the Protheans and brought about their extinction.

Also, protagonists in both series are heroic military personnel with the initials J.S.; John Sheridan (and John Sinclair) in *B5*, and Jane or John Shepard in *ME*.[8] As almost Christ-like martyrs, both John Sheridan and J. Shepard also die, but are henceforth resurrected. They are messianic heroes [9] who give up their lives for the livelihood of others; they also both make deals with ancient higher beings in order to save their respective intergalactic civilisations. In *B5*, John Sheridan dies on the mythical evil planet of Z'ha'dum, home planet of the Shadows, but is resurrected after a deal with the god-like Lorien, "the First One", who is supposedly the very first intellectual being in the Universe. Lorien remains (ostensibly) neutral between the forces of chaos and order: the Shadows and their followers, and the ancient beings of light known as the Vorlons and their followers, which includes, at the beginning of the series, the most advanced humanoid race, the Minbari. In *ME*, Commander Shepard dies in the beginning of the second game and is resurrected by the Illusive Man, a notorious leader of a group called Cerberus, a terrorist group that wants humans to claim a higher hierarchical place in the Galaxy. Cerberus opposes the Citadel and its Council. It is in a continuous war of terror with alien races and even the Systems Alliance, the representative body of humans. In the end of the series, it is revealed that Cerberus and the Illusive Man are in fact controlled by the Reapers, with their paranormal

---

[8]. Gender is one of the many external details you can choose at the beginning when playing *ME*. In this article, the case study plays were conducted as Jane Shepard. I would like to thank Juho Longi for acting as my test player for the article.

[9]. The archetypal heroes of *B5* have previously been studied, for example, by Moody & Schofield in 1998, and Iaccino in 2004.

powers of *indoctrination*. Also, in the end of the series, the resurrected Shepard is able to make a deal[10] with the collective consciousness of the Reapers, known as The Catalyst. In most cases, Shepard's actions bring peace to the Galaxy but also end Shepard's human life.[11]

The narrative plots in both series also resemble each other. Both emphasise the conflict of chaos versus order, battles of ideologies, question of free will, your own right to choose your path in the world. As major storylines, the protagonists fight against ancient evil threats which return once again to the Galaxy, while at the same time having to deal with militant, xenophobic, pro-human factions which are also striving for power and control: the Psi-Corps and Homeguard in *B5*, and Cerberus in *ME*. Humans are also aided in their fight by alien races who have earlier struggled against these ancient enemies themselves: the Minbari in *B5*, and the Turians in *ME*.

Most importantly, in both series, the most powerful enemies of these apparently evil races, the Vorlons in *B5*, and the Protheans in *ME*, are treated and viewed, at first, as "good", bringers of development, law, justice and order. Later, it becomes clear that these races have played a central part in the early development of most other races and have been manipulative, controlling, authorial, and are in fact totalitarian and amoral in many ways. In *B5*, it is revealed that the Vorlons artificially created the gene for telepathy on hundreds of planets. Their

---

[10]. In *ME 3*, the specifics of this deal, and the future fate of Shepard, depends on the choices made by the player. No matter what that deal actually is, this still acts as the end of the series.

[11]. There are many alternative endings for the series. The main storylines in these are usually called "Refusal" (make the deal and choose the future of the Galaxy), "Destroy the Reapers", "Control the Reapers", and "Synthesis" (of organic and synthetic life). Shepard remains alive as a human in at least in one possible ending, but most will result in Shepard either dying or changing form and becoming something more than human: a legendary creature for future generations, called "The Shepard", which is possibly play on words with "shepherd", being her/his new function for the Galaxy.

purpose in creating telepaths and PSI-forces was to craft future weapons for use against the Shadows, whose organic ships are, for some reason, vulnerable to telepathic interference. In *ME*, although the Protheans are extinct, a sole survivor of the race, named Javik, is later found in *ME 3*. In the discussions between Commander Shepard and Javik, it is revealed that the Protheans were manipulative and ruthless, savouring war and conquest, and employing the logic that "the ends justify the means". Javik explains that he and his people were (in part) moulded by the long struggle between the Protheans and the Reapers, stating that "War is our sculptor. And we are prisoners to its design." (*Mass Effect 3*, 2012). Javik knows only wartime and struggle, nothing more, and his moral outlook is accordingly shaped by this. In *B5* (Season 3, Episode 22), it is suggested that the Vorlons and the Shadows don't even remember when their ongoing war began or even who started it, but they are still determined to continue it, according to their own respective logic and agendas.

Portrayals of Evil in *Babylon 5* and *Mass Effect*

The Shadows in *B5* and the Reapers in *ME* are monstrous in their appearance, nature, and power. The Shadows are older than any known species. Their physical presence is variable: they can become invisible to mortal eyes, but sometimes also assume "forms" or exoskeletons which resemble spiders or praying mantises.[12] They are unfamiliar and uncanny; even their speech is a screech, reminiscent of noisy insects or horrific nightmare creatures. The Shadows come out from their hiding place (their home planet) every thousand years to spread chaos, and pit other species against each other, until only the most

---

[12]. In the *Babylon 5* Technomage Trilogy book series by Jeanne Cavelos, it is suggested that the Shadows are beings of pure energy and light, like their enemies the Vorlons. However, their true form isn't revealed in the original *B5* series.

powerful and "fit" survive. They destroy any unneeded species and create a forced evolution in the Galaxy. Their simple philosophy of destruction and devastation is unveiled by one of their human followers, Mr. Morden: "It's like knocking over an anthill [...] Every new generation gets stronger. The anthill gets redesigned, made better" (*B5*, Season3, Episode 22). So the Shadows use a strategy of "forced evolution" as their mode of operation. They oblige all races to wage bloody conflicts resulting in survival of the fittest, which is the model that evolution also follows.

The Reapers in *ME* are similarly ancient, and their origins stretches beyond the history of any known species. Players of *ME* learn of their existence from fifty thousand year-old data which their old enemies The Protheans have recorded. The Reapers, as well as the Shadows in *B5*, hide outside of known space, in so-called Dark Space, and only return after fifty millennia have elapsed. In the game series, it is once again time for the Reapers to return. In the cosmology of the *ME* game-world, the Reapers are monstrous "machines", gigantic in size and terrifying in their miles-long physical length. They were created long ago by a now (almost) extinct species called the Leviathan[13], who made the Reapers to serve as their AI machines, and utilised them to collect data and preserve all knowledge. At their core, the Reapers are highly sophisticated synthetic AI entities who "harvest" organic lifeforms and amalgamate them into their own bodies of existence. This is still their philosophy and function in the game series. During their long lifespan as a race, although they have their own private personalities, their collective consciousness has also "created" an almost omnipotent, non-physical AI creature called The Catalyst.

---

[13]. The players can learn from side missions of the game that there are still one (or more) of the Leviathan alive in the world, hiding in safe places from their own creations. The Leviathan themselves are giant sized aquatic cephalopod looking creatures.

So, how is evil portrayed in these series? The pivotal answer is that the perceived evil races are portrayed as strange and uncanny. The term "uncanny" (*unheimlich*) was first identified in Ernst Jentsch's article "Zur Psychologie des Unheimlichen" ("On the Psychology of the Uncanny", 1906). However, it was popularised by Sigmund Freud in his essay "Das Unheimliche" ("The Uncanny", 1919), where he expanded Jentsch's views and added new perspectives to the term. Unfamiliar elements are usually used in order to create horror, surprise and sublime scenarios (Korpua, 2015, p. 38).

To a human observer, these uncanny creatures look and sound different, and monstrous. The Shadows, with their spider-like forms and shrieking sounds, are uncanny, while their organic ships are feared by everyone in the *B5* universe. In the series, fighter pilot Mitch Harvey depicts the ships poetically: "It was jet-black. A shade of black so deep, your eye kind of slides off it. And it shimmered when you looked at it. A spider, big as death and twice as ugly. When it flies past, it's like you hear a scream in your mind." (*B5*, Season 2, Episode 22).

The Reapers in *ME* are gigantic, horrific and inhuman. They emit frightening sounds, but are also seemingly able to speak telepathically with organic beings. Their industrial-sounding, loud, rattling voices and huge squid-like forms are uncanny. But the most unfamiliar and horrific feature of the Reapers is their ability to indoctrinate organic beings. This indoctrination results in humanoids becoming fully controlled by the Reapers, as witnessed in the first game, where the Reaper called Sovereign is in control of the antagonist for that episode, a powerful Turian named Saren. In the first instalment of *ME*, a formerly controlled hive-minded insectoid creature named The Rachni Queen describes the process of indoctrination as "oily shadows" occupying its mind. Later in the series, the main protagonist Shepard is slowly being influenced by this process and has nightmares of horrific, oily shadow-figures, possible dystopian futures, and of the Reapers emitting a strange whispering sound. Even at the end of the series, in *ME 3*, the player cannot actually be sure whether Shepard has been indoctrinated into believing the Reapers and involuntarily becoming their aid, since there are oily shadows lurking about in the closing scenes of the game. Aesthetically, the whole concept of indoctrination is powerful and frightening. Most people are afraid of relinquishing control, losing their minds and their free will. So, this is clearly an evil ability to possess.

Battle of Ideologies

As previously touched on, the Shadows in *B5* favour chaos and survival of the fittest. They direct lesser species via elements of warmongering and aggressiveness. Then again, after their cyclical campaign for the destruction of lesser races is over, they permit the surviving races to prosper and thrive on the back of their victories and their new technological advances. As for their function, they seem to prefer technological advancement and dismiss morality, ethics, a humane perspective, and protection of weaker individuals. They worship chaos over patronising order and militarism over pacifism. Their main enemies, the Vorlons, are patronising and moralistic. Where the Vorlons act as good herdsman for the other species, the Shadows act as evil exponents of chaos and destruction.

Ideologically, the conflict with the Reapers in *ME* is even more interesting than the everlasting battle between the Shadows and the Vorlons in *B5*. This is because the Reapers see themselves as champions of order instead of chaos. From the point of view of their enemies –that is, any unharvested or non-indoctrinated people who are thinking for themselves– the Reapers are bringers of chaos and destruction, and altogether evil. The Sovereign, the very first Reapers one encounters in the series, clearly state as much: "We impose order on the chaos of organic evolution. You exist because we allow it, and you will end because we demand it." (*Mass Effect*). Here, the

Sovereign take chaos to mean confusion and disorganisation. More interesting still, their actions as destroyers of all other species will, if successful, inevitably lead to "chaos" as per its original meaning; i.e. a universe *devoid* of any (organic) living thing. This strategy can be considered, from our own point of view, as evil.

So, the Reapers impose the logic and thought-patterns of synthetic artificial intelligence machines on organic races. These organic lifeforms, seen from the point of view of the Reapers, are inferior, less reliable, illogical and feeble. The Reapers' strategy is to harvest and preserve all knowledge in the universe. They do this by absorbing all sufficiently advanced organic life into their own consciousness. This, of course, results in the extinction of those lifeforms, but this is not a dilemma according to the Reapers' ideology. They consider that all organic life will end sooner or later in any case, so the actual time and place of harvesting isn't important. What is important for them is "Continuing the Cycle", meaning the cycle of cosmic revolutions every fifty thousand years or so. This ideology is best portrayed by the Sovereign in the first *ME*. The Sovereign is contemptuous of organic lifeforms, viewing them as temporary, while the Reapers are eternal.

Both the Shadows in *B5* and the Reapers in *ME* are unfamiliar and monstrous to our eyes, but they act logically, according to their own private laws, functions and codes. As the Catalyst, the collective consciousness of the Reapers, declares in *ME*: "When fire burns, is it at war? Is it conflict? Or is it simply doing what it was created to do? We are no different." (*Mass Effect 3,* 2012). However, for the viewers and players, our own moral codes and humane approach doom them to be branded as evil beings. Their strategies and ideologies are viewed as immoral in the face of our own ethic codes, not least because they do not believe in free will. As a whole, their actions could be deemed as war crimes and crimes against humanity (and other races).

Spiritually they are empty, chaotic. Even physically, they are weird and uncanny; unidentifiable even.

The Reapers, as giant AI machines, force us to speculate on the morality of machines and their ethics, but also on the whole question of life and its meaning. Could an almost omnipotent synthetic being be considered as "living"? What moral rights do synthetic entities have? The Reapers could be seen as evil, since their actions fulfil the theological idea of moral evil. The theological concept of goodness is absent in their actions and so they would naturally be seen as advocates of "badness".

The Shadows in *B5* are in some aspects even more unfamiliar than the Reapers. With the Reapers, we know that they are machines created long ago who are merely acting according to their original coding. But the Shadows remain a mystery to the viewer. They come from the fringes of myths and nightmare stories. They are ancient and feared, but their background and history remains mostly unclear. We don't even know for sure whether they are organic or not; are they made of flesh and blood, energy, or something else? They have formed some kind of symbiotic relationship with machines, or are themselves partly machines. In the episode "Ship of Tears" (*B5*, Season 3, Episode 14), a human telepath who is implanted as a pilot on a Shadows spaceship, observes:

> "The machine says: 'kill, to protect.' The sign [of the PSI-corps] hurts us. We cannot hear the machine."
>
> "What machine?" the telepath responds.
>
> "Live. In my mind. I am the machine. We join, we fight. It is dark. Terrible. Help me, please, make it stop talking in my mind."

This voice inside his mind and merging with a living machine resembles the indoctrination process of the Reapers.

The chaos that the Shadows and the Reapers bring to organic

civilised species could indeed be seen as evil. As previously discussed, even the physical appearances and portrayals of both foes convey this sense of evil. Both series cleverly portray evil foes and villains as something completely alien to us; monsters who act in a manner that is fundamentally in opposition to our point of view and thereby effectively challenge and threaten our sense of morality and even our very existence.

> *Things fall apart; the centre cannot hold;*
> *Mere anarchy is loosed upon the world,*
> *The blood-dimmed tide is loosed, and everywhere*
> *The ceremony of innocence is drowned.* (*B5*, Season 2, Episode 2. The Narn Ambassador, G'Kar, prophesises the coming of the Shadows by quoting from "The Second Coming" by William Butler Yeats.)

Bibliography

Achell-Thompson, P. 1998. Shades of Darkness: Shadow and Myth. In Edward James & Farah Mendlesohn (eds.) *Parliament of Dreams: Conferring on "Babylon 5"*. Reading: University of Reading, Reading & Language Informat, pp. 71-79.

Babylon 5, 1994-1998. Television series. Created by J. Michael Straczynsky. United States of America: Babylonian Productions Inc. & Warner Bros.

Beale, S., 2013. The Problem of Natural Evil. *Catholic Exchange*. [online] Available at: <https://catholicexchange.com/the-problem-of-natural-evil> [Accessed 10 December 2018.]

BioWare. *Mass Effect*. [online] Available at: <http://www.bioware.com/games> [Accessed 10 December 2018.]

Booker, M. K., 2004. *Science Fiction Television*. Westport: Praeger Publishers.

Boyan, A., Grizzard, M. & Bowman, N., 2015. A massively moral game? *Mass Effect* as a case study to understand the influence of players' moral intuitions on adherence to hero or antihero play styles. *Journal of Gaming & Virtual Worlds*, Volume 7, Number 1, pp. 41-57.

Burks, R., 2018. Mass Effect 3 Ending Isn't as Bad as People Remember. *ScreenRant.com*, 26 November 2018. [online] Available at: <https://screenrant.com/mass-effect-3-ending-good-bad-controversy/> [Accessed 19 December 2018.]

Cgw.com, 2011. NewTek Honors. Visual Effects Artists at the Academy of Television Arts and Sciences. October 24, 2011. *Computer Graphics World* [online] Available at: <http://www.cgw.com/Press-Center/News/2011/NewTek-Honors-Visual-Effects-Artists-at-the-Acad.aspx> [Accessed 10 December 2018.]

Cowan, D. E., 2010. *Sacred Space: The Quest for Transcendence in Science Fiction Film and Television*. Waco: Baylor University Press.

Flescher, A. M. 2013. *Moral Evil*. Washington, D.C.: Georgetown University Press.

Harradence, M. 2011. The Mass Effect series has sold seven million units. psu.com, 22 April 2011. *Playstation Universe* [online] Available at: <https://www.psu.com/news/mass-effect-series-has-sold-seven-million-units/> [Accessed 10 December 2018.]

Holy Bible, 1978. New International Version. Colorado Springs: International Bible Society.

Iaccino, J. F., 2004. *Babylon 5*'s Blueprint for the Archetypal Heroes of Commander Jeffrey Sinclair and Captain John Sheridan with Ambassador Delenn. *The Journal of Popular Culture* 34:4, pp. 109-120.

Johnson-Smith J., 2005. *American Science Fiction TV. Stark Trek, Stargate and Beyond.* London & New York: I. B. Tauris & Co Ltd.

Korpua, J., 2015. *Constructive Mythopoetics in J. R. R. Tolkien's Legendarium.* Oulu: Oulu University Press.

Lancaster, K., 2001. *Interacting with Babylon 5: Fan Performances in a Media Universe.* Austin: University of Texas Press.

Mass Effect, 2007. Video game. Directed by Casey Hudson, designed by Preston Watamaniuk. Canada: BioWare.

Mass Effect 2, 2010. Video game. Directed by Casey Hudson, designed by Preston Watamaniuk. Canada: BioWare.

Mass Effect 3, 2012. Video game. Directed by Casey Hudson, designed by Preston Watamaniuk. Canada: BioWare.

Mazzotta, G., 2001. *Cosmopoiesis. The Renaissance Experiment.* Toronto: University of Toronto Press.

McCarron, K., P. 1998. Religion. Philosophy, and the End of History. In Edward James & Farah Mendlesohn (eds.) *Parliament of Dreams: Conferring on "Babylon 5".* Reading: University of Reading, Reading & Language Informat, pp. 131-144.

McGrath, A., 2011. *Christian Theology. An Introduction.* Fifth Edition. Malden: Wiley-Blackwell.

Merriam-Webster 2019. *Chaos.* [online] Available at: < https://www.merriam-webster.com/dictionary/chaos> [Accessed 21 February 2019].

Milton, J., 2003. *Paradise Lost.* Edited with introduction and notes by John Leonard. London: Penguin.

Moody, N. & Schofield, A. M., 1998. Reconsidering Gender and Heroism. In Edward James & Farah Mendlesohn (eds.) *Parliament of Dreams: Conferring on "Babylon 5".* Reading: University of Reading, Reading & Language Informat, pp. 50-60.

Ney, S. and Sciog-Lazarov, E.M., 2000. The Construction of Feminine Identity in Babylon 5. In: Elyce Rae Helford, ed., 2000. *Fantasy Girls: Gender in the New Universe of Science Fiction and Fantasy Television*. Boston: Rowman & Littlefield Publishers, Inc, 223-244.

O'Neil, G. 2000. *The High Frontier: Human Colonies in Space*. 3rd edition. Burlington: Apogee Books.

Rackham, H., 1938. *Pliny the Elder: Natural History*. Books I-II. Translated by H. Rackham. Harvard: Harvard University Press.

Sawyer, A., 1998. The Shadows Out of Time: Lovecraftian Echoes in Babylon 5. In Edward James & Farah Mendlesohn (eds.) *Parliament of Dreams: Conferring on "Babylon 5"*. Reading: University of Reading, Reading & Language Informat, 61-70.

Tolkien, J.R.R., 1999. *The Silmarillion*. Edited by Christopher Tolkien. London: HarperCollinsPublishers.

Tolkien, J.R.R., 2002. *The Book of Lost Tales. Part I. The History of Middle-earth. Volume 1*. Edited by Christopher Tolkien. London: HarperCollinsPublishers.

Vint, S., 2008. Babylon 5. Our First, Best Hope for Mature Science Fiction Television. In: J. P. Telotte (ed.): *The Essential Science Fiction Television Reader*. Lexington: University Press of Kentucky, pp. 247-265.

Ward, N. M., 2008. Mass(ively) Effect(ive): Emotional Connections, Choice, and Humanity. *Eludamos. Journal for Computer Game Culture*. 2008:2, 289-292.

West, M. L., 1988. *Hesiod: Theogony and Works and Days (A new translation)*. Translated by M. L. West. Oxford: Oxford University Press.

The Bloodlust of Elizabeth Báthory: From the Brothers Grimm to *American Horror Story*

Tatiana Fajardo

Abstract

This article aims to depict the evolution of the historic Hungarian Countess Elizabeth Báthory through her presentation in various pieces of fiction over time. To do so, four main characteristics of the Countess will be analysed in comparison to examples from popular culture: her notorious vanity and how it is echoed in the Brothers Grimm's *Little Snow White* (1812), her alleged bisexuality connected with Sheridan Le Fanu's Gothic novella *Carmilla* (1871-1872), her means of torture as illustrated in Alejandra Pizarnik's *La Condesa Sangrienta* (*The Bloody Countess*) (1965), and her role as a mother captured in season five of the TV series *American Horror Story* (2015-2016). Despite the fact that each characteristic emerges in all of the aforementioned fiction, each will be scrutinised separately with their corresponding narrative. In the context of Báthory's domains of wealth, authority and vampirism, a Jungian approach will be developed to examine the Countess's persona and the diverse archetypes she embodies.

Introduction

Countess Elizabeth Báthory was born in the Kingdom of Hungary, Habsburgh Monarchy, in 1560 as a member of the Báthory family, one of the most powerful dynasties in the region. She was the niece of Stephen Báthory, the king of Poland and grand duke of Lithuania as well as prince of Transylvania. Despite this aristocratic background and wealth, the clan was feared for its cruelty, and some of Elizabeth's relatives created a dark legend around their figures. For instance, Lady Klára Báthory, Elizabeth's aunt on her father's side, "has been remembered in the histories as an insatiable bisexual adventuress" (Thorne, 1997, p.147), and may have been the person who introduced Elizabeth to sadomasochism.

The alleged mental disorders in the family may have been the result of inbreeding among the kin, since they did not wish their blood to be fused with that of others (Thorne, 1997, p.83). Elizabeth is thought to have suffered from epilepsy and to have been deranged. The Countess is remembered as the most notorious of the Báthorys, primarily due to the rumour of her vampiric tendencies, a perspective this article will analyse. This version of her persona is based on the belief that she murdered more than 650 young girls, allegedly to obtain blood from the virgins in order to restore her youthfulness. She was condemned for her atrocious crimes and imprisoned in her own castle, where she died in 1614. But who was Elizabeth Báthory in reality? Was she the monstrous devil portrayed in novels, films and TV series? The legend of her persona has been employed in numerous narratives, yet there is little information about the historical figure behind them. This article will begin with the study of a popular fairy-tale by the Grimm Brothers, one of the earlier presentations of Báthory, and how she emerges in it.

"Mirror, Mirror on the Wall, Who's the Fairest of Them All?"[1]

The Brothers Grimm wrote a fragment named *Nach Einem Wiener Fliegende Blatt*, a pun which can mean 'a Flying Leaf', 'a Handbill' or 'a Rumour on the Wind…from Vienna', in which "the Brothers Grimm referred to a seventeenth-century folktale telling of an unnamed Hungarian lady who murdered eight to twelve maidens" (Thorne, 1997, p. 205), a softened echo of Báthory's myth. It is likely that one of their most

---
[1]. Grimm, 1812.

renowned characters, the stepmother of their *Little Snow White*, was also influenced by the aristocrat since there are meaningful similarities between the two female figures.

In the famous fairy-tale, the Grimm Brothers depict the consequences extreme vanity can trigger. Both the stepmother, as well as Snow White, emphasise the relevance of being young and beautiful. Vanity is a trait present in Countess Báthory, and the first section of this article will explore the existing connection between the tale and the aristocrat's life.

Nancy van den Berg-Cook claims how conceit is present in *Snow White* (n.d.). Through her explanation of the myth of Narcissus, she states that his self-devotion when he sees his image reflected in the water is employed to depict how "the surface of the water reflected the self, or at least the possibility of coming to know the self" (n.d.). Similarly, the mirror represents an entrance to the unconscious and, particularly in the case of the stepmother, a looking glass symbolises the Jungian archetype of the 'animus', the inner masculine side of a woman. It is interesting to note that most representations of the mirror in different versions of the story have Snow White's enemy being answered by a masculine face, or a depiction of male features.

David Tacey (2012, p. 162) explains that the "woman is compensated by a masculine element and therefore her unconscious has, so to speak, a masculine imprint. This results in a considerable psychological difference between men and women, and accordingly I have called the projection-making factor in women the animus, which means mind or spirit". Consequently, if the perspective of the answer the mirror gives the stepmother comes from her own unconscious, it can be argued that the woman depends on the patriarchal society which judges her according to her beauty and age. Interestingly, Raymond T. McNally (1985, p. 127) links the stepmother to Elizabeth Báthory and her need for staring at herself in the looking glass:

During the first official trial of Elizabeth Báthory on January 2, 1611, her young manservant Ficzko declared on the stand that the Countess kept by her side 'a mirror enclosed in a pretzel-shaped frame' and that 'supporting her head with her arms, she would gaze into the mirror for over two hours at a stretch'. The Countess also reputedly made incantations to the mirror.

As Maria Tartar explains, "The mirror image and the glass coffin, not surprisingly, have become the privileged sites for feminist interpretive projects. For Gilbert and Gubar, the magic looking glass and the enchanted glass coffin are "the tools patriarchy suggests that women use to kill themselves into art[2], the two women literally try to kill each other with art"" (1999, p. 77). It is significant that, when Snow White marries her Prince Charming, the Wicked Queen is invited to the wedding, yet is "forced to wear red-hot shoes in which she must dance until she dies" (McNally, 1985, p. 129). The reader believes this to be justified after the ill-treatment Snow White suffered from her stepmother, but does this not mean that she is capable of torturing someone?

In both the Grimms' tale and Báthory's life, husbands are absent. In the tale, Snow White's father dies, and Elizabeth, married to Count Francis Nádasdy at the age of 15, spent little time with her spouse as he continuously fought against the Turks and died after almost thirty years of marriage. If Prince Charming died when Snow White was in her forties, would Snow White begin to torment young girls simply because of their beauty and youth, as her stepmother did? The emphasised characteristic of her personality is her physical attractiveness as, even when she is dead, a glass coffin is used so everybody

---

[2]. The expression 'kill themselves into art' is employed by Gilbert and Gubar (1979, p. 36) as they consider the stepmother an artist because she is self-absorbed and creative as artists can be. Also, they explain that Snow White allegedly will change her glass coffin for the enchanted mirror in the future, as if the Wicked Queen could foreshadow Snow White's future. That's why they refer to art that way.

can admire her loveliness. But what about when she matures into a middle-aged woman?

Legend has it that Elizabeth Báthory may have pondered this, as McNally (1985, p. 40) depicts:

> Her German biographer R. von Elsberg (even) claims that Elizabeth sought to preserve her beauty for a potential suitor after her husband's death…Elizabeth was riding through one of her villages in the company of a young admirer, Ladislas, and came across an ugly old woman. Elizabeth turned to her male companion and asked, 'What would you do if you had to kiss that old hag?' The young man blurted out, 'Ugh! God save me from such a hideous fate.' Upon hearing that, the old hag shouted at Elizabeth, 'Take care, O vain one, soon you will look as I do and then what will you do?'

With this folktale, it seems Elizabeth changed from being the prettiest woman in the region, as has been alleged, to the brutal Wicked Queen who used her power to murder her young stepmother. Snow White is thirteen in the tale, and Báthory's victims were immature girls mainly between ten and fourteen who worked for her. In some versions of the tale, the stepmother embodies vampirism and cannibalism: "In Spain, the queen is even more bloodthirsty, asking for a bottle of blood, with the girl's toe used as a cork. In Italy, the cruel queen instructs the huntsman to return with the girl's intestines and her blood-soaked shirt" (Tatar, 1999, p. 74). Báthory's legend is notorious for her bathing in the blood of her young, virgin prey as a cosmetic anti-aging procedure. Nevertheless, her figure is also present in the abovementioned concept of vampirism, especially when linked to lesbianism or bisexuality. The following section will focus on how her persona may have influenced one of the most important novellas of Gothic literature: Sheridan LeFanu's *Carmilla*.

"I live in your warm life, and you shall die-die, sweetly die-into mine"[3]

In 1872, Irish Gothic writer Sheridan Le Fanu published his story *Carmilla* in a serial entitled *The Dark Blue*. The tale is narrated by Laura, a young motherless girl who leads an isolated life in a castle in Styria with her father, some governesses and the servants. The girl is disappointed when an expected visit by her father's friend General Spielsdorf and his niece is postponed. The General, whose intention was to stay with the family, explains to Laura's father that his young relative had suddenly become ill and died. Nevertheless, an accident occurs, and a youngster enters their lives: the apparently naïve Carmilla, who is, in truth, a vampire. Matthew Gibson (2007) analyses several possible sources for *Carmilla*; among them, one could be Dom Augustin Calmet's *Treatise on Vampires and Revenants* (1752), as well as

> William Sabine Baring-Gould's *The Book of Were-wolves* (1863). This work drew attention to Wagener's earlier researches into Erszebet Báthory, the Hungarian Countess who killed her female servants in order to rejuvenate herself with their blood, but who, in Wagener's account, clearly drew pleasure from inflicting sadistic sexual humiliation on her victims, 'especially if they were of her own sex'. The newly current story of Countess Báthory therefore helps to explain why Le Fanu's vampire is a lesbian as well as a Hungarian Countess.

Therefore, does Báthory's image in current popular culture relate to homosexual and vampiric relationships thanks to Le Fanu's *Carmilla*? James Craig Holte (1999) explains how female vampire films, especially some Hammer motion pictures from the 1970s such as *The Vampire Lovers* (1970),

---
[3]. LeFanu, 2012, p.27.

Lust for a Vampire (1971) and *Twins of Evil* (1971), help to illustrate this connection. Holte also states that "an equally attractive source for the development of the female vampire is the life of Elizabeth Báthory" (p. 166).

The eponymous Carmilla also belongs to the aristocracy, and her hidden bloodthirst emerges as the plot develops. The story relates how Carmilla and Laura belong to the same lineage: Le Fanu "makes vampirism, incest and homosexuality resonate" (Leal, 2007, pp. 38-39) in his tale. Whilst "several critics have noted how *Carmilla* is a rendition of Coleridge's fragment *Christabel*, which also features a female vampire, a motherless victim, obscure familial ties, and same-sex desire" (Leal, 2007, p. 39), Coleridge names one of the characters from his play *Zápolya* 'Bethlen Báthory', "an amalgam of Elisabeth Báthory's nephew Prince Gábor and his successor, Gábor Bethlen" (Thorne, 1997, p. 8). Therefore, the Romantic poet may also have been aware of the figure of the Hungarian Countess and her legend, and, consequently, Le Fanu could have been inspired by another piece of fiction by Coleridge's besides *Christabel*.

According to Jung and the aforementioned archetype of the 'animus', animus-inflated women tend to develop an exceptional rational instinct. Carmilla, perhaps in reference to the link with Elizabeth, represents the Jungian archetype of the fatal seductress, the Temptress; an active 'shadow' of the personality, which needs to have power over prey by using physical presence until there is no longer any interest in their victim, who, in Jung's theory, is male. Both Carmilla and Báthory embody this, being manipulative and methodical, yet with the notable difference that the victims are young girls. In reality, Elizabeth's sexual behaviour was not reported and cannot be verified, but it can be said that, from her position of complete power after the death of her husband in 1604, she would have been able to obtain whatever she wanted (Thorne 1997).

In Báthory's time, shapeshifting was believed to be real, and the Countess was credited with the ability to summon evil creatures in order to defeat her powerful enemies. It is therefore interesting to note that when Carmilla attacks Laura, she turns into a cat: "But I (Laura) was equally conscious of being in my room, and lying in bed, precisely as I actually was… I saw something moving round the foot of the bed, which at first I could not accurately distinguish. But I soon saw that it was a sooty-black animal that resembled a monstrous cat" (Le Fanu, 2012, p. 45). Pastor Ponikenus, the Lutheran Reverend at Čachtice, and ally of the Palatine against Báthory, claimed that Elizabeth was a sorceress and noted these words as hers: "God help! God help! You little cloud! God help little cloud! God grant, God grant health to Elizabeth Báthory. Send, send me little cloud ninety cats, I command you, who are the lords of the cats… send them away to bite King Matthia's heart, to bite my lord Palatine's heart…" (Thorne, 1997, p. 71).

Interestingly, when looking at these accusations of sorcery, the King owed Elizabeth money, and the Palatine Thurzó initiated the trial against her, accusing her of mass murder, witchcraft and high treason. After being found guilty of the "massacre of virgins" (Thorne, 1997. p. 57) in a trial in which she was never interrogated, Báthory was walled up in her castle until her death, her lineage ended once her nephew Gábor Báthory was murdered. Similarly, vampire Carmilla, whose real name is Countess Mircalla Karnstein, is finally defeated when she is sealed into her coffin full of blood and, consequently, her direct dynasty, although present with descendants such as Laura, becomes extinct. Therefore, in both cases, a patriarchal society corrals and ends with allegedly supernatural female powers which suppose a threat to the established order.

The fact that Mircalla rests in her blood-filled tomb and maintains her youth resembles Widow Nadashy's legend of Báthory's notorious gore baths: "Two old women and a certain Fitzko assisted her in her undertaking. This monster used to kill the luckless victim, and the old women caught the blood, in which Elizabeth was wont to bathe at the hour of four in the morning. After the bath she appeared more beautiful than before" (Sabine Baring-Gould, 1865, pp. 139-140). In reality, however, Báthory's blood-bathing first appeared in Jesuit Turóczi László's *Tragica Historia* in 1729. There is no mention of this practice in the original trial against her.

There are more similarities between Le Fanu's vampire and the Countess which support the connection between them. Where Báthory was aided by her servants, Carmilla had the support of two women: the so-called Countess who introduces the vampire to her victims, and the mysterious woman of the carriage who does not get out of it (Le Fanu 18-19). This lady resembles Báthory's confidante Anna Darvulia, "the Lady's guide and inspiration in her torturing" (Thorne, 1997, p.98), who was in charge of Elizabeth's domestic arrangements from around 1595 and who died before the trial.

The association between sorcery and vampirism is significant in *Carmilla*. Countess Karnstein, to maintain her façade, purchases "oblong slips of vellum, with cabalistic ciphers and diagrams upon them" (Le Fanu, p. 32) as an "amulet against the oupire" (p. 32). Similarly, in Hungary, aristocratic women such as Elizabeth, though not sorceresses themselves, could act as protectors to the crones known for their healing skills. Nevertheless, when one of the remedies did not work and disease spread uncontrollably, hysteria ruled and between 1529 and 1768 witchcraft trials took place in Báthory's country of Hungary. In the case of her charges of sorcery, it is worthy of notice that she was a Protestant, and had created enemies with other faiths, especially Catholics. Religion also relates Carmilla's lack of prayers to her scorn towards her labourer victims. When the funeral of a young girl occurs in front of Laura and Carmilla, the vampire claims: "She? I don't trouble my head about peasants. I don't know who she is [...] Well, her funeral is over, I hope, and her hymn sung; and our ears shan't be tortured with that discord and jargon" (pp. 30-31).

Similarly, Báthory despised peasant girls to the point of torturing them to death, or so her notorious legend declares. Alejandra Pizarnik's dark collection of poetic prose on the Countess describes in detail the alleged torment the Lady imposed on her prey. This section of the article will examine *The Bloody Countess*.

"More, more still, harder still!"[4]

Alejandra Pizarnik narrates Báthory's life in her short book *The Bloody Countess* (1965). Following French surrealist author Valentine Penrose's 1962 *Erzsébet Báthory la Comtesse Sanglante*, the Argentinian combines poetic prose, dark fantasy and journalism to depict the legend of the notorious Countess. From the very beginning of her narrative, Pizarnik focuses on the alleged torture which the aristocrat perpetrated to obtain eternal youth through blood. There is a brief analysis of how Penrose describes the Countess as a "gorgeous" criminal : "she (Penrose) inscribes the subterranean kingdom of Elizabeth Báthory in the torture room of her medieval castle: there, the sinister beauty of the night creatures summarises itself in a silent woman of a legendary paleness, of demented eyes, of hair with the luxurious colour of the crows"[5] (Pizarnik, 2014, p. 8). Pizarnik explores Báthory's alleged methods of torture, such as placing girls inside a cage with spikes, throwing frozen water at their naked bodies outdoors until they died, burning and mutilating them or employing the notorious Iron Maiden, a means of torture "often linked to the Middle Ages, though there is reason to believe that, in fact, it was not conceived until the

---

[4]. Penrose, 2000, 388 Position, Kindle Book.
[5]. Original text: "*Inscribe el reino subterráneo de Elizabeth Báthory en la sala de torturas de su castillo medieval: allí, la siniestra hermosura de las criaturas nocturnas se resume en una silenciosa palidez legendaria, de ojos dementes, de cabellos del color suntuoso de los cuervos*".

end of the XVIII century" (Torture Museum, 2015).

Báthory's prey were tortured at her castles and while she travelled in her carriage with the aid of her servants (Craft, 2009, chapter 13). Nevertheless, her favourite location to murder is said to have been the basement at her castle at Čachtice, nowadays western Slovakia. On the one hand, she may have chosen her basement to murder her victims as a means to hide her misdeeds; on the other, it is significant that an underground room corresponds to her 'underworld', a journey into her excessive subconscious. Elizabeth was able to mistreat the girls however she wished, since she was isolated in her castle. She lured them to her fortress, for "it was a great honour for a girl to be given a position in her (Elizabeth's) household, even that of a humble seamstress or chambermaid, and all her servants had come recommended for a particular skill" (Thorne, 1997, p. 31). However, the rumours of her cruelty spread and "poor families around Čachtice hid their daughters when they heard that the Lady was approaching" (Thorne, 1997, p. 31). In time, the Countess became bolder, and she began to attack noblewomen, which led her to her final destruction. However, Kimberly L. Craft explains how during the trial against the Countess it was said that some mothers gave her daughters to the Countess despite knowing of the girls' likely fate: "the Lady Szell had brought a girl, and one was also brought from Poland. The (wife of) János Bársony also brought a large, tall girl, the daughter of a nobleman, from where János Poliani lived; she was also killed" (Craft, 2009, p. 148).

It is relevant that at some point both Pizarnik and Penrose compare the aristocrat to the notorious 15th century serial killer of children, Gilles de Rais; Penrose (1962) states: "She (Báthory) knew nothing about remorse. Never did she, like Gilles de Rais after his crimes, roll about in her bed, praying and weeping. Her madness was her birthright. If she fell, it was not because she played a role unworthy of herself".

As has been employed in this article, Pizarnik begins each of her chapters with quotes to give a hint of the subject treated in her narrative. Yet there is an author whom she not only cites, but whom she also comments on at the end of her work and mentions alongside de Rais: French writer and libertine Marquis de Sade.

'Sadism' was so-named after the French author, and definitively established as a term by Freud in his 1905 *Three Essays on the Theory of Sexuality*. For French philosopher Michel Foucault,

> Sadism is not a name finally given to a practice as old as Eros; it is a massive cultural fact which appeared precisely at the end of the eighteenth century, and which constitutes one of the greatest conversions of Western imagination: unreason transformed into delirium of the heart, madness of desire, the insane dialogue of love and death in the limitless presumption of appetite (Foucault, 2001, p. 199).

Consequently, Pizarnik wisely compares the Countess to Sade and de Rais, since Báthory may have suffered from Sadistic Personality Disorder, as it was named in an appendix of the Diagnostic and Statistical Manual of Mental Disorders (DSM-III-R). It was removed from later versions of the manual. The disorder involves obtaining sexual pleasure from the discomfort or pain of others (Myers, 2006).

Báthory murdered ruthlessly for six years, from 1604 until 1610. She already tortured her servants while her husband was alive, and was indeed encouraged by him to do so, but the killings commenced after his passing. The question which arises is, why did nobody stop her before? The Tripartitum, the influential Hungarian law which reinforced the feudal system after a peasant revolt in 1514, gave full power to the nobles. Although rumours about Báthory spread, it was not until she slaughtered several noblewomen that actions against her were considered. Aristocracy held complete power over their peasants and servants. In this context, Báthory may have considered herself to be a goddess-like figure, above the law. For that precise reason, Penrose likens the Countess to the Hindu goddess Kali:

> the mythical representation and textualization of continuity. The countess literally (albeit unconsciously according to the narrator, Penrose) surpasses her limited existence by bathing in the blood of young girls which sustains her illusion of never dying; she thereby identifies with the continuity of the universe symbolized in the figure of Kali (Humpreys, 2003, p. 748)

Jung (1968, p. 82) also considers Kali as "the loving and terrible mother" in India, and the last section of this article will focus on how, in the TV series *American Horror Story*, a malicious vampire named the Countess can exhibit a similar duality by being a loving mother figure.

"I Save all my Children"[6]

The fifth season of *American Horror Story* (*AHS*), named *Hotel*, is full of serial killers. Viewers can find references to real murderers of the likes of H. H. Holmes, John Wayne Gacy or Aileen Wournos among others. The show creators, Ryan Murphy and Brad Falchuk, introduced the most ancient serial killer in their show so far: Countess Elizabeth Báthory.

In anticipation of the season five premier, the *Telegraph* (2015) penned about Lady Gaga's role: "Inspired – like many horror villainesses before her – by the real-life Countess Elizabeth Báthory, the 100-year-old character suffers from a rare 'haemophiliac virus', and combines her thirst for blood with a passion for fashion and an insatiable appetite for sex".

---

6. *American Horror Story*, S5, E4.

There are similarities between Báthory and Murphy's vampiric femme fatale version of the Countess of Blood. Craft (2009, pp. 64-65) states that "One particular gift Ferenc allegedly brought home to his wife was a device that resembled a hand of sharp claws that could be fitted over the fingers to cut, slash, and stab a victim". This not only echoes the animal shapeshifting in *Carmilla*, but also the Countess's glove in *AHS* with which she and her vampire creations murder their victims, since they do not have fangs to drain their prey. Moreover, "when servant girls passed out or were thought to be lazy, Ferenc taught Erzsébet how to insert pieces of oiled paper between their toes and then light the papers on fire" (Craft, 2009, p. 65). In *Hotel*, March (Evan Peters), the Countess's first husband, who is based on America's first serial killer H.H. Holmes, is depicted as the creator of a torture chamber at his hotel where he can murder as he pleases. She witnesses some of his killings and feels pleasure at doing so.

Is it possible therefore to believe that such cruel women can offer true maternal love? Authors such as Penrose (1962) and Craft (2009) believe so, since they emphasise letters Báthory sent to her husband regarding their children:

At your service, I write to you, my beloved Lord.

Regarding the children, I can report that Anna, thank God, is healthy, Kata has eye pain, and Orsika the mouth rot. I am healthy, thank God; only the eyes hurt me. God keep you.

Written at Sárvár, on the 8th day of the Month of St. James (July), 1596 (Craft, pp. 50-51)

Nevertheless, Báthory was hardly ever with her children; they were sent away to study in their youth, and as adults they lived with their spouses. It is believed that Elizabeth and Nadásdy had three girls and one son during their marriage, the first born after ten years of being together. Murphy's Countess is seldom seen with her new descendants, yet she kidnaps three boys and one girl to save them from neglect: "I could see where they were headed. A tragic, wasted life. I opened my heart and the children came to me willingly" (*AHS*, S5, E4). Must the viewer believe she loves these children? Is it her means of creating a pure race similar to the Báthory inbreeding? The show does not give any real answers.

As the plot continues, the audience learns of the Countess's attempted abortion in 1926, and how the child, Bartholomew, survived, as he shared her vampiric condition. She accepts the child into her heart, becoming fiercely protective and nurturing of him, despite the implication that he is deformed. The motherly instinct the Countess possesses is displayed again when her new husband Will Drake (Cheyenne Jackson) witnesses the hideous Bartholomew thanks to the Countess's former spouse James Patrick March, and Drake violently rejects the baby. Consequently, Drake is imprisoned by the Countess with the vampire Ramona (Angela Bassett), who kills him to consume his blood (*AHS*, S5, E9).

Báthory did not suffer an abortion per se, as authors such as the aforementioned Craft, Tony Thorne, and Raymond McNally illustrate. Nonetheless, there are differences in their telling of Báthory's transgression. All of them discuss how the teenage aristocrat had an affair with a young man when she was already engaged to Nadásdy: "Elizabeth had become pregnant. So, under the official pretext that Elizabeth had contracted some 'illness', she was spirited away to a remote Báthory castle in Transylvania, where Elizabeth gave birth to a daughter" (McNally, 1985, p. 29). However, Thorne (1997) and Craft (2009) analyse how the young man was named Ladislav Bende. They give an identity to her sentimental partner, with whom she maintained a supposed passionate love affair. Following R.A.von Elsberg's biography on the Countess, Craft (2009) depicts the alleged testimonies given by the Countess to the Church accusing Bende of abusing her. She did so in order to maintain her honour, despite the fact that the records of those reports were from 1609, when the Lady was 49 years of age.

In the presentation of both the real Countess and Murphy's vampire homage, both are assisted in reaching their aims. Where Báthory relied on her domestics to cover her crimes, the Countess in *AHS* assigns diverse tasks to her creations and underlings. Additionally, both women have employees who look after their children. McNally (1985, p. 33) describes how "the peasant woman Helena Jo, one of the 'accomplices' charged in the 1611 trial, was chiefly responsible for taking care of the infant Paul. Helen Jo was Paul's *dakja*, a term meaning 'wet nurse' as well as 'child nurse'". Similarly, the Countess in *AHS* employs two characters to feed and guard her vampire children: Iris (played by Kathy Bates), who is the mother of Donovan (Matt Bomer), one of the Countess's sexual partners; and Dr Alex Lowe (Chloë Sevigny), wife of detective John Lowe (Wes Bentley), and the biological mother of one of the Countess's kidnapped 'children'.

Taking into consideration the depictions of the Countesses here analysed, their roles as mothers remain ambiguous and arguably non-traditional. As the Countess states to the character of Nick, about her creation, later known as Elizabeth Taylor (Denis O'Hare), "we have two selves: one the world needs us to be: compliant, and the shadow. Ignore it and life is forever suffering" (*AHS*, S5, E5). This explains her behaviour in one scene with the police, when she acts as the perfect wife and stepmother of Lachlan (Lyric Lennon), Drake's son (E9). This behaviour echoes the Jungian archetype of the 'shadow', which "personifies everything that the subject refuses to acknowledge about himself and yet is always thrusting upon him directly or indirectly" (Jung, 1968, pp. 284-285). Jung employs the image of the mirror to introduce his concept of the 'shadow', as it shows the dark side the person does not want to accept. It is significant that Murphy's Countess, a stepmother in the series, calls back to Grimm's Wicked Queen, analysed in the first section of the article, coming, thus, full circle.

Conclusion

It is probable that we will never truly know what occurred at Báthory's castles due to the difficulties in finding any documents, let alone unbiased ones, as well as the language barrier which emerges for most scholars. Yet fiction and non-fiction continue to depict and analyse the haunting figure of the mysterious Countess. This article has illustrated the dark characteristics commonly linked to Elizabeth Báthory: vanity, lesbianism and vampirism, the torture of young women, and, finally, her less discussed feature of motherhood.

Jungian archetypes such as the 'animus' and the 'shadow' help to interpret her behaviour. An extremely powerful woman in a man's world, Elizabeth abused her power to ill-treat and murder those over which she ruled, although the number of victims varies from one source to another. What remains of her persona in popular culture has been studied through different narratives and more will follow as she continues to both fascinate and repel the public. It is the audience's task, therefore, to consider why they are so interested in the abovementioned features, what it reflects of society, and why an alleged serial killer who died more than four hundred years ago remains a current affair.

Bibliography

American Horror Story, 2015-2016. Season 5, *Hotel*. [TV Programme] FX.

Baring-Gould, S., 1865. *The book of were-wolves: being an account of a terrible superstition*.[e-book] Smith, Elder & Co. Available at: Internet Archive <https://archive.org/details/bookwerewolvesb00barigoog/page/n10> [Accessed 20 November 2018].

Craft, K. L., 2009. *Infamous lady: the true story of Countess Elizabeth Báthory*. [Kindle DX version]. Available through: Amazon.es <http://www.amazon.es> [Accessed 15 October 2018].

Foucault, M., 2001. *Madness and civilization: a history of insanity in the age of reason*. Routledge Classics, Psychology Press. Available at: Google Books <http://booksgoogle.com> [Accessed 2 November 2018].

Gibson, M., 2007. *Jane Cranstoun, Countess Purgstall: a possible inspiration for LeFanu's "Carmilla"*. University of Central Lancashire. [online] Available at: Internet Archive <https://web.archive.org/web/20090304171734/http://www.jslefanu.com/gibson.html> [Accessed 5 December 2018].

Gilbert, S. M. and Gubar, S. 1979. *The Madwoman in the Attic: The Woman Writer and the Nineteenth-Century Literary Imagination*. New Haven: Yale University Press.

Grimm, J. and W., 2005. *Little snow white*. [online] Available at: <http://www.pitt.edu/~dash/grimm053.html> [Accessed 20 November 2018].

Holte, J.C., 1999. Not all fangs are phallic: female film vampires. *Journal of the Fantastic in the Arts*, [e-journal] 10(2), pp. 163-173. Available through: JSTOR <https://www.jstor.org/stable/43308382?read-now=1&seq=4#page_scan_tab_contents> [Accessed 5 December 2018].

Humpreys, K., 2003. The poetics of transgression in Valentine Penrose's "La Comtesse sanglante". *The French Review*, [e-journal] 76(4), pp. 740-751. Available through: JSTOR <https://www.jstor.org/stable/3133083?read-now=1&seq=9#page_scan_tab_contents> [Accessed 10 November 2018].

Jung, C.G., 1968. *Collected works of C. G. Jung: the archetypes and the collective unconscious*. 3rd ed. [online] Available at: <https://archive.org/details/collectedworksof91cgju/page/n3> [Accessed November 2018].

Leal, A., 2007. *Unnameable desires in LeFanu's Carmilla*. [pdf] Syracuse: Syracuse University. Available at: <http://englishnovel2.qwriting.qc.cuny.edu/files/2014/01/Leal-names-desire-Carmilla.pdf> [Accessed 25 November 2018].

LeFanu, J. S., 2012. *Carmilla*. Bizarro Pulp Press.

Mcnally, R.T., 1985. *Dracula was a woman*. 3rd edition. London: Hamlyn Paperbacks.

Myers, Wade C., Burket, Roger C. and Husted, David S., 2006. Sadistic personality disorder and comorbid mental illness in adolescent psychiatric inpatients, *Journal of the American Academy of Psychiatry and the Law Online*. [online] Available at: <https://archive.is/20130415045910/http://www.jaapl.org/content/34/1/61.full.pdf.html> [Accessed 29 October 2018].

Penrose, V., 2000. *The bloody countess: atrocities of Erzsebet Báthory*. [Kindle DX version] Available at: amazon.es <http://www.amazon.es> [Accessed 5 November 2018].

Pizarnik, A., 2014. *La condesa sangrienta*. Libros del Zorro Rojo.

Tacey, D., 2012. Phenomenology of the self: the ego, the shadow; the syzygy: anima and animus; the self. In: D. Tacey, ed., *The Jung Reader*, 1st ed. Sussex: Routledge. Chapter 6.

Tatar, M. 1999. Introduction. In: M. Tatar, ed., *The Classic Fairy Tales*, 1st ed. New York: W.W. Norton & Company, Inc., pp. 74-96.

Telegraph Reporters, 2015. Lady Gaga in American Horror Story: Hotel: is she any good?. *The Telegraph*, [online] Available at: <https://www.telegraph.co.uk/culture/tvandradio/11915078/American-Horror-Story-Hotel-review-of-reviews.html> [Accessed 22nd November 2018].

Thorne, T. (1997). *Countess Dracula*. London: Bloomsbury Publishing plc.

Torture Museum. (2015). The Nuremberg Virgin. [online] Available at <http://torturemuseum.net/en/the-nuremberg-virgin/> [Accessed on 22 March 2018].

Van den Berg-Cook, N., (n.d.) *The magic mirror in Snow White*. [pdf] Available at: <https://www.cgjung-vereniging.nl/home/files/nancy_vd_berg.pdf> [Accessed 19 November 2018].

From Light to Dark – Using Gothic Styles to Visualise Evil in Architecture

Dominic Riemenschneider

Abstract

There are different reasons, strategies and forms for how the Gothic style, as a broad definition, is used within Fantasy storytelling.

This article will discuss representations of the Gothic within the visual modern Fantastic to visualise and characterise evil settings from an art-historical point of view. Using examples from a variety of media, the primary focus will be the connection between the architectural style begun during the Middle Ages in Europe and the ensuing views of the style by Romanticism and Historicism as well as its influences on the imagery of modern Fantasy and Science Fiction. Furthermore, strategies behind the presentation of the architectural elements will be discussed.

The examples to be discussed were chosen with the criteria of being built by an evil force or villain or to create an 'atmosphere of evil'. The other main consideration was that the architectural settings should feature obvious Gothic style motifs with a connection to an evil force.[1]

---

[1]. One might wonder why one of the most obvious buildings representing evil – *Barad-dûr* from Middle-earth, created by J. R. R. Tolkien – is not used as an example. It is, after all, an architectural manifestation of evil, built by Sauron, the evil force of this fictional world. However, in the visualisations, especially the movies by Peter Jackson, it has no explicit Gothic features in the understanding posited by this article. Orthanc, home of Saruman, with its obvious Gothic motifs, was not chosen as it wasn't built and designed by an evil force. Saruman became a villain centuries after he moved into this monolithic tower.

1. Gothic: A Term with many Faces

The term 'Gothic' is one that has assumed various faces throughout history, from an ancient European tribe that had a massive effect on the fall of the Roman Empire, to the black-clad subculture begun in the 1980s[2]; from haunted mansions and foreboding castles, to the cathedrals of the so-called 'Dark Ages', featuring walls filled with glass and made of light; from being associated with everything barbaric, ugly and coarse, to the 'Gothic sublime' of the Romantic era. The manifold and contradicting matter and objects associated with 'Gothic' makes it one of the most interesting and ambiguous terms in all fields of research.

In the context of the Fantastic, though, especially in Fantasy and Science Fiction, the usage of the term Gothic can in fact be clarified. It was strongly connected to the birth of modern Fantastic literature in the 18th century, with Horace Walpole's *The Castle of Otranto* (1764), the first of the Gothic novels still inspiring literature, art and movies today (Grein, 1995, pp. 18-26). With Mary Shelley's *Frankenstein* (1818), Edgar Allan Poe's work (e.g. *The Fall of the House of Usher*, 1839) and, later, Bram Stoker's famous *Dracula* (1897), the connection between horror and architecture found its foundation. Those, and of course many other authors, used old mansions and castles to give the supernatural, uncanny, and the evil a home. Mostly, those monuments were shown in a Gothic-influenced architectural style or borrowed architectural features from it. In combination with the Romanticist imagery of the 18th and 19th centuries using Gothic architecture, the connection between this and the Fantastic began[3].

---

[2]. A short overview of the different meanings of the term by Groom, N., 2012. *The Gothic: a very short introduction.* 1st ed. Very short introductions. Oxford: Oxford University Press.

[3]. Many examples, forms and mediums of Gothic in the Fantastic can be found in Bacon, S. ed., 2018. *The Gothic: a reader*. Oxford: Peter Lang.

When the Fantastic turned to more visual mediums to encourage a broader audience in the 20th century through movies and illustrations, comics, TV shows and fan art, and split into more distinct genres such as fantasy, science fiction, horror, and steampunk, the connection between Gothic-styled architecture and evil settings remained. It can be found in medieval-oriented fantasy, as well as in futuristic science fiction, with Gothic features and motifs used in a decorative manner or to construct an entire building. The forms range from historical representations to varied, enhanced, or transformed, as will be examined below.

2. Gothic Style and Features: The Basics

Before discussing how the connection between Gothic architecture and evil settings occurred, a short overview of the architectural style and its particular motifs is necessary. These motifs connect contradictory buildings and interiors from the Medieval period to modern architecture, varying from sacral to profane[4] and can be found across different continents. This makes the Gothic style perhaps one of the most commonly implemented architectural styles.

Gothic architecture, as represented in the Fantastic, mostly refers to the 'original' epoch of the Middle Ages. However, more commonplace, and perhaps more familiar, are the buildings of Gothic Revival and Neo-Gothic, constructed between the mid 18th century and the first quarter of the 20th century, primarily with a focus on English schools (Freigang, 2015, pp. 123-127) or the influence on Art Nouveau and Jugendstil[5]. Certainly,

---

[4]. By way of example, for the Medieval period: city halls, market halls, houses of the nobility; for the 19th century: justice palaces, train stations, schools, greenhouses, parliament buildings, museums, etc.

[5]. A well-known example is the Sagrada Família Cathedral by Antoni Gaudí in Barcelona, which combines Gothic elements with Art Nouveau. It also serves as the model for Gotham Cathedral in Batman's Gotham City, as embodied in the movies by director Tim Burton, and designed by Anton Furst.

these styles are all interdependent and can be referred to at the same time in one example from Fantastic media.

Gothic can be defined as a European epoch of art and architecture from the mid-12th century to around 1500, and is divided into distinct phases, as well as regional and national styles.

What is now called 'Gothic' first developed in France around 1140, but spread quickly all over northern Europe. Gothic-styled buildings can be found in Spain and Brittany, England, Germany, Scandinavia, the Czech Republic, Poland, Romania, and the Baltics. Therefore, it is also called 'International Style', as master builders and craftsmen travelled all over the continent to build, in particular, sacral buildings. The most famous examples are the cathedrals in France, but also in Spain, the Czech Republic, England, and Germany[6].

This Europe-wide activity did not create a unique appearance of buildings, but they all share features and motifs that obviously connect them to what we refer to as (Neo)Gothic architecture since centuries past.

Without exploring the full history of the Gothic architectural epoch, it can be stated that pointed arches and windows, buttresses and supporting arches, bundle pillars and ripped vaults are some of the most important and widely used elements of Gothic monuments. The style is further defined by the inclusion of colorful stained glass windows with longitudinal and pointed forms, and impressive round, rose windows; tracery in the windows, or as applications on walls, vaults and

---

[6]. Due to the limits of one article, the overview does not refer to important buildings themselves. The literature concerning this topic is manifold. Important works include Brachmann, C., 2013. *WBG Architekturgeschichte Bd. 1: Das Mittelalter (800–1500). Klöster – Kathedralen – Burgen.* Darmstadt: WBG, Wissenschaftliche Buchgesellschaft p. 149-319 or Toman, R. and Bednorz, A., 2007. *Gotik: Architektur, Skulptur, Malerei.* Königswinter: Ullmann.

the whole interior; and finials, pinnacles and crockets.

Another important aspect of Gothic buildings is the vertical orientation of structural elements, slender forms and an appearance of weightlessness. Due to new developments during the Gothic era in the understanding of construction and weight distribution, walls were no longer required to carry the full weight of the roof and vaults anymore, allowing for the placement of elaborate windows, bringing light into the space. Unimaginable new heights, widths and scales were reached during this time (Brachmann, 2013, p. 182-186).

These roughly sketched features of Gothic architecture are not limited to the Middle Ages. A Gothic revival occurred in the late 18th century, particularly connected to the art of Romanticism and the buildings of Historicism. Simultaneous to the beginning of Fantastic literature, buildings with Gothic features and styles appeared all over the world. The ideal example of this connection is one of the first Gothic Revival buildings, Strawberry Hill in Twickenham, England (1749), commissioned and designed by the first Gothic novelist, Horace Walpole (Bacon ed., 2018, p. 153-160).

Even 'modern' constructions from the 1930s, like warehouses and skyscrapers, still used echoes of the Gothic in external and internal decorations. A prominent example of the historical style, merged with modern materials and functions, is the Woolworth Building in New York City.

3. Examples

Before discussing how Gothic, as a broad term, has become synonymous with evil in general, four varying examples of Gothic-styled interiors and exteriors from Fantasy and Science Fiction will be presented. They are taken from different media and genres to emphasise the widespread presentation of Gothic forms and motifs, and to demonstrate how a variety of evil settings can be styled and characterised.

Bloodborne (Video Game, Horror/Fantasy, 2015)

The video game *Bloodborne*, developed by FromSoftware, was published in 2015 by Sony for PlayStation 4. It is a third-person action role-play game with a main character, called The Hunter, featured in a plot focused on combat and exploration.

The world of *Bloodborne* is centred around a decrepit, Gothic Victorian-era city named Yharnam, which came to be known for its medical advances, particuarly rgarding blood diseases. After a plague turn the population into monsters and nightmares, the city becomes decayed, mostly abandoned, and a place rife for evil to spread. Yharnam consists of varying districts and levels, and also features 'mandatory' dungeons with horrors to overcome.

The game sits predominently in the horror genre and is set in the 19th century, using actual architectural references in combination with artistic imagination and literary motifs; in particular, it features elements from Gothic novels such as Mary Shelley's *Frankenstein* and early horror authors like H. P. Lovecraft, and his fictional entities The Old Ones (Maher, 2018).

The city consists of many tall and representative buildings, with up to four storeys or more. A lot of viewing points, for example the Great Bridge or the towers of the Grand Cathedral, also use the city's silhouette, with its towers and spires as a background. All buildings follow the Gothic style of the 19th century, mostly in its English form, with pinnacles, finials and crockets being commonplace. The pinnacles are especially used as smaller endings for architectural elements such as portals and edges. They align with the bigger roofs and towers, with their demonstrably pointed and serrated designs. The basic elements of a Gothic style can be found everywhere in these interiors; smaller objects such as fireplaces or shelves are decorated with lancet arches and traceries.

A good example of exterior design is Oedon Chapel. The six storey facade is decorated with various Gothic architectural elements. All piers and edges end in pinnacles, and the bigger pointed arches over the portals and windows are filled with quatrefoils and other tracery elements.

The mentioned viewing points show the combined result of these vertical elements: by using one style, the city becomes a homogeneous, overwhelming mass of sharp edges and spikes, subtextually portraying the hostility the city holds for the player.

Besides the unifying architectural look and the narrow setting of the buildings, the dark and dirty colour scheme evokes the image of the city as one unit. Also, it is always either nighttime or sunset with a cloudy sky and foggy weather, supporting the atmosphere of horror and highlighting the sharp silhouette of the city.

Pathfinder (Roleplaying Game, Fantasy, since 2009)

What could possibly represent evil better than Hell itself? Fantasy and Science Fiction often refer to Hell, metaphorically or as a real place, for all the evil in the world, as a source of pain, suffering, and a lack of prospects. In the multiverse of *Pathfinder*, a fantasy roleplaying game by Paizo Publishing based on the 3.5 edition of *Dungeons & Dragons*, Hell exists as a setting and is described in the rulebook, *The Book of the Damned*[7]. Hell follows the structure of Dante Alighieri's famous *The Divine Comedy* (1321), with nine circled levels in a cone-shaped arrangement (Schneider, 2018, p. 136).

For the purposes of this article, the architectural setting of

---

[7]. The English version was published in 2017. For this article the German version is used: Schneider, F.W. ed., 2018. *Pathfinder: Das Buch der Verdammten*. Waldems: Ulisses Spiele GmbH.

the second level of Hell in *Pathfinder* is particularly important. This level is called Dis, the Infernal City, and is described as the most urbanised section of Hell, with the city itself at its centre and a Babylonian tower in its middle. The 'suburbs' are specified as a mixture of architectural styles from various settings within the multiverse, creating fantastic, but also pretty insane, scenery. The monuments, representative palaces, and towers defy the physical rules of architecture (p. 138).

Right:
Pathfinder, panorama view of the suburbs of Dis in Hell, ©Weston T. Jones, illustration for the rule book *The Book of the Damned*, German version 2018 by Ulisses Spiele GmbH, p. 134/135. ©2018 Paizo Inc.

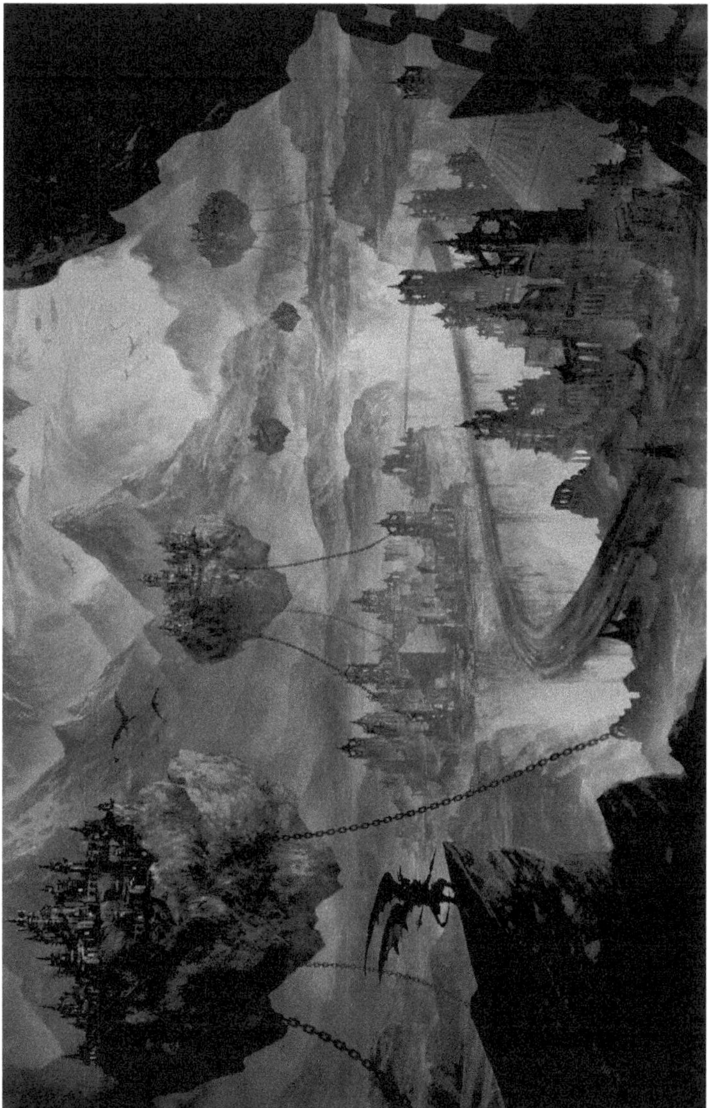

The illustration for this part of Hell shows a cavernous setting, illuminated by red lava streams. The buildings are arranged so as to compact areas, some on floating isles. Noticeably, there are two architectural forms dominating these areas: a few enormous, broad pyramids with little decoration and plain structures, surrounded by many towers with distinct heights, the Gothic style creating a contrast to the smooth pyramids. Four pillars on each edge of a tower with a pinnacle ending are connected to a taller one in the middle via supporting arches. This structure evokes an aggressive, claw-like association. Parts of the buildings appear to be in ruins.

The Abbey of Nevers, built by the evil and religiously fanatical Kytons, who fled from Hell to the Shadow Plane, is another example of a Gothic-styled evil setting in the game (Schneider, 2018, p. 162).

The illustration for this cathedral-like sanctuary, which is described as an ever-reconstructing maze, shows a high main building with three vertical parts and at least five horizontal levels heavily decorated with Gothic elements. Of special note is the two-storey portal, the windows in the shape of jutting arches and smaller friezes with pointed arches separating the levels. The main level is an open space lit by a rose window.

Right:
Pathfinder, facade of the Abbey of Nevers, ©Jay Epperson, illustration for the rule book *The Book of the Damned*, German version 2018 by Ulisses Spiele GmbH, p. 164. ©2018 Paizo Inc.

FROM LIGHT TO DARK: EVIL IN ARCHITECTURE   325

This symmetrical arrangement is aligned with smaller buildings and walls of different shapes, overtopped by monumental pillars with spires that hold supporting arches for the main building. These pillars and arches are of different heights and dimensions, giving the entire building an unsymmetrical look.

Dis, as the urban centre of Hell, and the Abbey of Nevers on the Shadow Plane, demonstrate two important contexts for Gothic receptions that will be important later: first, an urban setting with towers and representative housing; second, a religious context with references to cathedrals and other sacred buildings.

Jupiter Ascending (Movie, Science Fiction, 2015)

Following on from the previously discussed examples that represent historical Gothic elements, two examples of futuristic visualisations and settings will complete the overview of Gothic variations.

The first example is the space opera *Jupiter Ascending*, released in 2015, written, produced and directed by Lana and Lilly Wachowski. Its plot is set in our present time and follows the protagonist Jupiter Jones, a young woman without means from Earth, who is the genetic rebirth of Seraphi, matriarch of the House of Abrasax, the most powerful alien royal dynasty in the galaxy, and therefore her inheritor. Earth and many other planets were populated by ruling human and alien royalties to serve as resources to be harvested at some point in the future. In refineries, human populations are turned into a youth serum to allow the galactic elite to stay young and live forever. It is the most expensive and important trading material in the galaxy. The three children of Seraphi Abrasax, also her heirs, fight over control of their mother's inheritance and, therefore, over Jupiter as the key to securing that legacy.

All three of Seraphi Abrasax's children live, dress and act

more like gods than mere powerful human rulers. Kalique lives in a luxurious Byzantine-Oriental style palace, Titus resides in an extraordinary spaceship, and Balem rules from a monumental refinery inside the well-known storm of the planet Jupiter. All designs blend futuristic and modern styles with historical references to Gothic architecture. The spaceship and the refinery are of particular interest, as they are products of an almost magical technology and display many (historical) Gothic references at the same time.

Titus Abrasax tries to convince Jupiter to marry him to protect Earth from being harvested. The ceremony takes place in a traditional setting: a majestic Gothic cathedral. The central aisle with its arched ambulatories and two gallery levels is reminicient of a historical, stone-made church, only in monumental dimensions. This aisle is overdrawn by a gigantic vault made of glass and tracery. From the top gallery, huge clustered piers with a broad basis taper towards the top, carrying the vault, which is designed as tracery, with glass filling in pointed arches and geometrical Art Nouveau patterns. In the same style are the walls of the sanctuary, connecting the vault and the floor with an overwhelming view into space. They all combine in an organic, tree-like appearance with geometric and Gothic elements.

Furthermore, the concept art for Titus' private rooms show clearly how Gothic tracery is used to decorate walls, roof, entrances and windows. The concepts are similar to some historical references, though they are more disconnected from others; there is, however, a strong connection to English examples, with Art Nouveau abstraction in the second one.

Titus' ship is shown as the luxurious home of a rich libertine with a certain sense of style and privilege reflected in the dimensions, historical references and an iconography of wealth and power.

In contrast to Titus' seat of opulence is Balem's headquarters. He rules his planets and businesses from a gigantic refinery complete with a throne room. The main areas and landing pads are enclosed by a protective cover consisting of slim braces with pointed arches and geometric, pointed patterns; in its Neo-Gothic design, it is reminiscent of decorative greenhouses of the 19th century. The filling is not visible, the viewer encouraged to develop their own theories as to whether it may be special glass or an energy shield, or some other method.

The main factory building is a combination of industrial design and Gothic elements from medieval cathedrals, all on a monumental scale. The decorated pillars and pinnacles of Gothic cathedrals can be found everywhere on the outside of the building. Furthermore, pointed windows with tracery, decorative Gothic friezes, and other elements can be recognised. The concept art and production designs for the movie highlight these references to medieval sacred architecture with their vast piers and supporting arches, or pointed windows on the landing pads. The Gothic repertoire is also transformed and abstracted to create a more futuristic look and to vary the forms of the buildings.

Titus' throne room is designed as a basilica with three naves separated by geometrically decorated piers. The impression of an old church is supported by small, stepped, arched windows in the outside walls, which are apparently made of stone. The hovering throne lies in the sanctuary, a space with walls consisting of slim tracery with pointed arches, smaller lancets with trefoil endings, topped by a gigantic foil with radial ornaments. This broad and high sanctuary opens up a majestic view from the throne to the factory.

Ruthless power, humans as a resource, and near-immortality are the main aspects of Abrasax heirs and their homes. The combination of godlike might and behaviour, along with advanced technology, is reflected in the sacred and representative use of Gothic elements and architectural strategies.

Star Wars (diverse media, comics, Science Fiction, 1977 to present)

Our final example comes from one of the most widely known Science Fiction franchises in the world, ever since the release of the first movie in 1977: *Star Wars*.

The capital of the Old Republic, and later of the Galactic Empire, is Coruscant, a planet consisting of a single city. The most prominent building in this city of extremes is the Presidential Palace (later the Imperial Palace), one of the Twenty Wonders of the Galaxy. The palace was widely enlarged, restructured and fortified into an intimidating monument under Palpatine, who turned the Galactic Republic into a totalitarian dictatorship. Its highest level is outside the planet's atmosphere and was turned into a private sanctuary under the reign of Emperor Palpatine for his personal use (Andreson, 1997, pp.72-75; Carey, 2003).

The palace is a pyramid with manifold extensions, towers and piers. The outside cover is green-and-grey rock and mirrored crystals. Most new sections and reconstructions were specially designed by the Emperor himself.

One of these extensions is the Grand Corridor, an area with connections to the Senate, as well as the offices of important governmental members, and the landing pads. It is so huge that a whole Star Destroyer spaceship could fit into the space[1]. It was used for official receptions, and by senators and other visitors as a communal area for relaxation. That is one of the reasons why the Emperor lined the hall with trees containing hidden surveillance technology.

One comic, *First Impressions*[2], portrays wall designs

---

[1]. For comparison, the length of a Star Destroyer space ship of the Galactic Empire is 1600 meters, according to https://starwars.fandom.com/wiki/Imperial_II-class_Star_Destroyer (Accessed 26 March 2019).
[2]. Various authors, 2004. *First Impressions*. *Star Wars Tales* Vol. 4. Milwaukie., OR: Dark Horse Comics, Inc.

containing deeply carved windows with four slim lancet windows in the lower part, crowned by a round window with geometric pieces of glass. Each window ensemble is framed by vertical friezes that reach to the unseen vault; there are only technical instruments hanging down from above. The windows are decorated with small columns between the lancet openings and bigger elements at the transition to, and around, the round windows, all in the same greyish colour.

The entire design is a combination of Gothic elements and structures whose features appear futuristic and technological. With its dimensions, the already majestic window pattern of Gothic cathedrals is turned into a monumental, industrial version of this style.

4. Similarities & Differences in Fantastic Gothic Representation

The four preceding examples present similarities and differences in the use of Gothic styles and features in their visual world building. The Fantasy examples demonstrate a more historical representation of the medieval Gothic epoch or the Neo-Gothic style during the 19th century. It can be stated that these examples primarily focus on a medieval appearance in their fictional worlds, societies and technology levels. Even though the historical references are stronger in Fantasy than in Science Fiction, the Gothic elements cannot be reduced to simply being copied or drawing citations from a historical art point of view. They are always used to create something unique, fitting into the particular world building. At the same time, however, the visual references are rooted in history.

Science Fiction, with its potential outlook on a close or distant future, is not anti-historical per se, or lacking in references to historical styles, as the examples provided demonstrate. In the Science Fiction examples, however, the Gothic elements are used to construct a more explicit connection backwards, as in the wedding cathedral on a spaceship in *Jupiter Ascending*. However, this representation is detached from the historical context, becoming more abstract, enhanced, alienated or reduced.

But, why Gothic elements as a common thread in these totally different settings and fantastical contexts?

Gothic features should create a historical ambience for the recipient. In *Bloodborne*, the Victorian era is signposted in the architectural style of the buildings, as it is the epoch in which the game is set. Hell and the Infernal City of Dis in *Pathfinder*, with its mixture of pyramids and Gothic towers, is an eternal realm of contradictions and madness. The Abrasax family in *Jupiter Ascending* has been ruling for millennia (the matriarch is over 100,000 years old, while her children are at least 14,000 years old). Despite technological advances, their seats of power are filled with historic designs and references to underline their long reign. Only the Grand Reception Hall in the Imperial Palace in *Star Wars* is a relatively modern building within its fictional setting, and the Gothic-inspired design follows a similar premise to the other examples.

Before examining how Gothic references are used to create an atmosphere of menace, superiority and history, a brief look at how Gothic style is used to represent power and control is necessary, as it also influences the perception of evil.

It can be stated that dark forces and villains are evil due to their actions and the manner in which they attempt to achieve their ambitious but often diabolical goals. Most evil characters are also very powerful due to magical, political, economic and/or divine resources. So, when evil builds itself a home, that home needs to represent its architect's claims of power.

The presentation of power through architecture, both fictional and real, was always achieved through monumental buildings, decorative elements and the use of special materials (such as marble, gold and glass), thereby demonstrating great economic and technological resources. Gothic cathedrals are a prime example of this. In addition to the religious aspects of constructing a state-of-the-art monument over decades or even centuries, there was often competition during the Medieval Gothic epoch between cities and their rulers (bishops, lords, merchants) to have a more impressive church than the neighbouring city (higher nave, broader vaults, taller towers, richer interiors, or a larger area of expensive stained-glass coloured windows) (Toman and Bednorz, 2007, pp. 262-265; Brachman, 2013, p. 66ff). Aside from the dimensions, the interior and exterior decorations with their stonemasonry, statues and friezes would demonstrate the power and prosperity of the city.

As a matter of course, all architectural epochs competed with their own strategies and features. However, the Gothic style was one of the most successful, spanning from the end of the 18th century until the 1930s due to its rebirth through Neo-Gothic style and also its viability even today in new media shows.

All over the world, representative buildings were built with Gothic features, enhanced, developed further and integrated into new styles like Jugendstil and Art Nouveau. Even in the most modern symbols of architecture, skyscrapers, Gothic elements can be found in early iterations and during their breakthrough. Skyscrapers are used furthermore in fictional, and arguably real world, contexts as architectural symbols of power [3] in the same way cathedrals once were.

Considering the representational aspects and the necessary economic and technological resources, it is not surprising that

---

[3]. Good examples are Wayne Tower in Gotham City (DC Universe), The Aerium in Bay City (*Altered Carbon*) or the skyscrapers on Coruscant in the *Star Wars* universe. For examples from the real world, the skylines of New York City or Chicago, with their corporate towers, or newly built modern cities like Dubai or Abu Dhabi, can be named. See the author's article in Görden, M. ed., 2018. *Das Science Fiction Jahr 2018*. Berlin: Golkonda or the blog post from 76th World Science Fiction Convention about towers on www.arthistoryfantastics.com.

Gothic buildings are mostly an urban phenomenon. Only cities with the requisite human, intellectual and financial resources were able to commit to such demanding projects like cathedrals (Toman and Bednorz, 2007, p. 263).

With rapidly growing cities during the Industrial Revolution and the simultaneous Gothic Revival, the metropoles of the 19th and 20th century gained a new Gothic look as the style was used for many public and prominent buildings such as schools, train stations, churches, universities and city halls, as well as decorative elements on residential buildings (Freigang, 2015, p. 37). Of course, Historicism and Eclecticism used other styles too, but Gothic was one of the most popular. With the continuing growth of cities, the Gothic style became urbanised again and survived until the 20th century. In fictional worlds, Gothic representation never ended, as the examples show.

Many documents demonstrate how this style, particularly for sacred monuments, was seen as sublime, transcendent and illuminated, with its verticality, decorative elements, traceries and tremendous coloured glass windows. Therefore, it was the perfect style for paying homage to the Divine (Erne, 2012, pp. 126-129).

At the beginning of the Renaissance, another phase of opinion on Antiquity began. All European styles considered to not be classical or Mediterranean were dismissed. In art and architecture, this mode of thought remained mainstream until at least the end of the 18th century. One of the first critics of the Gothic style was the architect Donato Bramante (1444-1514), referring to it as the 'Germanic style' that is all 'unnatural and irrational'[4], its vertical tendencies not oriented to the human body, the gargoyles and other fantastic imagery, and the overall use of pinnacles, traceries, etc. This was the beginning of a centuries-long discussion about Gothic architecture.

---

[4]. 'Squat little figures, badly carved, which are used as corbels to hold up the roof beams, along with bizarre animals and figures and crude foliage, all unnatural and irrational'. Quote from Groom, 2012, p. 13.

The use of language like 'unnatural and irrational' is very interesting when discussing the reception of Gothic in the visual Fantastic, for it can be argued that its world building properties can be identified in this way – without the negative connotations, of course.

Giorgio Vasari, in the 1530s, was the first to use the term Gothic, also describing it negatively[5]. For centuries, these negative connotations stuck to the style until the Gothic Revival in the 18th century changed the course of the discussion. During the Industrial Revolution, Gothic style was revitalised with new ways of fabrication, new materials (iron, steel and, later, concrete), and new building types, allowing it to be transferred and transformed over decades, until it reached the 20th century.

5. How Gothic turned Dark

With the Gothic style being used for centuries as a representation of power, Divine contexts, and as a visible statement to the past, how has it come to be synonymous in the Fantastic with darkness, evil, and as characteristic of the homes of villains?

Since the birth of the modern Fantastic is closely linked to Gothic novels, the connection between dark and evil settings and Gothic-style architecture was established from the beginning. Horace Walpole, Mary Shelley and, later, Bram Stoker, Edgar Allan Poe and H. P. Lovecraft used historical, medieval buildings to house horror, the supernatural and evil. Literature is an imaginative art, which is why it is not necessary to give full architectural descriptions. The reader fills the imaginative free space with their own experiences and ideas of how a medieval castle looks.

When the Fantastic becomes visual, distinct references and receptions are needed. The 500-year-old evaluations of the Gothic by Bramante and Vasari give an idea of why the style

---

[5]. 'Monstrous and barbaric, wholly ignorant of any accepted ideas of sense and order'. Quote from Groom, 2012, p. 13.

was predestined to be linked with dark and evil contexts.

The serrated and pointed elements of Gothic buildings create an intimidating and menacing silhouette. The tall buildings and cathedrals are overwhelming, man-made mountains of stone, crafted to intimidate individuals with their presentation of power, be that divine, political, or financial.

The association between Gothic and prominent buildings, as seen all over Europe (and in Neo-Gothic form around the world), has been explored in some detail. The majestic features and towering elements, in combination with the extensive decorations, are illustrative of outstanding abilities, wealth, and power – in both fictional and real worlds. These traits, and the desire for control and intimidation, are often associated with mighty villains, or forces with special, outstanding abilities and vast resources.

Gothic style is often used to create a medieval-esque setting. This can be utilised to subtextually convey the ancient nature of evil in the fictional world. Even immortal forces or characters can be set in such ambience.

6. Conclusion: Thoughts on Gothic Representation in Evil Settings

Evil, in all its forms and guises, plays an important role in Fantasy, Science Fiction and other genres of the Fantastic. Sometimes, it can be identified easily by its nature (like Satan and Hell in *Pathfinder*, or Sauron in *The Lord of the Rings*). However, it also can be identified through the actions and goals of characters, which systematically turn them evil, step-by-step (such as Lord Voldemort in the *Harry Potter* series). Sometimes, it appears in forms familiar to the 'real' world: the oppressive power of a regime or government (*Star Wars*), the economic power of owning a rare resource (*Jupiter Ascending*), or technological and medical advancements turning against humanity (*Bloodborne*). Evil is a point of view.

It can be stated that the Gothic style, with the weight of centuries of varying connotations, is a natural setting for evil in all its subtleties and variations. The architectural strategies remain the same throughout the centuries, both in real and fictional worlds, being used in the visual Fantastic both for good and evil.

The distinguished and unique features of all Gothic styles, combined with special manipulations (such as light, surface, ambience, and condition) means this influential style is a favourite for representations of evil. However, based on a romanticised view of the past, from the late 18th century onwards, and the influence it still has on architecture, Gothicism will continue to endure in Fantastic media as the style of both good and evil, light and dark.

Bibliography

Anderson, K.J., 1997. *The Illustrated Star Wars Universe*. New York: Bantam Books.

Various authors, 2004. *First Impressions. Star Wars Tales* Vol. 4. Milwaukie., OR: Dark Horse Comics, Inc.

Bacon, S. ed., 2018. *The Gothic: a reader*. Oxford: Peter Lang.

Brachmann, C., 2013. *WBG Architekturgeschichte Bd. 1: Das Mittelalter (800–1500). Klöster – Kathedralen – Burgen*. Darmstadt: WBG, Wissenschaftliche Buch-gesellschaft.

Carey, C.R., 2003. *Star Wars Roleplaying Game: Coruscant and the Core Worlds.* Renton, Wash.: Wizards of the Coast.

Erne, T. ed., 2012. *Kirchenbau. Grundwissen Christentum*. Göttingen: Vanden-hoeck & Ruprecht.

Freigang, C., 2015. *WBG-Architekturgeschichte. Bd. 3: Die Moderne: 1800 bis heute. Baukunst - Technik - Gesellschaft*. Darmstadt: WBG, Wiss. Buchges.

Görden, M. ed., 2018. *Das Science Fiction Jahr 2018*.

Grein, B., 1995. *Von Geisterschlössern und Spukhäusern. Das Motiv des gothic cas-tle von Horace Walpole bis Stephen King*. Schriftenreihe und Materialien der Phan-tastischen Bibliothek Wetzlar. Wetzlar: Phantastische Bibliothek Wetzlar.

Groom, N., 2012. *The Gothic: a very short introduction*. 1st ed ed. Very short introductions. Oxford: Oxford University Press.

Kihara, D. and Sato, M. eds., 2017. *Bloodborne: artbook officiel*. Paris: Mana books.

Maher, C., 2018. *The Influence of Bram Stoker on 'Bloodborne'* (online). Available at: <https://bloody-disgusting.com/editorials/3525303/influence-bram-stoker-bloodborne/> [Accessed 2 December 2018].

Schneider, F.W. ed., 2018. *Pathfinder: Das Buch der Verdammten*. Waldems: Ulisses Spiele GmbH.

Stevens, D., 2000. *The Gothic Tradition*. Cambridge contexts in literature. Cam-bridge ; New York: Cambridge University Press.

Toman, R. and Bednorz, A. eds., 2007. *Gotik: Architektur, Skulptur, Malerei.* Kö-nigswinter: Ullmann.

Zahn, T., Stackpole, M.A. and Ezquerra, C., 2018. *Mara Jade: Die Hand des Impera-tors. Star Wars Legends* Vol. 37. Stuttgart: Panini.

The Inquisitor's Creatures: The Historical Roots of the Witch Trope and its Evolution Over the Centuries

Steph P. Bianchini

Abstract

Very few tropes in fantasy are as powerful and evocative as the witch, a figure portrayed both as the powerful sorcerer who commands the power of nature and/or resorts to magic to influence human destinies, and the evil creature in connection with, or possessed by, demons.

There is no shortage of literature and movies representing one, or many, versions of this popular myth. And, yet, the figure of the witch has a long and complex history, starting from antiquity, that has left a trail of blood and suffering over the centuries.

This paper aims at exploring the historical and philosophical roots of witchcraft –something more specific and time-defined than sorcery – as it emerged in Medieval and Modern Europe. Carrying out a brief exploration of magic in the Western world, starting in antiquity, until the last public executions for witchcraft in the eighteenth century, this paper highlights the often elusive, shifting character of the phenomenon, depending on the society and the period in which it took place. While 'witches' (as generally intended) have a long and distinguished presence in the lore of the Western world, witchcraft itself, with its paraphernalia of pacts with the Devil, black masses, and so on, is a more modern concept linked to philosophy (mainly Scholasticism) and to the Inquisition's practices, which eventually led to witch-hunts and widespread persecutions.

1. Introduction

'In 1507, when a severe famine strikes a small town in Germany, a friar arrives from a large city, claiming that the town is under the spell of witches in league with the devil. He brings with him a book called the Malleus Maleficarum—'The Witch's Hammer'—a guide to gaining confessions of witchcraft, and promises to identify the guilty woman who has brought God's anger upon the town, burn her, and restore bounty.

Güde Müller suffers stark and frightening visions—recently she has seen things that defy explanation. No one in the village knows this, and Güde herself worries that perhaps her mind has begun to wander—certainly she has outlived all but one of her peers in Tierkinddorf. Yet, of one thing she is absolutely certain: She has become an object of scorn and a burden to her son's wife. In these desperate times, her daughter-in-law would prefer one less hungry mouth at the family table. As the friar turns his eye on each member of the tiny community, Güde dreads what her daughter-in-law might say to win his favour.' (Mailman, 2007)

This is the blurb of Erika Mailman's excellent The Witch's Trinity, a novel of historical fantasy, which offers a surprisingly accurate and vivid portrayal of Germany's countryside in the Renaissance times, just a few years before the frenzy of the witch-hunts started in earnest. It also represents the perfect starting point for this analysis into the historical roots of the witch trope as an entity distinct from the sorcerer and the way it has dramatically changed over time.

As popular as sorcery might have been in the Middles Ages, contrary to the popular credence and a certain movie tradition, those were not the golden years of witchcraft.

If the trials are of any guidance in terms of how widespread the phenomenon truly was, in Europe the apex occurred well into the Modern Era, in the late XVI and XVII centuries, which saw the mass prosecutions in Trier (1581-1593), Fulda (1603-1606), Aix-en-Provence (1611), Würzburg (1626-1631) and Loudon in 1635, to mention only a handful of them. Moreover, and this is another black legend that crossed history but has no historical substance, these trials were *not* the work of the Roman Inquisition, which was generally sceptical, if not critical, of those processes (Tenenti, 1995). The depiction of the witch as a victim of the Catholic Church was a romantic creation of the 1800s, due to the influence of works such as Michelet's *La Sorciere*. A similar sceptical attitude was taken by the Portuguese Inquisition; even the Spanish one only tried once—in the case of the Basque Witches (1609-1611)—to seriously assess the veracity of the phenomenon.

A historical map of the process will show that the overwhelming majority of those trials occurred in Central and Northern Europe, and in countries of Reformation (in its various creeds), with the important exception of France, where the presence of Huguenots contributed to exacerbating the religious attitude of the people and caused, among other things, the massacre of St Bartholomew's night. Estimates regarding the number of trials and their victims vary, as will be discussed in more detail below.

From 1581, when one of the biggest witch-hunts was unleashed in the German town of Trier, until the mid-1600s, Europe saw fires burning regularly over the continent. It was only towards the second part of the seventeenth century that restraint and more thoughtful interrogation became increasingly common, the trials continuing only at the fringes (Scandinavian countries, the British Isles, the colonies), before generally disappearing at some point in the 1700s.

But how did these trials begin and why did they eventually end?

2. Magic, sorcerers, and witches. Not of the same kind

Although it might sound surprising, magic and witchcraft are not the same thing. Many scholars have highlighted the difference between sorcery and witchcraft, and the complex link between this shadow world and shamanism on the one hand, and heresy on the other.

According to Evans-Pritchard (1937), who first attempted an anthropological analysis of the role of magic in human societies, sorcery and witchcraft, are distinct phenomena, although both aim at influencing the environment in favour of humans. But, where the first is the practice of magic through the use of words, spells and complicated rituals, and can be learnt, witchcraft is power that resides in the individual. Witchcraft is not what a person *does*, it is what a person *is*, and it is with this quality that the witch, or the warlock, can work their magic. Sorcery, on the other hand, is

> a pragmatic, conscious practice, involving acts of magic and leading to personal power for the practitioner. Sorcerers typically must learn the texts, practices, rituals, or other components of magic as understood in their culture; such knowledge is esoteric and not normally available to everyone. Like other specialists documented in anthropology, such as shamans and diviners, the sorcerer may work on behalf of clients. (Moro, 2016)

In the Western world, the trope of the sorcerer/magician originates in Antiquity, with its rich tradition of magic in various forms, and whose literature immortalised powerful myths. The references are numerous, but figures such as *Odyssey*'s Circe or *The Golden Fleece*'s Medea are well-known examples of the stereotype of the sorcerer and magic itself, something that can be good or bad depending on what purpose it is used for.

The Roman world had its own share of magic and sorcerers (Apuleius's *The Golden Ass* is only one among many possible references), even though they generally had a negative view of such things.

Latin had two words for practitioners of sorcery: *striges*[1]

---

[1]. Ovid identifies them with nocturnal birds of prey. They were considered demonic creatures who could shapeshift into owls and suck the blood of children. "Illis (avibus) **strigibus** nomen; sed nominis huius / causa, quod horrendum stridere nocte solent" Ovid, Fasti (VI 139-40).

and *sagae*[2], and, while sagae held a less negative connotation, they were still accused of practicing maleficia of various kinds, including child sacrifices and other horrible feats.

The Roman laws on sorcery were severe, and they issued numerous regulations against magic (e.g. *Lex Cornelia de sicariis et veneficis*[3], at the times of Sulla, B.C. 82.). Moreover, there are historical mentions[4] of trials for *sortilegium*.

Medieval Europe inherited the Ancient Roman suspicion of magic, even though the Church initially dismissed it as superstition and relegated it to the more or less forgotten ancestral rituals and traditions. However, the Church itself absorbed, at least in part, the social function of magic[5] and, though discouraging of the practice, forbade the persecution of its users. As a matter of fact, in the Middle Ages, the Church was far more concerned about the proliferate and difficult battle with heresy, a problem that posed far more issues for the ecclesiastic order, generating enough political problems for the authorities to not overly worry about superstitious

---

[2]. Sagae were also seers who could warn people about future events. Cicero, *De divinatione* (I 21): "Sagire enim sentire acute est; ex quo sagae anus, quia multa scire volunt, et sagaces dicti canes. Is igitur qui ante sagit quam oblata res est, dicitur praesagire, id est futura ante sentire"

[3]. 'The law contained provisions for death or fire caused by dolus malus, and against persons going about armed with the intention of killing or thieving. The law not only provided for cases of poisoning, but also contained provisions against those who made, sold, bought, possessed, or gave poison for the purpose of poisoning.' (Smith, 1875, online)

[4]. Sources are quite limited for Ancient Greek opinions, both in terms of law and of process. A famous case was Theoris of Lemnos, mentioned by Demosthenes in *Against Aristogeiton*. For a more detailed discussion *on sorcery in the Ancient world*, see Collins (2011).

[5]. 'Prospective converts looked to Christian priests and monks to work magic more effectively than their pagan equivalents, and this remained a requirement as long as there were sizeable areas of Europe to be converted, that is, until at least the twelfth century. Saints played a major role in this preternatural activity. They worked wonders, cured the sick, expelled evil spirits and, when death took them, their relics continued the good work. Hence, amulets of all kinds, re-cast in Christian guise, pursued the miraculous or magical ends once sought purely by pagan magic.' (Maxwell-Stuart, 2000, online)

peasants.

The sources abound, both civilian and canonical, about a general condemnation of sorcery as superstition, as early as in *Edictum Rotharis Regis* (643), in the Longobard laws by Liutprand (728), and in *Capitularia de partibus Saxoniae* (the Saxon capitulary) by Charlemagne (785). The condemnation of the belief in sorcery contained in *Decretum Gratiani* (also known as *Canon Episcopi*[6]), compiled by the monk Gratian between 1140 and 1142 as a sort of Corpus Iuris Canonici, was later used by the Dutch physician Johann Weyer when he first spoke out against the witch-hunts that were ravaging Modern Europe.

When zealous Inquisitors were too quick to consider magic crimes as heresy, they were rebuffed by the central authorities. In the papal bull *Quod Super* of 13 December 1258, Pope Alexander IV warned against this practice, distinguishing between 'heresy' and 'divination and sorcery' (*Divinationibus et sortilegiis*), requiring the Inquisitors to stick to the first (the '*negotium fidei*') and leave the second to the civilian authorities. Only if there was a crime of heresy

---

[6]. The influence of the Canon Episcopi was twofold because, while it declared witches as non-existent, it also stated that the belief in them was heretical, which, it has been shown, was not what the papal bull of 1253 encouraged. 'It is also not to be omitted that some unconstrained women, perverted by Satan, seduced by illusions and phantasms of demons, believe and openly profess that, in the dead of night, they ride upon certain beasts with the pagan goddess Diana, with a countless horde of women, and in the silence of the dead of the night to fly over vast tracts of country, and to obey her commands as their mistress, and to be summoned to her service on other nights. But it were well if they alone perished in their infidelity and did not draw so many others into the pit of their faithlessness. For an innumerable multitude, deceived by this false opinion, believe this to be true and, so believing, wander from the right faith and relapse into pagan errors when they think that there is any divinity or power except the one God' [passage retrieved and translated here: <http://www.personal.utulsa.edu/~marc-carlson/witch/canon.html>. In this pagan depiction there is the early image of Sabbath which, under successive demonology, assumed a completely different image.

(*heresim saperent manifeste*[7]), were the ecclesiastic authorities authorised to intervene[8].

The picture is therefore quite clear:

> In the world of late antiquity or the early Middle Ages, it is impossible to define someone as a witch (as opposed, for example, to an amateur herbalist, a heretic or a scold), and none of the legislation of the time attempted to do so. Offenders were designated offenders by virtue of their performing various actions or wearing certain objects declared by the legislation to be condemned or forbidden. For all practical purposes, the 'witch' had not yet been invented. There were only practitioners of various kinds of magic, both male and female, who might belong to any rank of ecclesiastical or lay society, and whose actions might, or might not, bring them within the compass of canon or secular law, depending on external factors that were usually local but could, from time to time, be more general. (Maxwell-Stuart, 2000)

For the birth of witchcraft as a modern phenomenon, and the start of the witch-hunts, something else was required.

3. From Aquinas to the Malleus Maleficarum: Scholasticism, Demonology, and the Theoretical Construction of Witchcraft

Possibly the greatest contributor to the philosophical aspects of witchcraft is St. Thomas Aquinas. The philosopher, exponent of Scholasticism, elaborated a complex demonological system in his two works, the *Summa Theologica* and the *Summa against the Pagans or Summa contra Gentiles*.

Before the thirteenth century, theologians had no special

---
[7]. This "manifeste" (clear guilt) was defined to limit the discretion of the intervention of the Inquisitors.

[8]. Russell (1972) has been the first to establish the link between heresy and the social and philosophical construction of witchcraft as opposed to magic and sorcery.

interest in demons. Aquinas, with his *Treatise on Evil* in 1272, changed all that, arguing that the assault of demons on men was not an illusion, but a genuine fact[9], as were their attempts to make men commit sins. More importantly, Aquinas discussed the physicality of demons and their ability to interact with humans to persuade them to worship the Devil.

It is impossible to overstate Aquinas's influence on this matter. According to Cameron (2010), all the subsequent writers who explored the subject largely took Aquinas's conclusions in these areas as a given. Boureau (2006) has also convincingly shown that 'an obsession with the Devil[10] did not constitute an essential aspect of medieval Christianity, but it emerged rather suddenly between 1280 and 1330.'

This turning point was critical. If the belief in sorcery was a longstanding tradition from antiquity, the social construction of the witch[11] as the Devil's acolyte, and the Sabbath as a black mass, was a clerics' creation put, in most cases, into the mouth of the accused through torture (Mandrou, 1976), until it came out as a spontaneous "confession", as occurred in the mass

---

[9]. 'Two things may be considered in the assault of the demons–the assault itself, and the ordering thereof. The assault itself is due to the malice of the demons, who through envy endeavour to hinder man's progress; and through pride usurp a semblance of Divine power, by deputing certain ministers to assail man, as the angels of God in their various offices minister to man's salvation.' (Aquinas, Q114,1)

[10]. It is impossible here to even attempt a history of the concept of demons (or the *daimons* of Greek tradition). See Collins, 2011. It is important, however, to observe that if demons have a long and distinguished tradition in the Western world in general, and Christianity in particular, demonology as a discipline is a far more recent phenomenon.

[11]. The English word "witch" itself is misleading here. In the original Latin texts, the authors talk of "malefici", people who can be of either sex, while "witch" is always intended to denote a woman. Also, while in the "golden age" of the witch-hunt the majority of the accused were women–for many reasons, it is impossible to cover here–in other, more peripheral areas, men were the first to be indicted of these processes.

witch-hunts mentioned in the introduction[12].

Historians are divided about Margaret Murray's thesis of witchcraft as the re-emersion of pagan, pre-Christian cults, where 'witches were members of an old and primitive form of religion' (Murray, 1963, p. 34). Some dismissed it as a forced conclusion from flawed evidence (Thomas, 1971), while others (Ginzburg, 1974) partially accepted the whole idea but putting it into a more precise historical context, supported by processual sources (as will be shown in a following section).

There is, instead, widespread consensus about the fact that what had been considered, until the twelfth century, a form of superstition at best, and heresy at worst, assumed a completely different form once scholasticism came into the equation.

This shift from sorcery to witchcraft due to the philosophical support of the newly emerged demonology occurred at the end of the Middle Ages, and there are no reliable recorded instances of witch-hunts before then[13]. It was not a sudden change and,

---

[12]. There are other complex reasons, linked to the political and social conditions of those years, that helps explain this startling and growing fascination with Demonology as a new discipline. Boureau's work is exemplary in showing how this runs in parallel to a progressive halt of the progress of rational thinking in religion, as the 219 heretical propositions published by Stephen Tempier, bishop of Paris, in 1277, closely linked to Aquinas, also demonstrate.

[13]. There is a famous case of a witch trial in the 1200s, the processing of Angèle de la Barthe, which has been long considered the first of its kind in France and, on paper, at odds with what is explained above. Angèle was a Cathar–a heretic sect in the South of France–who was allegedly accused of witchcraft. Interrogated and tortured, she admitted to having entertained sexual relations with the Devil. However, no mention of what would certainly have been a spectacular trial remains in the Toulousan archives, otherwise quite rich in records of the heretical sources of those years. As observed by Cohn (2011), the earliest (and only) source of this story is a chronicle from 1455 by a councillor of the parliament of Toulouse, Guillaume Bardin, two centuries after the supposed events. Moreover, that chronicle has been found to be unreliable by modern local historians, since the 1700s. It is not the only case of inaccuracies or even gross fabrications of facts for those early times, which seem to have been "reinterpreted" later on with a quite different mindset and mutated historical period and worries. The trial of Angèle de la Barthe was at best a trial of heresy for Catharism but, most likely, it is just a legend of a trial that never happened.

while a few trials occurred in the 1300s (KieckHefer, 1989), they did not result in the massive and widespread phenomenon that took place two centuries later. Moreover, there have been cases where these supposed trials were shown instead to be hoaxes, such as the trials of Carcassonne and Toulouse in 1335, which have been debunked by historians as a posterior fabrication[14]. In those years, the Inquisition was still concentrating on the persecution of heretics. It was a long and slow process, with a few important milestones, which needed mutated political, religious[15] and social conditions to come to maturation.

Those milestones existed, first of all, in another papal bull, one century after *Quod Super*, with John XXII's[16] decree, *Super Illius Specula*[17] of 1329. It declared witchcraft to be heresy and required the Inquisition to put the accused on trial, thereby changing the previous approach. What happened in practice largely depended on the relationship between the civilian and the ecclesiastic authorities and, in general, 'the inquisitors showed little enthusiasm for carrying out even the limited instruction of the pope.' (Cohn, 2011, p. 186).

The 1300s saw famine, wars and the Black Death, which contributed to a climate of fear. Still, an examination of Inquisitors' manuals from the thirteenth century shows an interesting difference from later manuals–such as the 1478 *Malleus Maleficarum*–devoted to the topic. Both Bernardo Gui

---

[14]. See Cohn, 2011.

[15]. A few historians have pointed out eschatological tensions, for example in France and the Netherlands (Crouzet, 1990), in the widespread enthusiasm of witch-cleansing.

[16]. This Pope is well known in fiction, being portrayed both by Druon in *Les Rois Maudits* and Eco's *The Name of the Rose*. It seems he had personal motivations to target magicians and witches, if it is true that in his early years he had escaped a murder attempt by poisoning (Kors & Peters, 1972).

[17]. Hansen considers it the founding text of the new demonological obsession at the end of the Middle Ages and put it in this anthology of witchcraft sources. And yet, the magic sanctioned in the papal bull was of a different kind to later processes: there was still nothing here about Devil-worshipping women or the depictions of the Sabbath, which appeared at a later stage.

(1323) and Nicolau Eymeric (1376) left a marginal space for these practices and, when they did mention them, they talked about sorcerers and diviners but not witches. Both concentrated on heresy and the technical aspects of interrogations.

Even more interestingly, when Eymeric, in the *Directorium Inquisitorum*, discussed the invocations of demons, he did not assign them to common maleficium but to idolatry. Moreover, there is no mention of black Sabbaths or any other devil-related practices. This proves that, in those years, demons were instead considered a matter of necromancy, 'very much an elite art involving complex rituals and invocations' (Bailey, 2003, p. 34), and clearly outside the reach of common people like those who engaged in magic.

Eymeric's attitude reflects a more general position of the Inquisition in the 1300s: created as it was to chase heretics, the Inquisition had no interest in persecuting what it still regarded as superstition. It was only when cases raised a suspicion of heresy that action was taken.

By the end of the century, a few, occasional trials[18] by both secular and ecclesiastical courts occurred in various places in Europe, such as in Northern Italy, in the Pyrenees and in the North Sea. However, times were changing, and that shift, observed on a philosophical and theological level the century before, began effecting society as a whole. As Behringer (2004, p. 18) writes:

> We are reasonably confident today that the 'classical' doctrine of witchcraft crystallized during the middle third of the 15th century, shortly after the Council of Basel, primarily within a western Alpine zone centred around the duchy of Savoy.

---

[18]. One, analysed in the next session, was the case of Madonna Oriente, which occurred in Milan in 1384. The documents reveal the Inquisition was rather puzzled and indecisive about what to do with the two women declaring to have participated in a reunion with a "Dame Orient" or "Diana". They were eventually condemned and executed, but not by the Inquisition: it was left to the secular tribunal to take care of them (Cohn, 2000).

Nowhere is this more evident than in the work of Johannes Nider, a distinguished and highly respected Dominican theologian and reformer who participated in, among other things, the Council of Basel, persecuted heretics and wrote the first treaty on witchcraft, *Formicarius* (The Ant-Colony; 1435-1438), from which later and more famous manuals–the already quoted *Malleus* among them–have drawn heavily.

Nider was among the first to create this bridge between sorcery and necromancy, defining the "witch" as a woman having relations with demons. If magic-handling had been something common to both women and men before, witchcraft now emerged as a prominently female phenomenon and 'the crime of witchcraft no longer entailed just the practice of harmful sorcery against others, but took on terrible demonic and indeed diabolic overtones.' (Bailey, 2003, p. 5).

Another important event occurred in 1484 when Pope Innocent VIII issued the papal bull *Summis Desiderantes Affectibus*. This bull was allegedly issued at the explicit request of the Dominican Inquisitor Heinrich Kramer (also known as Henry Institoris), who had been denied the assistance to prosecute witches by the local authorities in his native Strasbourg. He gave a clear definition of witches[19], together

---

[19]. "[m]any persons of both sexes, unmindful of their own salvation and straying from the Catholic Faith, have abandoned themselves to devils, incubi and succubi, and by their incantations, spells, conjurations, and other accursed charms and crafts, enormities and horrid offences, have slain infants yet in the mother's womb, as also the offspring of cattle, have blasted the produce of the earth, the grapes of the vine, the fruits of the trees, nay, men and women, beasts of burthen, herd-beasts, as well as animals of other kinds, vineyards, orchards, meadows, pasture-land, corn, wheat, and all other cereals; these wretches furthermore afflict and torment men and women, beasts of burthen, herd-beasts, as well as animals of other kinds, with terrible and piteous pains and sore diseases, both internal and external; they hinder men from performing the sexual act and women from conceiving, ...they blasphemously renounce that Faith which is theirs by the Sacrament of Baptism, and at the instigation of the Enemy of Mankind they do not shrink from committing and perpetrating the foulest abominations and filthiest excesses to the deadly peril of their own souls, (...) the abominations and enormities in question remain unpunished not without open danger to the souls of many and peril of eternal damnation." (Papal bull, from the English translation of 1928).

with encouraging the Inquisitors in 'correcting, imprisoning, punishing and chastising' them.

Despite the harsh position of the decree, historians doubt it was responsible for the witch-hunts of the following century. As happened with previous papal bulls, the local ecclesiastic authorities showed disinterest in the matter and failed to cooperate with Kramer.

This lack of support had far-reaching consequences. Kramer, frustrated in his efforts to persecute the witches he had put on trial and eventually removed from his office by the local bishop, decided to take the matter into his own hands.

If Aquinas provided the theoretical foundation for demonology and Nider was responsible for the shift from sorcery to witchcraft, it was Kramer[20] who, in 1487, created the first, and by far the best-known, manual on how to deal with witchcraft: *Malleus Maleficarum* (The Hammer of Witches)[21].

It must be noted that the Roman Church was highly critical of the Malleus, banning it only three years after its appearance (1490). But the invention of the press and Kramer's relentless promotion assured its widespread diffusion, especially as an instrument of secular tribunals.

The road to mass persecutions was open.

---

[20]. James Sprenger is generally credited as co-author of the *Malleus*, but the authorship has been challenged by historians (Broedel, 2013).

[21]. While Kramer included parts of Nider's treaty in the *Malleus*, it is important to note that Nider had not intended his treaty as a means of practicing witch-hunting; his interests were those of a reformer, at a more systematic and theoretical level. Kramer had other purposes. 'The *Malleus Maleficarum* is one of the best-known treatises dealing with the problem of what to do with witches. It was written in 1487 by a Dominican inquisitor, Heinrich Institoris, following his failure to prosecute a number of women for witchcraft, it is in many ways a highly personal document, full of frustration at official complacency in the face of a spiritual threat, as well as being a practical guide for law-officers who have to deal with a cunning, dangerous enemy. Combining theological discussion, illustrative anecdotes, and useful advice for those involved in suppressing witchcraft, its influence on witchcraft studies has been extensive.' (Broedel, 2013, p. 3).

4. The mechanics of the trial. From pagan cults to the Sabbath

The 1500s and 1600s saw the golden age of witch-hunts. These occurred in waves of varied intensity, though not at the same moment or in the same places.

Many historians have attempted to estimate the numeric consistency of those trials and executions, arriving at widely different figures. Conservative estimates give 35,000 (Monter, 2002) or 40,000-50,000 deaths (Gaskill, 2010), with a suggested number of overall trials as high as 80,000 (Levack, 2006), 50,000 of which were in the Holy Roman Empire[22].

Nor were the trials the same everywhere; in continental Europe, records show that the secular authorities were particularly zealous in pursuing witches, whereas in Southern Europe it was a business often carried out by the ecclesiastic authorities, a fact that partly explains the differing outcomes[23]. The method of prosecution, however, remained the same: the mechanism of the trial, the interrogators relentlessly trying to force the doctrinal construction of a pact with the Devil, the narrative of the Sabbath, carnal congress with incubus and succubus, which the *Malleus Maleficarum* had been so accurate in describing, all drawn from a wide array of superstitions of various origins, many of which had little or nothing in common.

To better understand what transpired in those persecutions, it is beneficial to actually read the archival sources for these interrogations.

As often happened, when the procedure was handled by trained Inquisitors and not by civilian authorities, the

---

[22]. Including at times a variety of territories apart from Germany – e.g., Netherlands, Switzerland, Lorraine, Austria, including the Czech lands of Bohemia, Moravia and Silesia. This, by all accounts, is where the witch-hunt was at its fiercest.

[23]. According to the estimates mentioned above, only an estimated 1,000 executions took place across Spain, Italy, and Portugal, compared to 25,000-30,000 deaths in the Holy Roman Empire.

interrogation was accurate and punctilious, and although torture was allowed in all proceedings of justice–secular as well as religious–its use in cases such as these was less enthusiastic than the collective imagination assumes.

Ginzburg[24], examining the archives of North Italy, found many interesting similarities between cases, even in regions far away from one another, comparing the early declarations of the accused during the interrogation and what emerged later in the course of the process itself.

One case is especially telling in this sense, showing historians how much the technically defined "witch" was a creature of doctrine instead of a natural popular creation: the Benandanti ("Good Walkers") of Friuli, a region between Italy and Mittel-Europe, a place where ancestral agrarian cults mixed with Latin deities and Christianity.

In the archives of Friuli and the neighbouring Republic of Venice there are a century's worth of documents–from 1575, the date of the first interrogation, to 1680–regarding trials against the Benandanti, but the confessions and the handling of those cases at the beginning and towards the end are quite different.

In an examination of the first records, the Benandanti seemingly represented an agrarian cult of pre-Christian survival. The accused talked about their periodical (four times a year, at the change of the seasons) nocturnal journeys to the countryside, where they battled against witches and warlocks who threatened the crops. If they were successful, so were the crops[25]. Other Benandanti declarations from the same period

---

[24]. Ginzburg has authored numerous analyses of different witch trials that occurred over the course of a century, documents which remain in the archives. A few of them are mentioned in the list of references.

[25]. 'I am a benandante because I go with the others to fight four times a year, that is during the Ember Days, at night; I go invisibly in spirit and the body remains behind; we go forth in the service of Christ, and the witches of the devil; we fight each other, we with bundles of fennel and they with sorghum stalks.' Inquisitor Montefalco's record of what Moduco, one of the two first accused, declared in 1580. (Ginzburg, 1972).

alternately reported nocturnal processions with the goddess Diana, a claim already mentioned in the Milanese trials of Madonna Oriente two centuries before and covered in the *Gratian Canon*.

However, what clearly emerged from those interrogations was the conscious attempts the authorities made to conform them to the manifestations of witchcraft as informed by the demonology so popular in the rest of Europe at that time. However, the tribunal lost interest and treated the accused as either lunatics or impostors. It was only when the pressure produced results–and the Benandanti themselves were accused of dealing with the Devil–that they attracted the Inquisitors' attention[26]. This happened only thirty years after the first trials and the full, coherent description of a Sabbath dates to as late as 1634[27].

More follow along this line. In a startling inversion of means and ends, the Benandanti, people who fought evil sorcerers to assure a good crop, under pressure from the Inquisitors, slowly assumed features of the enemy they had meant to fight off. The transformation had taken half a century, but all the technical details of black Masses and pacts with the Devil were finally firmly in place.

5. Conclusions

Literature is a powerful mirror for the times, and nowhere is this demonstrated more clearly than in the evolution of the figure of the sorcerer/witch, as shown by Blomquist (2012) in her analysis of the trope, covering nine centuries of French literature.

---

[26]. The first instance of this new, demon-compliant version appears in 1618 with the prosecution of Maria Panzona of Latisana, who openly acknowledged having congress with the Devil.

[27]. This happened with the prosecution of Giovanni di Sion in Aquileia. Another important example, for the length and details of his trial, is Michele Soppe, who was condemned in 1649.

Starting with a positive depiction of the sorcerer–by Marie de France and Chrétien de Troyes, for example–influenced by the scholastic framework analysed here, it devolves into a malignant presence in the work of sixteenth and seventeenth century authors such as Pierre de Ronsard, Joachim du Bellay and François Rabelais, to mention a few famous names. However, as Blomquist (2012) herself states:

> It was not until the eighteenth century, through the works of Voltaire and the Encyclopédistes, that the rehabilitation of the witch began. By the twentieth century, Anne Hébert, Jean-Paul Sartre, Maryse Condé, and Sebastiano Vassalli began to rewrite the witch character by engaging in a process of demystification and by demonstrating that the "witch" was really just a victim of the society in which she lived.

The demonic addition to the trope would remain, however, and prosper. The literature of Romanticism and onwards presents many examples in this sense, starting with Lewis' *Monk* (1798) where a sorcerer, Matilda, summons the Devil to obtain his help.[28]

> The rise of witchcraft remains so fascinating and still so difficult to fathom, despite the vast array of scholarship devoted to it, largely because it was such a multifaceted and "multifactorial" phenomenon, drawing on and feeding off many other aspects of late medieval religious culture. (Bailey, 2003, p. 12).

This is probably the reason it is still not completely understood, although many studies have been devoted to it, especially over the last few decades. Much remains to be done,

---

[28]. Mario Praz (1966) has carried out an accurate analysis of the trope of the demonic female archetype – *La Belle Dame sans Merci*–in his well-known non-fiction book *La carne, La Morte e il Diavolo nella Letteratura Romantica*.

especially when reconstructing the history of it is like, at best, trying to compose a mosaic that is fragmented and, at worst, doing so with important missing tiles.

The same ferocity wasn't applied everywhere the witchcraft trials occurred, and a map of these trials returns us to a picture of a divided Europe. If Northern Europe was carrying out witch-burnings well into the 1600s, in Italy and Spain doubts and complexities had already started to seep in at the end of the 1500s. This was particularly the case when the central authorities of the Sant'Uffizio in Rome and the Supreme Council of the Spanish Institution in Madrid were called on to investigate procedures started by local, often civil (and non-religious) tribunals and, in a few cases, arrived at different conclusions and let the accused walk free (Romeo, 1990)[29].

A convincing explanation for this leniency has not been found, even though historians have observed that it was probably due to a series of factors. The most likely of these is the accuracy of the inquisitorial practice compared to the sloppiness of civilian tribunals, and a somewhat different attitude toward the crime of witchcraft itself (Prosperi, 1988).

As in other occasions in history, every place and case had its own characteristics and exceptions. Even in Germany, one of the areas most affected by witch-hunts and indiscriminate trials, there were instances of proceedings not resulting in convictions, as in the case of Rothenburg[30] (Rowland, 2003). However, for

---

[29]. In one of the ironies that history is often prone to, the Benandanti of Friuli benefitted from surprising luck: at the time, they fully fitted the superimposed scheme, but it was too late to be persecuted, at least in Italy. In 1650, the Roman Inquisition, assuming a more critical and sceptical attitude which was already being displayed by its Spanish counterpart, let them off the hook.

[30]. Rothenburg was an otherwise rather typical witch-hunt. 'As was the case in many other places in early modern Europe, most of those who were accused of or who confessed to witchcraft or who were formally questioned as suspected witches in Rothenburg were female. They ranged in age from eight to eighty-eight years but most were aged twenty-one and above, with those aged from around thirty to sixty – and perhaps particularly those in their fifties – most at risk of becoming the subject of a legal investigation into an allegation of witchcraft.' Rowlands, A. (2003)

the trials to finally end in the 1700s, radical changes in society and belief had to occur first: 'Trevor-Roper has said that it was necessary for belief in the Kingdom of Satan to die before the witch theory could be discredited.' Larner (2002).

If this is so, it means that the rise and fall of demonology as a belief was key to the transformation, or re-transformation, of witchcraft back into the sorcery from which it had drawn its origins a few centuries earlier, closing the circle and bringing to an end the persecutions.

Bibliography

Tomassetti, A., (ed.), *Bullarum, diplomatum et privilegiorum sanctorum Romanorum pontificum taurensis edition* (Turin 1858), pp. 663–666, no. XLVI.

Aquinas (sd). *Summa Theologica*. Online translation available at: <https://dhspriory.org/thomas/summa/> [Accessed 29 March 2019].

Bailey M.D., 2003. *Battling demons: witchcraft, heresy, and reform in the late Middle Ages*. Pennsylvania: Penn State Press.

Behringer, W., 2004.*Witches and witch-hunts: a global history*. Hoboken: Wiley-Blackwell.

Blomquist, L.T., 2012. *Rehabilitating the witch: the literary representation of the witch from the "Malleus Maleficarum" to "Les Enfants du sabbat"*. Doctor of Philosophy. Rice University. Available at: <http://hdl.handle.net/1911/70211> [Accessed 22 March 2019]

Boureau, A., 2006. *Satan the heretic: the birth of demonology in the Medieval west*. Chicago: CUP.

Broedel, H. P., 2013. *The Malleus Maleficarum and the construction of witchcraft: theology and popular belief*. Manchester: Manchester University Press.

Cameron, E., 2011. Scholastic demonology in the twelfth and thirteenth centuries. In: Cameron, E., 2010. *Enchanted Europe: superstition, reason, and religion 1250–1750*. Oxford Scholarship Online. Available at: <http://www.oxfordscholarship.com/view/10.1093/acprof:oso/9780199257829.001.0001/acprof-9780199257829-chapter-7> [Accessed: 30 December, 2018].

Cohn, N., 2011. *Europe's inner demons: the demonization of Christians in Medieval Christendom*. Chicago: University of Chicago Press.

Collins, D., 2001. Theoris of Lemnos and the criminalization of magic in fourth-century Athens. *The Classical Quarterly*, 51(2), p.477.

Crouzet, D., 1990. *Les guerriers de Dieu. La violence au temps des troubles de religion, vers 1525 - vers 1610*. Seyssel: Champ Vallon.

Evans-Pritchard, E., 1937. *Witchcraft, oracles and magic among the Azande*. Oxford: Oxford University Press.

Gaskill, M., 2010. *Witchcraft, a very short introduction*. Oxford: Oxford University Press.

Ginzburg, C., 1972. *I benandanti*. Torino: Einaudi.

Hansen, J., 1901. *Quellen und untersuchungen zur geschichte des hexenwahns und der hexenverfolgung im mittelalter*. Hildesheim: Olms.

Kierckhefer, R., 2011. *Magic in the Middle Ages*. Cambridge: CUP.

Kors, A. C. and Peters, E., 1972. *Witchcraft in Europe, 1100-1700: a documentary history*. Philadelphia: University of Pennsylvania Press.

Larner, F., 2002. Crime of witchcraft in early Modern Europe. In: Oldridge, R., *The witchcraft reader*. London: Routledge.

Levack, B. P., 2006. *The witch hunt in early modern Europe*. London and New York: Longman.

Mailman, E., 2007. *The witch's trinity*. New York: Three River Press.

Mandrou, R., (1976) *Magistrati e streghe nella Francia del Seicento*. Bari: Laterza.

Maxwell-Stuart P.G., 2000. The emergence of the Christian witch. *History Today*. Available at: <https://www.historytoday.com/pg-maxwell-stuart/emergence-christian-witch> [Accessed 25 November, 2018].

Maxwell-Stuart, P.G., 2011. *Witch beliefs and witch trials in the Middle Ages: documents and readings*. Hambledon: Continuum.

Michelet, J., 1862. *La Sorciere*. Biblioteque National de France. Available at: <https://catalogue.bnf.fr/ark:/12148/cb145579970> [Accessed 1 January, 2019].

Monter, W., 2002. *Witch trials in continental Europe, in witchcraft and magic in Europe*. Bengst: Ankarloo.

Moro, P., 2016. Witchcraft, sorcery, and magic. In: *The International Encyclopedia of Anthropology*. Available at: <https://onlinelibrary.wiley.com/doi/pdf/10.1002/9781118924396.wbiea1915> [Accessed 30 November, 2018].

Murray, M., 1963. *My First Hundred Years*. London: William Kimber.

Praz, M., 1966. *La carne, la morte e il diavolo nella letteratura romantica.* Firenze: Sansoni.

Prosperi, V., 1988. L'Inquisizione: verso una nuova imagine. *Critica Storica*,

XXV, pp. 120-134.

Romeo, G., 1990. *Inquisitori, esorcisti e streghe nell'Italia della Controriforma*. Roma: Sansoni.

Rowlands, A., 2003. 'God will punish both poor and rich': the idioms and risks of defiance in the trial of Margaretha Horn, 1652. In: *Witchcraft narratives in Germany: Rothenburg, 1561–1652*. Manchester: Manchester University Press. Available at: <http://www.jstor.org/stable/j.ctt155j5z9.11> [Accessed: 30 November, 2018].

Russell, J.B., 1972. *Witchcraft in the Middles Ages*. Ithaca, NY: Cornell University Press.

Smith, W., 1875. *A Dictionary of Greek and Roman Antiquities*. London: John Murray. Available at: <http://penelope.uchicago.edu/Thayer/E/Roman/Texts/secondary/SMIGRA*/Leges_Corneliae.html> [Accessed 28 November, 2018].

Thomas, K., 1971. *Religion and the decline of magic: studies in popular beliefs in sixteenth and seventeenth century England*. London: Weidenfeld & Nicolson.

Naming the Terror in the Forest: Evolution of The Horned God in Fantasy Fiction

Anna Milon

Abstract

Following Margaret Murray's contested work on European witch-cults, the Horned God has entered the public imagination as an amalgamation of the Greek Pan, Celtic Cernunnos, English Herne and the Devil himself: an anthropomorphic male deity with horns or antlers, associated with fertility, death, rebirth and wild spaces. He is presented in contemporary literature as an awe-inspiring guardian of the natural state of things. However, in works predating Murray, the Horned God has very different, much more sinister associations.

This paper will explore the transition of Horned God from frightening to inspiring and speculate as to the cause of this evolution of the character.

*

Panic! In the forest, a young woman encounters a grotesque creature – half-man, half-goat – and flees in terror, for she has just come face to face with the god Pan. The word "panic" originates from the god's name, arriving into English from the Greek 'πανικός', via the Latin 'panicus' and French 'panique'. Pan is said to possess such a frightful shout that all who hear it can't help but flee from him in terror. He is the source of the persistent unease one feels when one is alone in the woods, and is associated with unbridled sexuality and untamed wilderness. Despite his historic origin in Arcadia, in Peloponnese, Pan has been so popular with British writers as to become 'the most frequently cited male deity in the whole canon of English literature.' (Hutton, 1999, p. 43) Pan's heyday fell in the Edwardian period, between the 1890s and the 1920s (Merivale, 1969, p. 1). In 1930, Somerset Maugham writes

> Thirty years ago in literary circles God was all the fashion ... then God went out (oddly enough with cricket and beer) and Pan came in. In a hundred novels his cloven hoof left its imprint on the sward, ... But Pan went out and now beauty has taken his place. (pp. 66-67)

However, he did not stay away for long. Even though by the 1930s references to Pan had markedly decreased, the image of an anthropomorphic horned or antlered male deity remained popular.

This second bout of popularity is largely due to the work of Margaret Murray, an anthropologist writing on the history of witchcraft. In her 1931 book *The God of the Witches* Murray lists a variety of horned and antlered figures ranging from the Palaeolithic to the 16th century and from India to the British Isles, and concludes that they constitute an 'uninterrupted record of belief in a horned deity [which] shows that underlying the official religion of the rulers there still remained the ancient cult' of the Horned God. (p. 28) Despite the swift and damning debunking of these claims as 'based on deeply flawed methods and illogical arguments' (Simpson, 1994, p. 89), the notion entered the public imagination and stayed there. Murray's work opened the floodgates for writers who wanted to experiment with combining disparate deities into a single body of symbols: the Horned God. Murray was not the first to combine the facets of the Horned God. For instance, Stephen McKenna's 1926 novel *The Oldest God* assumes 'a virtually complete equivalence of Pan and the Devil' (Merivale, 1969, p. 175) and predates the publication of *The God of the Witches* by five years. However, her status as a scholar legitimised the use of the Horned God umbrella term in the eyes of many.

From then on, the Horned God became an ever-expanding amalgamation of Pan, the Devil, Robin Goodfellow, Herne the Hunter, Gwyn app Nudd and similar others. Their symbolic similarities made the association all the easier: all these figures are unambiguously male and to some extent connected with fertility, wild nature and chthonic forces.

While works that either repudiate Murray or chronologically trace the historical deities that make up the Horned God are many, there is scarcely any work done analysing the impact Murray's writing has had on present-day perception of the Horned God as a literary phenomenon. Although the symbolic association of the Horned God with wild spaces has stayed the same between his first incarnation as the Edwardian Pan and the post-Murray versions, the interpretation of his symbolism has shifted over time. In the Edwardian period, the god is perceived as dangerous and the nature he calls his own is incomprehensible to the human mind, often to the point of inducing madness. As time progresses, the Horned God gains a firmer foothold in the British mythological landscape, becoming antlered rather than horned, and becoming a less alien, less terrifying figure. By the 1960s he is a personage from the distant past, removed from all other characters' understanding and morals, but no longer associated with panic. At the turn of the 21st century his moral compass aligns with that of the protagonists; he remains 'Other', but now his behaviour if justified and understandable.

Merivale makes a distinction between the sinister and the pastoral versions of the Horned God in Edwardian fiction. A good example of the former would be Arthur Machen's *Great God Pan*, a concept so terrifying it renders any who behold him a 'hopeless idiot' (2009, p. 24), while the latter is best represented by Kenneth Grahame's Piper at the Gates of Dawn, a 'Friend and Helper' to the woodland creatures of *The Wind in the Willows* (2012, p. 130). But there is a certain degree of intermingling between the two: the sinister Great God Pan brings to mind pastoral scenes worthy of his Arcadian homeland in which a path weaves 'between ilex-trees, and here and there a vine climb[s] from bough to bough, and send[s] up waving tendrils and droop[s] with purple grapes' (Machen, 2009, p. 22); while the unthreatening Piper leaves the animals that encounter him 'cowed, stricken, and trembling violently.' (Grahame, 2012, p. 130)

The protagonists of *The Wind in the Willows*, Rat and Mole, meet The Piper at the Gates of Dawn in an eponymous chapter. The encounter prompts a sense of divine terror, conveyed powerfully by the image of 'the two animals, crouching on the earth' bowing their heads and worshipping the deity (p. 131). Grahame himself is careful to navigate the boundary between his Pan being fearsome and benevolent. The emotion he evokes is 'no panic terror – indeed [Mole] felt wonderfully at peace an happy – but it was an awe that smote and held him' (p. 130). Rat's dual reaction conveys the ambiguous nature of the Piper:

"Afraid! Of *Him*? O, never, never! And yet – and yet – O, Mole, I am afraid!" (p. 131)

Jane Darcy argues that this response is due to the Piper representing 'the immense and fearful power of the natural world' (Darcy, 1995, p. 219). However, the peaceful idyllic natural setting in which Rat and Mole encounter him does not correlate with the dangers nature can pose. Other than appearing near a weir, which Kimball sees as a threatening location because of its link to human industry (Kimball, 2002, pp. 55-56), the Piper is in no way identified with nature as a threat. Yet he still retains a sense of dread for both the characters and the readers.

Eleanor Toland writes of Pan as 'frightening, because he represented the guilty conscience of those who had destroyed the landscape with "dark, satanic mills"' (Toland, 2014, p. 10). However, such a viewpoint speaks more to the ecologically conscious reader in the 21st century than to the Edwardian Pan's contemporaries. Instead, the sinister Pan is a figure swift to deal retribution unto those who 'meddle frivolously with matters too mysteriously important for one's limited understanding' (Merivale, 1969, p. 171), but it is never specified what those mysterious matters are. If anything, characters encountering the Edwardian Pan suffer from a lack knowledge rather than from guilt, which comes with clarity. Arthur Machen uses the Great God Pan as a symbol occluding the terrible reality of existence that is normally hidden from human view, and Saki presents him as a surviving pagan deity inhabiting places where the 'worship of Pan never has died out', 'the Nature-God to whom all must come back at last.' (Saki, 2000, p. 162) In an encounter with Pan there can be no room for guilt, as it is supplanted by fear – the fear of nature and of the experiences on the fringes of the anthropocentric viewpoint which are so aptly represented by the Horned God's duality of god and animal.

One of the earliest notable post-Murray works featuring the Horned God is John Masefield's *The Box of Delights*, 1935. On his way home for the Christmas holidays, the protagonist, Kay Harker, falls into a dream within which fantastic events unfold. A gang of antagonists, who are a mix of high organised pistol-touting, airplane-cruising crime lords and an occult organisation (the ringleader actually summons a demon at one point), try to obtain a box of delights: a small case which appears to contain portals to multiple dimensions in space and time. One of these dimensions is home to Herne the Hunter. He acts as a benevolent cameo character who helps the protagonist and seems to belong to some group of good beings, identified by the 'lengthwise cross' ring on his finger.

After World War II, interest grew in preserving British folklore heritage, and it was not just Tolkien who was writing a 'mythology for England'. In the Horned God camp, interest shifted from the Classical Pan to the quintessentially English Herne the Hunter. Herne is a folk figure described as a man with stag's antlers on his head, riding his horse through

Windsor Great Park followed by two hellhounds and an owl. Shakespeare makes a brief allusion to him as to a hideous spirit rattling his chain in *Merry Wives of Windsor*, but his legend is not expanded upon until William Ainsworth does so in his 1842 novel *Windsor Castle*. However, it is only in the post-Murray period that Herne gains popularity in fantasy fiction as a facet of the Horned God.

Masefield's use of Herne is confounding. Though he pays homage to Shakespeare by describing the character wound with a chain with silver bells, there is little in the story to give Herne the mysterious terrifying aura other authors bestow on him. Although he does transform into a stag and transforms Will as well, there is no sense that this is a significant transformation, as it is too closely followed by the transformation into a bird and then a fish. In Disney's S*word in the Stone* a similar sequence of transformations bears an instructive nature, with Merlin using each form to deliver a lesson to young Arthur, but in comparison Masefield's sequence feels rushed and pointless. Herne does not bear any of the ferocity usually ascribed to him and that reduces his character to a status of mere supernatural helper.

However, Masefield's work ostensibly catalysed a sequence of children's books in which Herne's image consolidated into what we know today: the immeasurably ancient, cruel but just lord of the forest, Nature itself as we come full circle from Pan. Cooper's *The Dark is Rising* (1973) bears notable marks of similarity in composition and character grouping. In the eponymous second instalment of Cooper's *The Dark is Rising* series, Will Stanton discovers that he is one of the Old Ones, an ancient group of people who serve the Light just as the Rider and his retinue serve the Dark. These two cosmic forces are locked in perpetual combat and it is Will's task to unite six Signs of Power, which are a tool to aid the Light's fight against the Dark. Among the helpers Will encounters on his quest, there is the Hunter, a creature who is both recognised as one of the Old Ones and is not part of them. The triad of Merriman, Old Lady and Hunter in Cooper's novel are very similar to Masefield's Old Man, Lady and Herne. But where Masefield's Herne is a secondary character who appears as required by the narrative to aid the protagonist, Cooper builds to the revelation of her Hunter for the duration of the novel.

The Hunter wears a mask, the Caribbean provenance of which hints at the multicultural nature of the Horned God cultus:

> The head from which the branching antlers sprang was shaped like the head of a stag, but the ears beside the horns were those of a dog or a wolf. And the face beneath the horns was a human face – but with the round feather-edged eyes of a bird. (Cooper, 1973, p. 114)

Will gives it to 'the Hunter to put on. But the head was real.' (P. 198) Here Cooper's familiarity with Murray is most apparent, considering Murray's opening description of the Horned God is as follows:

> The figure is that of a man clothed in the skin of a stag. ... The face is bearded, the eyes are large and round, but there is some doubt whether the artist intended to represent the man-animal with a mask or with the face uncovered. (Murray, 1931, p. 13)

The Horned God is both man and animal, both same and separate.

The Hunter is instrumental in banishing the Dark after Will joins the Signs, but Cooper conveys the sense that his agenda is his own and not in service of the Light. When confronted by the Hunter, Will realises that his mouth is 'not the mouth of an Old One. It could smile in friendship, but there were other lines around it as well ... [that] told of cruelty and a pitiless impulse to revenge. Indeed he was half-beast.' (Cooper, 1973,

p. 198) Will is arrested by the merciless nature of wilderness the same way as the Edwardian characters who encountered the sinister Pan. But unlike the earlier writers, Cooper offers a compromise: this threat can be avoided, even utilised to the protagonist's benefit, as long as he understands that nature cannot be tamed or broken into servitude.

The logic of accepting a force that does not conform to the human order is even more pronounced in Alan Garner's *The Moon of Gomrath* (1963). The protagonists, Colin and Susan, unwittingly wake the Wild Hunt by lighting a fire atop an ancient mound. Presiding over the Hunt is Garanhir, Lord of the Herlathing, also referred to as the Hunter. He is an acolyte of Old Magic. When Susan asks what the Hunter does she is answered with,

> Do? He *is*, Susan. That is enough. There you see the difference between the Old and the High. The High Magic was made for a reason; the Old Magic is a part of things. It is not *for* any purpose. (Garner, 1963, p. 89)

High Magic represents power harnessed for human needs; to it 'the Old Magic was a hindrance, a power without shape and order' (p. 89). Garanhir, like Cooper's Hunter, 'is from a cruel day of the world. Men have changed since they honoured him.' (p. 89) Both Hunters are sentient beings that represent the primal order of nature. Humans have moved on from that order, but that does not make it wrong. While earlier texts associate the mysteriously important matters of the Horned God with threat of madness to all but a select few, post-Murray writing tends to present a more comprehensible if no less dangerous version of the character.

With the increasing ecological awareness and the understanding that humans pose a far greater threat to nature than the other way around in recent decades, the Horned God has become less of an unnameable evil in the woods and more of a representation of 'the guilty conscience of those who destroyed the landscape with "dark, satanic mills."' (Toland, 2014, p. 10) Toland's statement reads much more convincingly when applied to literature written in the atmosphere of global ecocide than the works written during the second industrial revolution.

Charles de Lint's *Into the Green*, published in 1993, exemplifies this shift of reader perspective from being fearful of the Horned God to sympathising with him. The protagonist of the novel, Angharad, is a travelling bard in a world that contains Hafarl, the Summerlord, a half-forgotten antlered deity of the old faith. During her travels, Angharad meets Pog, a hunchback village idiot ridiculed by his community. But when the two characters come together in a stone circle a mystic change comes over Pog, prompted by Angharad's music:

> Pog sang as he moved, a tuneless singing that made strange harmonies with Angharad's harping. ... When it took on the bass timbre of a stag's belling call, Angharad thought she saw antlers rising from his brow, the tines pointing skyward to the moon like the menhir. His back was straighter as he danced, the hump gone.
> It's Hafarl, Angharad thought, awestruck. The Summerlord's possessed him. (de Lint, 1993, p. 69)

The transcendent scene is interrupted by the villagers, 'the men from the inn who'd come, cursing and drunk, to find themselves a witch.' (p. 71) In their fear, the villagers slay Pog, who loses his stag-shape as the killers realise the full extent of what they have done. By attacking the wild they are harming their own. While Angharad shares a profound affinity with the Green, the source of natural magic and wonder, most other characters in the novel fear and resent it. Not only does this uphold the trend that only a select few individuals are receptive to the Horned God's mysteries, it also reflects the trend of the time: only a small percentage of individuals being open-minded enough to accept and align themselves with the natural order represented by the Horned God.

With the turn of the century the trend shifts, ecological concerns enter mainstream culture and small acts of awareness like recycling or planting indigenous species in one's garden become more and more common. An increasing number of readers align themselves with the ideas that the Horned God represents and that reflects on the characters. Patrick Ness's *A Monster Calls* (2015), the most recent work mentioned here, may seem as one least connected with the trend of Horned God narratives. However, the way the Monster describes himself identifies him firmly as a kind of Horned God:

> I am the wolf that kills the stag, the hawk that kills the mouse, the spider that kills the fly! I am the stag, the mouse and the fly that are eaten! I am the snake of the world devouring its tail! I am everything untamed and untameable! ... I am this wild earth, come for you, Conor O'Malley. (Ness, 2015, p. xx)

He evokes the Horned God's link to wild spaces, to the transformative cycle of death and rebirth and the violence inherent in the natural world. He is the earth seeking retribution against its wrongdoers. But his revenge is not against Conor. In fact, the Monster helps Conor accept the terminal illness of his mother and make peace with himself. In that instance, Conor does not find the Monster 'mysteriously important' or incomprehensible. He says, 'You look like a tree,' (p. 16) and that phrase both accepts the Monster's nature and unravels the shroud of terror that has veiled that which is natural and which is all around us: fields, glens and forests. Conor's perspective is the dominant one in the story; the reader thinks and speaks with Conor, accepting the awe-inspiring majesty of the natural world.

The Horned God, in his many guises, is too large a figure

to be dealt with in full in so short an essay. But in literature of approximately the last 100 years, his association with the wild has been evolving, and evolves still, to represent the general attitudes of his readership to the natural world. From the 'mysteriously important' figure in the woods, whose rough visage obscures the madness of life outside the human perspective, of the Edwardian Pan, he transforms into a vengeful effigy of humanity's past transgressions against nature and an urge to do better in the future. Sometimes understanding can come from as little as stopping to listen to the belling of a stag; and before you flee in terror from the forest, think whether the thing that scared you was just a gnarled old tree.

Bibliography

Ainsworth, W. H., 1842. *Windsor Castle*. London: Miller and Co Ltd.

Cooper, S., 1973. *The Dark is Rising*. London: Chatto & Windus Ltd.

Darcy J., 1995. The Representation of Nature in '*The Wind in the Willows*' and '*The Secret Garden*', *The Lion and the Unicorn*. Research Gate, [online] Available at <https://www.researchgate.net/publication/236713983_The_Representation_of_Nature_in_The_Wind_in_the_Willows_and_The_Secret_Garden> [Accessed 14 February 2019].

Garner, A., 1963. *The Moon of Gomrath*. London: Collins.

Grahame, K., 2012. *The Wind in the Willows*. London: Vintage.

Hutton, R., 1999. *The Triumph of the Moon*. Oxford: Oxford University Press.

Kimball, M. A., 2002. *Aestheticism, Pan and Edwardian Children's Literature*. CEA Critic, 65(1).

de Lint, C., 1993. *Into the Green*. New York: Tom Doherty Associates.

Machen, A., 2009. Great God Pan. In *Great God Pan and Other Weird Stories*. Welches, OG: Arcane Wisdom.

Maugham, W. S., 1930. *Cakes and Ale*. New York: Octopus Books Inc.

Masefield, J., 1957. *The Box of Delights*. London: Heinmann.

Merivale, P., 1969. *The Goat-Foot God: his myth in modern times*. Cambridge, MA: Harvard University Press.

Murray, M., 1931. *The God of the Witches*. London: Sampson Low, Marston & Co.

Ness, P., 2015. *A Monster Calls; from an original idea by Siobhan Dowd*. London: Walker Books.
\
Saki, 2000. Music on the Hill. In *The Complete Short Stories*. London: Penguin Classics.

Simpson, J., 1994. Margaret Murray: Who Believed Her, and Why? *Folklore* 105(1-2), pp. 89 – 96.

Toland, E., 2014. *And did these Hooves: Pan and the Edwardians*. Wellington, NZ: Victoria University of Wellington (unpublished).

Evil Rewritten: Witches in Revisionist Fairy Tales

Anna Köhler

Abstract

This paper explores the way that witches are presented in literary and cinematic retellings of three canonical fairy tales (*The Little Mermaid*, *Hansel and Gretel*, and *Rapunzel*). While witches in the classic fairy tales are stock figures with a clear dramatic role, presented as unambiguously evil, this simplistic portrayal has been challenged in literary revisionist short stories by writers such as Emma Donoghue, Tanith Lee, Amanda C. Davis, Leigh Bardugo, Catherynne M. Valente, and Melissa Lee Shaw, who contest the assumption that witches are wicked by nature. At the same time, various Hollywood productions have reimagined popular fairy tales, but largely stopped short of changing the dramatic role of the witch. This paper first discusses the way that witches are presented in the canonical tales and the specific type of evil that they represent: solitary, anti-maternal women who transgress the social order by exercising power outside of the domestic sphere. The subsequent section details three strategies that revisionist writers have employed to redeem the witch: reversing anti-maternal stereotypes, turning the witch from a stock figure into a complex character, and questioning storytellers and the act of storytelling itself. The final section contrasts these literary portrayals with the major conservative influence of Hollywood adaptations, which to this day preserve the image of the witch as an anti-maternal hag whose rightful death reaffirms the patriarchal order. These conflicting depictions of witches expose evil as a matter of perspective, determined largely by the stories we choose to tell over and over again until they become part of the public consciousness.

*

The wicked witch is a staple of many of the best-known and most beloved fairy tales in Western literature. She may occur in various guises – as a solitary crone, a cruel stepmother, an evil queen – but she is invariably wicked, usually without a particular motivation, and she is always female. An embodiment of feminine evil, the figure of the witch has become a site of cultural negotiation in feminist retellings and revisions of fairy tales, which cast doubt upon the things we take for granted about witches, and in doing so raise a number of questions. What sort of evil do witches in the canonical tales represent? How is this evil specifically feminine? Why do witches act the way they do in the tales – and who decides that witchcraft is wicked anyway? This paper will discuss the way that witches have been portrayed in contemporary retellings of three popular tales (the Grimms' *Hansel and Gretel* and *Rapunzel*, and Andersen's *The Little Mermaid*), both in literature and on film, and how this relates to shifting cultural notions of transgressive femininity. Witches in fairy tales – solitary, childless, independent, powerful – are female figures who reject patriarchal expectations of their time, and therefore pose a threat to the social order.[1] It makes sense, then, that feminist writers from the second half of the 20th century up to this day have found the witch a fascinating figure to explore to shed new light on familiar tales. Through this process, the witch has become representative of how society views women who transgress the patriarchal order.

The three canonical tales discussed here are cultural touchstones deeply embedded in the public consciousness, in part thanks to the Disney industry (although a Disney

---

[1]. In this context, it is important to note that fairy tales are not as simplistic in their portrayal of women as they are often made out to be (or as they may appear in their Disney versions), which makes sense considering that they were primarily told by women. However, the stock figure of the witch represents a specifically feminine type of evil at odds with hegemonic models of appropriate womanhood and is therefore, almost by definition, indicative of conservative forces within the fairy tale.

version of *Hansel and Gretel* does not yet exist), and as such have inspired numerous retellings in various media. They are therefore particularly suitable for the purposes of this paper, as a variety of literary and cinematic retellings provides a variety of new perspectives on the witch. The purpose of such retellings may differ: in his *Encyclopedia of Fantasy* (1997), John Clute differentiates between "twice-told" tales and "revisionist fantasy". Twice-told is a term that characterizes a tale "whose telling incorporates a clear retelling of the inherent story […] *foregrounding* the existence of a previous version of the tale now being retold. […] When a retelling also constitutes a substantive examination of the prior story – or of a corpus of stories – then the twice-told tale is also a Revisionist Fantasy" (Clute 1997, n. pag.). A twice-told tale, then, offers readers a new version of an old story, and is also considered revisionist if it critically engages with its source text. A revisionist fantasy need not be political in nature, though the tales discussed here – most written explicitly from a feminist standpoint seeking to question the portrayal of witches in the original tales – qualify as such. On the other hand, Disney adaptations such as *The Little Mermaid* (1989) or *Tangled* (2010), loose though they may be, qualify as twice-told rather than revisionist: their portrayal of witches is much more conservative than that of literary retellings.

Hag, sea witch, enchantress

The three canonical tales discussed here feature three rather different witches: a cannibalistic hag in *Hansel and Gretel*, a sea witch in *The Little Mermaid*, and a powerful enchantress whose status as a witch is up for debate in *Rapunzel*. All three have inspired multiple retellings and adaptations exploring the various witch figures in them. The Grimms' collection in particular, *Children's and Household Tales* (1812), has shaped today's idea of what the typical fairy tale is (cf. Zipes 2002), and with it conserved a specific image of the wicked witch from 18th-century oral folk tales (Dingeldein 1985, p. 59). This image is clearest in *Hansel and Gretel* (KHM 15): the witch is an old woman who walks with a crutch and lives alone in the woods, in this case, in a house made of candy constructed specifically as a trap for wandering children. When Hansel and Gretel come her way, she invites them in, feeds them and gives them beds to sleep in. When they feel safe, she locks up Hansel and makes Gretel help her fatten him up for the witch to eat. Notably, the witch is coded as inhuman: she has red eyes and a keen, explicitly animal-like sense of smell to make up for her bad eyesight. As is typical of the Grimms' witches, no motivation for her actions is provided – she wants to eat children because she is wicked, and she is wicked because that's how witches are. As various scholars have pointed out (e.g. Tatar 1987, p. 202; Dingeldein 1985, p. 55), the witch is also linked to Hansel and Gretel's stepmother, who convinces their father to abandon them in the woods: when they find their way back home after killing the witch, the stepmother has conveniently died in the meantime. No word is lost during the happy reunion about how their father agreed to send his children to their near-certain death. The figure of the stepmother in the Grimms' tales is closely related to the witch in that they represent the same kind of anti-maternal evil: instead of fulfilling the nurturing, loving role of the ideal mother, they pose a threat to children.[2]

Andersen's sea witch in *The Little Mermaid* (1837) is quite similar. Despite the underwater setting, she too lives alone in a house in the middle of a forest, though here the forest is

---

[2]. The vilification of stepmothers seems to be a deliberate editorial decision of the Grimms: the stepmother and evil queen in *Snow White* (KHM 53) was Snow White's biological mother in the first edition of the *Children's and Household Tales*, and only turned into a stepmother in subsequent editions. Maria Tatar (1987, p.201) argues that the decision was a response to the shifting audience of the tales, which were increasingly being read to and by children; the Grimms therefore felt they had to preserve the sanctity of the mother and replaced abusive mothers with stepmothers as intruders into happy family life.

made of "polyps, half animal and half plant" (n.pag.), whose tentacles cling to the bones of drowned sailors and the body of a strangled mermaid. Furthermore, the forest is surrounded by perilous whirlpools and barren rock, while the witch's house itself is "built of the bones of shipwrecked men" – all features associating the sea witch with danger and death before she is introduced to the reader. There is no physical description of the sea witch herself, but there are aspects of stereotypical witchcraft about her that are less prevalent in the Grimms' tales, including her cackling laugh and her brewing a potion in a cauldron. The concept of potion-brewing as a form of domestic, feminine magic has existed at least since classical antiquity if not longer (cf. Oberhelman 1980) and was cemented as a core feature of literary witchcraft through Shakespeare's *Macbeth*. Instead of using their kitchen magic to be nurturing (i.e. to fulfil the social role of mother), witches brew potions for their own selfish, often harmful ends. Andersen's sea witch is no exception: she knows that granting the mermaid's request – to give her human legs so that she may win over the prince she has fallen in love with – will only bring her grief, which is precisely why she agrees to help her. The witch is upfront about her intentions, the pain that the transformation will cause the mermaid, and the consequences should she fail to marry the prince, but the mermaid cannot be dissuaded. Only when the witch demands the mermaid's voice as payment does she hesitate – and then the witch goads her on, leading her to her doom. Like the redeyed witch in *Hansel and Gretel*, the sea witch is marked as an inhuman Other (in this case because she has black blood) and has no apparent motivation for her evilness. Although she is not responsible for the mermaid's choices – she does not attempt to trick her in any way – she clearly takes delight in providing the means to bring the little mermaid to her tragic end.

A rare more complicated witch is featured prominently in the Grimms' *Rapunzel* (KHM 12) – in fact, it is questionable whether she is a witch in the strictest sense at all. In the original

German, she is not referred to as *Hexe* (witch), but rather as *Zauberin* (female wizard), which is commonly translated into English as witch or enchantress. Compared to the Grimms' other witches, she is unusually complex: the woman is widely feared for her considerable magic powers. She demands the newborn Rapunzel from her parents in retaliation for the father entering her garden and stealing her vegetables, but has no intention of harming the child, promising that she means to raise her as her own. No motivation is given for her later act of locking Rapunzel in the tower, which has left plenty of room for speculation in revisionist approaches to the tale. Furthermore, the *Zauberin* remains unpunished, alive and in power by the end of the tale. This enchantress, then, does not seem to represent quite the same kind of anti-maternal evil that other witches do. While locking Rapunzel up is a reprehensible act, it is left up to the reader to decide whether this might have been for selfish reasons or possibly born out of a desire to protect Rapunzel. She also makes an active decision to raise a child. Nevertheless, she clearly functions as the antagonist of the story, but she is not evil in the same unequivocal way that other fairy-tale witches are. Her comparative complexity has made her a particularly attractive figure for writers revisiting classic fairy tales.

Through the figure of the witch, canonical tales have preserved certain historical anxieties about the social role of women. Heidi Breuer (2011), who traced the establishment of the wicked hag as the default witch back to the Renaissance, argues that the literary wicked witch is the result of increasing anxieties about women achieving a degree of economic and social independence (pp. 109-110): an old, childless woman who lives alone (suggesting financial independence) and wields power outside of the domestic sphere poses a threat to the patriarchal order and must, therefore, be a wicked witch. In the canonical fairy tales, the witch (and closely related stock figures like the stepmother and the evil queen) therefore became the go-to character type to explore the notion of non-nurturing, anti-maternal women – women who are not only childless, but actively seek to bring harm to children. They represent a specifically feminine type of evil, that of women transgressing the social order by rejecting the fundamental female role of motherhood and exercising power outside of the home.

Revisionist approaches

Second-wave feminism brought with it a renewed interest in fairy-tale scholarship to the extent that modern fairy-tale criticism has largely been driven by feminist concerns regarding the socializing power of fairy tales, i.e. the way in which fairy tales consumed during childhood impact our conceptions of gender roles.[3] In addition to scholarly work, this movement brought forth numerous revisions of canonical tales that examined, above all, the role of women in the tales. These revisionist tales take various approaches to the witch, reinventing and in many cases at least partially redeeming her. To do so, writers have employed several strategies, of which three recurring ones are explored here. As the witch is fundamentally marked as an anti-maternal type of evil, the most obvious approach of redeeming her is to make her care for others, particularly (her own) children. Second, authors may choose to challenge the witch as a simplistic stock character (as necessitated by the structural nature of canonical fairy tales) by turning her into a complex figure with a backstory that she may tell in her own voice, thus humanizing her. Finally, some revisionist tales approach the witch by questioning the foundations of the fairy tale, i.e. storytellers and the act of storytelling itself, by exploring who has a stake in telling

---

[3]. For a thorough survey of the development of feminist fairy-tale scholarship, see Haase (2004b). While "[a]wareness of the fairy tale as a primary site for asserting and subverting ideologies of gender is evident throughout the genre's history" (Haase 2004a, p.vii), feminists in the 1970s propelled such discussions into the public spotlight on a scale not seen before.

stories about wicked witches, why witchcraft is considered evil by definition, and who decides that someone is a witch in the first place. These strategies are, of course, not mutually exclusive – while some tales rest primarily on one of these methods, others employ all three.

Reversing anti-maternal stereotypes

Challenging the anti-maternal connotations of fairy-tale witches is the most straightforward way of reversing the fundamental aspect of what makes witches wicked. Revisionist tales employ this strategy to differing degrees: in Tanith Lee's *Rapunzel* (2000), the witch is a genuinely good person who cares for Rapunzel and takes her on as an apprentice witch after her parents sell her into the witch's service. Rapunzel states that the witch "was better than any mother to me" (p. 10) and learned the craft of healing from her, reversing notions of witchcraft as harmful by definition. Here, it becomes a tool of caring for others. In *The Sea Hag*, Melissa Lee Shaw (1999) portrays the witch from *The Little Mermaid* as the mermaids' mother, betrayed and imprisoned by their father who took almost all her power from her and lied to his daughters about their mother's fate. When Coral, the youngest mermaid, approaches the sea hag for the spell that will give her legs, the hag drives up the cost of the spell to dissuade her and demands her voice out of sentimentality because she has been kept from her daughter all her life. Ultimately, however, the hag loves Coral too much to deny her anything. The tale ends in an act of maternal sacrifice when the sea hag, who can shapeshift and live both in the sea and on land, gives up her own human form to heal Coral's crippled legs so that she may find happiness with the prince. Again, witchcraft is reimagined as a way of caring for others. The witch, rather than taking delight in harming children for her own selfish gain, is a mother prepared to do anything for her daughters' happiness. Emma Donoghue takes a slightly different approach in *The Tale of the Cottage* (1999), a retelling of *Hansel and Gretel*. There is no mention of the woman living alone in the cottage in the woods being a witch at all; she is a genuinely kind woman who takes in Hansel and Gretel when they come to her door in need. She only turns on Hansel when he repeatedly sexually harasses and then assaults her, locking him up with the intention of killing him. Gretel frees him in secret, but decides to stay and live with the woman herself. Donoghue thus questions the motives that witches may have for their supposedly wicked actions (which I will discuss in more detail in the following section) and portrays a woman who is both caring and willing to defend herself.

These tales make a point of showing witches as independent, solitary women who are neither selfish nor cruel. However, redeeming the witch by simply turning her from an anti-mother into a loving, caring woman does not challenge the misogynist assumption that something must be wrong with childless women. Donoghue takes this up in *The Tale of the Kiss* (1999), the backstory she invents for Andersen's sea witch: in this version, the sea witch is a woman who decides to leave her village behind and live on her own because she is barren and wants to avoid being ostracized for it. Donoghue's sea witch does not wrestle with her infertility and is able to gain people's respect, give both help and curses to those in need, fall in love with a woman, and live a fulfilling life without ever expressing a desire to have children, or thinking herself lesser for it. Donoghue thus creates a witch who is childless, independent, neither particularly kind nor nurturing, and powerful, and is in no way punished by the narrative for who she is.

Complicating the witch

The second major strategy of reimagining witches is to take advantage of her status as a stock character of the fairy tale. Since very little is known about who these witches are, how they came to be witches and why they act the way they do, they are a near-blank canvas and can be turned into complex characters with a backstory and a voice, as already suggested in Shaw's *The Sea Hag* and Donoghue's *The Tale of the Kiss* and *The Tale of the Cottage*. Breaking with the generic restraints of the traditional fairy tale allows revisionist writers to come up with elaborate backstories that are not necessarily incompatible with the original version(s): these complicated witches may still be wicked, but are humanized through a voice of their own and challenge the notion of pure, irredeemable evil.

Donoghue's entire collection of retold fairy tales, *Kissing the Witch* (1999), is built upon this concept. Each tale is told by a character from the previous one, and so the witch from *Rapunzel* used to be a little girl whose brother was taken by a mysterious snow queen; the witch from *Hansel and Gretel* was once the princess from *Donkeyskin*, making her a survivor of rape and incest and further validating her response to Hansel's harassment; and the witch from *The Little Mermaid* receives the backstory mentioned above, the only original tale in Donoghue's collection. In each case, the sympathetic history gives the witch a life prior to the one that readers are familiar with, shedding light on her motivations and rejecting her status as a stock character representing one-dimensional feminine evil. Shaw's version of the sea witch is similarly redeemed through a backstory that shows her as the betrayed Spirit of the Sea, trapped by a power-hungry man who claimed to be in love with her so he could steal her powers and now uses the magic she taught him to keep her trapped and away from their daughters.

Other stories, however, turn witches into complex and largely sympathetic figures without disputing their villainous potential. Leigh Bardugo's *When Water Sang Fire* (2017) is an elaborate coming-of-age tale about an ambitious mermaid's search for identity and her attempts to gain social status despite being an outsider amongst her people. Aside from her name,

Ulla (the diminutive of Ursula, the name of the sea witch in Disney's adaptation of *The Little Mermaid*), there is little in the tale to indicate that she will become the villain of another story. By the end of the tale, Ulla, blinded by ambition and seeking to create a powerful spell, has become complicit in a murder and been betrayed by her accomplice and closest friend, Signy, who leaves her to die to become queen of the mermaids. Only then is Ulla's future as the sea witch revealed. She survives and lives in exile, awaiting her chance for revenge:

> When Signy gave birth to daughters – the youngest born with her mother's bright-ember hair – Ulla rejoiced. She knew they would be cursed as their father to long for what they shouldn't and cursed as their mother to give up what they most held dear in the hope for something more. She knew that they would find their way to her in time.
> The storm had brought Ulla to the cold shelter of the northern islands, to the darkened caves and flat black pools where she remains to this day, waiting for the lonely, the ambitious, the clever, the frail, for all those willing to strike a bargain.
> She never waits for long. (p. 273)

With revenge for the injustices inflicted upon her as her motive, the sea witch becomes sympathetic despite her faults and her willingness to punish a daughter for her mother's sins – her actions, while still reprehensible, are humanized. Catherynne M. Valente follows the same strategy in her retelling of *Hansel and Gretel, A Delicate Architecture* (2010), the account of a girl who is revealed to be the witch of another story at the end of the tale. Valente's protagonist, Constanze, is the daughter of a skilled but solitary confectioner who makes everything in his house out of candy and teaches Constanze his trade, which feels "almost like magic" to her (p. 148). He also teaches her to eat "sugared plums with a fork of sparrow bones; the marrow left salt in the fruit, and the strange, thick taste of a thing once alive in all that sugar" (p. 144). The father frames this act of eating bone marrow as an awareness and appreciation of the human labour required for the harvest of sugar cane, and warns her never to forget it. When Constanze asks him about her mother, he tells her that he created Constanze from sugar. She does not believe him, but one day he takes her to court in Vienna, where he fell out of favour years before, presents her to the empress, and reveals that she is in fact one of his candy creations, made to regain his place at the empress's side: "'[Y]ou may have her, you may have the greatest confection made on this earth, if you will but let me come home, and make you chocolates as I used to, and put your hand to my shoulder in friendship again'" (p. 150). Constanze, horrified at this betrayal, is hung up on the kitchen wall for years, with her fingernails, hair, blood and eyelashes used to sweeten the empress's food: "I grew old on that wall, my marzipan skin withered and wrinkled no less than flesh, helped along by lancings and scrapings and trimmings. My hair turned white and fell out, eagerly collected" (p. 152). Over time, the cannibalistic violation of her bodily autonomy turns her into a crone, and she manages to escape only after her father and the empress have died. She begs villagers for sweets and builds a cottage in the woods from them. Even after years of abuse, she cannot escape the need for her father's approval:

> I hated and loved him in turns, as witches will do, for our hearts are strange and inexplicable. He had never come to see me on the wall, even once. I could not understand it. But I made my caramel bricks, and I rolled out sheets of toffee onto my bed, and I told his ghost that I was a good girl, I had always been a good girl, even on the wall. (p. 157)

It is her need for his approval that sparks her desire to eat something that will remind her of the sugar cane harvest and sate her hunger "for something living and salty and sweet amid all my sugar" (p. 157). She laments that she cannot manage to catch a sparrow, and the tale ends as two children approach her cottage.

While the tales that recast the witch as a kind, caring, altruistic figure challenge readers to question their fundamental assumptions about fairy-tale witches, stories like Bardugo's and Valente's don't seek to redeem the witch by making her good or nice, but rather ask readers to consider the roots of evil, how it is not inherent in anyone but can be created through the selfish and cruel actions of others. These witches have been hurt and as a result are willing to hurt others, be it for revenge or validation, creating a cycle of evil. They no longer serve to demonize non-maternal, independent and/or powerful women because they are too complex to be reduced to a one-dimensional type of unadulterated evil. Instead, these witches illustrate that evil can be brought out in anyone and ask readers to question why people – or supposedly one-dimensional characters in well-known stories – may commit evil acts.

Questioning storytellers and the act of storytelling

Finally, the third major strategy of reinventing the fairy-tale witch is to question the fundamentals of the fairy tale: storytellers and the act of storytelling itself. This includes questioning who the storyteller is and what motives they may have to tell a story a certain way (or to certain people), who decides that a woman must be a witch, and why witchcraft is considered wicked in the first place. This is the strategy behind the tale-within-a-tale concept of Donoghue's collection, making the witches themselves storytellers and giving them a chance to win over their audience by telling their story in their own words. The mechanics of storytelling, the process of how a story comes to be, are highlighted in other stories as well. In Tanith Lee's *Rapunzel*, a rather ordinary story (a young prince returns home from a war, and on the way meets and falls in love with a young woman) is transformed into the tale as written down by the Grimms because the prince's father, who loves stories, demands an explanation for why the prince's journey home took him so long. The prince feels guilty about turning the kind witch who took Rapunzel in into a wicked crone, but Rapunzel reassures him that "the old lady would have laughed" (p. 18). In Shaw's *The Sea Hag*, the mermaids are convinced that the witch is wicked because of the tales their father told them. When the sea hag tells her own version of the story – of her lover's betrayal, her own imprisonment, the sea king's cruelty – the mermaids (and readers with them) are forced to reexamine familiar tales and see them in a new light. The act of telling her own story leads the witch's daughters to find some love for her in their hearts, and their love breaks the spell that keeps the witch imprisoned and powerless. Here, the act of telling her own story is, quite literally, empowering. *The Sea Hag* not only reclaims the witch as a positive figure, but shows that from a different perspective the sea king may become the villain. Bardugo's *When Water Sang Fire* functions similarly, revisiting not only the witch's moral alignment, but that of other characters from the original tale as well. Evil becomes a matter of perspective, depending on who tells the story.

The mechanics of storytelling are also the underlying concept of Amanda C. Davis's spin on *Rapunzel, The Peril of Stories* (2013). The entire tale is made up of bedtime stories that the witch tells Rapunzel as Rapunzel makes requests for how the story should go, which escalates into a fight over the story. Initially, it is the story of how a young girl's cruel parents give their daughter away to a beautiful wise woman; the woman and the girl live together happily ever after. When Rapunzel asks for a man to be introduced to the story, the storyteller makes him a rapist, a narrative tool to punish the girl in the story for disobeying the wise woman. The girl then sees she was wrong to let the man into the tower and never disobeys again, and so she and the woman live happily ever after. However, Rapunzel next asks for a version of the tale in which the girl is in love with the man. The storyteller is reluctant, but then tells her a story about the wise woman taking away the girl's things for being so silly over a man and supposedly ungrateful to the woman, and the girl sees the error of her ways. Rapunzel is still not satisfied with this version of the tale and interrupts with the ending of the Grimms' version: the girl goes after the man, heals him with her tears, has twins with him, and goes on to "live in a castle far away from the wise woman" (p. 28). The witch shouts at Rapunzel for taking over the story in ways she disagrees with. She then apologizes, but in the same breath threatens to throw Rapunzel from the tower.

Davis's witch is very much in line with the original version, in that she attempts to manipulate Rapunzel so that she will stay with her. She can easily be read as a contemporary take on evil (i.e. abusive) mothers. Nevertheless, this retelling subverts the fairy tale genre as a whole by highlighting, as the title indicates, the peril of stories. Storytellers, Davis suggests, have an agenda that determines which stories they tell and how they tell them – revisionist writers included. The witch notably never refers to the woman in her stories as a witch, but only ever stresses how beautiful and wise she is, and how foolish and ungrateful her daughter would be to disobey her. Her bedtime stories are emotionally abusive attempts to make Rapunzel feel guilty for even thinking of leaving the tower. Stories, especially those consumed during childhood, shape the way we think, and Davis's tale is a warning not to accept what we hear unquestioningly. This in turn may lead readers to reconsider the canonical tales as well.

Witches in Hollywood films

Despite numerous literary attempts to reclaim and redeem the witch, reversing her connotations of anti-maternal evil, the wicked old hag remains the default witch of the popular consciousness. This is in no small part due to Hollywood adaptations of the source texts, which have a much greater reach and thus pop-cultural impact than any of the short stories discussed here. The major adaptations covered here are Disney's *The Little Mermaid* (1989), Disney's version of *Rapunzel*, *Tangled* (2010), and the action-horror film *Hansel & Gretel: Witch Hunters* (2013). While each of these films deviates significantly from its respective source text, the function of the wicked witch as the antagonist is kept intact.

While Disney's *The Little Mermaid* expands the role of the sea witch, Ursula, it does so not to make her sympathetic, but to increase the threat she poses to the protagonist. Her past is merely hinted at: Ursula mentions that she used to live in the palace and was banished by the king, Triton. As a result, she carries a grudge and deliberately targets Triton's youngest daughter, Ariel, to bring him down. When she learns that Ariel is in love with a human prince, she is the one who presents her with the idea of becoming human and suggests a deal that sets Ariel up to fail so that Ursula may win her soul. She is not a passive watcher, but continues to scheme and attempts to marry the prince herself to stop him from falling in love with Ariel. Ultimately – after Ursula temporarily succeeds and gains Triton's powers – she is killed by the prince and the patriarchal order is restored.

The witch in *Tangled*, Mother Gothel, is a similarly conventional villain: the film turns the ambiguous character of the enchantress from the Grimms' tale into a vain, selfish woman who poses as Rapunzel's mother and keeps her locked up in a tower, ostensibly to protect her, but in reality for her own selfish gain. In this version, Rapunzel's hair has magical healing powers that it loses when it is cut. Gothel, ultimately revealed to be an old hag, is kept young and alive by the powers of Rapunzel's hair and wants to keep it for herself at all cost. Zipes (2012, p. 77) cites this movie as an example for how, despite feminist efforts, "the culture industry continues to produce the stereotypical evil bitch/witch".

Hansel & Gretel: Witch Hunters, which "depicts the hunting of female witches as an infantile game" (Zipes 2015, p. 74), tells the story of Hansel and Gretel as grown-up professional witch hunters after the (somewhat altered) events of the original fairy tale. The primary antagonist is the Grand Witch, who – together with the witches she leads – kidnaps children to sacrifice them for a spell that will make witches immune to fire. The depiction of witches is entirely stereotypical, though it does leave room for the concept of good white witches who do not harm humans – Gretel is revealed to be one, as was her mother (not stepmother), who only abandoned her children in the woods to protect them from the townspeople who had found out that she was a witch and were coming to kill her. By replacing the figure of the stepmother with a loving biological mother, the film associates anti-maternal evil entirely with wicked witches.

None of these films engages critically with its source material, at least not with regard to the figure of the witch – they are very much twice-told rather than revisionist. As a result, they perpetuate centuries-old views of evil femininity by transporting them unquestioningly into the present. These films (and other recent Hollywood retellings, e.g. *Snow White and the Huntsman* [2012], *Oz the Great and Powerful* [2013]) lack the truly complex and/or heroic witch figures we find in literary reimaginings of the fairy tale, instead keeping the hag witch as a representative of non-maternal evil alive and well. Breuer (2011, p. 151) ascribes this ongoing production of conservative witchcraft narratives to a patriarchal desire to keep women confined by gender roles:

> Just like medieval and Renaissance writers, contemporary Americans are invested in the maintenance of censures against child-less [sic] women, especially ones who possess power and autonomy, as do each of the witches in these films. When they watch films like these, children learn that older, single women are anomalies, monsters who need to be tamed or perhaps chased off a cliff.

Conclusion

The contrast between the way that witches are portrayed in cinematic and literary retellings indicates that the negotiation of gender roles and evil femininity through the figure of the witch is ongoing. Hollywood films constitute a strong conservative influence, whereas the short stories discussed here variously reclaim the witch as a kind, misunderstood figure, as a maligned empowered woman, or as a complex, well-meaning woman driven to villainy by a combination of choice and circumstance. The black-and-white morality of Hollywood films is juxtaposed with the nuanced view of evil presented in literary tales that explore not only what evil means, but how it may come to be and how it may be used as a label to discredit those who transgress the social order. This tension exposes evil as a matter of perspective: the same person can be interpreted as evil personified, threatening both the lives of innocents and the rightful social order, and as an empowered woman choosing to live outside an oppressive system. The stories we tell one another determine which interpretation becomes culturally dominant, particularly those we tell children. Unlike the animated films produced by Disney, the literary retellings discussed in this paper are not addressed to children, which further limits their power to rehabilitate the witch in the popular consciousness. Metanarratives such as those written by Donoghue, Davis, and Lee explore the mechanics of storytelling and the goals that storytellers seek to achieve, thereby highlighting that storytelling is always to some extent a political act. The fairy-tale witch still functions as a representation of how society views women who transgress the patriarchal order – but the hegemonic view of the witch as evil has been weakened through feminist efforts, including the practice of rewriting canonical tales, resulting in conservative and progressive portrayals in pop culture alike. These revisionist approaches have not only granted the witch a degree of redemption, but also led to a deeper engagement with and understanding of the mechanics of the fairy tale as a whole.

Bibliography

Andersen, H.C., 1837. *The Little Mermaid*. Translated from Danish by J. Hersholt. Available at: <http://www.andersen.sdu.dk/vaerk/hersholt/TheLittleMermaid_e.html> [Accessed: 19 November 2018].

Bardugo, L., 2017. *The Language of Thorns: Midnight Tales and Dangerous Magic*. New York: Imprint.

Breuer, H., 2011. *Crafting the Witch: Gendering Magic in Medieval and Early Modern England*. New York: Routledge.

Clute, J., 1997. Twice-Told. In: J. Clute and J. Grant, eds. *Encyclopedia of Fantasy*. [online] London: Orbit. Available at: <http://sf-encyclopedia.uk/fe.php?nm=twice-told> [Accessed: 30 November 2018].

Davis, A.C., 2013. The Peril of Stories. In: A.C. Davis and M. Engelhardt. *Wolves and Witches: A Fairy Tale Collection*. Alpena, MI: World Weaver Press, pp. 25–28.

Dingeldein, H.J., 1985. 'Hexe' und Märchen: Überlegungen zum Hexenbild in den Kinder- und Hausmärchen der Brüder Grimm. In: S. Früh and R. Wehse, eds. *Die Frau im Märchen*. Kassel: Röth, pp. 50–59.

Donoghue, E., 1999. *Kissing the Witch: Old Tales in New Skins*. New York: Cotler.

Grimm, J. and Grimm, W., 1812. *Kinder- und Hausmärchen*. [online] Halle: Hendel. Projekt Gutenberg. Available at: <http://gutenberg.spiegel.de/buch/kinder-und-hausmarchen-7018/1> [Accessed: 21 November 2018].

Haase, D., 2004a. Preface. In: D. Haase, ed. *Fairy Tales and Feminism: New Approaches*. Detroit: Wayne State University Press, pp. vii–xiv.

Haase, D., 2004b. Feminist Fairy-Tale Scholarship. In: D. Haase, ed. *Fairy Tales and Feminism: New Approaches*. Detroit: Wayne State University Press, pp. 1–36.

Hansel & Gretel: Witch Hunters, 2013. [film] Directed by Tommy Wirkola. Germany, USA: Paramount Pictures.

Lee, T., 2000. Rapunzel. In: E. Datlow and T. Windling, eds. *Black Heart, Ivory Bones*. New York: Avon Books, pp. 5–19.

The Little Mermaid, 1989. [film] Directed by Ron Clements and John Musker. USA: Disney.

Oberhelman, S., 1980. Greek and Roman Witches: Literary Conventions or Argrarian Fertility Priestesses? In: F.E.H. Schroeder, ed. *5000 Years of Popular Culture: Popular Culture before Printing*. Bowling Grenn: Bowling Grenn University Popular Press, pp. 137–153.

Shaw, M.L., 1999. *The Sea Hag*. [online] Originally published in: E. Datlow and T. Windling, eds. *Silver Birch, Blood Moon*. New York: Avon Books. Available at: <http://www.melissashaw.net/Sea_Hag.htm> [Accessed: 30 November 2018].

Tangled, 2010. [film] Directed by Nathan Greno and Byron Howard. USA: Disney.

Tatar, M., 1987. *Von Blaubärten und Rotkäppchen: Grimms grimmige Märchen, psychoanalytisch gedeutet*. Translated from English by A. Vogel, 1990. Munich: Heyne.

Valente, C.M., 2010. A Delicate Architecture. In: E. Datlow and T. Windling, eds. *Troll's-Eye View: A Book of Villainous Tales*. New York: Penguin, pp. 144–158.

Zipes, J., 2002. Towards a Definition of the Literary Fairy Tale: Introduction. In: J. Zipes, ed. *The Oxford Companion to Fairy Tales*. Oxford: Oxford University Press, pp. xv–xxxii.

Zipes, J., 2012. *The Irresistible Fairy Tale: The Cultural and Social History of a Genre*. Princeton: Princeton University Press.

Zipes, J., 2015. *Grimm Legacies: The Magic Spell of the Grimms' Folk and Fairy Tales*. Princeton: Princeton University Press.

The Fictional Scientist as a Dichotomy of Good and Evil in Contemporary Realist Speculative Fiction

Sean Z Fitzgerald

Abstract

Fiction writers continue to utilise science and scientists to embody both 'good' and 'evil', often in parallel depictions. The design of a scientist character – as at once representing the potential villain and the potential hero – with the capacity to personify evil or at least exhibit a sinister streak, has been a prevalent theme throughout literature from R.L. Stephenson's *Strange Case of Dr Jekyll and Mr Hyde* (1886) to H.G. Wells' character of *Dr Moreau* (1896) through to Michael Beard in Ian McEwan's *Solar* (2010) and the character of Benedict Lambert in Simon Mawer's *Mendel's Dwarf* (1997). In these terms, it is perhaps too simplistic to describe a main or principal character in a fictional narrative as exclusively one thing or the other, as any effective characterisation should look to deliver a complex, multilayered construction rather than a one-dimensional figure. I approach this critical examination on the evolution of evil in fantasy and science fiction from the perspective of a fiction writer who specialises in writing against the backdrop of *doing* science. Currently I am engaged in creating a collection of fictional stories about scientists and the scientific process in the field of genetics that characterise professional scientists as both altruistic and selfish. Alongside such established characters as detailed previously, my own creations do exhibit elements of evil, although I wouldn't necessarily describe them as evil individuals. I would hope that my (scientist) characters are complex enough to balance good and evil as they do what they believe is right even though, ultimately, it may be for the wrong reasons. This investigative piece considers scientists in fiction – specifically contemporary realist speculative fiction – and how their characterisations embody evil and evil tendencies in relation to the way science is delivered to a readership. It further considers if this places the reader in a position where they are required to empathise with a character even if they are regarded as dubious or evil.

Introduction

In the research and preparation for writing a collection of genetic science-based stories, there were many common and recognisable factors identified across a number of relevant works of contemporary fiction, ranging from William Boyd to Andrea Barrett to Allegra Goodman. One key element of what I refer to as *contemporary realist speculative fiction* – a shorthand description of realistic, science-based speculative fiction that has its origins in contemporary science practice and theory, and is maybe speculating 2-5 years ahead – is the characterisation of scientific personnel within a narrative. With this in mind, as I developed each story, there was a conscious effort made in designing the nature of the principal characters and their relationship to the process of engaging with practical science, to approach the characterisations from a left field perspective as I considered this would allow more latitude in portraying characters that both a readership and myself would readily engage with. This decision enabled me to put together a collection in which I consider the personality traits and backgrounds of my fictional scientists from across a broad range of choices. So, within stipulated boundaries, I refer to both professional and amateurs who either work or have a proven interest in the scientific process with some level of academic or professional training in the processes of undertaking science as *scientists*, even if they have not been professionally engaged in the business of doing science. This allowed me (within the collection) to have central characters that drive elements of the narratives, who are as diverse in their scientific background as anthropology research assistants, outsider bio-hackers, medical doctors, professors of biology, surveillance and security experts, government scientists and registered nurses. This approach enables an expanded choice of scientific personnel to help in the development of narrative story strands. The range of characters that can be used to populate each story offers a variety of opportunities both to deliver defined (simplistic) roles of heroes and villains but also to present the fictional scientist as a dichotomy of good and evil, where it is seems unfeasible to have one aspect without the other.

Through my fiction collection I have approached this critical examination of whether the contemporary fictional scientist is presented as a force for good or evil or – which may be a better reflection of everyday experience – a combination of both. This analysis is designed to address key aspects through a series of distinct perspectives that present an appraisal of the moral compass of the contemporary fictional scientist. It considers if and how a reader willingly identifies or empathises with a character who they perhaps find equally repellent and intoxicating, as is in the cases of Michael Beard in Ian McEwan's *Solar* (2010) and Benedict Lambert in Simon Mawer's *Mendel's Dwarf* (1997).

The fictional scientist in writing contemporary science-inspired fiction

From recent studies of scientists in fiction, notably by Roslynn D. Haynes (2003), Soren Brier (2006) and Jon Turney (2009), there is recognition of an image of fictional scientists in a popular culture frame that often leads to their portrayal as self-serving, morally vague characters of dubious motive. Both Turney (2009) and Charlotte Sleigh (2011) comment that the literary image of scientists is now starting to be readdressed in the light of contemporary works by authors such as William Boyd (*Brazzaville Beach*, 1990), McEwan (*Saturday*, 2005) and Richard Powers (*Generosity*, 2011). This trend, which features scientific characterisations along with aspects of professional science and scientific research subject matter (including a high proportion of genetic-based material), continues to thrive with a range of successful novels represented by authors and works such as Allegra Goodman (*Intuition*, 2009), McEwan (*Solar*, 2010), Edward Docx (*The Devil's Garden*, 2011), Richard P. Marshall (*Antisense*, 2013), Andrea Barrett (*Archangel*, 2013), and Tracy Chevalier (*Remarkable Creatures*, 2009). The nature of a fictional scientist's character is both an important aspect of creating a plausible fictional scenario for science to take place in, and in establishing a sympathetic protagonist which readers may identify (and even empathise) with.

Haynes (2003) identifies a 'Pandora stereotype' (p. 251), which she considers as the default position for the portrayal of scientists in mainstream fiction. She argues that this could be standing in the way of more socially acceptable (and sympathetic) science-inspired fiction, which features scientists, their work, and their private lives, alongside that of lawyers, journalists, forensics officers, police officers, detectives, and doctors, as recognisable (professional) protagonists existing in a fictional world.

Within popular literature, the portrayal of the fictional scientist from the Romantic period to the present-day can be traced back to two points in the culture of the nineteenth century: a speculative scientific fiction and a theoretical scientific non-fiction. In 1818 Mary Shelley's *Frankenstein: Or, the Modern Prometheus* was published, with its eponymous central character Victor, a proto-scientist (natural philosopher) possessed equally of madness and genius, presented as a man willing to abandon his humanity in search of 'empirical truth' (in this case, the (re)creation of life). Forty-one years later, in 1859, when Charles Darwin (based on work with and independent of Alfred R. Wallace) published their joint theory of Evolution to The Royal Society, it reached both a generalist audience (due in part to an established print media), as well as the specialised one it was originally intended for. According to Gillian Beer (1983, p. 149) *On The Origin of Species* (1859) had a tangible effect on popular, published fiction from that era as it focussed the attention of established authors such as George Eliot, Thomas Hardy and Charles Kingsley to include aspects of the new theory in both the structure and content of their post-Evolution works such as *Middlemarch* (1871), *Tess of the d'Urbervilles* (1891) and *The Water Babies* (1863) respectively. Throughout the following twentieth century, the view of the 'scientist' was shaped through a popular culture which was best suited to use the image and preconception of the scientist and science, to imaginative extremes, through the genres of science fiction and fantasy, across the forms of fiction novels and stories, pulp fiction, comic-book fiction and the film and television industries. By the end of the twentieth century and on the cusp of the twenty-first, the image of genetic science and the 'genetic scientist' had fared no better. Referred to as 'Frankenfoods' in 1992 by Boston college professor Paul Lewis[1], genetically modified organisms (GMOs) were the subject of many newspaper and media outlet headlines (and continue to be so with the ethical and societal issues surrounding GM crops). However, in the beginning years of the twenty-first century, there appears to be a more concerted effort on behalf of scientists, governing bodies/councils and the media to provide (medical) genetic science with the opportunity to help

---

[1]. Aneela Mirchandani (2015).

an often sceptical public gain the information it needs to make an informed decision. This sea change had emerged in the so-called 'designer babies' debate and is happening currently with the very recent emergence of the *Crispr-cas9* gene editing-technique[2] (launched in 2012 and first used on human embryos in April 2015). Understandably, this technique and the issues surrounding it are now present amongst many genetic-related news and related feature items. In part, the marginal (positive) shift in the media's attitude in reporting on the *Crispr-cas9* may be due to the medical contexts in which this breakthrough genetic science and resultant technology will be used.

According to Haynes, contemporary (literary scientist) authors such as Susan M. Gaines (*Carbon Dreams*, 2000), Jennifer Rohn (*The Honest Look*, 2010) and John McCabe (*Paper*, 1999 and *Snakeskin*, 2001) who consistently produce science literary fiction (aimed at the mainstream), try to offer a more balanced view of science and scientists, presenting both the positive and the negative, and are '…concerned to engage with the process of "doing science" and to indicate realistically how actual scientists think and behave in the intense atmosphere of a research laboratory' (2014, p. 6). In contrast, more generalist literary writers such as McEwan (*Solar*, 2010 and *Saturday*, 2005) or Boyd (*Brazzaville Beach*, 1990 and *Ordinary Thunderstorms*, 2009), or genre fiction writers such as Kathy Reichs (*Grave Secrets*, 2002) or Neal Stephenson (*Zodiac*, 1988 and *Reamde*, 2011) make use of

---

[2]. The *Crispr-cas9* gene editing technique makes use of a biological function of the cellular defence mechanism, in which a cell replicates the code of the attacking bio-organism. This is used as a 'key' to unlock the code (break open the chain), with the aid of a protein called *Cas9*. The result of this is that strands of DNA can be edited in situ and targeted precisely, with new information inserted or simply a section removed. For more detailed information on both the techniques offered by *Crispr-cas9* gene editing method and the issues surrounding the use of this technique, particularly in medical genetic science, see articles by: Penny Sarchet and Michael La Page (2011), and Heidi Ledford (2016) for discussions on human genome editing and *Crispr-cas9* gene editing respectively.

scientific characters and protagonists but not always in the most sympathetic manner, and not always in the interests of presenting (genetic) science in the best light. As Haynes (2014) points out, McEwan has both used sympathetic and caricatured approaches to his fictional scientific protagonists to suit the demands of his respective storylines. In his 2010 novel, *Solar*, the main protagonist (Michael Beard) is a self-serving and duplicitous research physicist who sees nothing wrong in furthering his flagging research career by any means. In contrast, the neurosurgeon character (Henry Perowne) at the centre of McEwan's 2005 novel, *Saturday*, is presented as a good person in all senses of the word according to Haynes' critique of the novel's main protagonist:

> In this highly sympathetic portrait, McEwan explores the subtle interaction between Perowne's scientific rationalism, his compassion, his deep emotional relationship with his wife and adult children, his sense of his privileged social position...
> (Haynes, 2014, p. 6)

Whilst in the case of the genre fiction writers, Reichs' pathologist-detective main character, Dr Temperance Brennan in *Grave Secrets* (2002) and Stephenson's battling environmentalist character, Sangamon Taylor, in his novel *Zodiac* (1988), exhibit the trademarks of being scientists but without undertaking much science beyond the procedural aspects of their respective professional interests. Often the focus for these characters is on driving the story forward through plot revelations rather than extensive observations and insights into being a scientist/researcher. The point here is that the more generalist writers (of both literary and genre fiction) tend to use the scientist/researcher template as a means to an end, rather than trying to portray an authentic scientist (as much as it is possible to do with a fictional character), where there would be both positive and negative aspects to their personalities and actions. This balance is illustrated through the main character of Dr Darren White in McCabe's *Paper* (1999), a disillusioned DNA laboratory researcher who is good at his job but is being driven to unpleasantness and insanity by its tedium. Ultimately he has to undergo a whole life shift in which he examines his relationship to science in order to regain his purpose, identity and sanity.

In either paper, 'From Alchemy to artificial Intelligence: stereotypes of the scientist in western literature' (2003), or 'Whatever happened to the "mad, bad" scientist? Overturning the stereotype' (2014), Haynes does not propose any special treatment in the portrayal of realistically fictional scientists. Instead she calls for a fair and balanced representation, somewhere in between the virtuosity of McEwan's character of Perowne and the inhumanity of H.G. Wells' sinister and evil Dr Moreau[3].

As a starting point for this, it is worth noting that in the discussion of scientists, science and contemporary fictional literature, the North American author Carl Djerassi (biochemist and inventor of the contraceptive pill) wrote his novel *Cantor's Dilemma*, in a newly self-termed style of 'science in fiction', in 1989. Djerassi helped pave the way of the scientist-turned-novelist, in the area of plausible science and contemporary fiction. This was followed up with a collection of novels and, latterly, plays dealing mostly with the 'business of doing science'. Since then, other scientists-turned-novelists (or literary scientists), have added to Djerassi's initial work across a whole range of different fictional (but factually-based) scenarios and settings (including 'Lablit'[4], a collection/grouping of predominantly scientist-originated fiction hosted

---

[3]. Further investigations may look at the sociological and philosophical considerations of how portrayals of genetic science/scientists and the culture of science are represented both in contemporary literary and genre fiction to consider whether they really are a reflection of the society which creates them.

[4]. See Rohn (2005) http://www.lablit.com .

online). While contemporary authors such as McCabe, Rohn, Goodman, McEwan, Barrett and Stephenson all write about the practice of doing science in a popular fictional format, there still remains something of a barrier to the presentation and marketing of popular fiction which deals with this topic[5].

Constructing fictional scientists and fact-based speculative science

The following section offers perspectives on the construction and portrayal of (genetic) science and the scientist in speculative fiction writing.

Previous studies into the publics'[6] perception of fictional scientists range across different types of media rather than concentrating solely on the written word. Haynes (1994, 2003 and 2014), David A. Kirby (2003), Christopher Frayling (2005), Frans Saris (2006), Russell (2010 and 2014), J.M. van der Laan, (2010b), and Jill A. Fisher and Marci D. Cottingham (2016) are key examples of these studies as they consider the stereotypical character and personality of fictional scientists (from across types of media including literature).

Haynes identified seven 'primary stereotypes' (2003, p.244) of scientists who are represented in literature; for my proposed study, the representations offered by the latter two:

---

[5]. Although the work of the popularly successful author Michael Crichton would fall into this category his work had, and still continues to have, a market of its own outside of the Lablit oeuvre. Works such as *The Andromeda Strain* (1969), *Jurassic Park* (1991) and *Prey* (2002) would still fit into the family of novels about the practices of science and its associated technologies.

[6]. It is common in the academic treatment of 'science communication' to intentionally refer to 'the public' in the plural term of 'publics' to signify that the make-up of society is many layered when it comes to a relationship with science. There are public audiences who are scientists and those who have no interest in science at all, and then everywhere in between. It is often difficult for one blanket term, such as 'public' to describe all of the varied standpoints. However, in this body of work, the singular term will be used to refer to the general public as one homogenous entity.

'The scientist as adventurer' (2003, p. 250), and 'The mad, bad, dangerous scientist' (2003, p. 251) would be the most relevant. Of these two (fictional) stereotypical scientists identified by Haynes, perhaps only the 'scientist as adventurer' would offer a suitable and positive way forward for any mainstream popular science-as-fiction literature. However, in reality none of the fictional scientist stereotypes identified by Haynes may be useful in realising a contemporary body of what Russell refers to as 'popular, socially-realistic [science] literature' (2009, p. 35). Though Haynes in an earlier investigation does allude to some hope in terms of a more engaging scientist *stereotype* emerging:

> 'There have been some important studies of idealistic scientists, and it is significant that these characters are evaluated by their authors almost wholly in relation to their contribution to the community, rather in terms of their scientific expertise' (1994, p. 294).

This correlates to the approaches I have used in creating an original collection of genetic science-inspired stories[7]. One key element that is identifiable across the five discrete pieces in the collection is that I distinctly use two main protagonists in each of my stories. In an individual story there is a defined role each of these protagonists fulfils, in relation to them either being a scientist or working within the field of science or technology. Haynes identifies a generic counterpoint to the 'mad scientist' (2003, p. 251), which is prevalent in fiction from Shelley's writings up to the present-day. Within my creative practice, I represent both Haynes's 'scientist as adventurer' (p. 250), who provides a sympathetic version of a scientist (or science), who

---

[7]. The collection comprises a techno-thriller ('The Commuter Lab'), a medical-based science romance ('The Patient Experiment'), a creation-fiction ('A Common Thread'), a techno-evolution fiction ('NUCA: Beginnings in vivo') and a fiction of self-discovery ('An Invisible Fix').

is fair but flawed and is more concerned with altruism than prestige, and her 'mad, bad, dangerous scientist' (p. 251), who is out of control and exhibits elements of evil as well as good (and through this, adds heightened danger and dramatic tension to the storylines). These represent the two main protagonists of each story in the collection. This enables me to present both a main (positive/good) protagonist within each of the individual stories who is engaged in science but not (as yet) a fully-fledged scientist (if you take Rohn's doctoral distinction)[8], together with an equally central but morally dubious main (negative/evil) protagonist.

Mawer in an article for *Nature*, 'Science in Literature' (2005), considers the fictional scientist's role in written fiction. As the author of *Mendel's Dwarf* (1997), in which a brilliant but deceitful geneticist confronts his own chronic condition head-on, Mawer is uniquely placed to contribute to a discussion about where (genetic) science-as-fiction may be heading. He says, with his notion of the 'supremacy of imagination' (2005, p. 298), that fiction can and should be used to deliver the exciting elements of science to the general reader, in a way circumventing the reality and sometime laborious nature of scientific endeavour. Mawer considers that both the concept and actuality of 'science' has always been used as effective descriptors in literature but now, speaking specifically of science-as-fiction, he says: '[It is] only recently that some writers have made the scientific process the very focus of their work' (2005, p. 298). In making this point, he draws attention to the validity of science literature as a fair representative of

---

[8]. Rohn (2010b) only defined fiction authors as 'scientists' if they had achieved doctoral status. If this were to be accepted, it could mean the same definition being applied to their fictional counterparts. From a creative viewpoint, the quasi- or proto-scientist characters that I make use of – the outsider or maverick who are not part of the scientific elite or establishment – are the more interesting, as they operate outside of the rules but are less morally ambiguous, as none of their intentions could be seen as being motivated by evil.

science. Mawer goes on to say: 'It is important not to be misled by the use of the word fiction here. Fiction does not stand as the antithesis to fact. Good fiction points towards truth, which is after all, only where the scientist is trying to go' (2005, p. 298). With the 1997 novel *Mendel's Dwarf* and continuing up to his recent fiction publication *Tightrope* (2015), Mawer highlights pertinent moral and ethical concerns and poses questions of acceptance, rights to decide over life-changing treatments, access to (scientific) information and ultimately decisions over life itself. From within a narrow focus of genetic science, I support the idea that science-inspired fiction is one suitable platform in which to address a diverse range of contemporary societal issues. These could be ethical ones, such as decisions on what information from an individual's sequenced genome is held in the public domain, or moral ones, such as should 'three-parent designer babies' be allowed to be conceived if it means creating an unalterable and unnatural combination of genetic information to be passed onto future generations[9].

The role of philosophy of science in developing science-inspired fiction

Here, the focus is on how science-as-fiction is perceived from within the context of a philosophical and socio-philosophical perspective.

On a fundamental level, science can be considered as a process through which nature is investigated. Scientist and empiricist Lewis Wolpert refers to science as '...the best way to understand the world [to] gain insight into the way all nature works in a causal and mechanistic sense' (1997, p. 9). In this sense, it is seen as central to the process of understanding science in literature, as it helps to explore the process of scientific enquiry which ultimately results in the establishment of accepted scientific practice.

---

[9]. Just one of the issues I raise with the story, 'NUCA: Beginnings *in vivo*'.

If considered in the field of fiction, Wolpert's definition of science (above) presents the reader with something physical or tangible to reflect upon when offered a storyline which deals with science or a resultant technology. From the perspective of a writer, what is harder to establish with a readership is how the laws, theories and principles which seek to explain the natural world are constantly in a state of revision through new observations and interpretations[10]. Russell questions how it is that these provisional facts or 'matters of facts' (2017, p. 2) give rise through interpretation to the laws, theories and principles which seek to explain the natural world, and which are themselves superseded or adapted through new observations and interpretations. (The premise was mentioned earlier with regard to the evolution in the principles of physical sciences from Newton to Einstein.) This is the area of 'Philosophy of Science', which seeks to investigate the robustness of scientific interpretations and provides a framework to test and analyse whether the claims and proposals of scientists stand up to academic and intellectual scrutiny. As an example of how elements from the philosophy of science could be represented in literature, Turney (2009) explains how McEwan in his novel *Enduring Love* (1997) uses aspects of both game theory and evolutionary theory to describe his characters' actions and their justifications of those actions (in relation to their responses to the pivotal 'balloon' incident). This is an atypical (almost metaphysical) approach, as for the majority of pieces of science-as-fiction it is more likely that the processes under consideration would be more concrete especially in the area of genre fiction. As Russell (2017, p. 3) indicates, it is the 'shop work' which is dealt with in popular fiction literature as it is more practical to examine through the actions and thoughts of a protagonist how they carry out their primary goal. In most instances, it is more practical to examine how genes are spliced or how genetic material is recovered from a crime-scene

---

[10]. As an example, the evolution of the principles of physical sciences from Newton to Einstein to String Theory.

sample, through the actions and mechanical processes which can be seen to obtain results directly through those actions.

Russell (2017) raises a further issue that it is often scientists responsible for a particular body of knowledge that are overly critical of fiction which deals with realistic science. Indirectly, an author (writing science-as-fiction) may be overly cautious as they tread a thin line between being plausible and appealing to both a scientific and non-scientific readership. On the one hand, this balancing act demands of scientists that they need to appreciate that the delivery of scientific information in fiction is not as it would be in a scientific textbook or paper. And of general readers, that not all science delivered in this type of writing will be one hundred percent (empirically) accurate. The scientific content should be plausible within the constraints of the fictional world which has been created, even if it is based on a factual, recognisable and realistic one. It is this 'plausibility' which is the main key to the acceptance of both the character of the scientist and the scientific 'facts' or situations which are dealt with in the narrative. If this notion of plausibility breaks down within a story, due either to an aspect of a scientists' character or the scientific information, then the illusion of the fiction dissolves, and along with it any acceptance or trust (believability) in the science and, importantly for here, the process of undertaking science.

Beer in *Darwin's Plots* (1985, p. 3) considers that even these elemental or fundamental problems, from whichever era, are considered can never be fully appreciated by the proposer of a scientific theory or a solution. She draws on Thomas Kuhn's work, *The Structure of Scientific Revolutions* (1962, p. 52), in which he says that ideas often put forward may contain speculations which may not initially be considered a 'scientific fact'. In her Introductory Chapter (p. 4) Beer considers that a scientific theory contains much more of relevance than is suspected at the time of its formulation. Beer puts forward an argument concerning narrative structure in relation to the development of new scientific ideas in Darwin's *On The Origin of Species* (1859). She argues that:

> ...evolutionary theory had particular implications for narrative and for the composition of fiction. Because of its preoccupation with time and with change, evolutionary theory has inherent affinities with the problems and processes of narrative.
> (Beer, 1985, p. 7)

It is with this hindsight that Beer seeks to establish clear links between the process of scientific theories and discoveries and the structure of narrative fiction: 'Evolutionary theory is first a form of imaginative history. It cannot be experimentally demonstrated sufficiently in any present moment. So it is closer to narrative than to drama' (p. 8). Beer's point is that that the development of scientific reasoning, and the focussing of this through the whole concept of evolution, led to a subtle change in the way Victorian novelists such as Eliot and Hardy were to use aspects of (evolutionary-inspired) science in their approach to narrative construction, analogies and metaphors. In science-inspired fiction (such as the work in my collection) the exploration of contemporary science should be used to question the value, morals and ethics of science. Sleigh with her book *Literature and Science* (2011) argues that in fiction the concept we know as 'science' is able to go beyond what is factually correct or can be empirically proven, and helps take in the totality of what needs to be discussed in any contemporary discussion of a scientific issue within a society.

An example of this in context is examined by Russell (2010, pp. 279-280) as he considers Jane Gregory's arguments that in the 1950s scientist and broadcaster Fred Hoyle used his influence and profile to promote his own secondary career as a science fiction writer, in which he put forward serious ideas on various theories centring on '...life-from-space' (p. 280). What is unusual about this was that Hoyle in the 1950s used the medium of science fiction writing as a test-bed for his ideas, which he could neither prove nor put forward with any real justification to the general scientific community. His book *The Black Cloud* (1957) is probably the best known work from this period of Hoyle's 'unproven' theories. By laying the groundwork Hoyle was able to put out his ideas into a general and scientific readership, and this opened up the opportunity for him to publish credible scientific papers two decades later in accepted science publications (including the respected journal *Nature*) repeating many of the original concepts and theories which he had used as the basis for his science fiction writing. Russell goes on to say that Hoyle's manipulation of the media and the science press came to an abrupt end in the 1980s when he spoke up in support of a group of creationists at a court hearing in Arkansas: 'In the end Hoyle's life-from-space thesis moved from respectable heterodoxy to crackpot vision in the eyes of the scientific establishment' (2010, p. 280).

Essentially our understanding of science has been reorganised by considering the image of science from a socio-philosophical perspective, and as a result has led to reevaluate both what science is and what it represents. By extension, this is also true of the role of scientists in society and their fictional counterparts.

Communicating scientific knowledge within science-inspired fiction

This section examines how both current and established 'scientific knowledge'[11] and provisional new (cutting-edge)

---

[11]. The term 'scientific knowledge' can be both a catch-all term and a misleading one. It is very subjective and depends at which academic and intellectual level an individual accesses the information required. I use the term in this study to suggest an interest which goes beyond the general knowledge of everyday life to understand 'why' a particular (natural or otherwise) physical effect or event happens. For example, if I used the *Water Cycle*, on a general level a person would be expected to realise that seawater is absorbed by rising air over the oceans and this forms clouds, and these in turn deposit (filtered/fresh) water back onto land. If the same natural physical event is considered with a more in-depth look as to why the seawater is initially absorbed through the natural methods of evaporation and why this occurs, then this would be to access or gain and use scientific knowledge.

scientific knowledge are communicated within a (genetic) science-inspired fiction.

Whilst current and established scientific knowledge is located mostly in published textbooks, the cutting-edge often exists in the form of written scientific papers customarily published in peer-reviewed academic journals but now increasingly in an online capacity too. These repositories (physical and virtual) are where the collection of what is referred to as scientific knowledge is housed and so to enable science to progress (i.e. new hypotheses to be developed and tested), it relies on the peer-to-peer communication of this knowledge between scientists in their role as the 'practitioners' of science. Where scientific knowledge is used within a piece of plausible science-inspired fiction, it is as likely to propose *new* claims (both fictional and unsubstantiated) as well as to use reputable empirically-based ones. In fiction, both are given an equal footing within the design of the story-world. For established scientific knowledge ('science') this seems to go against the whole nature of proving and testing sound and reliable empirical evidence. For convincing science-inspired fiction, in order to develop the story in a credible manner, it is often necessary to go beyond what is wholly accepted as correct or proven. However, in carrying out the research for my collection, a conscious effort has been made to stay within the confines of plausibility. Again this is a subjective claim and one which I hope to justify through bringing the background research as faithfully as possible into the individual stories.

As an author of genetic science-inspired fiction, it is important to have defined views on both scientists and science. After all, it is the author who ultimately controls the personalities of the fictional scientists. It is he/she who uses these characters as instruments for what is to be communicated. In the case of my own writing, this comes through as aspects of a scientist's (or proto-scientist's) character, their ambitions and how they relate to scientific culture (within the context) in which they exist. This latter point, on the cultural significance of science-as-fiction, Russell (2010) comments that the authentic world of science has been explored in situ and relationships drawn out between how science and society interact but '...the cultural significance of science in fiction has been relatively neglected'. He concludes that '...readers can learn much about science and its culture from fiction' (p. xiii). This relates directly to the development of the 'outsider' (or proto-scientist) characters that I make use of in my collection. The personalities, ambitions and drive of the characters of Peter ('The Commuter Lab'), Jake ('The Patient Experiment'), Judith ('A Common Thread'), John ('NUCA') and Ute/Uwe ('An Invisible Fix') all are able to freely observe, react, and comment on the culture of (genetic) science because they are on the outside or periphery. They view it with a healthy cynicism which a reader may or may not empathise with. From my own perspective as a reader I enjoy thinking that I am on the edge – on the outside looking in – as this is the place (I feel) to achieve a more-informed view.

When approached as an academic discipline, the history of science communication is one fraught with complications. Whether the aim is to address a deficit or just to impart new information as a result of groundbreaking research (as with the developing *Crisper-cas9* gene editing technology), the issue of trust always appears. Recent circumstances surrounding areas in which science and its communication (or lack of), such as GMOs, BSE and MMR[12], have just served to undermine the public's trust in science (and of scientists). As a sociologist of science, Stephen Yearly sees a double meaning in the phrase: 'Trust in science'. He says it can refer both '...to the public's trust in scientific expertise, and to the role of trust within the scientific enterprise itself' (1998, p. 3). When science and scientist characters are examined in works of fiction, the issue of trust is never too far away. From the perspective of a reader or a writer,

---

[12]. Genetically-Modified Organisms (crops), *Bovine Spongiform Encephalitis* (in cattle), and Measles, Mumps and Rubella (vaccination) respectively.

the question of how far should a fiction *trust* both the science and the scientists it comes into contact with – whether factually-based or purely fictional – is a challenge, as it depends on how the author wishes science and scientists to be represented.

Whilst many attempts at communicating scientific knowledge can have positive effects, there are also numerous instances that deliver an unhelpful combination of confusion and mistrust. In terms of fiction writing. this may affect how contemporary science and scientists are perceived, more so if fictional scientist characters are presented as either one-dimensional entities motivated only by reward, or more complex characters who are morally ambiguous when it comes to making decisions that to an outside observer/reader appear to be motivated by evil or dubious intentions.

Concluding remarks

Along with other key elements of human endeavour in society reflected or reimagined through tales of fiction and their fictitious characters, those scientists – amateur or professional – who populate science fiction, fantasy and speculative fiction will naturally represent the broad spectrum of any contemporary society. Complexity in purpose and design have moved the emphasis away from the one-dimensional 'bad' or archetypal evil scientist character, but there lingers a stereotyped image of the scientist as a clinical, almost inhuman individual that persists in works of fiction, as it does in society. From a science fiction viewpoint – particularly a speculative one – beginning with Shelley's creations of the dangerous, driven scientist and the unwitting monster (a passive victim) shaped as a result of scientific actions and reckless imagination, up to the sympathetic but monstrous character of Mawer's Benedict Lambert, who fulfils both altruistic and narcissistic roles, there is an argument to be made that there has been (in part) an evolution of evil intent in the make-up and portrayal of fictional scientists.

Bibliography

Barrett, A., 2013. *Archangel*. New York: W.W. Norton & Company.

Beer, G., 1983. *Darwin's Plots: Evolutionary Narrative in Darwin, George Eliot and Nineteenth-Century Fiction*. London: ARK Paperbacks.

Boyd, W., 1990. *Brazzaville Beach*. London: Penguin Books.

Boyd, W., 2009. *Ordinary Thunderstorms*. London: Bloomsbury Publishing.

Brier, S., 2006. Ficta: Remixing generalized symbolic media in the new scientific novel. *Public Understanding of Science*. 15 (2), pp. 153-174.

Chevalier, T., 2009. *Remarkable Creatures*. London: HarperCollins.

Crichton, M., 1969. *The Andromeda Strain*. London: Jonathan Cape.

Crichton, M., 1991. *Jurassic Park*. London: Arrow Books.

Crichton, M., 2002. *Prey*. London: HarperCollins.

Darwin, C., 1859. *On the Origin of Species*. Reprint 2008. Oxford: Oxford University Press.

Djerassi, C., 1989. *Cantor's Dilemma*. New York: Doubleday.

Docx, E., 2011. *The Devil's Garden*. London: Picador.

Fisher, J. A. and Cottingham, M. D., 2016. This isn't going to end well: fictional representations of medical research in television and film. *Public Understanding of Science* [online]. Research Paper published online, pp. 1-15. DOI: 10.1177/0963662516641339. Available at: <http://pus.sagepub.com/content/early/2016/04/04/0963662516641339.abstract> [Accessed 6 April 2016].

Fitzgerald, S. Z., 2016. NUCA: A beginning *in vivo*. *Holdfast Magazine* [online]. Available at: <http://www.holdfastmagazine.com/nuca-brexitlit/4592952439> [Accessed: 11 September 2016].

Fitzgerald, S. Z., 2017. Published Writing: Fiction. *Creative practice website* [online] Available at: http://www.seanzfitzgerald.com> [Accessed: 12 January 2018].

Frayling, C., 2005. *Mad, Bad and Dangerous?: The Scientist and the Cinema*. London: Reaktion Books Ltd.

Gaines, S. M., 2000. *Carbon Dreams*. Berkeley, California: Creative Arts Book Company.

Goodman, A., 2009. *Intuition*. London: Atlantic Books.

Haynes, R. D., 1994. *From Faust to Strangelove: Representations of the Scientist in Western Literature*. London: John Hopkins Press Ltd.

Haynes, R. D., 2003. *From Alchemy to artificial Intelligence: stereotypes of the scientist in western literature*. Public Understanding of Science. 12 (3), pp. 243-253.

Haynes, R. D., 2014. Whatever happened to the 'mad, bad' scientist? Overturning the stereotype. *Public Understanding of Science* [online]. Published online before print, 10 June 2014, pp. 1-14. DOI: 10.1177/0963662514535689. Available at: <http://pus.sagepub.com/content/early/2014/05/30/0963662514535689> [Accessed 11 June 2014].

Hoyle, F., 1957. *The Black Cloud*. Reprint 2010. London: Penguin Modern Classics.

Kingsley, C., 1863. *The Water Babies*. Reprint 1995. London: Penguin Books.

Kirby, D. A., 2003. Scientists on the set: science consultants and the communication of science in visual fiction. *Public Understanding of Science*. 12 (3), pp. 261-278.

Kuhn, T., 1962. *The Structure of Scientific Revolutions*. Chicago: University of Chicago Press.

La Page, M., 2011. Read me a genome. *New Scientist* [online]. Daily news, 16 February 2011. Available at: <http://www.newscientist.com/article/dn20137-read-me-a-genome.html#.VRRBS47-XhI> [Accessed 23 March 2011].

Ledford, H., 2016. CRISPR: gene editing is just the beginning. *Nature* [online]. 531 (7593), pp. 156-159. Available at: <http://www.nature.com/news/crispr-gene-editing-is-just-the-beginning-1.19510> [Accessed 22/07/16].

McCabe, J., 1999. *Paper*. London: Granta Books.

McCabe, J., 2001. *Snakeskin*. London: Granta Books.

McEwan, I., 1997. *Enduring Love*. London: Jonathan Cape.

McEwan, I., 2005. *Saturday*. London: Jonathan Cape.

McEwan, I., 2010. *Solar*. London: Jonathan Cape.

Marshall, R. P., 2013. *Antisense*. N Charleston, South Carolina: CreateSpace Independent Publishing Platform.

Mawer, S., 1997. *Mendel's Dwarf*. London: Doubleday-Transworld Publishers Ltd.

Mawer, S., 2005. Science in Literature: Interview. *Nature*. 434 (7031), pp. 297-299.

Mawer, S., 2015. *Tightrope*. London: Little, Brown Book Group.

Mirchandani, A., 2015. *The Original Frankenfoods: Origins of Our Fear of Genetic Engineering* [online]. Genetic Literacy Project. Available at: <https://www.geneticliteracyproject.org/2015/02/10/the-original-frankenfoods> [Accessed 25 May 2016].

Powers, R., 2011. *Generosity: An enhancement*. London: Atlantic Books.

Reichs, K., 2002. *Grave Secrets*. London: Heinemann.

Rohn, J., 2005. *Lablit.com: the culture of science in fiction and fact* [online]. Available at: <http://www.lablit.com> [First Accessed 7 September 2009].

Rohn, J., 2010. *The Honest Look*. New York: Cold Spring Harbor Laboratory Press.

Rohn, J., 2010b. More lab in the Library. *Nature*. 465 (7298), p. 552.

Russell, N., 2009. The New Men: scientists at work in popular British fiction between the early 1930s and the late 1960s. *Science Communication*. 31 (1), pp. 29-56.

Russell, N., 2010. *Communicating Science: Professional, Popular, Literary*. Cambridge: Cambridge University Press.

Russell, N., 2014. What Did Scientists Do All Day? Scientists at Work in British Fiction from the 17th to the Mid-20th Century. In: *Fiction Meets Science Working Paper 1* [online]. Bremen: University of Bremen, June 2014. Available at: <http://www.fictionmeetsscience.org/ccm/cms-service/stream/asset/Working%20Paper%201%20Russell.pdf?asset_id=1142002> [Accessed 30 October 2014].

Russell, N., 2017. [est] *The history of science in fiction* [wt]. London: [n.k.]

Sarchet, P., and La Page, M., 2011. Human gene editing has arrived – here's why it matters. *New Scientist* [online]. Focus. Available at: <https://www.newscientist.com/article/mg22630194-200-human-gene-editing-has-arrived-heres-why-it-matters/> [Accessed 17 March 2016]

Saris, F., 2006. *Science through the looking glass of literature* [essay]. LabLit.com (online). Available at: <http://www.lablit.com/article/90> [Accessed 25 October 2009].

Shelley, M., 1818. *Frankenstein: Or, the Modern Prometheus*. Reprint 1993. Hertfordshire, UK: Wordsworth Editions.

Sleigh, C., 2011. *Literature & science.* Hampshire, UK: Palgrave Macmillan.
Stephenson, N., 1988. Zodiac. New York: The Atlantic Monthly Press.

Stephenson, N., 2011. *Reamde*. New York: William Morrow (HarperCollins).

Stephenson, R. L., 1886. *Strange Case of Dr Jekyll and Mr Hyde and Other Tales of Terror*. Reprint 2003. London: Penguin Classics.

Turney, J., 2009. Science Communication in Fiction. In: Holliman, R., Thomas, J., Smidt, S., Scanlon, E. and Whitelegg, E. (eds.) *Practising Science Communication in the Information Age: Theorising professional practices*. Oxford: Oxford University Press, pp. 166-177.

van der Laan, J.M., 2010b. *Frankenstein* as science fiction and fact. *Bulletin of Science, Technology & Society* [online]. 30 (4), pp. 298-304. Available at: <http://bst.sagepub.com/content/30/4/298> [Accessed 3 September 2010].

Wells, H.G., 1896. *The Island of Doctor Moreau*. Reprint 2005. London: Penguin Classics.

Wolpert, L., 1997. In praise of science. In: Levinson, R. and Thomas, J. (eds.) *Science Today: Problem or crisis?* London: Routledge, pp. 9-21.

Yearly, S., 1998. Trust in Science. *Science and the public*. S802: Part B. Milton Keynes, UK: The Open University, p. 3. (Open University MSc Science course material.)

Author Biographies

Dr Teika Bellamy is the award-winning managing editor of Nottingham-based independent press, Mother's Milk Books, which publishes books that celebrate femininity and empathy, with a view to normalizing breastfeeding.
As the editor of the popular series of dark fairy tales, *The Forgotten and the Fantastical*, she is delighted by the fact that 'Teika' means fairy tale in Latvian. Her poetry and short fiction, published under the pen-name, Teika Marija Smits, has appeared in various places including *Mslexia*, *Brittle Star*, *Strix*, *LossLit*, *Shoreline of Infinity* and *Reckoning*.

Steph P. Bianchini is an Italian academic based in the UK. She's an Associate Professor and a member of the Royal Historical Society, and she has worked over the last ten years on projects in social sciences, international relations, and humanities.
She blogs about sciences, speculative fiction, and history at earthianhivemind.net and has a book coming out in 2019 with Macmillan about the space sector.
As a fiction writer, Steph is a member of HWA and writes under the byline Russell Hemmell. Her short stories and poetry have appeared in 70+ publications, including *Aurealis*, *Flame Tree Press*, *The Grievous Angel*, and others.

Octavia Cade is a New Zealand writer. She's had over 40 short stories published, in venues such as *Clarkesworld*, *Asimov's*, and *Strange Horizons*. A non-fiction collection on food and horror was published in 2017, and several papers on speculative fiction have been published in *Scandinavica*, *Horror Studies*, and the *BFS Journal*. She's won three Sir Julius Vogel awards, and has been shortlisted for a BSFA award. She attended Clarion West 2016.

Alice Capstick completed her undergraduate degree at Monash University before continuing her interest in the figure of the dark hero in her PhD, which examines the development of the figure from the early modern period through to contemporary fantasy.

A J Dalton (the 'A' is for Adam) is an international author of fantasy and science fiction. He has published ten novels, including the *Empire of the Saviours* trilogy with Gollancz and *The Book of Angels* with Grimbold Books. He runs the Metaphysical Fantasy website (www.ajdalton.eu), where there is advice for aspiring writers and plenty to entertain fans of SFF. In addition to his creative publications, he writes academically about current science fiction and fantasy, and contributed an article to *Gender Identity and Sexuality in Current Fantasy and Science Fiction*, published by Luna Press Publishing.
Completing and publishing his PhD in Creative Writing last year (*The Sub-Genres of British Fantasy Literature*, published by Luna Press Publishing), Adam is now a Senior Lecturer in Creative Writing for Falmouth University.

American by birth and British by marriage, **Sharon Day** began her international academic career as an exchange student to Japan in 1980; returning for college and then again after graduating law school in New York City, as an expat to Tokyo with her British husband. After repatriating to London in 1997, Sharon was drawn to the Occult and joined The Honourable Fraternity of Ancient Freemasons (Freemasonry for Women), thereby becoming the fourth generation of Freemason in her family.
In later years, she discovered a vocation in Alexandrian Witchcraft and her search for training and experience took her from London to Australia, to the United States, and back to London, where she became the personal student of Maxine Sanders, a prominent Witch and co-founder of the Alexandrian Tradition. She was initiated in 2013, took her higher degrees in 2016, and currently leads The Coven of the Stag

King in London with the benefit of Mrs Sanders' guidance.

Sharon's ongoing endeavours include Craft teaching; giving talks and interviews; authoring several publications; and evolving her brainchild, an online historical archive and timeline of Alexandrian Witchcraft (alexandrianwitchcraft.org). She is also a Trustee of the 'Friends of the Museum of Witchcraft and Magic', a charity which supports the Museum in Boscastle, Cornwall (friendsofthewitchcraftmuseum.co.uk).

Matthew J. Elder is a PhD candidate and tutor at the University of Waikato in Hamilton, New Zealand. He is also Reviews Editor at Fantastika Journal.

His research interests include contemporary fantasy literature, magic, and identity construction. Sacrifice in long-form contemporary fantasy is the subject of his doctoral research. He finds hope in the notion that exploring impossible worlds might help make our own world better.

Tatiana Fajardo completed her MLitt in the Gothic Imagination at the University of Stirling (Scotland), writing her dissertation on the employment of art and science in Patrick McGrath's novels.

She began a blog in which she discusses her literary, cinematic and artistic interests in 2017. Passionate about Gothic literature, her blog post on Dracula's "Bloofer Lady" was published by Sheffield University. Some of her essays have been translated into Swedish and published by Rickard Berghorn, both on his online Weird Webzine and in his printed books *Studier I vart* (2018) and *Två fantasistycken* (2018). These include her analyses of Ridley Scott's *Blade Runner* (1982) and Ingmar Bergman's *Hour of the Wolf* (1968).

She presented her study of the employment of Romantic poets in the TV series *Penny Dreadful* (2014-2016) at the IGA conference in Manchester in August 2018. (1968). Her article on Victor Sjöström's *The Phantom Carriage* (1921) is forthcoming on Weird Webzine..

Tatiana combines her work as a researcher with her job as an English teacher in Spain.

Dr. Sean Z. Fitzgerald holds a PhD in creative writing practice from the University of Winchester, England. His thesis, 'Writing Genetic Science-Inspired Fiction in Contemporary Society', concentrates on the contextualisation and practice of writing genetic fiction. The research practice undertaken for his doctorate has produced a collection of novelettes and novellas that explore and speculate through contemporary and near-future fiction, the possible impacts and consequences of manipulating genetic code.
His short fiction can be found in publications such as: *Holdfast Magazine*, *The Honest Ulsterman*, *The Ham* and *Written Tales* and scholarly work in papers such as 'Practice-based creative writing methodology' delivered at Cardiff Metropolitan University and 'Writing genetic fiction' for the *Frankenstein Unbound Conference*, Arts University Bournemouth.

Jason Gould is a writer of fiction and non-fiction, in prose, script, and for the screen. Born in Hull in 1971, he has been shortlisted for a British Fantasy Society Award, received several honourable mentions, and holds an Honours degree in Creative Writing. He can be found on Twitter @jasongoulduk.

Lucinda Holdsworth is a freelance fantasy editor based in Glasgow. Obsessed with all things fantastic from a young age, Lucinda endured a B.A. in sensible literature from The University of Nottingham, before moving on to the good stuff at the University of Glasgow with an MLitt in Fantasy.
She is currently working towards a PhD in English Literature and Theology at the University of Glasgow. Her research interests include religious fantasy, gender and comics. In her free time, Lucinda enjoys screaming at the news in despair.

Anna Köhler is a PhD student at the Chair of British Literature at RWTH Aachen University, Germany.
She holds an MA in English Studies and Communication Science and has worked as a translator, editor, and library assistant. She is

particularly interested in how fantasy reflects real-life discourses on social issues, and is currently researching the way in which cultural models of gender are negotiated in contemporary fantasy literature through magic and magic users. Her research interests include feminist approaches to literature, cognitive literary studies, worldbuilding, and anything that will give her an excuse to buy more books.

Dr. Jyrki Korpua (Finland), PHD in Literary studies. Lecturer and researcher at the University of Oulu, Finland. His research interests include fantasy and science fiction, worldbuilding, classical mythologies, J. R. R. Tolkien's fiction, Kalevala, Bible studies, utopian and dystopian fiction, graphic novels, and game studies. At the moment he is working on the international Tove Jansson Companion project funded by Kone Foundation.

Rostislav Kůrka is a Prague-born theologian with lifetime interest in fantasy, sci-fi, writing and world-building. His greatest success among wide public came unexpectedly in the form of *LotR* musical which spread among the Czech fan community after TolkienCon 2004.
In the academic field, his chief interest has been the Hebrew Bible and its historical background. While focusing on the importance of story in Judeo-Christian tradition, his interest in fantasy storytelling has managed to seep into his research, as it occasionally still does.
He currently lives in Finland, trying to find future balance between his academic interests and hobbies. He also contributes to ScififantasyNetwork.com as a *Star Wars* editor.

Kim Lakin-Smith writes Science Fiction, Fantasy and Historical fiction for adults, young adults and children. Her short stories have appeared in numerous magazines and anthologies, including *Interzone*, *Black Static*, *Celebration: 50 Years of the BSFA*, *Behind the Sofa: Celebrity Memories of Doctor Who*, *The Mammoth Book of Ghost Stories by Women*, *Solaris Rising 2*, *Resurrection Engines*, *Best British Fantasy 2013*, *Sharkpunk*, *The Mammoth Book of Dieselpunk*, and more.

Her short story, 'Johnny and Emmie-Lou Get Married' (*Interzone*, Issue 222) was shortlisted for the 2011 British Science Fiction Association award and her novel, *Cyber Circus*, was shortlisted for both the British Science Fiction Association Best Novel and the British Fantasy Award for Best Novel 2012.

She is also the author of *Tourniquet, Queen Rat, Autodrome*, and *Underneath This Burning Sun*. Kim's non-fiction centres on issues of gender, sexuality and otherness, with a particular passion for the social renegade.

Robert S Malan is an editor, non-fiction and horror writer. He runs freeflowedit. Shortlisted for the Nommo Awards 2018 for his graphic novel *Quest & The Sign of the Shining Beast*.

Anna Milon is a Russian-born, London-bred PhD student at the University of Exeter with the thesis revolving around the Horned God in modern fantasy content. Outside academic pursuits, Anna holds the role of Education Secretary for the Tolkien Society and an assistant editor position of Exclamat!on, a University of Exeter based peer reviewed journal. She is a firm believer that free time is best spent with a good fantasy book, a mug of Lapsang Souchong and her cat, Sherlock.

Thomas Moules is currently a freelance academic, with a BA(Hons) in English Literature from Anglia Ruskin University and an Mlitt in Fantasy Literature from the University of Glasgow. They have written and presented papers on a variety of topics and plan to return to academia to study for a PhD.

Katarina O'Dette is a fantasy writer and PhD student in Film and Television Studies at the University of Nottingham. Her research interests include fantasy television, production studies, and genre theory. She holds a BFA in television writing from the University of Southern California and a MLitt in Fantasy from the University of Glasgow.

In addition to earning responsible degrees, she serves on the organising committee of GIFCon, and has led a research station on Harry Potter at the Hunterian Museum, co-led seminars on fantasy television at the University of Glasgow, and worked as a Television Academy Foundation intern in the writers' room of Syfy's *Haven*.
Her work can be found in *From Glasgow to Saturn*, *Fantastika*, and *Slayage: The Journal of Whedon Studies*.

Dr. C. Palmer-Patel received a doctorate from Lancaster University, UK in 2017.
Her first monograph, The Shape of Fantasy (Routledge, 2019), examines structures of post-1990 American Epic Fantasy. Palmer-Patel is head editor of *Fantastika Journal* (www.fantastikajournal.com), a journal that brings together the genres of Fantasy, Science Fiction, Gothic/Horror, among others. Palmer-Patel currently resides in Edmonton, Alberta, Canada.

Dominic Riemenschneider is an Art Historian with a Magister Artium degree, a self-funded Ph.D. candidate at the University of Mainz and an independent scholar living in Berlin. His work and research are focussed on the connection between the Fantastic, its imagery and the roots in actual art & architecture, history and society. The strategies of visualization but also the reasons and ways of reception are his main interest. In his homepage *Art History Fantastics* he bundles all his ideas, projects and publications.

Barbara Stevenson is a fiction writer based in Orkney. She studied creative writing as part of a BA from the Open University. In 2016 she won the Scottish Association of Writers 'Castles in the Air' award for a fantasy short story. Her background in veterinary medicine has led to a growing interest in the portrayal of animals in fairy tales and folklore.

Lightning Source UK Ltd.
Milton Keynes UK
UKHW021326040619
343840UK00006B/579/P

9 781911 143918